Architectural Practice and Procedure

Architectural Practice and Procedure

A manual for students and practitioners

Hamilton H Turner
Late Fellow of the Royal Insitution of Chartered Surveyors

revised by
John Hamilton Turner MBE
Fellow of the Royal Institution of Chartered Surveyors

in association with
Reginald James Maynard
Fellow of the Royal Institution of Chartered Surveyors

with a foreword by
Bernard M Feildon OBE

FSA, FRSA, AA Dip(Hons), RIBA

ERRATUM

We regret that the opening pages of Chapters XXI and XXIII have been transposed.

Chapter XXI *The builder's foreman* should be on page 172 and Chapter XXIII *Fees* on page 178.

B T Batsford Limited

© John Hamilton Turner 1974

First published 1925
Second edition published 1931
Third edition published 1945
Fourth edition published 1948
Fourth edition reprinted 1950
Fifth edition published 1955
Fifth edition reprinted 1960
Sixth edition published 1974

ISBN 0 7134 2799 X hard cover
ISBN 0 7134 2826 0 limp edition

Computer composition in England
by Eyre and Spottiswoode Limited
at Grosvenor Press, Portsmouth
Printed by The Anchor Press Ltd, Tiptree, Essex
for the publishers B T Batsford Limited
4 Fitzhardinge Street, London W1A 0AH

Contents

Genesis of this book; Fitness of a quantity surveyor to
write it; His relations with the architect; Preliminary survey
of the ground to be covered; Obtaining work; Making
surveys; Information required in plans; Specifications; Bills
of quantities; Approximate estimates; Contracts;
Inspections of Works in Progress; Certificates for payment;
Extras; The quantity surveyor; The client; The builder,
foreman, clerk of works and workmen; Fees;
Responsibility; Sanitary work; London Building Acts; Light
and Air; Dilapidations; Reports on property; Arbitration;
Fire Insurance

Methods of obtaining commissions; Through friends; As the
result of actual work; By specialisation; By luck; From
solicitors; Competitions; Other methods (such as public
service) and their abuse; The value of opportunity

School training must be supplemented by office training;
Variety of methods in architects' offices; Assistants and
their duties; Hints and advice on the performance of these
duties; Importance of industry; Setting up your own
practice

Papers relating to an architect's practice; Importance of a
proper system of filing and correspondence; The 'packet'
and 'jacket'; Use of index or reference numbers; Number
book of papers; Copying of letters; Separate letters for
separate jobs; Record of interviews; Enclosures with letters;
The writing of business letters; Binding and storing of
papers

chapter

Foreword to the sixth edition

I was delighted when John Hamilton Turner asked me to write a Foreword to the sixth edition of *Architectural Practice and Procedure*, for I, like many hundreds or perhaps thousands of architects, have over the years been brought up with his father's lectures and book in the matters concerning architectural practice. I felt that there was a very distinct loss to students when the fifth edition went out of print some years ago.

Architects oldest text book, *Vitruvius*, contains admirable advice on professional practice which has not dated, likewise the passage of time since this book was published has in no way lessened its value, both to the young architect starting in practice and indeed to those of us who have had many years of experience.

This book tends to deal with the smaller jobs and practical aspects of architecture which those joining large practices may miss, but which are the grass root work of architects of which it is essential to have a mastery.

New techniques such as the invaluable RIBA Work Method, and sophisticated programming may be introduced but, as *Vitruvius* shows up, the nature of the client does not alter. Hamilton Turner helps us architects with the art of client management which is part of the art of architecture.

By retaining the original form John Hamilton Turner, in association with Reginald James Maynard has in my view acted wisely, but naturally all the rates and prices and the other matters have been brought up to date so that as now presented this sixth edition is a valuable and necessary volume for both the student and practitioner to have available for ready reference.

June 1974   Bernard M Feilden

Foreword to the fifth edition

My acquaintance with the late Mr Hamilton H Turner began about 1926, when he was appointed as Quantity Surveyor for the new Horticultural Hall. I found that for him the preparation of a meticulously correct and complete Bill of quantities was regarded as, almost, a thrilling as well as a satisfying undertaking. And I soon discovered that he knew far more about the business and procedural side of architecture than any architect I had known — let alone myself.

If I avoided being caught on the wrong foot in those early days of practice, it was largely due to the wise counsel of this friend and adviser.

His son, John Hamilton Turner, now guides me in the far more complicated world of post-war building. He has a mastery, not only of new and old building legislation, but also a keen awareness of the precautions necessary to the drawing up of contracts in a time of scarcities and rising costs.

·The fund of knowledge contained in *Architectural Practice and Procedure* was first made available to the public in 1925, and since then, successive editions of the book have kept pace with the changes that have concerned the profession.

Now a fifth edition, embodying the most recent developments which affect architectural practice, is being presented and I am happy to have the privilege of wishing it well and of recommending it to every practising architect.

January 1955   John Murray Easton

Foreword to the first edition

Many branches of the work of an architect and a quantity surveyor are so interwoven that it is essential there should be a mutual confidence and respect between them. Years ago, when I first began to practise as an architect, I was advised by my father to look for and find a quantity surveyor of about my own age with whom such relations could be established. By a curious coincidence, a day or so after this advice was given me, a quantity surveyor bearing an introduction from an uncle of mine came to see me. He explained that he was just opening an office in London after some years' work in the provinces. Could I put any work his way? I happened to have one of those little alteration jobs so aptly described later on in these papers as the frequent beginning of an architect's practice, just in the state when it was ready for quantities. I handed it over then and there to the author of this book, and the happy association then begun has continued, certainly for my benefit, up to the present time, with the exception of a few war years, when absence of building and absence abroad made a brief gap in it. After the war I believe I suggested Mr Turner's name as the best man for the course of lectures now happily embodied in book form.

It is, therefore, with a peculiar pleasure that I recommend to every architectural student the practical wisdom of its contents. If occasionally the author exposes with good-nature and good-humour the weakness of the architect, the advice he gives for avoiding these weaknesses will not only be valuable to architects, but will, I hope, lessen the burdens of the quantity surveyors who come after him and work for architects who have taken his advice to heart.

December 1924   Maurice E Webb

Preface to the sixth edition

When I was asked by Batsford, at the suggestion of the Royal Institute of British Architects, to consider a new edition of this book I was confronted with an immediate problem as to whether it could be brought up to date after the number of years which have elapsed since my revision in 1955, or whether the only way to present it usefully would be a completely new work. After many consultations I was persuaded that a revision maintaining the original 'fatherly' style would best meet the gap caused by the book going out of print a year or so ago. Accordingly this is what I have attempted to do with the skilful aid of my colleague, Reginald James Maynard, now senior partner of the firm of Hamilton H Turner and Son which my father founded in 1904 and which I carried on for twenty years after his death, to become the firm's consultant as I now am. I am hopeful that the result will prove as helpful to both students and practitioners as previous editions have been over the years since the lectures which are its basis were originally delivered in 1921.

I have received valuable support in parts of the revision from Mr W H R Barker, my solicitor, Mr J Dufton, the District Surveyor for Westminster, Mr Bob Garratt of the Architectural Association and Mr D H G Forest concerning Fire Insurance. To them all I extend my appreciation of their help.

Retaining the original style and yet modernising the text wherever vitally necessary for current reference, in for example such matters as pricing, has meant the retention in some cases of imperial dimensions and measurements. Only where such does no harm to the educational value of the text has this been done, for example the report on property to be purchased cannot be changed to metric dimensions when it is dated 1962. The principle of report writing is clearly shown by this example but of course in producing a report today the architect would have to decide whether to give sizes in imperial or metric measurements (or both). Likewise in the *Inventory of Household Effects* no attempt has been made to up-date the style or prices because every case will be different and costs continue to change from day to day, so that every case must be considered on its own merits at the time it is undertaken. In the *Form of List of Market Prices* I have of course brought the rates up to date, but here again I must caution the reader to realise that changes are occurring every day and all rates should be checked against current market prices at the time they are used.

With these qualifications I trust the sixth edition of this book will be as useful and acceptable as its predecessors.

19 Queen Anne's Gate   JHT
Westminster, SW1
Spring 1974

Preface to the fifth edition

It was always my father's intention that I should carry on the work of revision when he was no longer able to do so. When he died in October 1949, the fourth edition had only recently been published, but so great was the demand that I was asked by the Publishers in 1950 to consider a revision. Pressure of work at that time made it impossible for me to act with sufficient speed and for that reason the fourth edition was reprinted.

Perhaps it is fortunate that the work of revision was postponed, for I am confident that the new edition now offered will be of considerably greater value since upon such matters as London County Council By-laws, the notes in connection with war damage practice and naturally in all the many references to prices the volume is now up-to-date. I have also been able to make reference to the Landlord and Tenant Act 1954 and the Housing Repairs and Rents Act 1954 which only came into force recently, while the revision of the type Specification with particular reference to British Standards will, I am sure, be helpful.

This short preface gives me an opportunity of emphasising my father's warning 'You cannot be too careful' in any matters concerning Architecture and Building. I must also claim association with his awareness that perhaps not everyone would agree with him on points of detail. This applies to me also. Nothing, however, has been said in this revised edition without very considerable thought, and it is my hope that the book in its present form will prove still more useful than before.

19 Queen Anne's Gate   JHT
Westminster, SW1
Spring 1955

Preface to the fourth edition

The rapid exhaustion of the third edition of my book has enabled me to revise such portions of the work as appeared necessary, and to add to the chapter on *Dilapidations* a Form of Proof of Evidence which is always required when a dispute is taken to a Court of Law. Some notes on the procedure to be followed in War Damage Practice, written by my son, John H Turner MBE, FSI, have been included which, though they cannot hope to be exhaustive, should prove helpful in what is, at the moment, a very arduous and somewhat perplexing subject. A Form of Specification for making good war damage in a small house has also been included.

It is hoped that the work in its revised form will prove still more useful, especially to those who, after long absence from their office in consequence of national service, may wish to refresh themselves in certain branches of their professional practice.

19 Queen Anne's Gate   HHT
Westminster, SW1
November 1947

Preface to the third edition

The fact that the second edition of *Architectural Practice and Procedure* is now exhausted, has given me the opportunity to carry out a complete revision of the work. I have examined each chapter in detail and made whatever changes have seemed necessary since the publication of the second edition in 1931.

The latest RIBA Form of Contract has been dealt with in detail and a short form of contract for minor works, where the standard form seems to long and elaborate, will be found in the *Appendix*. The chapter on the *London Building Acts* has been almost entirely rewritten and much new data has been introduced in the chapter on *Approximate Estimates*. I have also included a Schedule of Condition of Repair of Property, and an Inventory and Valuation of Furniture and Household Effects.

It is most gratifying to me to have received so many assurances that my book has proved useful, and of value, and I hope that the present revised edition will give help to all those who are able to consult it on the many intricate details connected with a responsible exacting profession.

I am greatly indebted to my friend, Mr Walter H Godfrey, FSA, FRIBA, whose kindness and many valuable suggestions have given me the opportunity to revise the textual wording and give it greater clearness and exactitude. I also wish to place on record my appreciation of the great help I have received in the present revision from my son, John H. Turner, FSI.

19 Queen Anne's Gate   HHT
Westminster, SW1
January 1945

Preface to the second edition

The early demand for a further edition of this work has given me the opportunity of carefully going over the text and embodying a number of corrections and revisions necessary for bringing the book up to date. Additions have been made to several chapters, such as that on the *Responsibility of Architects*, and the chapter on the *London Building Acts* has been entirely rewritten in order to bring it into accordance with the recent changes in building law. In addition, an entirely new chapter has been added on *Fire Insurance*, defining the position of the architect in regard to this important subject.

I am glad to think that the favourable reception of the book shows that it has proved of some value to the architectural and surveying professions, and I trust that in its revised form it will continue to be found of practical utility.

19 Queen Anne's Gate   HHT
Westminster, SW1
April 1931

Preface to the first edition

It has often occurred to me that a book dealing with the more prosaic side of the work and practice of an architect and surveyor might be acceptable. When, therefore, I was asked in 1921 to deliver lectures bearing upon this subject to the students at the Architectural Association in London, I decided to prepare my papers in such a way that they could be utilised as the nucleus of the book which I had in mind. In preparing the lectures for publication I have consulted many of my friends among architects and surveyors, and I desire to acknowledge here my indebtedness to them for many valuable suggestions and for the assistance they have so generously given to me.

I should like to draw the special attention of my readers to the list of books which will be found in the *Appendix*, for I can confidently recommend these as being, in my opinion, the most satisfactory works upon their respective subjects.

19 Queen Anne's Gate   HHT
Westminster SW1
December 1924

Chapter I
Introduction

This book is the result of a series of lectures on the business side of an architect's practice, delivered to the students of an Architectural School in London. The lectures, which were taken down in shorthand[1] when first delivered in 1921, have since been revised, but it has not been considered necessary or advisable to alter their form, as the facts which it is desired to present to the reader remain the same, whether in the style of a discourse or in that of a book.

There is so much to learn in the technique of an architect's profession that few students receive adequate instruction in the business methods which are so necessary to efficiency and success. Architecture is a life study, and a working knowledge of historical styles and building construction, together with the means of expressing his compositions on paper, is in itself sufficient to tax the full powers of the young architect. It is, however, nonetheless true that an artist's training is by itself quite inadequate to fit a man for business life, and the ordinary practice of an architect turns as much, if not more, on business aptitude as upon his powers of design. Just as architecture is mistress of the arts, nearly all of which are called upon to minister to her widespread enterprises, so building, being a practical necessity of public and private life, touches a thousand matters of a purely utilitarian nature. Prices, contracts, by-laws, the nature of sites, materials, plant, trade-customs, rights of light and air, legal responsibility, negotiation with builders, merchants, clerk of works, and workman — these and a host of other intricate problems await the architect. With so much preoccupation ahead of him, with the certainty that hours of precious time, which he would devote to his drawing-board, will be occupied with this very prosaic business, he will be well advised to be armed at all points, and to be prepared to deal with this all too necessary side of his profession with ability, promptitude, and despatch. To this end his office procedure must be efficient and fool-proof; he must take more than one leaf from the business man's book and perfect his machinery and routine.

A little careful thought and a determined adherence to a tried procedure will set him free from hours of worry; his creative work will

---

[1] It is an interesting 'domestic' fact that whereas I attended all my father's lectures in 1921 and am responsible for this sixth edition in 1974, the shorthand typist referred to is Miss Freda Haines who has typed all the current revised drafts likewise over 50 years later. This could be a unique record. JHT

thus have a vigour and freshness which otherwise he will be in real danger of losing.

It is the function of the quantity surveyor to make a study of all the severely practical sides of the architectural profession. He takes pains to keep his knowledge up to date, not only in the important province of prices, but in the general conditions of the building trade, the status of contractors and merchants, the bearing of legal decisions, and many similar matters. It is the privilege and the pleasure of the quantity surveyor to support and inform the architect when desired, on this practical side of his work, and in the confidential relationship which ensues, he gains an inside experience covering many varieties of precept and practice. In some ways, like the looker-on who sees most of the game, he realises perhaps more than the architect the importance of mundane things — system, procedure, and the like — and if he turns his observation to good use, his services are quickly recognised at their full value. It is in the role of guide, philosopher, and friend to those who are putting their feet on the first rung of the ladder of their professional ascent, that I have taken upon myself the task of putting together this book. Those who have already made the ascent, among whom I number not a few as my friends, will perhaps differ from me on points of detail, but on broad principles will, I believe, endorse the importance with which this subject should be invested.

Everyday architectural practice has been treated in the following pages with as little theorising as possible, the practical problems being solved by examples drawn from actual practice, and presented as if they were matters of ordinary routine. The student is asked to imagine himself engaged, for example, in writing, copying, and filing a letter, interviewing a client, placing a contract, drafting a specification, making a report, or preparing an approximate estimate. I have endeavoured to take nothing for granted, and have paused to explain simple terms or details of procedure which doubtless are well known to many of my readers, but the omission of which might mystify others.

I propose to give a general idea of the ground covered, and to touch lightly upon the various points dealt with, in an endeavour to create, if not enthusiasm, at least a desire to know more of this by no means uninteresting subject. We must first consider what happens at the beginning of the practice of an architect. The starting point is obviously the obtaining of work, and for a young architect this is one of the most difficult things of all. It may be interesting to know how some architects have obtained work in the past. The practical problems which arise are then touched upon in order to make it clear that the preparation of a drawing, although an important thing, is only one of the many steps which go towards the actual carrying out of a building scheme. Some advice as to the working of an architect's office is offered. My own experience is drawn upon as to the various ways in which business is conducted, and in this connection I have something to say upon the subject of the orderly filing and recording of papers, drawings, catalogues, etc.

One of the first things a young architect may be called upon to do is to make a survey of an existing house with a view to carrying out alterations and additions. Some of the difficulties which are met with are indicated, and advice is given as to how mistakes can be avoided. It is very easy to go to a house with a drawing-board, tee-square, and all the necessary implements and stay until you have measured and plotted the survey; but if only a limited time at the house is available, and in that time all necessary measurements have to be taken to enable the survey to be plotted in the office, with no further chance of taking more dimensions on the site, then the matter is quite different. I well remember when I was twenty-one having to survey an awkward site for a building adjoining the main line of an important railway, and in order to get the correct frontage line it was necessary to include in the survey a bridge across the railway line at an oblique angle. I should have appreciated greatly any assistance that could have been given me as to how to avoid any difficulties in piecing together the survey upon my return to the office.

Many architects have told me that it would be a good thing to make clear to the young architect the kind of information that should be contained in plans to enable the quantity surveyor properly to prepare the bills of quantities. This I endeavour to do; and may I deprecate, in passing, the ingenuity displayed by some draughtsmen in selecting a section line which avoids the staircases and the difficult parts of the roof, for it is a subject on which quantity surveyors have been known to wax eloquent.

It was considered that the students would want to hear something about specifications. Perhaps, however, when I think of my student days, this was an unwarrantable assumption. Nevertheless, the specification is the strongest possible evidence as to whether an architect has a proper knowledge of building materials and construction, and it is as important, in its way, as the drawings themselves. It has fallen to my lot to write specifications for almost every class of work, and by showing how I myself proceed, I endeavour to indicate the easiest and most satisfactory way. I give the following list of specifications as interesting evidence of some of the unfamiliar subjects for which one may be called upon to write an intelligible and correct technical description:

Show-cases	Automatic telephones
Carpets and blinds	Electric clocks
House furniture	Groynes
Carving and gilding	Repairs to a pier, and pile driving
Garden work	Tall chimney
Vestment presses	Road-making, sewers, etc
Terrazzo flooring	Caulking of deck floor
Electric lighting	Animal houses
Restoring ancient castle	Underground spirit tanks
Granolithic staircases	Reinforced concrete jetty

The preparation of bills of quantities and what they purport to be will be dealt with. Bills of Quantities are naturally a very important subject to the quantity surveyor. Some people think that his work consists solely in taking out quantities, but this is far from correct. He has many other duties to perform, although the bills of quantities are his chief work. If I could have my way, I would put all students through a short course of quantities. I know an architect who spent a year in a quantity surveyor's office, and in speaking of this to me, he said; 'I look upon that time as the rottenest period of my life'. I asked him what he did, and he replied 'I squared dimensions all the time'. Now squaring dimensions is not exactly an interesting task for an architect, or for anyone else, and I do not mean that twelve months should be so spent. I mean a course of quantities judiciously prepared and made as little uninteresting as possible. The information thus gained would, I am sure, be very useful to the architect. It will be shown how modern quantities are prepared and how easy it is to understand the principles which are followed. Schedules of prices are also described.

A very important subject is the making of approximate estimates of building schemes. It is a difficult subject for a young architect with little experience and no data to refer to, so I have endeavoured to give some real help in this direction. Methods of obtaining tenders, including the form of invitation generally used, and the form of tender, are also dealt with. It may seem sufficient simply to ask the builders to tender, but it is much better to have correct forms for these matters.

The subject of contracts is an all important one, and various forms generally in use will be discussed.

Inspections of works in progress then claim attention, and the sort of things to which special notice should be directed are pointed out. Frequently an assistant who is sent to report on the progress of a building comes back knowing very little about it. He has made no notes of the condition of work, the number of men employed, or the way in which the work is being carried out, and he finds much difficulty in explaining to the architect what is happening. The method of making a useful inspection and report will be indicated.

Something is said as to the issuing of certificates for payments on account, and also of final certificates, and the important matter of variations is dealt with. It is very seldom that a job of any size is completed without variations either by way of additions or omissions. If the variations are omissions, and result in a saving, there is no cause for worry, but if they are additions, as is usually the case, and result in extras, then an architect has all the worry he wants, unless he has been very careful. The difficulties which arise in connection with 'extras' cause the architect more trouble and deprive him of more sleep than anything else in connection with building. The way to keep straight in the matter of variations is indicated. The meaning of prime cost and provisional sums is discussed, and how they are arrived at and treated. The position of the various sub-contractors and specialists is also examined.

It is certain that the reader will want to know something about the quantity surveyor and his work, and also about that very important person, the client. Endeavours have been made, therefore, to explain their positions.

A few remarks are included about the builder, the builder's foreman, the clerk of works and the workmen. Something is said about the attitude of the architect towards each of these classes of men, whose co-operation is essential to the carrying out of any work, and who are worthy of more respect and consideration than is sometimes given to them. The position and duties of the clerk of works and of the foreman are explained, and a list is given of the qualities they must possess to enable them to carry out their work efficiently and to the benefit of all concerned.

An important matter dealt with is that of fees. Architects must be paid for their work, and the amount of their fees is usually based upon a scale approved by the Royal Institute of British Architects, but there are the fees and charges of the quantity surveyor, the various consulting engineers, the district surveyor and other people. A subject not lightly to be dismissed is the important one of responsibility. This is a very real thing, and a clear idea is necessary as to the legal position of the architect. Some remarks are given upon the law of copyright, which it is hoped may be useful.

The subject of sanitary work and drains is considered, the testing of both new and old systems being dealt with.

Attention is drawn to some of the intricacies of the London Building Acts, with which we must be acquainted if we build in London. I may say at once that I make no claim to be an authority on this difficult subject, but, nevertheless, I do know what practical action to take on matters that come under the various Acts governing building works in London, or at any rate where to get the necessary assistance or information. An architect who was making some alterations to an existing building, asked me to deal with the questions arising in connection with the adjoining buildings. The case was a very complicated one, and in it there were many points of interest. This has been dealt with as a special case, and explanations have been given as to how all the difficulties were surmounted.

Some remarks are included on the law of Light and Air. Although questions relating to this and to the London Building Acts are distinct, yet they often have to be dealt with together. The subject of dilapidations is illustrated by a copy of a schedule and an explanation as to how it was made, and some remarks will be found bearing upon the question of leases, etc. Sometimes it occurs in the practice of an architect that he will be called upon to support his schedule of dilapidations in a Court of Law. This matter is also dealt with.

Another subject which is considered is the reports upon property which architects and surveyors are occasionally called upon to make. A client desiring to purchase a property asks to be advised as to its structural and sanitary condition, and also as to its value. A copy of a recent report will be found and also a list containing the information usually required. When a lease of property is to be negotiated and one of the conditions is that your client will be responsible for handing it over at the end of the lease in as good a state of repair as when the lease was granted, it is a wise precaution to have a report made upon its condition, and this point has been dealt with. Architects are often called upon to act as arbitrators, especially in small matters connected with contract work. Some knowledge is therefore requisite of the Law of Arbitration and the usual procedure to be followed.

Fire insurance relating to old and new buildings has been referred to, especially with a view to assisting the architect in dealing with any claims that may have to be made.

Sufficient has now been said to give some idea as to the extent and variety of the practical knowledge which an architect must acquire. I know of no work which deals with all the matters to which I have referred. Although here I am able to touch only the fringe of some of them, I do offer this book as an outline of the whole subject and as a serious contribution to a larger work[2] — a well considered textbook which we may contemplate in the future — based on the practical experience of many architects and surveyors.

When delivering the lectures upon which this book was founded I was often accused of giving too frequently, the warning, 'You cannot be too careful'. I have been reminded of this accusation again and again, but when I contemplate on the great importance of my subject I feel that this warning cannot be repeated too often.

[2] Since this introduction was first written there have been several works published concerning architectural practice and procedure notably that by the Royal Institute of British Architects itself entitled *Handbook of Architectural Practice and Management.*

Chapter II
How work is obtained

It is obvious that, unless you can obtain commissions, you will have no opportunity of putting into practice the knowledge you are now acquiring: a few remarks on this subject may therefore be welcome. I can imagine the pleasure you all experience in designing and drawing beautiful buildings, but very few people are so fortunately placed as to be able to do this without receiving payment in the way of fees. You must therefore have some idea as to how clients are obtained. It is by no means sufficient to put up a brass plate and to sit in an office expecting that jobs will rain in upon you. I can assure you that the matter is one that demands a great deal of careful thought and attention, and I hope that the methods I shall mention may be of assistance to you in the future.

I have noted a few clearly defined ways of obtaining work, and will now deal with them under separate headings:

(a) Through friends
This is one of the most usual sources, especially in the case of beginners. It is therefore to your advantage to enlarge the circle of your acquaintances at every opportunity. Personality is of as much importance as professional ability, and there is no doubt that in your profession a great deal depends on your ability to make friends who will interest themselves in your career. I was asked recently to give an approximate estimate for the extension of a large house, and in this case the architect told me that the client was a friend of his.

I repeat that you should lose no opportunity of making friends. Commissions come from unlikely quarters. I know an architect who obtained the nucleus of a quite good practice as the result of friendly chats with a builders' merchant from whom he occasionally bought wood and other odds and ends.

(b) As the result of actual work
The manner in which you design and carry out any work entrusted to you will play a vital part in the success or otherwise of your practice. I want to impress upon you the importance of doing your best in the small cases as well as in the more important ones. If, for instance, you are asked to add a garage or other small extension to a house, lay yourself out to satisfy your client. Such a job cannot, of course, be made to pay, but it may very likely be the means of extending your practice considerably.

Many years ago one of my friends designed a small church in Cardiff.

He had almost forgotten about it when, many years after, a clergyman called upon him and asked if he would design a similar one for him. Again, an architect was asked to advise a client upon the purchase of certain property, and he carried out his work so thoroughly that the client recommended him to one of his friends who desired to make an extensive addition to his house; thus by his careful work in a small case he obtained a much larger commission.

(c) By specialisation

I think it is always well for the young architect to study some particular branch of his profession, and endeavour to know all there is to be known of, say, one class of building. He may then become known as an authority on the subject on which he has specialised. But you must be careful not to over-specialise, and so have difficulties in carrying out work outside the class in which you are specially interested. A friend of mine made a special study of Old Peoples Homes, and in order to add to his collection of examples, made measured drawings of some houses that were subsequently pulled down to make way for a street improvement. When it became necessary to employ an architect he was commissioned to design the new buildings. The Royal Institute of British Architects runs a Clients Advisory Service which receives a large number of enquiries each year from prospective clients wishing to be put in touch with suitable architects.

(d) By luck

An architect, who has now ceased practice, was in the train on his way to London. He got into conversation with a fellow traveller, and when he arrived at Victoria he had a sanatorium in his pocket. I prepared the quantities for this building, and that is how I learnt of the incident. I found out afterwards, however, that the architect had heard that the building of a sanatorium had been mooted, and purposely got into the compartment where his fellow-traveller was, so perhaps there was less of luck than of business acumen in this incident.

In another case I was asked to prepare the quantities for a large seaside hotel. The architect who designed it obtained the work through another architect who was living near the site, but did not feel sufficiently competent to design the hotel himself.

(e) From solicitors

A good deal of work comes to architects through solicitors. For instance, the preparation of schedules of dilapidations, reports on the value of properties with a view to purchase or mortgage, questions regarding light and air, easements, encroachments, party walls and other matters involving legal points. Although the jobs are often small ones, it is impossible to tell what they may lead to. I therefore again advise you to take as much care over a small job, which may not mean much in the way of fees, as over a large one. You will find that the kind of work which comes through solicitors is very good practice; it usually requires special care, and sometimes may land you in the law courts. One experience as a witness under cross-examination will be of great value to you, besides enlarging your sympathies with all those who are subjected to this ordeal.

(f) Competitions

Going in for competitions is a method of obtaining work with which, no doubt, you are well acquainted. I advise you to enter for competitions whenever you find a subject which appeals to you. If you have a chance to enter into a competition where the number of architects is limited, the advantage will be great, and you may obtain a fee sufficient to pay for your work, even if you are not placed first. You will, however, find difficulty in getting chosen for limited competitions and so you must enter for the open ones. At the date of this sixth edition, 1974, there are regrettably very few competitions — at least ones of moderate size. Large ones now tend to be more international and call for very great resources. You are more likely therefore to be engaged on competition work as an assistant in a large office or consortium. You must guard against the temptation to neglect the small work that you have in hand. It takes time to tackle all the problems which arise, to overcome the difficulties which beset the architect in designing buildings to suit the requirements as set forth in the particulars supplied to competitors. Remember that 'a bird in the hand is worth two in the bush' but, on the other hand, the training to be obtained by working on a competition is excellent, and no time thus spent should be looked upon as lost. The Royal Institute of British Architects issue regulations governing the promotion and conduct of architectural competitions; these regulations must be carefully complied with.

(g) Other methods and their abuse

An architect once jokingly remarked to me that a good way of securing a commission was to go about with your eyes open. There is much more in this than a mere pleasantry. The man who trains his faculties to be always acute and responsive to what is going on around him is the man who will win through. The finest school for such intensive training is public service, and although I do not advise any architect to overburden himself with public duties outside his profession, I do think that he will be wise to take part in such activities as far as possible. Do not be afraid of serving on committees, church councils, or other bodies which have sound objects of public utility in view. You will learn much of human nature, you will be training yourself in diplomacy, you will be making yourself known, and you will be taking that best of tonics — the feeling that you are being of use to your generation. Such duties are sometimes, I am afraid taken up with the sole idea of getting work (like the man who joined a religious body when they acquired a site for their church), but a motive so dubious will in the end defeat its object. But duties taken up for the more praiseworthy purpose of fitting oneself for life and being of service to others will most assuredly not go without reward.

A tradesman who opens a shop endeavours to obtain customers by attractive window display, by advertising special articles, by punctual delivery of goods, and so on. The architect must always have regard to the Codes of Professional Conduct of the Royal Institute of British Architects and the Architects Registration Council; he is debarred from exhibiting his designs in a shop window and also from direct public advertisement; therefore, as it is necessary that he should become known, other methods have to be employed. I have offered a few suggestions, with the object of leading you to give careful thought to the matter. The future may sometimes look pretty hopeless to a man without influence, but I think the few examples I have given will show you that a practice often results from very trifling incidents. Never lose heart, therefore, but be quick to grasp the slightest opportunity that offers itself, and when it comes, as assuredly it will come, put every ounce of your weight into it and work harder than ever you have worked before to produce the finest effort of which you are capable. You may then rest assured that, whatever befalls, you will have the satisfaction of knowing that when the opportunity came you were ready for it and made the very best use of it in your power.

Chapter III
The working of an architect's office

My remarks about the working of an architect's office are only intended to give you some idea of what you may expect when you commence working with an architect.

When during your course of study you go into an office for the first time, try to believe that the architect has at least some little knowledge of his business. Do not deceive yourself or adopt the attitude that because you have spent several years as a student of architecture, you know all there is to be known, for I may as well tell you, whether you like it or not, that the knowledge you have gained there will only suffice to start you upon your career, and that the things you are ignorant of are so many that if you realised what you don't know, and the vast amount of knowledge there still remains for you to gain, you would feel quite unequal to the task before you.

Architects' offices are worked in various ways. The management of a large office with many assistants differs from that of one with, say, a single assistant. In many large offices the junior assistants see the principal only occasionally, and have to work under the orders of senior assistants, which procedure may well be met in group practices where half-a-dozen or more architects form a group, but not a partnership, and use common facilities for technical and administrative staff, whilst in smaller offices there is continual touch between the principals and all their assistants.

Do not get into the habit, which I am afraid many assistants do, of thinking that the principal just swaggers about, working only when he likes, that he always has a good time, and that his fees roll in with very little effort on his part. I should like to be able to make you realise that whatever salary an assistant gets, it is as much as he is worth; but my experience of architects' assistants is that they usually feel they are underpaid, and are apt to contrast their salary with the percentage 'raked in' by the principal. They either forget, or probably have little idea of, the amount of the architects' expenses or of his total responsibility.

Upon entering an architect's office you could well be called upon to develop principal sketches, and you will find plenty of scope in this for showing what you are made of. Time is one of the really important things in an architect's office, as it is in most other places, and I strongly advise you to cultivate the ability to work rapidly. Then you will be asked to detail certain parts of a building from the small scale plans, and this is where real ability counts. You may be sure that when details are required there is no time to waste, and so I advise you in your studies to make full use of your opportunity to acquire this most necessary knowledge. I once heard an architect say, when the question of the reduction of staff was being considered, that a certain man must be retained because of his ability to detail accurately and rapidly. There is no time nowadays to waste in any business, and therefore the assistant who can work quickly and accurately is bound to get on. Many assistants waste time by trying to get their own ideas adopted. I suggest that you try to drop your individuality for the moment and concentrate on carrying out the wishes of your principal.

Some architects design their buildings to a small scale and also prepare a large scale detail of one portion of the building. An assistant then draws further details, following the small scale plan and the typical detail, with datum lines running right across the paper. You will probably find that your early tasks will be something like those I have outlined.

Surveys will have to be made of existing buildings; and as in large offices it is not often that the principal has time to do this, one of your jobs may be to make a survey. You will find in chapter VI some remarks on surveys, which I hope may be found useful.

The time will doubtless come when you will be asked to write a specification. You may feel quite incompetent to do this but you will make a very great mistake if you do not rise to the occasion, doing the very best you can and in the shortest time, working in the evenings and far into the night if necessary. It is wonderful how easy and interesting the writing of specifications can become if careful attention is given to details and to the technical wording of other specifications which come before you.

In a small office you will, of course, have to do everything that comes to hand, from drawing plans and details to posting letters, and this will give you a splendid all-round training.

I remember one office where the principal did no designing at all, he was very clever indeed at getting work, but no good at designing or drawing; therefore his chief assistant did all that work for him. I advise you to avoid an office of that sort; your object should be to gain experience from a capable principal.

A large office will no doubt have a special staff for such clerical work as typing of letters, the registering and recording of papers and plans, making arrangements for obtaining photo prints, and attending to all matters not concerned with actual drawings. You will probably have nothing to do with this part of the office, but nevertheless I advise you to go about with your eyes open, and you will see much that will help you later on. I am referring in chapter XIII to consortia between not only contractors but also professional offices. In the case of architects, consultants and quantity surveyors a consortium may more normally take the form of a group practice in which independent firms are associated together sharing office expenses including technical staff and such an arrangement can at times be helpful to one's clients and beneficial to oneself and it can exist with equal effect in small as well as large offices.

Sooner or later you will be engaged on working with consultants of various types, in co-ordinating their drawings and details with your own and in checking working drawings of sub-contractors and specialists all of which operations call for great care and experience.

Whatever office you go into, try to earn the reputation of being a worker. There is a temptation in a large office to slack, and you may think it does not matter, but I can assure you that under the present stress of living there is no room even in the largest concern for a slacker, and that, sooner or later, he will get thrown out. On the other hand, the worker who tries to make himself indispensable will find little difficulty in keeping and improving his position.

With the training you have received I am sure you will be welcome in any architect's office, provided you make up your mind to try to do a little better than anyone else, and remember that you still have much to learn.

In the introduction to this edition I have referred to the *Handbook of Architectural Practice and Management* published by the RIBA and I would particularly like to draw your attention to the Plan of Work for design team operation which although forming part of the main handbook is published separately. You should use this Plan of Work as a check list to ensure that you properly conduct contracts from inception to final feed-back of information.

Notes on running your own practice contributed by Bob Garratt of The Architectural Association.

The introduction of the RIBA Practical Training Scheme in 1964, details of which can be found in the front of each RIBA Practical Training Logbook, has gone some way in coping with the expectations of young architects in the offices as well as ensuring an overall view of running both a job and an office. In the following paragraphs I will try to give a very brief outline of what to watch when starting a practice.

First a warning — most clients are no longer individuals. You will work in a capitalist society in which the old-style 'patrons' who helped protect *your* interests have virtually vanished. Clients are mostly companies concerned with rapid return on their investment or government departments desperate to stay within their prescribed cost limits. So it is likely that from the start your practice will be under pressure from clients to reduce your fee whilst, simultaneously, increasing the service you give them. This gives them a cheaper service whilst offering you vague promises of further jobs. Do not succumb. Not only is it against the professional codes but it can be financially disastrous to your new practice because you cannot plan for, or put in the bank, promises.

With interest rates so high on borrowed money the most important thing to do, once you have a job, is to ensure that you do not go broke during the running of it. The technique to handle this is to record each month the amount of money you receive from fees and set against this the amount of money you are paying out on wages, papers, drawings, rent, insurances and other running costs. Provided the income each month is equal to or more than the expenditure, then you are at least solvent. The simple chart you have then devised shows your 'cash-flow'. This must be revised each month as unforeseen events occur, and I guarantee that they will. Although some people find this task a bore, it can prove extremely helpful when talking to your bank manager or clients as they will both understand that you appreciate how to handle money and this usually means that if you really need to borrow then it will be easier for you than for those who vaguely 'think they will make a profit'.

Sadly clients can be very tardy at paying fees and if you have no income but considerable expenditure this is the fastest way of going out of business. So when you accept a job from a client send him a copy of the RIBA Conditions of Engagement and Scale of Fees, suitably marked to show just what service he is going to get for his money. To these papers you should add a note that a percentage will be charged, say 5% per month, on fees unpaid after one month. This may sound hard on the client but my experience is that this clause has never yet had to be implemented because the client then understands that he must play his part in keeping your organisation effective so that you can put your full attention in providing him with the best building you can design and build.

The most difficult part of starting a practice for young architects is getting the first jobs, as you will have gathered in Chapter II, and there are no hard and fast rules here except that you should only attempt jobs of which you have some specialist knowledge and about which you feel moderately confident of being able to handle. As you cannot directly approach clients, except local authorities through the RIBA Practice Information Sheets, obtainable from the RIBA, it is important that your schemes are well publicised — and not just in the professional press. Remember that there will be people interested in every one of your schemes both in the vicinity of the building (where the local and regional news media will publicise it if it is of sufficient merit) and in the trade press of the industry or service organisation for which the building or scheme is designed. All of these can be valuable to you especially at the start of your practice. Once you have some jobs it is essential that you keep a weather eye open on regional, national and international governmental movements to see whether changing policies will mean more or fewer jobs from your present sources. If things look doubtful see what building types the new policies will be favouring and educate yourself in the problems of these.

When handling the administration of a job follow the routines set out in the RIBA Job book at least until you have enough experience to decide whether to develop your own procedures. Remember to watch the monthly 'Practice Notes' in the RIBA Journal as the courts take these as current best practice. Should you be so unlucky as to end up in court over alleged professional incompetence and you are not following these advised procedures you will severely weaken your own defence and this could have costly effects on your practice.

A lot of time, and some money, must be spent in properly setting up the practice — especially if it is to be a partnership. The partnership deed must be handled by a solicitor experienced in such matters, and it should not just deal with the pleasant aspects of who is to be paid what but should cover the unpleasant aspects (which seem inconceivable at the start of a practice) such as what happens on the death of a partner, especially to his wife and family. Your solicitor should also help you register the name of your practice. You will need a good accountant. One who does not just prepare accounts at the end of each year to comply with the tax and company laws but one who will help you set up simple financial information systems, like cash-flows, that will help you monitor your monthly progress. And do not forget all the insurances you will need for professional indemnity, employees, third parties, premises etc. These can well be arranged through the Architects Benevolent Society at 68 Portland Place, London W1.

And finally, do not forget your staff. They are your strongest asset and need to be treated as such. Do not be bombastic to them and let them work out job problems for themselves. Remember what it was like when you were an assistant and try to do better than your ex-boss. If you immediately give them solutions to all problems you will show that you do not trust their judgement. And if you do not trust them why are you paying them?

I hope this does not make running your own practice too terrifying or depressing. I do not want to put you off with dire tales of finance problems, insurances going wrong, or wicked clients. Most of the problems concerned with running a practice that you could meet *are* avoidable with a little thoughtful planning. And if you do this planning at the start of each job and once a month to see how the whole practice is going you will have about 28 days a month to enjoy your professional skills in designing to the best of your ability.

Chapter IV
Keeping and recording papers

My next subject is the keeping of papers, and by this I mean the systematic filing and recording of correspondence and other papers relating to an architect's practice. I am afraid the subject is one which is not calculated to awaken intense enthusiasm, but I hope I shall at any rate make it plain to you how necessary it is to have a simple and efficient system of keeping papers.

I am convinced that most assistants and young architects commencing practice do not realise the amount of clerical and routine work which is connected with a practice, nor do they foresee that unless this work is carried out in an orderly manner confusion will soon reign supreme. Let me therefore show you one of the means whereby you may be saved from all the petty annoyance and worry inseparable from mislaid papers, thus keeping your minds free to soar into those realms of artistic ecstasy which befit the young enthusiast, but regarding the existence of which an architect of my acquaintance recently professed profound scepticism.

I propose to explain in full detail the system of keeping papers which has been in operation in my own office for many years, and which has always been found to be absolutely efficient. I should like you to take special note of what I am going to say, as I am sure this system, based on that which at one time obtained in a government department where I served for several years, is a really good one and able to fulfil all the needs of an architect, whatever size his practice may be.

Briefly, the system is to have a set of papers for each job, and where the works are large, as many sets or 'packets' as are found necessary. For example, a cottage or a small alteration job will require only one packet of papers, but a large building like Australia House will require many sets. The general idea is to keep different subjects distinct and separate, and in a large job — the contract, say, for the constructional steelwork — may well be sufficiently important to warrant a separate packet. As a matter of fact, there are in my office over 100 packets in connection with the building of Australia House.

The 'packet' is formed gradually, and consists of the various papers, such as letters received, copies of letters written, specifications, estimates, and variation orders. On top of the packet is placed a double sheet of plain foolscap (or A4 if preferred), which we call the 'jacket', at the bottom, as a backing, is a envelope in which are kept all rough drafts or letters, reports, etc. The whole packet is tied round the middle with a piece of tape and always kept the same size. We generally call the whole bundle or packet the 'papers'.

When a client commissions you to design and build a house, for example, the name is at once written upon a blank sheet (the jacket) folded down the centre the long way of the paper. A number is assigned to the job and placed at the top right-hand corner of the jacket. A further number is placed immediately below the first number with a line between, thus, $\frac{235}{622}$. The top number represents the actual number of the packet, and in this case would mean that there were already 1234 other packets in the office. The lower number represents the month and year that the commission was obtained, 6 meaning June, and 72 meaning 1972. This double number is placed upon all letters and other communications, reports, etc, and therefore no difficulty is ever experienced as to where to place loose papers which may be found lying about in the office.

A number book or index is kept which shows the name of the job, the number given to the packet, the description of the work, and also the number of the recorded bundle where the packet can be found after it has been put away at the termination of the works. I shall deal with the recording later on.

I think the examples given on pages 34 and 35 showing the first page of the jackets, and also a page of the number book, will assist you to understand the system.

The first item to enter on the jacket is the origin of the work. It may be the receipt of a letter from a client asking you to design a cottage. A short précis or epitome is written on the jacket, with the date of the letter, or, if the commission is given verbally, a short report is written upon the jacket, with the date, and initialled. Then follows in order of date a short précis of all letters received and written.

The précis of the letters received is entered on the left-hand side of the fold of the jacket, and the précis of the letters despatched on the right-hand side. In addition to the packet number every letter or paper is given a special number, the first letter being numbered 1 and all others consecutively, whether received or written. In this way it can easily be seen whether all the letters are in the bundle. As the letters arrive they are numbered and afterwards fastened together, the latest letter always being on top and the first letter at the bottom. Carbon copies are kept of all letters written and are given a number in the same way as incoming letters. When the 'jacket' is filled up with entries, another sheet is added and tied to it. Never omit to date all documents and papers. You may be surprised to hear we often receive even letters with no date on them.

Before leaving the subject of letters, there is one other point which, if attended to, will save a lot of time. Seeing that we have a separate jacket of papers for each job, it is essential to the system that no extraneous matters should be introduced. Never write about more than one job in a letter. Sometimes I receive a letter referring to three or four different jobs, and this causes much trouble. In such cases we number and file the letter with the packet for the job first mentioned by the writer, and we make copies of such portions of the letter as relate to other subjects. After numbering the copies they are kept in their proper jackets, with references on the respective jackets showing where the original letter is filed. In my

$\frac{547}{448}$

The Anchorage, Slocumpton.

14 April 1916. Interview with Miss Blank who instructed me to carry out certain alterations and additions to the above house, made appointment for the 15th. inst. at Slocumpton

J.S.J. $\frac{14}{4}$

15.4.16 Letter from Miss Blank putting off appointment until 19th. (1)

16.4.16. Letter to Miss Blank acknowledging (2)

19.4.16. Visited The Anchorage. Slocumpton and took particulars   Expenses £2.3.6

J.S.J. $\frac{21}{4}$

27.4.16. Letter to Smith & Sons asking for estimate for grates. (3)

28.4.16 Letter from Smith & Sons giving quotation for grates. (4)

3.5.16. Miss Blank approved drawings and gave me instructions to obtain tenders. Cost not to exceed £1,000.

J.S.J. 3/5/16

2.6.16. Invitations to tender sent to following :— (5)
1. Jones & Co.
2. Robinson & Son
3. Smith Bros.
4. F.K. Thomas
5. Brown & Sons

Note   The dotted line represents the fold in the paper

NUMBER BOOK OF PAPERS

No of Papers	Name	Description of work	Papers recorded in Bundle numbered
539	St Mary's Church	New reredos	75
540	General Hospital	Additions	61
541	Willesden	New factory	
542	The Anchorage, Slocumpton	Alterations and additions	37
543	The Square, South Acton	New motor-garage	60
544	Westburton	Proposed new wing	
545			
546			

own practice I am most careful not to write about more than one job in a letter, but I am unable to say the same of all my clients.

In addition to keeping letters in the packets of papers, we put in it everything else connected with the job, such as variation orders, approximate estimates, copies of reports, small plans, specifications, contracts, and bills of quantities.

I have not yet explained the full use which is made of the jackets. Many architects and surveyors keep no written report of their interviews, possibly only a short note in a diary.

It is very wise always to write on the jackets a short report of your interviews, and if done at once there is very little trouble. I want to make a strong point of keeping notes of interviews, as it is most important. Some little time ago I was a witness in a case in the County Court, and the habit of keeping records of interviews proved very useful to me. A witness on the other side had described an interview between us, and his evidence did not agree with my recollection of what had taken place. When I was called upon to describe the interview, I asked permission to refer to my papers, and was able to read the report I had written immediately after the interview; this was accepted in preference to the evidence of the other witness, who had kept no notes, but had trusted only to his memory. The fact that the report was written upon the jackets, and was in its correct position of date, also helped to show that it had been written at the time. This illustration will show you almost as well as anything the value of the system.

Interviews are of various kinds and with all sorts of people. You should keep notes of all interviews with tradesmen and especially record their promises and what they say they can do. It is extraordinary what differences of opinion can arise in a short time about such things, and unless you have a record of what was actually said you may be placed in a difficult position. Make a list of full names and addresses of all persons present at an interview or conference. See that your staff keep a record of all calls and interviews and also the substance of telephone messages.

The jackets are also useful for keeping accounts of your expenses. When you visit a client at his house in the country, or go to inspect the works, you will incur railway fares, out-of-pocket expenses, taxi or car hire, car mileage etc. You will find that the jackets are a convenient place on which to enter the amount of your expenses. You can, of course, if you prefer it, keep an expenses book, but I think it is more convenient to keep the record on the jackets. But, whatever you do, be sure it is done systematically, as it will sometimes be a difficult matter to make up your account of expenses if the items have not been recorded at the time.

You must be very careful about enclosures with letters. There are plenty of systems for dealing with enclosures, and one of the special things we do in my office is in connection with this. It is most important to be able to tell definitely what enclosures were really sent with a letter, say twelve months ago. For example, a letter is written to a client, and enclosed are three or four estimates, or perhaps letters. It may be quite easy to remember for a week or so what enclosures were put in the envelope with the letter, and you may have a list put at the end of the letter, but even with this precaution it may still be difficult to know definitely what was enclosed. It has often happened that a firm has been unable to say for certain what enclosures were sent with a letter. It may be quite clear that, say, two or three enclosures were sent, but the difficulty lies in identifying the actual enclosures and so we get over the trouble by writing at the top of our copy of each enclosure something like the following:

Enclosure with letter to $\cdots\cdots\cdots\cdots\cdots\cdots\cdots\cdots\cdots\cdots\cdots\cdots$

dated $\ldots\ldots\ldots\ldots\ldots\ldots\ldots\ldots\ldots\ldots\ldots\ldots\ldots\ldots\ldots\ldots\ldots$ No. $\dfrac{21}{235}$

or

Enclosure ith letter from $\cdots\cdots\cdots\cdots\cdots\cdots\cdots\cdots\cdots\cdots\cdots\cdots$

dated $\ldots\ldots\ldots\ldots\ldots\ldots\ldots\ldots\ldots\ldots\ldots\ldots\ldots\ldots\ldots$ No. $\dfrac{4}{542}$

The result of this action is that we always know, and are able to prove, exactly what was enclosed with any letter coming into or going out of the office. There have been cases, however, where letters have been sent in which it was stated that certain documents were enclosed, and where, as a matter of fact, the enclosures were left out. This is the human element coming in and upsetting all our careful arrangements. To make such an occurrence as unlikely as possible, a second clerk should see that the letter and enclosures are all in order before they are sealed, and in this way we get as near perfection as possible.

Whilst on the subject of letters, I should like to say that it will pay you well to give a good deal of study to the art of writing a business-like letter or report. This is a subject to which little attention seems to be directed, and one frequently reads a rambling, slipshod epistle, which properly edited, could have been expressed far more clearly in half the number of words. It takes a long time to acquire the ability to write a good letter or report — in fact, some people never learn to do it. Therefore take every opportunity of studying well-expressed correspondence, reports, leading articles in newspapers, etc. Endeavour to criticise them, to boil them down to improve upon them. Do not disdain to write drafts of your own letters or to re-write them as often as is necessary. Try to place yourself in the position of the person who is to receive the letter. I often ask one of my assistants to read, and give me his honest opinion, of one of my reports before I send it, in order to satisfy myself that everything is clear.

Now we come to the recording of papers. When a job is finished and all accounts paid, the time has arrived to put the papers away, and this can be done in two ways. One way is to tie up the papers just as they are and put them into a cupboard or upon a shelf, and the other (and better) way is to go through the packet and take out and destroy all drafts and unwanted copies in order to make the packet as small as possible. See that all the letters are in order, and bind them into book form. When we consider the work is important, we send the correspondence to the binder, and have the letters bound in a simple manner, but with less important work the correspondence is bound in the office, and so whenever we want to refer to a particular job we can always rely upon finding all the papers, which we have put away in a good workmanlike manner. The packet is then wrapped up in brown paper, a number is placed upon the bundle in a prominent position (cloak-room numbers do very well for this) and the bundle is placed upon a shelf. If the packet of papers for a particular job is small, we put several together to form a fair-sized bundle, and in the number book or index, already described, we enter the number of the recorded bundle where the papers have been placed, so that it takes only a few moments to find any particular packet.

I am anxious that the simplicity of this system should appeal to you all. As you are aware, a verbal explanation is never so convincing as an actual experience. I therefore advise each of you (whether you have any present need or not) to get a few letters, etc, together, and to make a few packets as a test in order to impress these counsels of mine on you memory.

The system needs no elaborate filing cabinets, no card index; no drawers are necessary, no hunting up in cupboards or on shelves for letters or reports; everything (except plans) will be found in the packet of papers, the whole case quite complete. I can illustrate this simplicity by supposing that I have to go to Aylesbury tomorrow, and am leaving home at 7 o'clock in the morning. I have had a very busy day, and have not managed to spare a minute to look up the papers I require to take with me. As I leave the office, for perhaps some social function, the packet of papers relating to the job is given to me, and I shall now be able to go through the whole matter this evening at home, with the certain knowledge that I have before me every paper connected with it. This I think, illustrates my point very well, and when some day you happen to sit at a conference and witness the embarrassment of one of the members who has mislaid several of his papers, you will have reason to thank me if I have persuaded you to adopt a system which saves you from trouble.

I do not want my advice to be regarded as simply a counsel of perfection; to me it is a vital necessity of successful business. There will be many who will find it difficult to keep a good system going at first. My advice is never to allow initial failures to make you abandon it. Begin again and acquire gradually the habit of system, and you will soon find it of real value.

There are, of course, many other efficient systems for the keeping and recording of papers. Some of them proprietary and others prepared from individual experience so that before setting up you own office discuss the problem with as many people as you can so that the system you do adopt in the end is the one which suits your own needs best.

Chapter V
Catalogues and price lists

Every architect should have a well-selected supply of catalogues. These are very easily obtained, but somewhat difficult to keep in a manner which admits of ready reference. Some system should be adopted, even if it is a poor one, rather than no system at all. If you have a large staff and can delegate to one of your assistants the duty of keeping a catalogue system in order, the matter is simple, but this is seldom the case in the ordinary architect's office.

One of the difficulties about catalogues is that there is no uniformity of size, and this makes the filing of them very troublesome. In many of the offices I know, the catalogues are all over the place, and the architects trust to luck to find the right one when they want it. In my own office the catalogues are kept in a large book-case. Each catalogue is numbered in such a way that the numbers may be seen at a glance without moving the catalogues; the bound books stand on end, and the thin catalogues or paper ones are laid flat, with the number marked on a paper slip pasted to the catalogue.

An index is kept both in names and in trades or materials, and as far as time will permit, this index is kept up to date. When revised catalogues are obtained, the old ones are put in the waste-paper basket. In practice, it is my experience that, after referring to a catalogue, it is not always put back into its proper place, and sometimes it is taken out of the office and is not returned. It is seldom, therefore, that perfect order, such as a quantity surveyor aims at, reigns.

I make a practice of having the catalogue book-case put in order not less than once a year, and the index corrected; but I must admit that even with this system it is sometimes quicker to obtain a new catalogue from the manufacturer or merchant than to look for the one that happens to be missing. The best advice I can give is, put your catalogues in a book-case, number them and have an index, and as time permits go through the book case and bring the whole up to date.

One of the objects of having a good supply of catalogues is to be able to obtain quickly the prices of various articles. Some years ago it was usual for merchants to send out their catalogues fully priced, but now the general practice seems to be to leave out the prices. I should like to warn you, moreover, that where prices are given you must not rely too much upon them, for they vary so rapidly that they are generally quite unreliable, especially, too, as the amount of the discounts given is seldom stated. These discounts vary from 2½ to $33^1/_3$% or more and therefore unless you know the correct market price and the amount of the discount you cannot know the real price of the article. Prices are changed by the merchants without any notice being given to the architects. I therefore suggest that you should get written quotations whenever occasion requires, and note on your catalogues the prices and date. Although we do not now act upon this advice as prices vary from day to day, it may be that in the future prices will again become stablized and you will be able to keep the prices in your catalogues up to date.

In chapter XVII it will be explained that manufactured articles and fittings required under a contract, for which monetary provision has been made, are charged net, that is, after the deduction of trade discount. This discount is given by wholesale firms for the benefit of retail traders, but the contractor is not a retailer, for he is remunerated by the profit on his contract and therefore the architect should see that his client gets the full benefit of this discount. Trade discount should not be confused with cash discount to which the contractor is entitled, and if your contract is the standard form of building contract (1963 Revised 1973), this cash discount will be 5% if the materials or goods are to be supplied by a nominated supplier for fixing by the contractor.

There are some very admirable general catalogues available for your reference such as *The Architect's Standard Catalogues* which cover such a wide field of materials that the need for scores of individual catalogues is less than it used to be, but I find that my staff still prefer to read the catalogue dealing with the material they are actually describing as prepared by the manufacturer.

Instead of preparing your own catalogue system you can of course today subscribe to firms who specialise in providing technical libraries of catalogues for professional offices and these firms undertake to keep your library up-to-date.

For an architect starting in practice and for small offices I still advocate the personal collection system, for handsome though the libraries are, they create a state of affairs like the position of a man who owns a complete *Encyclopaeadia Britannica* — you know it's all there but you don't know what there is.

Chapter VI

Surveying sites and buildings

No doubt you have all made some progress in the art of surveying and levelling, but you may not have had many opportunities of putting your knowledge to practical use. I am now going to give you some hints which I have found useful in my own experience and which will enable you to proceed with confidence when you have sites for new buildings to survey or existing buildings to measure for alterations.

The first thing I wish to impress upon you is to place no reliance on your memory. Make a note of all the information you obtain before you leave the site. It is the only safe way, and may sometimes save a second expensive journey.

You will find it very helpful on going to make a survey to take with you a form containing a list of questions on the various points to be considered. Some years ago I saw a form used by Government surveyors, and with this as a basis I composed a document which we use in my office. It is as follows:

Proposed . . . . . (*describe work*) . . . .
. . . .
. . . . Date . . . .

PARTICULARS OF SITE, ETC

1 *Plan of site*	*Notes*
The site is to be surveyed and plotted to a convenient scale. Note any buildings adjoining the site, and state whether there are any windows overlooking the latter, and whether it is likely that any right of light and air has been acquired thereby.	
The survey and plan should include all necessary particulars of adjacent properties and roads and of all walls, fences, etc. Note exact position of trees, etc, which it is desired to retain.	
Show correct aspect of site. If the site is a large one an Ordnance map will be found most useful. Visit office of Local Authority and obtain a tracing of the site from an Ordnance map. The surveyor to the Authority will generally assist you with local information and let you see maps and plans of the district.	

2   *Levels*

Levels of the site, abuttals and approaches to be taken and referred to Ordanance datum where possible, and checked by the existing bench marks.

Show bench marks on plan. If an arbitrary datum is unavoidable it should be plainly so marked on the drawings, and some permanent mark selected, such as the step of a door.

The number of section lines will depend upon the surface conditions of the site and the proposed position of the buildings.

The section lines must be marked upon the survey plan, and the reduced levels at the points taken written thereon and enclosed in circles.

If preferred the site can be contoured, but generally the site divided into, say, squares of 8 m will be convenient, with extra levels taken where any special features occur.

3   *Surface, subsoil and trial holes*

Describe general character of site — grass, arable land, trees, etc.

Dig trial holes near the site of proposed buildings and mark positions on plans. Describe subsoil.

State depth at which a good foundation can be obtained.
State whether surplus excavated material can be deposited on site and show position on plan. If not, give approximate distance to be carted.

4   *Position of building*

Show on plan the best position for the buildings, and state your reasons.

5   *Foundations*

Will concrete be required for foundations? If so, describe materials and state proportions.

If foundations will be on rock give some description.

It is sometimes useful to consult a geological map to see the general nature of the ground.

6   *Walls*

Where should the stone or bricks for walls and facings be obtained?

Obtain particulars and probable cost of same, and of all carta and labours involved as far as they can be easily ascertained.

7   *Portland cement and lime*

Describe and give prices of Portland cement and lime.

State prices whereby the cost of stone-walling or brickwork in cement mortar may be compared.

8   Sand

Describe and give prices of sand, and state where it may be obtained.

9   Water

How can water for the works be obtained?

How should the building be supplied with drinking-water?

If company's water is obtainable, show on plan the position of mains, and state whether supply is constant or intermittent and whether lead or iron pipes should be used. Some Authorities require special pipes.

If water is likely to be obtained by sinking a well, give particulars of wells in the neighbourhood and any other information obtainable. State if analysis is desirable.

Ascertain, if possible, the degree of hardness of the water, and state if there are any local difficulties in using the water for hot-water supply.

10   Gas and electric mains

If gas and electric current can be obtained, show on plan the position of mains.

11   Drainage

How should sewage be disposed of?

Show on plan position and direction of sewer (if any). State depth and give other particulars. If the depth cannot be obtained by actual measurement, ask local authority, and get the depth from them in writing.

Do the authorities require a separate system of drains for soil and rain water?

Will the site require surface drainage? How will this drainage be disposed of?

12   Boundaries

What kind of boundary fences and gates will be required? Will any road or path-making be necessary.

13   Generally

Give any other information which will facilitate the preparation of the particulars for the contract.

14   Local Authorities

Obtain a copy of local by-laws and regulations. The Borough (or Rural) Surveyor will, no doubt, assist with information in connection with questions Nos 1, 3, 6, 7, 8, 9, 10 and 11.

Notes

I suggest that you should always take a copy of this form with you and endeavour to fill in replies to all the relevant questions, and if you are wise you will revise the form periodically to meet your own requirements.

The Standard Form of Building Contract (1963 revised 1973) makes the client responsible for the correctness of the setting out of the works at ground floor level so that surveys should be absolutely correct, therefore do not be in a hurry. Before you commence a survey, take a good look all over the site, note any unusual features and decide where the lines of your survey are to come. If you are not careful you may find your main line — the line upon which possibly your whole survey is to be based — running directly into a tree or some other obstruction, and much time will be lost in circumventing the obstruction. Take all your dimensions very accurately, and see that all points are properly tied. If the site is a sloping one do not forget to allow for the slope in your measurements, as you will remember plans are drawn on the level. Endeavour to divide up the site into triangles as large as possible, and do not spare your measurements. It is better to have too many than too few.

It is always desirable to make full use of Ordnance maps, which are very reliable, but you must always make your own survey. You can, in the first place, make an enlarged sketch from them, and when your survey is plotted, a comparison with the map will show whether you angles are correct.

In getting your levels be sure to finish up on the point from which you start; reduce your levels while you are on the field; you will thus know whether they are accurately taken, and you will arrive at the office with your mind at rest and your book complete. Be very careful when you change the position of the level to see that the reading staff is held on a solid object. If there is no Ordnance survey bench mark near the site, you should select an arbitrary permanent mark to start from, such as a doorstep or a mark on a gate-post. Note this point carefully on your plan so that it can be found readily at a later date if required. Write all your levels, dimensions and information very clearly in the level book otherwise, if the survey is not plotted immediately after it is made, you may have great difficulty in setting up your sections. You may sometimes have to employ a man to hold the staff who has little idea as to how to hold it vertically. You can, of course, see whether it is vertical one way, but unknown to you it may be leaning towards or from you. It is always well, therefore, to ask such a man gently to move the staff backwards and forwards, and you thus read the highest figure where it swings through the vertical point. As Ordnance bench marks are very valuable to all surveyors, I should like to plead with you to have them re-cut in all cases where, owing to the pulling down of buildings, they are destroyed. I think however that the Ordnance Survey Office, Romsey Road, Maybush, Southampton desire to be notified when a bench mark is likely to be affected by building operations, and prefer that in such cases the mark should be wholly defaced so as to avoid the users of the mark being misled by false levels.

The original Ordnance Survey of Great Britain was related to a datum of mean sea level at Liverpool. All revised levels, however, are now related to a similar datum at Newlyn, Cornwall, and it is important for you to be sure to which series of levels any bench-mark you propose to use is related. To be up to date your levels should wherever possible relate to Newlyn and if you are in doubt you can obtain advice from the Ordnance Survey Office.

In measuring buildings always take running dimensions on lines as long as possible in addition to the detail measurements, also plenty of diagonals. Take great care to get the thickness of walls on each floor, and to mark the thicknesses carefully upon your survey sheet. Always measure doorways and windows in the same way. For doorways, take the width of the door itself, and if necessary make a detail sketch of the plan of the doorway with full measurements. For windows, take the width between the outside reveals, and make larger sketches if necessary. Be very careful in getting the heights of the rooms and the thickness of the floors. First obtain the heights from floor to floor on the staircase, and then measure the heights of the rooms. It must not be assumed that the joists are of equal depth throughout.

It is often impracticable to take the height of a room against the wall on account of the projection of the cornice. It is, however, easy to reach the flat ceiling by putting your rod against the edge of the door when opened into the room.

In large buildings where steelwork is to be used extensively it is customary for the steelwork engineer to make the survey. I remember seeing on the engineer's site plan for Australia House a dimension of $115' \, 3^{13}/_{16}''$ and another of $73' \, 7^{13}/_{16}''$. I think you will agree with me that this shows great care, but I fancy these dimensions were calculated, and not the result of actual measurements. By kind permission of the architect I am able to show you a copy of this plan and also a copy of an engineer's plan for some alterations to a building, showing a very careful survey made for the purpose of indicating the exact positions of new stanchions and steelwork.

I expect you are all aware that measuring tapes and chains are liable to vary in length according to the moisture in the air, temperature and by constant use. These should always be used for accurate work. It is a good plan if you live in London to check your tapes and chains periodically at the standard measurement scale in Trafalgar Square. I remember on one occasion, many years ago, setting out six small houses with a measuring tape that had stretched $6''$. Fortunately the mistake was found out before the houses were erected. On the other hand, a tape which had not been used for several years was found to have shrunk $3\frac{1}{2}''$ in $40' \, 0''$, and this shrinkage was also uneven, but I believe the manufacturers have now improved the shrinkage factor. If you have a lot of surveying to do, it would be wise to set up standard marks on the pavement outside your office, so that you can check your chain or tape as often as you like, not only its full length, but each $10' \, 0''$ also.

I should like to give you a word of warning in connection with the use of any surveying instruments depending on the swing of a magnet — for instance, the magentic compass. A friend of mine was using one, and seeing that the workmen who was assisting was interested, he allowed him to look through the instrument. The bearing which the workman obtained by no means agreed with that booked by my friend, and at last it was

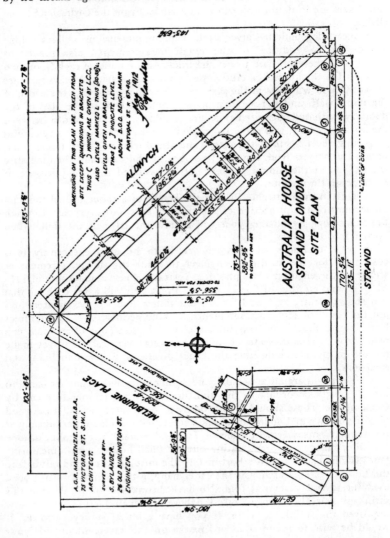

discovered that the man had a large iron key in his pocket. Be careful in the use of such instruments not to stand near iron fences or other objects which will deflect the magnet.

The best way to avoid mistakes in surveys is to take plenty of measurements and to tie them together as fully as possible. In theory one diagonal may seem all that is necessary, but in practice it is wiser to take several as a check, especially if your building is irregular. In a survey which

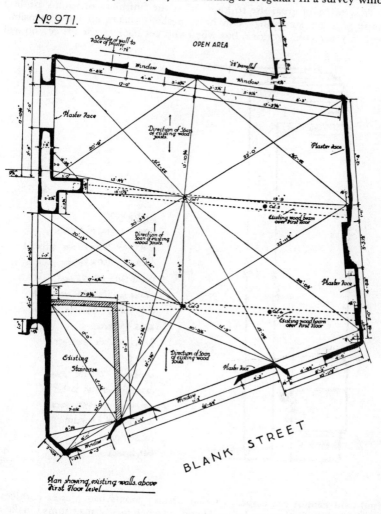

I made recently of some rather straggling buildings, I measured every diagonal I could find, although I knew that many might prove superfluous; but it does not take long to measure an extra line or two, and the want of one single dimension may sometimes make it difficult to plot the survey.

Always get your lines as long as you can, measure carefully, and record your dimensions distinctly. Sketch your plan as large as possible on sheets of paper not less than say A4 size. Make separate details of all special work, using your general sketch for the leading dimensions only.

It is often of great use to know what the finishings of rooms are in a house you are surveying. You have, perhaps, taken all the dimensions necessary for your sections, but when you get back to the office you will

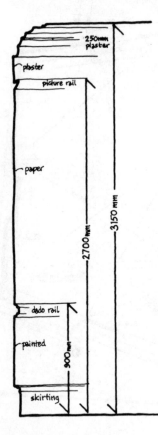

DINING ROOM
floor - softwood boards
skirting - 225 x 25 mm softwood
dado rail - 100 x 25 mm   "
picture rail - 50 x 25 mm   "
plaster cornice - 250mm girth
dado filling - painted
walls - papered
frieze - white emulsion
ceiling -   "   "
woodwork - painted cream
cased frames and sashes
softwood six panel doors
wood mantel - painted
register grate
tile hearth

find you cannot remember whether certain rooms had plaster cornices, picture rails, skirtings or dados. Therefore when measuring rooms I make a sketch section with a short list of the finishings. It takes very little time to put in the heights, describe the cornice, picture rail, dado, etc. It is extraordinary how often information is wanted on the very points which have not been noted, but if you follow my practice you will find much time will be saved in the end.

In making surveys you will come across many things of interest. Many years ago one of my assistants was sent, in the month of January, to a large Georgian house in Surrey to make an estimate for repairs and decorations. The windows of the drawing- and dining-rooms were very large, with boxed shutters and back flaps. The shutters were in the boxings, and upon opening them to examine their condition he was astonished to find that the whole space of the boxings, the backs of the shutters and both sides of the back flaps were covered with a dense mass of blue-bottle flies packed four or five deep. It was not a very pleasant sight, and he quickly closed the shutters.

On one occasion I had to survey a house in Bath which had been partly destroyed by fire, a plan being required for production in the police court, where the owner was charged with setting fire to the property for the purpose of obtaining the insurance money. Among other things I found a bedroom measuring only 6′ 0″ x 3′ 0″, with bed complete, and also a small separate staircase to it. I thought that was a record for size, but I have since discovered a bedroom of similar size in the Euston Road, London.

More important to the architect than these matters of curiosity are unexpected forms of construction and unusual materials. In some South Coast towns a form of hanging tile is largely used which gives the appearance of a solid brick wall, and as these tiles have a vitreous surface so often found in brickwork near the coast, the illusion is sufficient to deceive an expert unacquainted with the local methods. What appear to be brick buildings are really timber framed and tile hung, a vital matter to the correct survey of the building.

You will often have to find the height of buildings that you cannot actually put a measuring tape upon, and the following method will be sufficiently accurate for many purposes. If the facing is of brick the courses can be counted, and the full height can then be determined by measuring the height of four courses or the number of bricks, say in 5′ 0″ and using this as a divisor. As a check the sections of the iron rainwater pipe can be counted and then multiplied by the length of one section, which you should measure, but which is usually 6′ 0″ in older buildings.

Photographs are of great value in connection with surveys. These can often be obtained of the buildings you have to survey, but you will generally find that the portions you particularly require are not shown. Some little time ago I prepared the quantities for an extensive alteration to a large house near Lichfield. The architect had given me a very fine set of plans to work from, and I spent five days at the house. During my stay I took sixty photographs, and from these, on my return, I discovered all sorts of things about the house which in spite of all the care I had taken had been missed on my inspection. The result was that the quantities and specification were very complete and accurate. I therefore strongly advise you to study the use of a camera and to take your own views. Not only will you find this is a help in surveying, but in your leisure time you will be able to accumulate a store of interesting photographs of architectural interest.

Finally, I would ask you to train yourself in the art of noting down everything that you can observe when surveying a house. The floor boards, unless there is a counter floor, will show you the run of the joists, the position of gullies and manhole covers will assist you to trace the drains. Always mark upon your plans the position of beams and roof trusses, also the heights of all the steps and their direction, and note any variation in the height of the rooms. The more information you can collect, the easier will your subsequent work become, for a good survey is an essential prelude to a sound practicable scheme.

Chapter VII

Drawings

The preparation of drawings in obviously a subject upon which you may be inclined to say that an architect could advise better than I can, but there are some points on which I think a quantity surveyor has the advantage. He may not be able to tell you how to design your buildings or how to draw the plans, but he should be able to tell you what kind of information the drawings should contain to enable the builder to carry out the work in accordance with the desires of the architect.

Quantity surveyors see a great variety of drawings and obtain an intimate knowledge of the plans prepared by different architects. They are therefore in a position to say what drawings are the easiest to follow when preparing the quantities, and thus which will best meet the builder's requirements.

The *taking-off*, as it is called, of the quantities has to be done from the architect's drawings, and if these are not correct it is obvious that the quantities will be inaccurate; therefore one of the first things to re-memeber is to prepare your plans accurately. If you have an entirely new building to design, there is no excuse for drawing incorrect plans, but if you are designing some alterations and additions to an existing building the matter is a little different. A good deal depends upon your survey. If that is correct, then there should be no difficulty, but frequently the survey is made in a great hurry and is far from being complete; moreover, you will not always be able to uncover important constructional members, such as masked timbers, steel, etc, and there is thus little chance of your drawings being wholly satisfactory.

I have no doubt you can all turn out excellent work, but good or smart drawings are of little use unless they are also correct. Try to cultivate the habit of understanding what you draw. If you are working to $^1/_8{}''$ scale, (or 1:100) see that everything you draw is really correct to that scale. Do not show one door opening $3' \ 0''$ wide and another at a different width if you mean them both to be the same. See that the chimney breast upon an upper floor has something below it to stand upon. I remember once seeing a plan in my office upon which was shown a fireplace on an upper floor with absolutely nothing below it and no indication as to how it was to be carried. Show the floor joists on the plans in their proper position and see that the floor boards go the right way. It is easy to have them run the wrong way of the room, and although this is not, perhaps, a terrible mistake, yet anyone of small technical ability may notice it and criticise you. You may be interested to know that a quantity surveyor is rarely satisfied with the way in which joists and rafters are shown on plans; he always calculates the right number required and never relies upon the number indicated upon the drawings. It is a useful thing to mark on your plans in what way the floors are to be finished and also the line where one kind of floor ends and another commences. If there is no roof plan, show the position of ridges, valleys, hips, etc, on the top floor plan; this will be of much assistance to the builder. Always show on the plans which way the doors are to open. This will at the same time make it clear which openings are to have doors. I was once called in to help settle a dispute where the architect had specified that all openings were to have doors. He had omitted to give on the plans the information I have just referred to, and it was contended that certain of the openings were never intended to have doors. The drawings and specification therefore seemed to be at variance, and a dispute arose which proved very difficult to settle. I think this will show how important it is that the drawings and specification are in absolute agreement.

In another case the connection of a drainage system to a public sewer had been shown on the plans, but not specified; this also led to a dispute, so I advise you to be very careful in such matters. Do not gaily draw the drainage system without a thought as to whether it is practicable. You will be wise to set out some of the manholes to a large scale in order to see whether there is sufficient room in them to take all junctions. As a rule drains are shown by single lines, and all seems well in a small manhole with several junctions. Set it out, however, to a large scale, and you may find that a much larger manhole will be required. Unless your quantity surveyor noticed such matters, extras would often be involved.

Rainwater pipes are often omitted on plans and elevations. I suppose architects consider the straight lines spoil their elevations and so leave them out, but the builder has to put them in. You will be wise always to show these pipes and also all the soil, ventilating and other pipes. This will enable you to form a correct judgment as to where these pipes will be least objectionable.

It is well to remember that buildings when erected look quite different from those shown upon drawings. I often hear architects say that their buildings look much better than they expected, or the reverse. No doubt it requires a good deal of training to foresee how a building is coming out, and it is always a safe plan to set up perspectives of designs containing unfamiliar features.

If after you leave the architectural School you happen to go into a Government office, such as the Department of the Environment or the Ministry of Defence, you will find that drawings are prepared very carefully indeed, and are not sent to the quantity surveyor until practically everything has been threshed out. In a private office, however, circumstances will not always permit of this. Often you will find that the drawings and estimates are required in a great hurry; the client will not wait, and requires the work to be commenced at once. This may mean that your drawings will be lacking in that perfect accuracy which the quantity surveyor hopes for and dreams about. In a case like that, of course, it cannot be helped, and everyone must make the best of a bad job. I am afraid, however, that some offices have a habit of turning out incomplete and slipshod drawings. This is very unfair to everybody and causes no end of trouble. 'Once well done is twice done', and it is safe to say that time spent upon the accurate preparation of drawings is never lost. Although it is difficult to satisfy an impatient client, it pays in the long run if you can get him to understand that his building will be completed more quickly and with less worry to himself if the drawings are well thought out and accurately finished.

An architect recently said to me that it would be a very useful thing if I could make clear exactly what drawings a quantity surveyor requires for the preparation of quantities. He added: 'When I send you plans you always return them saying that all the important things are left out'. This is, of course, an exaggeration, but it contains a certain amount of truth. It is seldom that a quantity surveyor gets as complete a set of drawings as he desires. This is not because the architect has not the ability to make them, but because there is generally a 'big rush' on when the time comes for quantities. In order that the quantities may be taken out accurately, the surveyor requires a complete set of plans, elevations and sections, and sufficient details to a larger scale to enable him to measure everything; even full-size drawings are required of specially difficult or intricate portions of the work. If you realise that the very smallest detail has to be measured in order to get a satisfactory bill of quantities, and will try to put yourself in the place of the man who has to do it, I feel sure you will have no difficulty in settling what drawings are necessary. For example, when you are making your sections you will take your lines through those portions of the building which contain the difficult and unusual features. Then, again, do not make your large-scale details totally different from your small-scale drawings. This occurs not only before quantities are prepared, but often later on, because the details have not been sufficiently visualized at first. It makes it very difficult for everyone to have, say, one design of doors on the small-scale plans and quite another design on the larger-scale details. See that the chimney-stacks are large enough to take the required number of flues.

I remember an occasion when I was given a complete set of drawings for some alterations to a large house drawn in freehand to $1/8''$ scale and with very few details. Nothing I could say would induce the architect to give me anything else, but it was clear to me that he would have to elaborate his details later on, and that the result of putting off doing this would be many unnecessary variations. I mention this in order to show you what not to do. Make a practice of getting your drawings well and finally thought out, so that when the contract is signed you will have no need to make revisions. I have often seen plans altered many times when the work was in hand simply because this had not been done. Circumstances necessitate so many variations when the works are in progress that it is all the more important to avoid unnecessary changes due to slipshod original drawings.

Small-scale drawings are as a rule drawn in pencil and then traced, photoprints are obtained, and these are finished in whatever way the architect desires: sometimes sets are coloured or tinted for the benefit of the client although drawings are not normally coloured for issue as working drawings. It is a good plan to get all your drawings as nearly as possible of the same size. This means that the drawings are simple to keep in order. In any case, to avoid extra expense, you should make your tracings to one of the sizes given by photo printers in their catalogues. A difference in size makes it difficult to keep count of all your drawings, and I repeat, therefore, that as far as possible all plans should be kept to one size. References to BS 4000-1968 will give you information on sizes of papers both in metric and imperial units.

It will be obvious that all drawings should have the title upon them, and it is best to keep the same title all through the job. Do not forget to date all your drawings; this is most essential. All the drawings should be numbered. There are different systems of doing this — in fact, no two architects seem to use the same system. Adopt a simple system of numbering your plans and stick to it. One architect I know has two numbers and a letter to all his drawings, thus, 17E4. The first number is that given to the job; the letter which follows represents the scale of the plan — E for $^1/_8{}''$ (or 1:100), H for $^1/_2{}''$ (or 1:20) and F for full size — the number at the end is the number of the drawing, commencing with 1. A record book is kept showing where each copy of the various drawings has been sent, and the original tracing never leaves the architect's office.

It seems unnecessary to say that you should keep correct copies of all plans sent out, but I have often noticed when in architects' offices that no copy at all is available when required. The pressure of business is continually making this and other essential precautions of prudent practice difficult. A very real effort is necessary to do the right thing and avoid the evil consequences of omission. In any case the contract drawings, that is those signed by the client and the contractor, should never leave the office, nor should they be altered or defaced by any subsequent working on them. Keep tracings or photoprints for any revisions or explanations which it may be necessary to make during the course of the work and make sure that all revisions are clearly defined at each issue.

You will find no difficulty in keeping your drawings if you adopt a simple system. I think the best for current plans is an ordinary set of shallow drawers in which the plans lie flat. But there are also proprietary systems of plan storage which can be employed when large numbers of drawings have to be referred to and handled frequently in the course of a job. Then when a job is finished the drawings relating to it can be collected and made into a roll, with a brown-paper cover bearing the name of the job in large letters, with a number on each end of the roll. If the numbers of the rolls and the names of the jobs are entered in a register you should have no difficulty in finding any drawing you want at a moment's notice; alternatively the drawings can be micro-filmed and stored releasing valuable storage space for other uses.

If the client has appointed a quantity surveyor you will find it a very useful plan to keep a record of all drawings passing between the two offices. It is extraordinary how easy a thing it is to lose plans, and it is a good thing to be able to trace to which office the blame should be attributed.

In conclusion I cannot recommend you too strongly to prepare your details well. You ought to be able to draw anything that you want carried out; and the details of special features should always be done before your $^1/_8{}''$ scale plans are completed. It may be a counsel of perfection, but it is only in this way that you can be sure of getting your drawings right.

Chapter VIII

Specifications

A Specification is a document which is, as a rule, prepared to accompany a set of drawings, to explain in detail what materials are to be used and what methods of construction are to be carried out. In theory, it may be unnecessary to include in a specification such details as are clearly indicated and described on the drawings, but in practice it is the rule to make the specification complete in itself, and I think this is a wise plan.

There are, of course, many books on the subject, but I believe the statement which I read in an American book some time ago is quite true, viz: 'no satisfactory treatise on specifications has yet been written', but by the sensible use of books such as *Specification* published by the Architectural Press and the more recent *National Building Specification* distributed by RIBA Publications Limited young architects should have no difficulty in writing a specification.

You will say, I expect, that specification writing is a dull job and one to be avoided as much as possible, but I tell you frankly that if that is your view you are quite wrong, for in endeavouring to describe in detail the work you desire to see carried out you will experience a very real pleasure if you only make up your minds to produce a document as complete in all its detail as your drawings will no doubt be.

In the first place the ability to write a specification pre-supposes a knowledge of building construction and of materials and their uses, and added knowledge in these subjects will lead to greater facility and definiteness in specification writing. But in addition to technical knowledge it is desirable to cultivate the gift of expressing oneself clearly and crisply. A useful plan is to write a report on any subject and then to study it with a view to boiling it down to the fewest possible words, setting out the paragraphs in the best order. It is wonderful how quickly improvement follows this method.

Many years ago I began to compile a type specification. I took as a basis a specification I had already written, and had this bound and interleaved with plain white sheets; then, as time passed, I added more clauses, with the result that the original document at last outgrew itself and I had to remodel my type. But this type specification lasted a long time and proved to be of the greatest use. I strongly recommend each one of you to prepare a similar type specification, and for this purpose I suggest that you write out the specification given in the *Appendix* (page 242), leaving plenty of space between the clauses, and have the whole bound. This will make a good nucleus and give you room to write in fresh clauses whenever you so desire. If you become thoroughly interested, as I think you will, you will always be on the look-out for some fresh clause or for an old one expressed in a better way than the one you have in your type.

I think it may be of interest to you to know that at the present date my own type specification now comprises four thick, bound, foolscap volumes and contains about 990 pages, with 1820 clauses. It is still increasing in size.

Specifications are usually divided into sections. The first section is headed Preliminaries or Generally, and consists of all the clauses containing general directions applying to the whole work and not only to a particular trade. Then follow the various trades, preferably in the same order as in the *Standard Method of Measurement of Building Works* : Demolitions and Alterations, Excavation and Earthwork, Piling, Concrete Work, Brickwork and Blockwork, Underpinning, Rubble Walling, Masonry, Asphalt Work, Roofing, Carpentry, Joinery, Structural Steelwork, Metalwork, Plumbing and Engineering Installations, Electrical Installations, Plasterwork and other Floor, Wall and Ceiling Finishings, Glazing, Painting and Decorating, Drainage and Fencing. The first stage, therefore, of writing a specification is to divide up your work into different sections or trades and to take care that all the work which is to be carried out by a particular trade is included under its proper section. Thus it follows that anything to do with lead must be written in the section headed Plumbing and Engineering Installations, and anything to do with plaster in the section headed Plasterwork, and so on. Sometimes you will find it necessary, for the sake of clarity, to refer to some detail in a section to which it does not properly belong, and when you do so, be sure also to specify it in the correct section, so that the various tradesmen may have no difficulty in finding the description of their particular work.

We will suppose that you have been commissioned to build a small house in the country, and we will go briefly into the work of writing the specification in detail. In chapter VI some hints are given as to the kind of information you would require to obtain on the site. Now if you have filled in the form I suggested, you will have a good deal of material ready for use in writing the specification.

The method I advise you to adopt is to follow in imagination the whole process of erecting the building from its commencement to its completion, and the first thing to be done is to get together as complete a set of notes as you can. These notes should be written in your words without any attempt to put them into the correct technical phrases as employed in the finished specification. The following notes were supplied to me by an architect when he asked me to write a specification for a small house. They illustrate very well the kind of notes you should make.

Notes for Specification

Time for completion, 9 months
No clerk of works required

Continued

Contingencies — £250
Cement concrete for foundations
Fletton bricks in gauged mortar
Facing bricks red sand-faced
Concrete paving in yard, scullery, etc
Red tile paving in kitchen and passage
Steps in red bricks, with tiles between, all in cement
Plain red chimney-pots
Grates and mantels as follows:

Sitting and dining rooms	£100 each
Two best bedrooms	£75 each
Other bedrooms	£50 each

Slate damp course
Brick paving to verandah
Slate shelves in larder
Two rainwater butts
Asphalt flat to balcony
Stoneware drains
Manholes as usual
Sand-faced roofing tiles fixed with galvanised nails
Red ridge tiles
Timber roof and floors, see details
Roof boarded with felt
Skirtings generally 75 mm x 19 mm
Wood-block floor in hall
Metal windows with softwood surrounds
Architraves generally 75 mm x 25 mm
All doors in softwood
Trap door to roof
Provide a coke-hopper
Coal boards as usual
Picture rails 50 mm x 25 mm
Dado rail in kitchen
Outside louvre shutters to windows of south elevation
Staircase in softwood, oak handrail
Dresser in kitchen
Two tiers of shelves in larder and scullery
Linen-room shelves as usual
Bench in garage
Tanks in roof to be lagged
Cast iron gutters and rain-water pipes
Pc sum of £100 for railing to balcony
Pc sum of £175 for entrance gates and railings
Hot-water service as usual
Cold water from company's main in road
Radiators in hall, drawing and dining-rooms
Pc sum of £400 for electric wiring and fittings

Continued

       Grade 5 lead to flats
       Water supply as usual
       Pc sum of £50 for three lavatory basins; £50 for the bath
       Ordinary plastering
       Plaster cornice in hall, dining and drawing rooms
       Tiled dado in kitchen and scullery
       External walls stucco, rough surface
       White glazed tiles at back of shelves in larder
       4 mm sheet glass, selected quality
       Painting generally four coats

Now the first operation in building a small house will be the clearing of the site, and so you write in your notes:

       Clear the site

The next thing to be done will be to take off the turf and vegetable soil, and your note will be:

       Cut up the turf and clear away the soil

Then the ground must be excavated for the foundations, so you say:

       Dig the trenches

Some of the excavated material will have to be returned and filled in around the foundations, so you put in your notes:

       Return, fill and ram

Then will follow a note as to the disposal of the surplus excavated material. This note can be:

       Cart away surplus material or
       Deposit surplus material on site

You will now be thinking of the foundations, so you say:

       Put in the concrete

And then will follow the walls, and you make a note:

       Build brick (or stone) walls

This will naturally make you think of the damp-proof course, so you write:

Damp-proof course

And the way the walls have to be finished on the outside will at once occur to you, and you put down:

Facing of walls

and follow with all the various additional points, such as:

> *Brick arches*
> *Window sills*
> *String courses, etc.*

and so you continue with your notes until you cannot think of anything else, and lastly you put down:

Leave building clean

You will find that, as you gain experience, this system of notes can be dispensed with, but I am sure it is the best way of learning to write a specification.

Now, when you have made a complete set of notes you are in a position to write out the clauses in correct technical language and in doing so your type specification will prove of the utmost value, but I advise you to think out your subject very thoroughly and not be satisfied until your notes are very full and complete.

In order to make the system quite clear I will give you a few of the clauses which will grow out of the notes:

Clear the site

The site of the building to be cleared of bushes, fences, and all rubbish, and the turf and vegetable soil removed to a depth of 150 mm and wheeled and deposited in a convenient spot. Any uneven parts of the site to be filled in and rammed, and the whole left ready and at the correct level to receive hard core.

Dig the trenches

The trenches, etc to be excavated to the widths and depths shown on the drawings or as may be directed by the Architect, and the surplus material carted away.

Damp-proof course

A damp-proof course formed with two courses of stout new Welsh slates in cement to break joint to be laid on all walls at proper level with bed of cement under and over the same and the outer edge pointed with a flush band in cement mortar.

Facing of walls

The whole of the outside walls and chimney stacks, etc, to be faced with the best selected 75 mm red sand-faced bricks to be obtained from an approved maker pc £40 per thousand net delivered to site.

Leave building clean

The whole of the premises to be left clean, perfect, and watertight at completion to the satisfaction of the architect.

When I have to deal with a large Contract I always suggest to the architect that he should have every door and window opening numbered consecutively on the plans. I then obtain from him complete particulars of what he requires and in due course the quantities are prepared and the specification written. In this way all doubt is eliminated as to what is required and no items are likely to be omitted. The finishings to the various rooms are dealt with in the same manner. In order that you may be provided with a suitable model when you are engaged upon a large contract, I have included three typical pages from one of the specifications recently written, which will indicate to you the kind of information required for windows, doors and internal finishings. Study these sheets carefully and you will be well repaid if you follow the method, since it is a very important insurance of accuracy.

I have now explained my method of making specification writing easy, and I believe that if you tackle the work in this way you will find that after a little practice many of the troubles and difficulties which now, perhaps, loom large will vanish. But you will no doubt appreciate the point I referred to at first, that unless you take every opportunity to increase your knowledge of materials and construction you will never acquire the facility to draw your details correctly or to write a clear and correct description of the work. I expect you all know that a quantity surveyor has to obtain from the drawings and specification, or notes, the quantities of all the various materials and labour required for a building, and unless the drawings are accurate, the details workmanlike, and the specification or notes clear, he will not get the correct information, and will be put to much unnecessary trouble.

When the specification has been completed and typed it is a good plan to make an index of the clauses, and if you do so be sure that it is complete and correct. A poor or incorrect index is worse than useless and only causes annoyance to everyone concerned. As a rule, I find that specification writers are very lax in this matter, and seem to think that anything will do.

I think it may help you in your work if you remember that the preparation of a specification for an actual job is a very different thing from writing one in the examination room. Whereas in the latter case you will have to rely entirely on your own knowledge, in the former you will have the advantage of being able to consult, not only your own type, but also many other specifications. If you happen to start your career in a

SCHEDULE OF WINDOWS

Number on Drgs	Casement or sash	Frame	Window board, linings, etc	Pelmets	Sundries
1 2 3 4	Metal	88 mm x 75 mm softwood rebated, moulded and grooved, with 138 mm x 75 mm rebated, moulded, weathered and grooved oak sill	225 mm x 38 mm softwood moulded, 25 mm x 16 mm softwood bed mould	138 mm x 32 mm softwood moulded and rebated front, 138 mm x 25 mm softwood soffit, Plastic curtain track and brackets pc £1 per metre including runners	4 mm specially selected quality sheet glass in metal beads
5 6 7	56 mm teak casements, 56 mm x 32 mm moulded and rebated division bars, 25 mm x 16 mm movable beads	125 mm x 88 mm teak, rebated moulded and grooved, with 175 mm x 88 mm rebated, moulded, weathered and grooved teak sill. Teak scribing fillets 50 mm x 25 mm	225 mm x 38 mm teak, moulded, 25 mm x 16 mm teak bed mould, 25 mm teak rebated linings 100 mm x 38 mm teak moulded architrave	—	6 mm float glass. Casement fastener pc £1 each, and stay pc £1 each. 100 mm bronze metal butt hinges pc £1.50 per pair
52	50 mm softwood moulded sashes with 50 mm x 22 mm rebated and moulded sash bars	Ordinary softwood cased	150 mm x 150 mm quarry tiles. 25 mm softwood linings, 57 mm x 25 mm softwood moulded architrave	—	Best flax sash cords iron weights brass-faced pulleys. Sash fastener pc 75p each, two sash lifts to each sash pc 35p each

SCHEDULE OF DOORS

No on Drgs	Position	Door	Size	Frame or linings	Fanlight or sidelight	Ironmongery	Architraves	Sundries
31	Ground Floor	Type 'B' teak, open and glazed	975 mm x 2100 mm	Teak 106 mm x 100 mm moulded and rebated frame fixed with 6 No. 25 mm x 3 mm galvanised wrought iron holdfasts	—	Single action floor spring and top centre pc £17. Mortice dead lock pc £3. Two push plates pc £1 each. Grip handle pc £4. Two kicking plates pc £1.50 each	Teak 100 mm x 25 mm moulded, 38 mm x 19 mm splayed softwood grounds one side	Cast aluminium socket shoes pc £5 each for door frames. 6 mm float glass in wash leather. 19 mm x 16 mm teak movable beads. 25 mm x 6 mm wrought iron weather bar. 75 mm x 75 mm moulded teak weather fillet
32	Ground Floor	Teak 56 mm thick two panel door, the lower panel 56 mm thick with vertical edges of styles and the front of panel moulded and the back of panel bead and butt, the upper panel open, rebated and prepared for glass with 56 mm x 30 mm rebated and moulded division bars to form nine panes with marginal lights	975 mm x 2250 mm	Teak 175 mm x 100 mm rebated stop moulded on face and beaded frame fixed with 8 No. 25 mm x 3 mm galvanised wrought iron holdfasts. 175 mm x 100 mm teak mullion and 125 mm x 100 mm stop rebated, beaded, part twice moulded and part once moulded head	Teak 56 mm thick, moulded and rebated sidelight with 56 mm x 30 mm rebated and moulded division bars, 25 mm x 13 mm teak movable beads and 6 mm float glass in wash leather	Three 100 mm double steel washered brass butts pc 75p per pair. Mortice night latch pc £4. Twelve extra keys pc 25p each	Teak 100 mm x 25 mm moulded, 75 mm x 19 mm splayed grounds one side. 32 mm x 25 mm teak scribing mould to sidelight	Cast aluminium socket shows pc £5 each to door frame, 6 mm float glass in wash leather, 19 mm x 16 mm teak movable beads. 25 mm x 6 mm wrought iron weather bar. 75 mm x 75 mm moulded teak weather fillet. 175 mm x 32 mm plain teak linings and backings one edge tongued into teak frame

SCHEDULE OF FINISHINGS

Room	Floor	Walls	Ceiling	Skirtings	Picture rail, etc	Paintwork	Sundries
Drawing-Room	Softwood sub-flooring. Oak parquet in long strips	Plastered and emulsion paint.	Plastered and emulsion paint. 250 mm plaster cornice	225 mm x 32 mm in two pieces moulded	150 mm x 32 mm wrought softwood china shelf grooved for plates on shaped brackets at 1.20 mm centres	Flooring wax polished Woodwork painted four coats	—
Own Bedroom	32 mm Softwood grooved and tongued. Resilient quilt sound-proofing to joists	Plastered and emulsion paint	Plastered and emulsion paint. 200 mm plaster cornice	150 mm x 19 mm softwood moulded	75 mm x 25 mm softwood moulded picture rail	Flooring stained and wax polished. Woodwork painted four coats	
Kitchen	150 mm x 150 mm buff tiles	Plastered and emulsion paint above 100 mm x 100 mm white tiled dado 1 m high. Expanded metal angles	Plastered and emulsion paint	150 mm x 150 mm coved tile	100 mm x 25 mm softwood moulded chair rail	Woodwork painted four coats	Thin iron plate on floor under boiler

large office, you will probably be able to consult a specification applying to a job very similar to that on which you are engaged. This of course, will be a very great help, but particular care is needed to see that clauses which do not apply to your particular work are not inserted, and that new or additional clauses which may be required are put in. As an example I may mention that in one of my own specifications for a house in Sussex, I worked from a specification I had once written for some alterations to a house in Park Lane, London. I will leave you to imagine what I felt like when the architect asked me to explain why I had specified that a temporary roadway 200 yards long was to be constructed from Park Lane to the site.

Finally, let me impress upon you once more the need for definiteness. I have seen a specification so loosely prepared that one clause such as the following would be almost as useful: 'Provide all materials and workmanship required and complete the work to the satisfaction of the architect'. Avoid such expressions as 'in a proper manner', 'as required', and so on. It is for you to define the 'manner' and the 'requirement'. The builder, being a practical man, looks for information, and if he finds instead evasion, he is likely to conclude either that you are lazy and careless or that your knowledge is imperfect. Therefore, if you come to a point on which you are uncertain, then is the time to hunt round for information until you know definitely the 'requirement' and the 'manner' of execution, and are able to write an unmistakable description.

In the opinion of the American writer whom I have quoted above, the standard of specification writing is much higher now than it was fifty years ago. I sometimes refer to a specification I wrote a long time ago and I find that the documents which now come before me and which I myself write are much more carefully prepared. I do not think this should cause you any uneasiness, because, while it is necessary nowadays to reach a high standard, the facilities for acquiring knowledge rapidly are infinitely greater than those which were available fifty years ago.

Chapter IX
Bills of quantities

In a later chapter I shall tell you something about the quantity surveyor and his work. I now propose to give you some insight into bills of quantities, not so much with the object of showing you how they are prepared, but rather to indicate their use and purpose. And, first, I think we should understand what a bill of quantities is or purports to be. I will give a definition which I think will make it quite clear:

> A bill of quantities is a document prepared by a quantity surveyor to enable a builder to estimate the cost of a building or other work as shown on the drawings and described in the specification prepared by an architect, and consists of items which give in detail the quantities and descriptions of the various materials and labour required to carry into effect the intentions of the architect.

A bill of quantities, to be of any real value, must be absolutely accurate. Every item of labour and materials should be included and set forth in the bill in a manner that will be clearly understood by the builders who are asked to tender. The detailing of every item will not add to the cost of the work. It will give the builders a feeling of security in pricing the bill, as they will know that the quantities have been carefully taken out, and you can thus rest assured that really competitive tenders have been obtained. Loosely prepared or indefinitely worded quantities make it necessary for the builders to protect themselves by including covering amounts.

Mistakes are easy to make in preparing a large bill of quantities and sometimes very difficult to detect until the work is being carried out. It must be remembered that a surveyor generally has a very short time for the preparation of his quantities; but the builder who carries out the work has plenty of time for criticising them, and does not fail to bring to notice, and quite rightly to charge for, any item omitted.

When, however, a builder sees in a bill of quantities items such as one softwood staircase 3' 0" wide to rise 9' 0" complete, it naturally makes him a little sceptical as to the accuracy of the work, and if he gets the contract you may be sure that plenty of claims will be made. The above insufficient description actually occured in a bill of quantities some years ago.

Bills of quantities are prepared upon slightly different systems in different parts of the country, but it is the London system that we shall shortly examine, and not those which obtain in the north of England and Scotland.

In 1922 the *Standard Method of Measurement of Building Works* was published by the then Surveyors Institution and National Federation of Building Trades Employers. This standard method was founded upon the practice of the leading London Quantity Surveyors and it provided a very useful guide to students and others who desired to acquire a working knowledge of the preparation of bills of quantities. Since 1922 there have been a number of revisions to the *Standard Method of Measurement* and all bills of quantities should be prepared in accordance with it, following of course the latest metric edition which was published in 1968 by the Royal Institution of Chartered Surveyors and the National Federation of Building Trades Employers. As from 1939 the RIBA Standard Form of Building Contract has laid down that bills of quantities should be prepared in accordance with the principles set out in the *Standard Method of Measurement* unless it is expressly stated to the contrary.

You may ask what is the good of having quantities at all. The architect prepares drawings and writes a specification, and surely, you may say, these give sufficient information to enable the builder to make up an estimate. Such an idea is quite erroneous. An experienced builder may be able to form an approximate estimate from the plans and specification, but it is impossible for him to arrive at a definite figure without quantities. It is true that tenders can be obtained, and that contracts are often entered into in cases where no quantities have been supplied, but this means that each builder tendering for the work has been obliged to have quantities prepared for himself, often by one of his own surveyors. This involves an immense amount of labour, and is very unfair to the builders. In a case where, say, twelve builders are invited to tender, twelve separate bills of quantities have to be prepared. Such quantities also would not be anything like as accurate as those prepared by a qualified surveyor. It is possible, and indeed, it often happens, that a low tender is received as a result of this system, but the unfortunate builder not infrequently discovers, after the job has commenced, that he has obtained the contract owing to serious errors of omission in his quantities. The natural consequence is that he will do his best to minimise his loss by putting in inferior workmanship and using materials of a poorer quality than those specified. Thus, although the job may appear to have been carried out more cheaply than if quantities had been supplied, this is not really the case, because either the quality of the workmanship and materials will be inferior or the difference in cost will be borne — as a loss — by the honest victim, the builder. It sometimes occurs that builders who have not been supplied with quantities ask a quantity surveyor to prepare a proper bill, a copy of which is supplied to each builder who is to tender, the quantity surveyor's fees being added to the tender in each case, thus the client has to pay for the quantities and does not have the benefit of the services of the surveyor.

I think it is absolutely correct to say that, if you are trying to get work of the best quality carried out, it is cheaper in the long run to have the quantities prepared, provided, of course, that they are properly prepared by a qualified surveyor. Quantities enable the builders to tender upon an equality. They show exactly what sort of work is required and the exact amount of work to be done and materials to be used, and each builder competing is furnished with a copy of the same quantities. It is not sufficiently realised that the preparation of an estimate involves the builder in a considerable amount of risk. Even when proper quantities are prepared it is very easy in pricing them to make errors both in figures and in judgment. Tenders based upon the same quantities always show some latitude in prices, even for exactly the same work, but tenders prepared without quantities are more widely divergent; therefore anything that can be done to ensure that the builders will tender upon the same basis is all to the benefit of the client. There is only one way to prepare a reliable tender, and that is to base it on quantities supplied by a qualified surveyor.

One other consideration which shows the necessity for having quantities is the limited time within which the client often requires tenders to be obtained. If the builders have to prepare their own quantities it means that each one would have to be supplied with a copy of the drawings and specification, unless, of course, the client was prepared to wait for the tenders until each builder in turn had been given the opportunity of having the original documents in his possession for several days.

It seems hardly necessary to say how important quantities are where variations upon the contract have to be adjusted. Without quantities the settlement of accounts is often extremely difficult, but with quantities the matter becomes one of comparative ease.

Quantities are extremely useful should the lowest tender amount to more than the client is prepared to spend. When you have such a case you can ask the builder to produce his priced copy of the bill, and in a very short time you will probably be able to make out a statement which will show the client the possibilities of reducing the amount of the tender to the sum he desires to spend.

We must now consider very briefly the procedure usually adopted by surveyors in preparing their quantities. The first stage is called *taking-off*, and consists of obtaining from the drawings and noting on sheets called the *dimensions* the correct measurement of every item of work in each trade and extracting from the specification — or the notes supplied by the architect — the information necessary to explain to the builder the exact description and quantity of work which will require to be done to complete the job to the satisfaction of the architect and client. All the items have to be fully described by the 'taker-off', such as 'excavate to trenches not exceeding 1.5 m deep and get out', with separate items describing the disposal of the excavated materials. To 'take-off' a door may mean not less than twelve separate dimensions, involving seven or eight different trades, and all must be enumerated in a regular and consecutive manner.

The second stage consists of *squaring the dimensions* so taken-off, which means multiplying the separate sets of dimensions together in order that the figures so obtained shall give the cubical, superficial or lineal contents of the item. The third stage is called *abstracting*. This consists of transferring all the squared dimensions, and of course, the lineal dimensions and 'numbers' also to sheets called the *abstract*, which are ruled in vertical columns. Abstracting, to be done properly, requires a great deal of experience, and it is of importance to get the items arranged in the abstract as nearly as possible in the order in which they will appear in the bill. As some items occur only a few times in the dimensions and others occur fifty times or more, it will be seen that this part of the work must be done carefully to avoid confusion. The fourth stage consists of *casting up the items* on the abstract and reducing the dimensions to the respective denominations required to comply with the *Standard Method of Measurement*. The last stage is called *billing* and consists of writing the finished bill of quantities from the abstract in the form with which architects and builders are familiar. All these operations have to be checked and sometimes cross-checked. It will be seen, therefore, that something like eight separate operations are involved in the preparation of an ordinary bill of quantities.

The specimen sheet on page 71 from one of my own bills of quantities may be interesting to you, it is set out in what is really the traditional method. In recent years there have been many attempts to rationalise the wording and setting out of bills of quantities and my own office now prepare bills in an elemental form as distinct from trade by trade using the principles of a phraseology introduced by Fletcher and Moore and in order that you may compare the difference the specimen sheet written traditionally has been reproduced on page 72 using the modern phraseology technique.

There are, of course, other types of bills of quantities being prepared and one of these uses constructional operations as the basis for setting out the document. Computers have also had an effect on the format and young architects would do well to discuss their first project in which bills of quantities are to be prepared with their quantity surveyor to ensure that they understand the methods to be adopted. You will note that every item can be found by reference to the page number and the serial letter. This system has been found of great assistance, especially when measuring variations, since by using number and letter there can be no mistaking the item, whereas if reference is made to the number of lines from the top or bottom of the page, errors may occur. I prefer this method of indicating the items by letters to that sometimes employed of numbering each item in consecutive order throughout the bill. It has not been an unknown occurrence for the number of the item to be mixed up with the quantity in the next column, for which reason also it is wise to omit the letter 'I'.

It is essential that architects should have at least a working knowledge of the details of bills of quantities and be able to say how the principal items should be presented. The quantities of every material or mixture of materials are stated in the bills under units or denominations which have been arrived at by custom and are now practical universal. The following list contains some of the principal items and unit measurements which should be known by every architect:

Excavation. . . . . . Per cubic metre (m^3) Concrete. Per cubic metre (m^3)
Reinforcement. . . . . Per kilogram (kg)
Brickwork and blockwork. . . . . Per square metre (m^2)
                                   reduced to one brick in
                          thickness where appropriate
Facings. . . . . Per square metre (m^2)
Arches, cornices, string cornices,
  plinth courses, copings, etc. . . . . Per linear metre (m)
Drains. . . . . Per linear metre (m)
Manholes. . . . . .Measure in full detail.
Gullies, etc. . . . . Per number (No.)
Stonework. . . . . Per square metre (m^2)
                                   stating the thickness.
Slating and tiling. . . . . Per square metre (m^2)
Hips, valleys, eaves, etc. Per linear metre (m)
Structural timber. . . . . Per linear metre (m)
Flooring. . . . . Per square metre (m^2)
Roof boarding. . . . . Per square metre (m^2)
Roof felting. . . . . Per square metre (m^2)
Windows. . . . . Per square metre (m^2)
Doors. . . . . Per number (No.)
Door frames. . . . . Per linear metre (m)
Skirtings. . . . . Per linear metre (m)
Wall panelling. . . . . Per square metre (m^2)
Steelwork. . . . . Per kilogram (kg)
Iron eaves gutters and rainwater
  pipes. . . . . Per linear metre (m)
Sheet metal roof coverings. . . . . Per square metre (m^2)
Lead pipes. . . . . Per linear metre (m)
Plaster. . . . . Per square metre (m^2)
Cornices and mouldings. Per linear metre (m)
Glass. . . . . Per square metre (m^2)
Painting. . . . . Per square metre (m^2)

SPECIMEN PAGE OF TRADITIONAL BILL OF QUANTITIES

7 BLANK STREET

BRICKWORK

@ £   £

*Fletton brickwork in cement mortar
    as described*

A   Half brick wall as skin of hollow wall.   40 m^2

B   One brick wall.   28 m^2

C   One brick wall as skin of hollow wall.   40 m^2

*Damp proof courses consisting of two
courses of stout Welsh slates laid in breaking joint, bedded in cement mortar and
pointed on exposed edges.*

D   Horizontal damp proof course on brickwork.   3 m^2

E   Ditto ditto but 112 mm wide.   10 m

Sundries

F   Form 50 mm cavity between two brick skins
of hollow wall including tying skins together
with zinc coated mild steel ties 203 mm long
to comply with BS 1243 type (a) built in
every 900 mm horizontally and 450 mm
vertically and staggered and for keeping the
cavity clear of mortar droppings.   40 m^2

G   Hole through hollow wall consisting of a one
brick skin, a half brick skin with a 50 mm
cavity between for large pipe on rake and
make good.   2 No.

Carried to collection £

SPECIMEN PAGE OF BILL OF QUANTITIES USING THE PRINCIPLES OF FLETCHER AND MOORE PHRASEOLOGY

7 BLANK STREET

		@ £	£

BRICKWORK

Fletton bricks in cement mortar

Half brick thick

A	Skins of hollow walls	40 m^2

One brick thick

B	Walls	28 m^2
C	Skins of hollow walls	40 m^2

DAMP PROOF COURSES

Two courses Welsh slates; breaking joint; bedding in cement mortar

Horizontal

D	Exceeding 225 mm wide	3 m^2
E	112 mm wide	10 m

Sundries

Forming cavities in hollow walls, wall ties, zinc coated mild steel, 203 mm long, BS 1243 type (a), built in every 900 mm horizontally and 450 mm vertically and staggered, keeping cavity clear of mortar droppings

F	50 mm wide	40 m^2

Holes for pipes, large, on rake.

G	Hollow wall; brick skin, half brick skin, 50 mm cavity.	2 No.

Carried to collection £

Chapter X
Schedules of prices

A schedule of prices is a detailed statement governing the cost of materials and labour; in other words, it is a scale of prices for supplying materials and performing work for which the actual amount to be paid by the client will be ascertained by measuring and pricing each item according to the scale. It is an alternative to a bill of quantities – a poor alternative, but one that is sometimes adopted in cases where time is short and where the client is content to to proceed on the architect's approximate estimate of the cost of the work.

The procedure which is usually adopted, when it has been decided to obtain tenders by means of a schedule of prices, is for the architect to prepare the drawings and specification, and the quantity surveyor then to prepare the schedule or statement of all items of work and materials which he thinks will be required in connection with the job. No quantities are included, but simply a description, and a column is provided in which the builders, who are invited to tender, enter against each item the rate at which they are prepared to carry out the work or supply the materials. I have given in the *Appendix*, page 312, a complete schedule of prices for a new building which I think will illustrate clearly my meaning. In cases where no quantities are supplied it is a very useful thing to have a similar document filled in and sent to the architect by each builder with his tender, and this schedule can be used as the 'Schedule of Rates' referred to in clause 3 of the Standard Form of Building Contract (1963 revised July 1973) without quantities.

One of the disadvantages of a schedule of prices is that it cannot be stated definitely before the work is commenced how much it is going to cost. It is obvious that as the schedule contains no quantities it cannot be used as the basis for a lump sum contract; and I have noticed that when a contract is based on a schedule of prices there seems very little incentive to keep down the cost of the work, but rather a tendency to increase it first on the part of the architect, who does not hestitate to revise the plans and even to alter the work after it is actually built, and then on the part of the builder, who, although an approximate figure may have been mentioned to the client, knows that he will be paid for all the work he actually does; and therefore whose only care is to see that the cost of the work to himself is less than the amount he will be entitled to receive when the work has been measured up, as it must be, and priced according to the schedule rates.

There are several forms of schedules of prices, the ideal form being the usual bill of quantities, and, if there is sufficient time, I always advocate this. Failing this, the best alternative, if time permits, is to prepare a schedule with the addition of approximate quantities, so that the builders have a good guide in filling in the rates; and by moneying them out one is able to decide to whom the contract should be let, and to form an approximate idea of the total cost of the work. It should be clearly understood that such quantities do not accurately indicate the amount of work required — in fact, many of the quantities and descriptions may be included simply in order to obtain rates applicable in the event of contingencies arising which have not been foreseen. Nevertheless, such a schedule is better in every way than one which gives no indication of quantities, but it requires a good deal of experience to prepare. I remember among others a contract for additions to a house in Surrey in which a schedule with approximate quantities was used. The whole work was carried out satisfactorily and with the advantage that the client knew at the commencement very nearly the amount he would have to pay.

If you have a large building scheme to carry out, and have not much time to get the contract particulars prepared, it is a good plan to recommend your client to have the foundations of the building constructed under a schedule of prices, and then, while this work is being carried out, there will be plenty of time for the completion of your plans and details and for the preparation of proper quantities for the buildings above ground. This plan is often adopted, and is usually highly successful.

When you receive a tender based upon a schedule of prices without approximate quantities you must be careful how you act. Where bills of quantities have been supplied it is nearly always satisfactory to accept the lowest tender, provided the prices in the quantities are first scrutinised to see that no serious clerical errors have been made. But with a schedule of prices the case is different. The architect or surveyor must make a careful examination and analysis of the rates filled in by the builders tendering in order to arrive at a conclusion as to which of the schedules it will be advantageous to adopt. It is by no means an easy thing to do. It may, for instance, be found that a specially low price has been entered against an item of which there will be only a very small quantity and a high price against an item of which a large quantity will be required; thus a schedule which on the face of it appears to be low one may really be deceptive. There are many ways of analysing schedules of prices, but none better than to prepare a rough statement with approximate quantities and price it out at the various rates tendered by the competitors. These approximate quantities can be prepared while the builders are pricing their schedules and thus little time will be lost.

Certain very comprehensive schedules of prices are issued by Government Departments including the Schedule of Rates for Building Works (Metric Edition) 1969 prepared by the Ministry of Public Building and Works (now the Department of the Environment). Copies of these are obtainable from Her Majesty's Stationery Office. I am fairly well acquainted with these schedules and find them very useful when I have one to prepare myself. These schedules differ, however, in one respect from those we have been discussing. The rate for every item is printed in the schedule as issued to the competitors; and in tendering they have to take the schedule as a whole, and to state whether they will adopt the printed rates for any work ordered to be done or what percentage above or below such rates they require or offer.

The Department of the Environment occasionally accepts estimates of separate percentages for each trade or groups of trades which appears to me to be a wise proceeding in view of the different circumstances in which builders are placed and the fluctuations of prices which continually take place.

It is seldom the case that every item of work required in a building is given in a schedule of prices, however carefully prepared, and it is therefore necessary to know how to deal with work not specifically mentioned. The methods generally adopted are to value all such items at rates proportionate to the prices in the schedule where the work is of a similar character and executed under similar conditions. Where the work is so dissimilar as not to admit of this method then prices (usually called *Star* prices) are agreed with the contractor, based upon the normal amount of labour and materials necessary to produce the result obtained. Daywork prices should only be agreed to in exceptional cases. The following extract from the Schedule of Rates for Building Works to which I have referred and reproduced with the permission of the Controller of Her Majesty's Stationery Office and also a page of a plumbing schedule as issued by me to competitors, will, I hope, be interesting:

WROUGHT SOFTWOOD CASEMENT WINDOWS TO B.S.644 PART 1

Rates for the following include

Generally

.. for windows without glazing bars.

.. for projecting sills 5¼ in. x 2¾ in. (133 mm x 70 mm) extreme of two members tongued together as BS alternative 'A' or of single member out of the solid.

.. for cranked butt hinges and hanging opening portions: but not for fastenings.

Each

Item	1 2 ft 6¼ in (768 mm) £	2 3 ft 6¼ in. (1 073 mm) £	3 Height 4 ft 0¼ in. (1 226 mm) £	4 4 ft 6¼ in. (1 378 mm) £	5 5 ft 0¼ in. (1 530 mm) £
Window 1 ft 5¼ in. (438 mm) wide					
3314a .. with one opening light	2.700	3.000	3.100	–	–
Window 2 ft 1¼ in. (641 mm) wide					
3314b .. with one opening light	3.000	3.300	3.500	3.900	4.200
3314c .. with two opening lights	–	–	–	4.700	5.100
Window 4 ft 0¼ in. (1 226 mm) wide					
3314d .. with two opening lights	5.200	5.800	6.000	6.300	6.700
Window 5 ft 11¼ in. (1 810 mm) wide					
3315 .. with two opening lights	6.300	–	–	–	–
3316 .. with three opening lights	–	8.300	8.600	8.900	9.200
3317 .. with four opening lights	–	–	–	10.000	10.500
Window 7 ft 10¼ in. (2 394 mm) wide					
3318 .. with four opening lights	–	10.300	10.900	11.400	11.900

Per opening light

	£
ADD where opening light hung on one pair of easy-clean hinges	0.360
3319 in lieu of one pair of cranked butts	
3320 in lieu of one and a half pairs of cranked butts	0.240

Lead Pipes to conform in all respects with BS 602.

Lead waste and ventilating pipe and fixing complete with and including orna-mented double lead tacks soldered to the pipe not more than 1 metre apart, the tacks fixed with 75 mm brass screws to and including oak plugs or blocks let into face of wall. All joints in the running length to be included for in the rate which is also to include for pipes either in chases or elsewhere. Bends in pipes are to be priced separately.

Nominal bore (mm)	32	40	50	65	75	90	100	115	125
Price per metre									

Lead waste and overflow pipe all as in last item but in short lengths and not including joints or tacks.

Nominal bore (mm)	32	40	50	65	75	90	100	115	125
Price per metre									

Flushing and Warning pipes all as in first item.

Nominal bore (mm)	12	20	25	32	40	50
Price per metre						

Labour in forming bends in lead pipes.

Nominal bore (mm)	12	20	25	32	40	50	65	75	90	100
Each										

Soldered joint to fitting.

Nominal bore (mm)	12	20	25	32	50
Each					

Chapter XI
Approximate estimates

There is nothing, in my opinion, which affects more vitally the initial relations between architects and clients than the furnishing of approximate estimates. Your reputation will depend not only upon your ability to design buildings to satisfy requirements, but also upon the accuracy or otherwise of the estimates which you present, and which, of course, are the basis upon which your clients usually authorise you to proceed.

You are, no doubt, aware that there are many systems of making approximate estimates. I shall indicate a certain number and explain how they operate, but perhaps the first thing to get quite clear is what we mean by the term *approximate estimate*.

The word 'estimate' means 'a statement of the probable cost of carrying out any work', and the qualifying word 'approximate' implies that the estimate is not 'exact', but as near an approach to exactness as one can get in the initial stages; it must be reasonably accurate and is valueless if it proves too far out. Therefore when we use the words 'approximate estimate' we mean, 'a statement of cost, prepared by a competent person, to give a client some reasonably accurate idea of the expenditure to which he will be committed, if he decides to proceed with a scheme which has been prepared in accordance with his instructions'.

An approximate estimate is the basis upon which an architect is allowed to proceed, or is commissioned by his client to prepare the working drawings and specification and to obtain tenders. It follows therefore that it is a most important matter and must not be delegated to a junior.

I am well aware that a client, when he has made up his mind what it is he wants, is usually in a great hurry to have the work put in hand. He often has little idea of the amount of careful work entailed on the part of the architect before tenders can be invited, and in order to meet his wishes the architect is sometimes inclined to give too little time to the preliminaries. I wish to impress upon you most strongly the desirability of informing your client that time, trouble and money will be saved by allowing a sufficient period for close consideration of the preliminary designs and the probable cost of the work.

It will happen probably, when you first discuss a proposal with a client, that he will ask what it will cost to carry out the scheme. You will find that it is a wise plan in such circumstances to temporise, otherwise you will run the risk of misleading him. Do not commit yourself to any figure at this stage, as it should be obvious that you cannot produce figures on the spot; endeavour rather, to ascertain what amount your client is prepared to spend. Your attitude should be that the sizes of the rooms, etc, and the nature of the work will depend greatly upon the amount of money available. One of my architect friends told me a few years ago, that when he was faced with this question of estimates, his reply was twofold, either, 'Tell me the accommodation you require and I will tell you what it will cost', or 'Tell me how much you have to spend and I will tell you what you can get'. Both replies are reasonable, but many business men are reluctant to disclose what they are prepared to spend, even if they have any clear idea of the matter at all.

The moment when you first meet a new client is really an important one, and some careful thought on the matter will repay you. It is essential that you should win confidence, and not only be frank but convince your client of your frankness and the disinterestedness of your advice. Remember that the man-in-the-street, and particularly the 'business' man, is often entirely ignorant of professional procedure and etiquette. For instance, he may think on the analogy of the market place, that you get commissions from builders and merchants (not suspecting that your self-respect alone will prevent this), or, again, he may imagine that you are out to make the cost high and so to increase your legitimate fee. You must be prepared to be misjudged (quite unintentionally) at first, and you will only remove such misconception by convincing your client, in the most tactful way, that you are guided solely by a consideration for his interest, both in the cost and quality of the work. I was once asked, quite seriously, by the friend of a lady who had commissioned an architect to design a small house for her, to tell him what commission, other than the usual scale fees, the architect would get from the builder and merchants. The point is that professional status, and all that it implies, is not as generally understood as it should be, and you must be prepared to overcome any scruples of delicacy to make your position quite clear.

Many experienced architects and surveyors develop a faculty of sensing the value of work from very little information, but this faculty only comes from real knowledge of the cost and value of work. If an approximate estimate is made too high for safety it may result in important work being abandoned in its early stages and if it is made too low — perhaps in the hope that whatever the tender at a later stage may be the client will proceed with the work — the result may be the entire abandonment of the work and a difficult situation for all concerned.

A little reflection will show you that practically no important work is proceeded with until an approximate estimate has been furnished. One very seldom, if ever, comes across a client who instructs his architect to go ahead with a scheme without first having received some idea of the cost. Architects will often be asked to say what a certain work will cost and will make a shot on the spot. This shot will be registered by the client and soon becomes to him a definite figure, and later, a nightmare to the architect. I want to warn you against doing this if you can possibly avoid it. One of my friends was asked to give an estimate for garden work, lawns, paths, rock gardens, etc, and after much pressing by his client gave a figure entirely as a shot. The amount he gave was not acceptable to his client and that was the last he heard of the work. He will be more careful next time, I feel sure, though if in conversation one is asked these questions one must reply and if one declines the result may possibly be the same.

It must be remembered that full information is never available when instructions are received to prepare an approximate estimate. One's imagination has to play a great part because the information is generally meagre and innumerable problems are waiting to be considered. There is no time for accurate plans, details, elevations, or sections, one must rely on rought sketches, if any, and it sometimes occurs that not even a site has been decided on. It can easily be imagined how difficult all this will make the preparation of a reliable estimate.

Having obtained your client's instructions as definitely as possible, you can proceed with the preliminary drawings, and form your approximate estimate. You must be prepared for one very important and almost invariable contingency, which has an awkward repercussion on approximate estimates, and that is, that after the client has agreed to the architect proceeding with his working drawings he will tend to add to the original instructions and in a short time a formidable list of additions will have been made to the original design. Rooms made 'just a little' longer, the ground floor 'just a little' higher, an additional bathroom added, floors to be of oak and outside doors of oak to be provided, also the floors to be soundproof. If the architect does not warn his client of the additional cost of these things in good time he will find explanation difficult when the tender comes in, but if you have a quantity surveyor he will develop his approximate estimate into a 'cost plan' and keep you advised of the additional cost of these modifications.

Moreover, it is well to remember that a client will almost invariably forget the word 'approximate', and assume that the early figures given to him were quite definite ones, and his opinion of your capacity will vary in proportion to their degree of accuracy. This is a real difficulty, inescapable from the practice of an architect, and nothing but experience will teach you how to meet it.

When the tenders are received, if your preliminary estimate is found to have been too low, your client may refuse to proceed with the work, or, as an alternative, you may have endless trouble in revising the drawings, etc, in order to bring down the cost. If, as a third course, the client elects to accept a tender in spite of the additional expense, he may feel that he is not getting full value for his money. In any case the result is unsatisfactory to all concerned.

There is less difficulty where the approximate estimate is found to have been too high. When tenders are obtained and are lower than your approximate estimate your client will generally feed satisfied that he is getting a good bargain. I hasten to add that you must never deliberately make your estimates too high. My experience, however, is that, perhaps almost subconsciously, approximate estimates are often made too low in order to please a client and induce him to proceed. It is far more pleasant to find your estimate agreeing with the average figure given by the builders tendering than 10% above the highest or below the lowest tender. The architect who is able to make a close estimate, and then to carry out the work without extras (except such as the client requires), is one who will be recommended from client to client and deserves to prosper.

We must now consider in detail the various systems used in the preparation of approximate estimates, and it will be well to have them in tabulated form.

(a) Cubing.
(b) Superficial area of floors.
(c) Rough or grouped quantities.
(d) Detailed accurate quantities of one bay of a large building.
(e) Price per unit of accommodation.
(f) Other special systems less well known.

(a) The Cubing Method   This consists of obtaining the actual cubical contents of a building and multiplying the result by a given sum per cubic metre. It works out with surprising accuracy provided you known the class of building intended. The law of averages is so constant that structures of entirely divergent form and plan are found to cost practically the same amount per cubic metre as long as they are of the same class, namely, churches, hospitals, schools, factories, houses, etc. The standard system for arriving at the cubical contents of a structure is, to take the total length and breadth of a building outside the walls and the height from the top of the concrete foundations to half way up a pitched roof and $2'\ 0''$ (600 mm) above a flat roof. Certain other matters have to be attended to such as chimneys, bay windows, etc, but it will not be necessary to include the projections of ordinary plinths, cornices, etc, or the footings. The diagram will, I hope, make the matter clear. The projection of bay windows, porches, turrets, unusually elaborate chimney stacks, lantern lights, etc, must also be measured and included in the cube.

You may perhaps be puzzled to know what to do with all the nice little projections with which some architects like to adorn their buildings – cornices, pilasters, dormer windows, etc. Well simply ignore them unless the projections are of a very special character or unusually large, in which case you must take them into consideration and the best way to do so is to treat them as extras to the cube and allow a sum of money for them.

You should make a practice not to vary from whatever system of cubing you adopt, for if you do, your records, at the price per cubic metre, will lose their chief value, which is comparative. The cubing, which is practically mechanical, is the basis upon which you make your calculations, and the vital importance of not changing the basis will become obvious.

Should you be interested in a building having many unusual features, different levels, some parts much more elaborate than others, etc, it will be necessary to keep the various parts of the building separate so that the rate per cubic metre can be properly assessed. In the case of a large school in Shropshire, erected some years ago, for some reason (architectural I think) the architect had a parapet $6'\ 0''$ high all round the building. The building was cubed in the usual manner at $2'\ 0''$ above the level of the flat roof and ordinary quantities were prepared and priced for the parapet, the amount being added to the estimate.

The cubic contents of a building being ascertained the important thing is to decide what rate per cubic metre is to be adopted, and this is where

the real difficulty begins. Until you have had a lengthy experience and have accumulated a variety of records of actual costs, you are bound to find this a difficult matter. It is therefore essential to begin at once to keep systematic records of prices and actual costs of buildings, not only of your own works, but whenever you can obtain such information. It is a good plan in recording to note against the particulars of your approximate estimate the actual cost per cubic metre of the building as carried out with notes as to any variation in the work which affects the comparison.

On the following page will be found a specimen sheet of my record book of approximate estimates, which although now out of date will give you an indication of the layout I recommend.

(b) The next system we must consider is the method of estimating by taking the superficial area of floors and this is becoming more used than the cube method. This consists of measuring the actual area of each floor within the external walls in a building and multiplying the total area by a given sum per square metre. It is just as important in this method that the measurements should always be taken in the same way as in the cubing

RECORD BOOK OF APPROXIMATE ESTIMATES

Date	Name	Particulars as estimated			Particulars as contract			Particulars as carried out			Remarks
		Cube Feet	Rate	Estimate	Cube feet	Rate	Contract Amount	Cube feet	Rate	Cost	
1923 13 Jan	Dean Lodge .. Addition of drawing room, dinning room, and bedrooms	20 160	2/6	£2520	20 160	2/7	£2604	21 382	2/7	£2762	Brick walls, oak windows, lead lights, oak doors and floors
8 Mar	City of London .. Block of offices	805 559	3/-	£120 833	805 559	2/11	£117 477				
10 May	Croydon .. New house	26 634	1/7	£2108	26 634	1/6	£1997	27 428	1/7	£2171	Bathroom added
14 Aug	Mayfair .. Two new houses	154 250	2/6	£19 281	154 250	2/5½	£18 960				

method. For instance, if in one case, in, say, a large building, you measure all over the floors including the staircases, and in another building you omit the staircases, your fundamental basis will change. It is therefore vital that you keep the same basis every time, otherwise your data will be inconsistent. When you have calculated the floor areas you must then decide the question of the rate per square metre which is often difficult. Everything depends on the class of building. It will be obvious that a building such as a warehouse can have storeys which vary a great deal in their height and yet contain the same floor area. Buildings which from the outside look very much alike may have the floors spaced quite differently. It will be apparent that the building with the greater number of floors in the same height will be the most expensive and therefore you have to be very careful how you fix your rate. We have records in our office of buildings which look very similar from the outside but which differ considerably in their cost, owing to the fact that one building has more floors in it than the other and yet the total height is the same.

(c) The method of rough or grouped quantities consists of taking out approximate quantities for a building and requires usually more particulars than is given in the architect's original sketches. It is really a system based on builder's quantities where labours are not given in detail, but included in the various items of materials. These rough quantities can be produced in a tenth of the time taken to prepare the ordinary bills of quantities, for which a surveyor is responsible, but when they are priced in a manner which includes all labours they form quite a reliable method of approximate estimating.

You should cultivate the practice of remembering the prices of the leading items of work and materials. If you occasionally look up the prices in bills of quantities, and study the lists which are published periodically in the technical papers, you will very soon acquire a good working knowledge which you will find exceedingly useful. As a further help it is desirable to keep a record of leading items, and to note against each of them the prices given in the bills of quantities for each of your own works. You will thus have a personal store of information as to the variations and fluctuations which occur. If you obtain grouped and priced quantities for a whole building you will get an accurate and fairly satisfactory approximate estimate and you will always find it a great help in checking the other methods. As a guide the following list of inclusive prices calculated as current in December 1972 may be of assistance, but as prices are constantly changing, the list, to be of value, must be continually and carefully revised at short intervals.

List of Inclusive Prices 1972

(for work in London)

Excavating trenches of ordinary depth wheeling and loading into carts and carting away.	£3.50 per m^3
Cement concrete in foundations (1:2:4) and wheeling and depositing in trenches and ramming.	£10.00 per m^3
Stoneware drains (102 mm diameter British Standard) and laying, including digging trenches of ordinary depth, cement concrete bed and haunching, filling in and ramming and carting away surplus material.	£3.00 per m
Brickwork in Fletton bricks, laid in gauged mortar, in walls one brick thick and including all angles, rough cuttings, and similar labours.	£6.40 per m^2
Ground floors, including hardcore, concrete layer, sleeper walls, air bricks, wall plates, softwood joists, and grooved and tongued softwood flooring.	£7.00 per m^2
Ground floors, including hardcore, reinforced concrete layer floated with cement to take linoleum, etc.	£5.00 per m^2
Upper floor, including softwood joists, plates, herring-bone strutting, concrete hearths, softwood flooring, skirting, plaster ceiling.	£8.30 per m^2
Roofs, including wall plates, softwood rafters, purlins, ridges, tilting fillets, eaves fascia and soffits, boarding, felt, battens, tiles, etc, flashings and gable boards, iron gutters, rain-water pipes, brick gable walls where necessary, with facings and stone copings.	£15.00 per m^2 of horizontal surface covered
Flat roofs, including concrete and steel joists, centering, cement screed and asphalt, one brick parapet walls with stone coping, iron rain-water heads with rain-water pipes.	£12.50 per m^2 of horizontal surface covered

Ordinary softwood cased windows and sashes in small squares glazed with 3 mm sheet glass, and with softwood linings, architraves and window boards, all painted four coats, and with sash fasteners and lifts.   } £17.00 per m^2

Ditto ditto but in oak, fumed and wax polished inside.   } £35.00 per m^2

50 mm six-panel, both sides flush moulded softwood doors size 730 mm x 2040 mm overall, with 38 mm rebated softwood linings, 75 mm x 25 mm softwood architraves both sides and painting four coats, brass mortice lock and furniture, steel hinges and finger plates.   } £50.00 each

Six-panel, both sides flush moulded oak doors, with 38 mm rebated oak linings, 75 mm x 25 mm oak architraves both sides, all oak fumed and wax polished, brass mortice lock and furniture, brass hinges and finger-plates.   } £100.00 each

Plasterboard ceilings with scrimmed joints, 5 mm one coat plaster and paint two coats emulsion.   } £1.50 per m^2

Studded partitions in fir, plasterboard both sides, two coats emulsion paint and with softwood skirting.   } £6.25 per m^2

75 mm clinker concrete partitions, plastered both sides, two coats emulsion paint and with softwood skirting.   } £6.00 per m^2

Staircase in softwood with strings, risers, treads and balusters, oak newels and handrails, well-hole casing, quarter spaces, etc, all softwood painted, the staircase 900 mm wide and rising 2600 mm.   } £275.00 each

Cold-water supply, including connection to company's main, stopcock, length of pipe from road to house, and all internal work, including cistern in roof and all services exclusive of cost of sanitary fittings.   } £40.00 per sanitary fitting

Central heating and domestic hot-water supply, including boiler, supply cistern, insulated cylinder and all pipes, radiators and connections. } £800.00 for 4 Bedroom house

Gas supply, including connection to company's meter, gas-pipes, etc, ready for fixing fittings. } £4.50 per point

Electric light wiring, in PVC insulated and sheathed cable protected by light gauge conduits where buried from the company's meter to the various points, excluding fittings. } £8.00 per point

Red brick boundary walls one brick thick with concrete foundations, two courses of tiles and brick on edge coping, the wall 1350 mm high out of ground. } £40.00 per m

Park pale fencing fixed complete, with stout oak posts 3 m apart, two oak arris rails and pales 1350 mm high. } £3.00 per m

Paving to yards in granolithic concrete on ordinary concrete layer and hard core. } £4.00 per m^2

Ditto ditto but with 50 mm York stone paving instead of granolithic concrete. } £15.00 per m^2

Covering walls with 152 mm x 152 mm x 6 mm white glazed tiles on a cement bed. } £4.25 per m^2

Plastering walls with lightweight gypsum plaster and painting two coats emulsion paint. } £1.40 per m^2

Covering roofs with 508 mm x 254 mm slating to BS 680 laid to a 76 mm lap, including battens. } £5.20 per m^2

Covering roofs with handmade tiles laid to 64 mm lap, including battens. } £5.50 per m^2

Painting new work, four coats, including knotting, priming and stopping. } £1.15 per m^2

Painting old work, two coats, including well rubbing down the existing work. } £0.90 per m^2

Emulsion paint, two coats. } £0.35 per m^2

(d) A method we sometimes employ when the client asks for an approximate estimate which will be more accurate than the estimate arrived at by the cubing or floor area system is to take out accurate and detailed quantities for one bay in a building, such as a hall, where there are many bays of similar construction, and to price the quantities at current rates exactly as ordinary quantities are priced by a builder when preparing a definite tender. This method will give you an accurate price for one bay and it can then easily be applied to a building as a whole. You must, of course, realise that in doing this you cannot simply multiply the result you have obtained by the number of bays in the hall, because the bay for which the quantities have been prepared may be a bay in the middle of the hall and the end bays will have additional walls and doorways, windows, etc, quite different from the intermediate bays; these must, of course, be allowed for. You will understand that the quantities must be prepared by a person fully qualified to prepare ordinary quantities, otherwise the result will be quite useless.

(e) The next method to consider is the price per unit of accommodation. This system practically speaks for itself, as it consists of acquiring a knowledge of prices per unit, such as Hospitals per bed or department; Schools per scholar; Churches per sitting; Theatres, Cinemas, Halls, etc, per seat; Flats per room, etc. This method is useful as it forms a comparison with the other methods, but it should only be used as a check because the complexity of present day buildings prevents reliable estimates being prepared on this basis.

(f) I believe there are some other less known systems of preparing approximate estimates, used by some architects and surveyors, but I think you would be well advised to concentrate on and acquire a good knowledge of the methods I have dealt with in some detail, for then you will be equipped with valuable information which should enable you with confidence to advise your clients when the time comes. The Storey Enclosure system of approximate estimating introduced to the Royal Institution of Chartered Surveyors in April 1954 is an example of a different method of approach which no doubt deserves careful consideration, but it is more the type of system that would be used by the quantity surveyor than the architect. You should also be aware of the vast amount of information on costs which is published by the Building Cost Information Service of the Royal Institution of Chartered Surveyors and which is available on subscription to architects.

I think it may now be of some help to you if I point out various factors which must be taken into consideration in arriving at the rate upon which to base your estimate for whichever type you decide to adopt. For instance there is the style and finish of the building. It may have to be designed as a very plain building, or for want of a better term in what I call the Houses of Parliament style; the inside finishings may have to be specially elaborate; the joinery and floors of oak; ceilings and cornices may have to be in fibrous plaster; expensive materials may have to be used such as marble floors, expensive grates and mantelpieces and special decoration, etc. Then again there may be difficulties with the site, the ground may be at a considerable slope, or the building may have to be erected on bad ground involving piled foundations, or on clay involving extra depth, or all the roof space occupied by bedrooms, etc. The rates of wages and the cost of materials in different parts of the country must be taken into consideration and can easily affect the cost by as much as 10%. Then again the size of the structure affects the rate, for a small building is pro- portionately more expensive than a large one. A scheme with many detached buildings all alike may be cheaper than one large building giving the same accommodation; a building with many circular rooms or peculiar roofs is more expensive than with ordinary rectangular shaped rooms and simple roofs, a single storey building is often more expensive than a building with two or more floors giving the same accommodation and the situation of a building — near a railway station or some distance away from a main roadway — will make a difference to the rate. Facilities at the site can affect prices; where there is plenty of ground for the builder to put his materials and to move about it is obviously cheaper than if the whole site is built over, as often happens in towns. Further matters have to be considered which will affect the estimate very considerably; for example, scarcity or abundance of work; rises or falls of wages; rises or falls in the cost of materials and in what manner and under what form of contract the work is to be carried out. You will see therefore what a great variation there can be in the rate to be chosen in making approximate estimates and the quantity surveyor, who, as a rule, has a wide experience of country prices as well as those in London, and is accustomed to prepare estimates under all the conditions I have mentioned, should be of considerable assistance in coming to your aid when occasions arise. I am trying to impress upon you all that the chief difficulty in preparing approximate estimates is to decide the correct rate and therefore the necessity of keeping as full and reliable records as possible, so that you may have plenty of past experience to draw upon, is very important.

It is not unlikely that one of your first jobs will be to design some alterations to an existing building. The preparation of an approximate estimate for this class of work is often extremely difficult and requires a good deal of knowledge and experience. I think the most satisfactory way is to prepare an estimate of the genuine additions on one of the methods I have described and then make a detailed list of the proposed alterations, putting against each item the amount you think the work will cost. You should make your list at the building itself going into every part of it and make a comprehensive rough bill of quantities which should be priced as you proceed.

You may have to make an approximate estimate for reconditioning a building and you should proceed exactly in the same way that I have just described.

The architect is personally responsible for the approximate estimate (unless he has notified his client that his quantity surveyor has prepared it) and it is important that he should possess the necessary ability to prepare it, and with increasing experience he will gain the necessary confidence. At the same time, it is obvious that the architect can never acquire that intimate knowledge of prices which comes to the quantity surveyor in the ordinary way of business. In normal circumstances it is seldom that a quantity surveyor cannot estimate within 5% of the real value. It is therefore to the advantage of the architect to avail himself of the surveyor's services in connection with the preparation of all such estimates, for which, by the way, he makes no charge, if they are prepared on the cube or floor area basis. But make sure that the surveyor is given sufficient time, or his figures cannot be expected to be reliable; and further, if your own estimate does not agree with his, do not present your own until you have threshed the matter out with the surveyor and come to an agreement.

I have already referred to the difficulty experienced when tenders are found to be too high, and methods have to be taken to reduce the estimates. One of the ways of cutting down the cost is to omit a portion of the proposed building, but it is not easy to convince a client that the omitted portion of the building cannot be priced at the same rate as the whole of the scheme. If, for example, you are estimating the cost of a public hall and the rate is £100 per m^2, you must not calculate the saving of one bay at £100, otherwise when the tender is received you will be surprised to find that the amount of the saving in only about £70 per m^2.

Another very important point — and one which I think is frequently forgotten — is to make it quite clear to your client what is and what is not included in the amount of the approximate estimate. You will find it a help to study carefully the following letter, which was sent by a surveyor to an architect some time ago.

Dear Sir

I have made a careful approximate estimate of the probable cost of erecting the proposed building in accordance with your sketch plans prepared to a scale of 16′ 0″ to the inch. I have assumed that the ground floor level will be 2′ 0″ above the top of the concrete foundations, the ground floor storey 10′ 0″ in height ffrom floor to floor and the first floor 9′ 0″ The approximate cubical contents are 79 400′ 0″ which at 1/6 per foot cube would cost £5955. To this amount should be added the cost of a garage, £250 and a conservatory £150. It should be noted that nothing is included in this estimate for the following services: garden work, tennis lawns, etc, roads, paths, fences and gates, lavatory basin in each bedroom, oak panelling in library, electric cables, water and gas mains, electric light fittings, drainage and sewage disposal, architect's fees and expenses, clerk of works' salary, and quantity surveyor's fees.

Yours truly

John H. Jones

I have not updated this letter because the principle wording is still applicable, but you should note that the architect's fees are specially mentioned as excluded from the estimate. I am sure it is always advisable that the client should be made aware of this because, in 99 cases out of a 100, when a client is told how much the building is going to cost he will assume that the sum includes architect's fees.

The current RIBA Conditions of Engagement are quite clear on the method of calculating architects' fees for the preparation of estimates, which are covered by Work Stages B – D.

There are many useful records that can be kept and that will be of great value to you in making approximate estimates. I do not pretend that it is a complete list, but those I am now going to mention are almost all indispensable and you can, of course, add to them as need arises. These lists are chiefly skeleton ones, given solely as a guide to help you in your own work. You must, of course, realise that all the prices are subject to constant revision and must be looked upon as examples and not for use in preparing an estimate.

(a) THE ACTUAL COST OF BUILDING. (ESPECIALLY USEFUL IF YOU HAVE HAD EXPERIENCE OF THE BUILDING IN QUESTION)

Date	House	Total cost			Rate per foot cube
		£	s	d	
1936	Cambridge (House)	3 444	0	0	1/4½
1937	Bewlie (House)	9 760	0	0	2/4
1938	Rowfant (House)	4 845	0	0	1/9
1948	Lewisham (Shops and Flats)	13 368	0	0	3/6
1950	Croydon (House)	3 871	0	0	4/1
1950	Surrey (Church Hall)	6 500	0	0	2/9½
1951	Kensington (Flats)	30 544	0	0	3/9
1952	Reading (Changing Rooms)	10 800	0	0	5/2½
1954	Sussex (House)	10 998	0	0	5/3

Note   The rates per foot cube would be expressed today as a rate per m^2 and the floor area noted.

(b) THE PROPORTION OF LABOUR TO MATERIALS

Trade	Labour	Materials and Plant
	per cent	per cent
Excavator	90	10
Concretor	17	83
Bricklayer	30	70
Drainlayer	33	67
Mason	50	50
Roofer	20	80
Carpenter	30	70
Joiner	60	40
Steel and Ironworker	23	77
Plasterer	60	40
Plumber	25	75
Glazier	15	85
Painter	50	50

We have found that, in a general way, two-thirds of the cost of a house can be assigned to the carcase and one-third to the finishings.

(c) THE PERCENTAGE COST OF THE VARIOUS TRADES. THE FOLLOWING LIST GIVES THE AVERAGE FOR THE FOUR HOUSES RECENTLY ERECTED. IT MUST BE NOTED THAT THE PERCENTAGE COST WILL DIFFER IN ALMOST ALL BUILDINGS

Excavator, Concretor and Bricklayer	27.00
Drainlayer	4.35
Mason	2.75
Tiler	4.75
Carpenter, Joiner and Ironmonger	26.25
Steel and Ironworker	4.00
Plasterer	9.75
Plumber, Hot Water, Gas and Electrical Installations	16.25
Glazier	2.65
Painter	2.25
	100.00

(d) THE COST OF MATERIALS IN THE LONDON AREA (1973)

Description	Unit	Rate
		£
Ballast	tonne	1.52
Shingle, ¾" gauge	tonne	1.57
Sand (washed)	tonne	1.57
Portland Cement	tonne	9.32
Bricks, Flettons	1000	12.25
Bricks, Stocks (2nd Hard)	1000	32.25
Bricks, Engineering (Class B)	1000	32.10
Stone, Portland	m³	30.65
Clinker Concrete Blocks, 3" thick	m²	0.75
Slates, 20" x 10"	1000	136.50
Roofing Tiles (hand made)	1000	42.00
Asbestos Cement Sheeting (corrugated)	m²	0.80
Timber, Softwood	m³	42.00
Joinery Deals	m³	55.00
Structural Steel	tonne	90.00
Steel Reinforcing Rods	tonne	100.00
Sheet Lead	tonne	221.50
Lead Pipes	tonne	226.50
Coarse-Plaster (white)	tonne	15.76
Keene's Cement (pink)	tonne	20.89
Sirapite (fine)	tonne	16.28
Clear Sheet Glass (Ordinary Glazing Quality),3 mm	m²	1.40
Gloss oil paint	5 litre	3.50
Emulsion paint	5 litre	2.95
Solignum	5 litre	0.55

The following analysis of wages is from 'Cost Information File' (*Building*, 6 July 1973) compiled by the Building Cost Information Service of the Royal Institution of Chartered Surveyors. Copyright The Builder Limited and the Royal Institution of Chartered Surveyors 1973.

Cost Information File: BCIS Subsection: (c) WAGES-1

WAGES

All-in Labour Rates

The "all-in" hourly rates used in the Measured Rates section have been calculated in accordance with the Institute of Building, Code of Estimating Practice. The build-up of the rates are shown in Table 1.

A 30% addition for plus rates was calculated as the average "bonus" payment being made in the construction industry from the Department of Employment's statistics on average weekly earnings and hours worked*. It is obvious that this figure, while average, is unlikely to be typical, there being a wide variation in wage rates actually paid. In order to assist those readers who find this addition inappropriate, we have shown in Table 2 the all-in hourly rates calculated using other levels of plus rate addition.

The basic rates used are those for the London region. Basic rates for other regions are shown in Table 3. The basic rates for Building workers are those promulgated by the National Joint Council for the Building Industry on the 14th September 1972 and operative from the 18th September 1972. Basic rates for the Plumbing Industry are those promulgated by the Joint Industry Board for Plumbing Mechanical and Engineering Services on the 23rd October 1972 and operative from the 2nd April 1973 (the operative date was postponed from the 1st January 1973 by the freeze).

In the Measured Rates section the labour constants include for a plumber and mate, the rate being taken as that of an advance plumber and an apprentice aged 18.

*Department of Employment Gazette Statistical Series, Table 122.

TABLE 2
All-in Rates for Craftsmen with Differing Plus Rate Allowances
Percentage Addition for Plus Rate

	10%	20%	30%	40%	50%	75%	100%
Basic rate	67½p	67½p	67½p	67½p	67½p	67½p	67½p
Plus rate	7p	13½p	20½p	27p	34p	50½p	67½p
Total rate	74½p	81p	88p	94½p	101½p	118p	135p
All-in rate	100p	109p	118p	126p	134p	154p	174p

TABLE 3
Basic Wages
Craftsmen, Labourers, Apprentices and Young Male Labourers
Per 40 hour week

	London & Liverpool District Rate £	Grade A Rate £	Scotland Rate £
Craftsmen	27·20	27·00	27·00
Labourer	23·20	23·00	23·00

A Guaranteed minimum bonus of £2·60 for craftsmen and £2·20 for labourers (50% for apprentices and trainees) is payable where bonus earnings fall below this level.

England & Wales	Scotland	% of Crafts.	Rate £	% of Crafts.	Rate £	% of Crafts.	Rate £
Apprentice	Year						
Age 16	1	40	11·00	40	10·80	45	12·15
17	2	60	16·40	60	16·20	55	14·85
18	3	80	21·80	80	21·60	75	20·25
19	4	85	23·15	85	22·95	85	22·95
20		90	24·50	90	24·30		

Young Male Labourers	% of Labs.	Rate £	% of Labs.	Rate £	% of Labs.	Rate £
Age 15	33⅓	7·86½	33⅓	7·66½	33⅓	7·66½
16	45	10·55	45	10·35	45	10·35
17	66⅔	15·53½	66⅔	15·33½	66⅔	15·33½
18	100	23·20	100	23·00	100	23·00

Watchmen, the rates per shift for watchmen engaged on building sites are £4·06 in London and Liverpool District, and £4·02½ in Scotland and Grade A Districts.

TABLE 1
All-in Hourly Rates

	Building Craftsmen	Building Labourer	Plumbing Technical	Plumbing Advanced	Plumbing Trained	Apprentice aged 18
Total hours worked per year	2193	2193	2193	2193	2193	2193
Inclement weather 2% of total hours	44	44	44	44	44	44
Total Productive hours per year	2149	2149	2149	2149	2149	2149
Hours non-productive overtime per year	111½	111½	160½	160½	160½	160½
Days sick per year	5	5	5	5	5	5
Days public holiday per year	6	6	6	6	6	6
Sick pay: per day	75p	75p	+	+	+	+
Tool money: per week	10p	10p	15p	15p	15p	15p
Annual holiday with pay contribution	£1·80	£1·80	£2·59	£2·22	£2·02	£1·50*
Trade supervision: per hour	7p	6p	11p	9p	8p	6p
Basic hourly rate	67½p	57½p	91½p	76½p	68½p	52p
30% plus rate	20p	17½p	27½p	23p	20½p	15½p
Total hourly rate	88p	75p	119p	99½p	89p	67½p
Basic wages (Total hourly rate × hours worked)	1929·84	1644·75	2609·67	2182·04	1951·77	1480·28
Non-productive overtime (Total hourly rate × Non-productive hours)	98·12	83·63	191·00	159·70	142·85	108·34
Sick pay (days sick × sick pay)	3·75	3·75	+	+	+	+
Working rule agreement (49 weeks x tool money)	4·90	+	7·35	7·35	7·35	7·35
Annual holidays with pay (49 weeks × contribution)	88·20	88·20	134·68	115·44	105·04	78·00*
Public holiday with pay (No. of days × 8 × total hourly rate)	42·24	36·00	57·12	47·76	42·72	32·40
Sub-total	2167·05	1876·33	2999·82	2512·29	2249·73	1706·37
Graduated pensions	80·08	68·12	76·44	76·44	65·52	37·96
C.I.T.B. levy	15·00	3·00	45·00	45·00	45·00	9·00
National insurance	54·60	54·60	54·60	54·60	54·60	54·60
Sub-total	2316·73	2002·05	3175·86	2688·33	2414·85	1807·93
Severence pay Add 1%	2339·90	2022·07	3207·62	2715·21	2439·00	1826·01
Employers liability & third party insurance Add 1·2%	2376·98	2046·33	3246·11	2747·79	2468·27	1847·92
Trade supervision	153·51	131·58	241·23	197·37	175·44	131·58
Cost of supervision x hours worked Total cost	2530·49	2177·91	3487·34	2945·16	2643·71	1979·50
Cost per hour (total cost ÷ no. of productive hours)	**£1·18**	**£1·01**	**£1·62**	**£1·37**	**£1·23**	**£0·92**

***This is an estimate, actual contributions depend on individual indentures**

(f) THE PERCENTAGE OF THE TOTAL COST FOR ELECTRIC LIGHT AND POWER INSTALLATIONS

Building	Cost of Building	Percentage of total cost for electric light and power installation
	£	%
House, Rowfant	4 845	2.97
House, Stow-on-the-Wold	13 660	1.54
Army Hostel	11 292	2.13
Public House	7 247	3.31
Men's Club	15 690	2.26
Mansion (reconditioning)	39 566	14.70*
Residential School	14 875	1.21
Fire Station	40 611	7.16*
Flats (London)	130 500	2.62
Students' Hostel (London)	220 000	6.66*
House (Sussex)	10 998	2.82

*These amounts include the cost of light fittings.

(g) THE PERCENTAGE OF THE TOTAL COST FOR HEATING AND HOT WATER SERVICES

Building	Cost of Building	Percentage of total cost for heating and hot water services
	£	%
House, Rowfant	4 845	5.72
House, Stow-on-the-Wold	13 660	5.04
Army Hostel	11 292	4.58
Public House	7 247	4.55
Men's Club	15 690	5.67
Mansion (reconditioning)	39 566	12.35
Residential School	14 875	3.50
Fire Station	40 611	5.38
Flats (London)	130 500	2.88
Students' Hostel (London)	220 000	5.07
House (Sussex)	10 998	7.09

(h) THE PERCENTAGE OF THE TOTAL COST FOR STEELWORK. IT WILL BE SEEN THAT THE PROPORTION OF STEELWORK VARIES WITH THE NUMBER OF STOREYS AND OF COURSE WITH THE DIFFERENT FLOOR LOADING REQUIREMENTS

Type of building	Situation	Total cost of work	Percentage of total cost for structural steelwork
		£	%
Multi-storey offices	London	250 000	12.00
Multi-storey stores	London	35 000	13.71
Two-storey workshops	Cambridge	52 500	12.95
Multi-storey hostel	London	220 000	7.95
Multi-storey laboratory	Cambirdge	232 000	7.84
Two-storey laboratory	Cheltenham	170 000	5.29

Chapter XII
Tenders

The preparation of your contract particulars being completed and approved by your client, the next stage is the obtaining of tenders for the carrying out of the work. It is essential that the competing builders should be given definite and detailed information upon which to make up their tenders, and, of course, that each builder should be given similar particulars, otherwise the tenders will be unsatisfactory, and you will be laying up trouble for yourself as the work proceeds. If anything in your contract particulars is lacking or indefinite the builder whose tender is accepted will have misunderstood your intentions, and when it turns out that more work is required than he has provided for in his tender, an extra will be demanded, and your troubles will begin. One of the reasons why quantities are prepared is to enable all the firms tendering to compete upon the same definite basis.

If during the time tenders are being obtained it is found that some alteration is necessary in the particulars sent out, it is, of course, essential that all the builders invited to tender should be notified, and you will be wise to ask for an acknowledgement of your communication.

We will assume that your contract particulars (drawings, bills of quantities and conditions of contract) are prepared and the quantities are ready to be issued. The next procedure is to make up a list of builders to tender. An architect with a well organised practice has no trouble in doing this, as there is probably what amounts to a queue of builders always waiting for the chance of tendering for him, but at first it is a matter requiring a good deal of inquiry and consideration. You can consult the Architects Standard Catalogue which contains a list of builders in different parts of the country or you can consult the National Federation of Building Trades Employers who would I am sure supply a list of builders in the particular district in which you are interested. It is really essential to invite builders of equal standing for the same job chosen for their suitability for the particular contract, any one of whom could be entrusted with the work, and if you are in any serious difficulty in making up your list, one of your brother architects will, I am sure, be only too pleased to help you.

To invite the builders to tender is an easy matter. A simple invitation form which is often used and upon which you can model your own letter is as follows:

Date . . . . . .

Dear Sir

I am writing to invite you to tender for the erection of a proposed factory and office building at . . . .
for . . . . The buildings are expected to cost of the order of £ . . . . . . and bills of quantities are being prepared by . . . . who expect to be able to issue copies to firms tendering by . . . .   Tenders are to be delivered to me not later than first post on . . . .   An early reply to this letter will be appreciated.

Yours faithfully

. . . .

It may be preferable in some cases to give the floor area of the building instead of quoting an estimate of the cost. It is desirable that all the tenders should be made out in the same form. The following example illustrates a form in common use:

FORM OF TENDER
Proposed erection of a new house at Slocumpton
for Jonas Brown Esq

To
John W. Smith Esq
Architect
New London

Sir

We hereby agree to enter into a contract to execute and complete the whole of the works required to be done in connection with the above in strict accordance with the drawings, bills of quantities and conditions of contract prepared by you and to your entire satisfaction for the sum of . . . . (£   )

It is understood that neither the lowest nor any tender will necessarily be accepted.

We are, Sir
Yours faithfully
Signature . . . .

Address . . . .
Date . . . .

I always advise that the tender form should contain the clause I have written at the end, 'It is understood that neither the lowest nor any tender will necessarily be accepted'. A similar clause is usually put both in the specification and the quantities, the object being to safeguard the client from any claim being made in the event of all the tenders being declined or of a tender being accepted which is not the lowest. It is a good plan also to send each builder an addressed envelope, with the name of the job on the top edge.

If you wish to make your invitation to tender and the tender itself more formal, and this may well be advantageous in the case of larger work, you can follow the Code of Procedure for Selective Tendering 1972 published by the RIBA for The National Joint Consultative Committee of Architects, Quantity Surveyors and Builders.

It sometimes happens that a client will insist upon accepting a tender which is not the lowest, and this always seems to me unfair in cases where you have made a careful selection of builders and invited them to tender. The preparation of a tender usually involves a great amount of work, and the only stimulus that the builder has is the chance of being the lowest and getting the work. It is quite a different matter when you advertise for tenders. In this case you cannot be sure that all the builders are really trustworthy, and you may receive the lowest tender from a firm whose reputation is not very high. If, after making enquiries, you are dissatisfied, you need have no hesitation in passing over such a builder. The above remarks appear to me, and I hope also to you, convincing, but I must point out that you may not always find it easy to convince your clients. I have attended committee meetings where these points have been discussed, and failed to convince them of the fairness of my views. I leave you to judge whether the fault lay with me or the committees.

It will be necessary to decide what length of time is to be given to the builders for the preparation of their tenders, and many things will have to be taken into consideration. If contractors are not allowed sufficient time to make necessary inquiries and obtain quotations for the special articles required, it is likely that their tenders will be higher than would otherwise be the case. On the other hand, clients are generally in a hurry to know how much the work is going to cost them, and will put pressure upon you to get in the tenders at the earliest possible date. Three or four weeks is probably the minimum period required, but in the case of large or intricate jobs a longer period will be necessary.

The question of opening tenders now arises. As a rule the tenders are received by the architect and opened by him, and it is essential that the matter should be conducted in a perfectly straightforward way. Some architects make a practice of having the builders present. In some offices the tenders are receivable by the first post on a certain day, and in others they are received at noon. Occasionally the client desires to open the tenders himself. This, I think, should be discouraged; the builders certainly prefer that the architect should do this. If the client insists, you must give way but you should make a point of being present at the opening. Tenders were recently received for a large building in London. They were opened by the clients at a board meeting at which the architect was not present. The first intimation that he received was that a tender about the fifth from the lowest had been accepted. As this was a limited competition, and by invitation, the builder whose tender was the lowest was naturally upset. He protested so vigorously that the builder whose tender had been accepted asked to be allowed to withdraw it. This, I think was the correct course to pursue. A short time ago tenders were invited for a small school building. The committee charged with carrying out the work asked to have the tenders delivered to them and did not invite the architect to be present at the opening. After the tenders had been opened the committee requested the architect to obtain a tender from a builder who had not been previously invited. Without having the power to refuse, the architect advised the committee against the proceeding on the grounds (a) that it was not in accordance with professional procedure, and (b) that, although he had no doubt as to the right intentions of the committee, he would be quite unable to convince the contractors of his own good faith. This, I think, was a very subtle way of putting the matter.

Before accepting a tender you must make sure that there are no obvious mistakes in it. Care should be taken to check the rates quoted in the bills of quantities and to see that none of them is excessively high compared with average current prices. I have referred to this in chapter XIII, page 105, and given instances where this precaution was not adopted and the result.

When you have received your client's instructions to accept a tender it is always a wise proceeding to accept it subject to a proper form of contract being entered into.

You may receive two tenders of exactly the same amount. If they are not the lowest it will not matter, but if they happen to be the lowest, then the fair thing to do, I think, is to send the tenders back to the builders, inform them of the fact, without disclosing the name of either to the other, and to ask them to submit a revised tender by a certain specified time.

Sometimes you will receive tenders too late — that is, after the time fixed for their receipt. You must be careful in dealing with such tenders or you may lay yourself open to a charge of unfairness. Late tenders should only be opened in cases where no tender has been received in proper time, or, if the tender has come through the post, where the postmark shows that it was posted before the time of opening. I think that, with the above exceptions, tenders received too late should not be opened, but returned to the builders. This, however, is not always done. The reason for all this care is that builders, as soon as the latest time for posting their tenders has passed, are apt to discuss the matter with other competitors and perhaps disclose the amount of their tenders. An unscrupulous competitor thus has a chance, if he has not posted his tender, of putting in a lower figure.

When a tender has been accepted, I think it is due to the builders that they should each be thanked for the trouble taken in tendering and that a list of the tenders should be sent to them; but it is advisable to delay sending the list until after the contract is signed, especially if the lowest tender is much below the next.

You may be surprised to hear that it is not always possible to get genuine tenders from builders. For example, if a contract is in progress at a house, and you wish to obtain tenders for further work, the builder who is carrying out the original contract will sometimes arrange with the other competitors that their quotations shall be higher than his own. There is, I think, a feeling among builders that additional work of this kind should be given to the original builder without competition, and provided that fair rates can be obtained, it seems to me that there is a good deal to be said for this view. In a case some years ago an architect invited a firm at Glasgow to compete for some work in Kent, as he thought that otherwise he would not get genuine competition. The result justified his fears, as the Glasgow firm's tender was much the lowest, and they carried out the work.

Much talk is heard at times about collusion among builders when tendering. It is, however, just as natural for builders who know they are estimating for the same job to make some mutual arrangement to avoid undercutting each other as for two friends in a sale-room to agree not to bid against each other. There are, in fact, certain organisations in existence in various parts of the country which have been expressly formed for facilitating such mutual arrangements between builders. The remedy is to take precautions to keep secret the names of the builders tendering. Request your clients to preserve silence on this matter, and, when inviting tenders, arrange definite appointments on separate days for the necessary inspection of the site or building by the contractors. A little forethought will often prevent collusion, which is as troublesome as it is human.

Chapter XIII

Contracts

I think it will be obvious that one of the most important documents in connection with the carrying out of work of any sort is the contract agreement. It is always necessary to have a contract in some form or other; it may be only a verbal one, or it may consist simply of a tender and a letter of acceptance, but the better the form the fewer the difficulties which will arise.

When I speak of 'contract particulars' I mean the drawings, specification and form of contract, also the quantities where they form part of the contract. When, therefore, you are preparing your drawings and specification you must not forget to think about the form of contract. It is a good plan to fill this up whilst you are writing the specification, and in any case most of the provisions must be settled before the contractors can give definite tenders.

Two forms of contract (with and without quantities), dated 1963 but revised in 1973 and issued by the Joint Contracts Tribunal, are in general use among architects at the present time. The Joint Contracts Tribunal is composed of membership from the Royal Institute of British Architects, the National Federation of Building Trades Employers, the Royal Institution of Chartered Surveyors and various other organisations who have an interest in the formation of a standard form of contract for construction purposes. They are sometimes referred to as the RIBA Contracts, but that is no longer technically correct. Copies of these standard forms can be obtained from the Institute and each one of you should possess copies and make a thorough study of them. They are in reality variations of the same document and the one which I propose to examine in detail is the Standard Form of Building Contract — Private Edition with Quantities; it should not be difficult for you to fill in the other where quantities are excluded, if you study well my remarks about the first. The present standard form is the result of many revisions over the years. It is certain to be revised again (in fact it is reviewed by The Joint Contracts Tribunal every six months) but I do not think our time will be wasted, as many of the clauses must be included in any new form. I repeat that one of the forms is used when quantities are included in the contract, and the other is for use where quantities are excluded. I will explain later the reason for the two editions. A word of warning, however, that whereas the earliest RIBA form that anyone practising today can remember, ie the 1909 edition, covered only 10 pages, the form current in 1973 runs into 28 pages so that it is obvious that an enormous number of variations and additions to the text have been made. The 1909 edition (there were earlier ones) presumed a very good deal of understanding and loyalty between the architect and the builder who followed the architect's wishes and sometimes idiosyncrasies without making financial claims at every turn and still in most cases came out with a profit and an enhanced reputation. The present 1973 edition began its life as it were in the 1931 revision which was the result of discussions between architects and contractors at which time the quantity surveyors were not consulted. As a result quite a number of provisions appeared in the 1931 edition which in my opinion were greatly in favour of the contractor and enabled him to begin the claims process which is so prevalent today. Indeed you will find as your practice grows that some contractors even have claims departments or claims consultants whose job it is to watch the way the architect behaves so as not to miss the slightest opportunity of making a claim for additional payment.

Of course circumstances have changed considerably over the many years from 1909 to the present time, and a simple example of the changes may serve to illustrate my point. I have referred to the Builder and later changed this title to Contractor, the significance here being that the old time 'builder' set out to erect the building more or less with his own hands and as such was offering the skilled services of all trades from his own organisation and employees, whereas the modern builder is more correctly described as a 'contractor' being someone who employs perhaps very little of his own labour, but arranges for the work to be done by sub-letting plastering, painting, etc and even excavations, concrete work and bricklaying to mention only a few of the trades required to complete the whole contract. The builder, for instance, supplied scaffolding from his own yard, sending on to the site so many poles, putlogs and ropes and being always ready to send more if necessary without any thought of extra cost. The contractor today, however, makes an estimate of the amount of steel scaffolding he thinks he will need and gets an estimate from a sub-contracting scaffolding firm for supply, erection, dismantling and for a stated hire period and if he finds he needs more or that the hire period is extended he never considers he might have under-estimated the requirements, but upon receiving extra invoices from his sub-contractor therefore proceeds to seek additional payment by making a claim.

So you must be very careful indeed even though I still advocate the use of the Standard Form that you do nothing which can produce a claim situation or your clients with you yourself as their agent may find an arbitration on your hands or even perhaps as the modern trend a High Court case to settle the dispute.

There are, of course, many other forms of building contract in use, such as those used by Government departments (Form CCC/Wks/1) and local authorities (for example, The Greater London Council's own form) and it is probable that you will, sooner or later, come into contact with them. You will find it useful to study these special contracts without delay, some of which can be obtained from HM Stationery Office, others from the RIBA. No doubt your quantity surveyor will be able to supply information on most of the special forms in use if you care to ask him.

The standard form of building contract is divided into two parts, the first being the 'Articles of Agreement' and the second the 'Conditions'. The only difficulty that arises as regards the first part is to describe correctly the nature of the intended work. If it is 'to carry out certain alterations and additions' or 'to erect and finish complete a certain building', the matter is simple, but if the work to be done is very complicated you may not find it easy to cover the ground in a concise statement which will really express the work which is to be done under the contract. On page 3 the employer and the contractor must sign in the presence of witnesses. It is usual for the employer to sign on the upper part of the page. If you are dealing with a committee as clients, you should have the contract signed by every member, as in such a case it is advisable to take every precaution. The drawings and bills of quantities should also be signed, and in order that they may be properly linked up with the contract a short endorsement should be used, such as, 'This is one of the drawings referred to in the contract dated . . . . 19 . .', or 'These are the bills of quantities referred to in the contract dated . . . . 19 . .'. It is advisable also to have the specification signed in a similar manner, although where quantities form part of the contract the specification is not a contract document. Both employer and contractor should sign each endorsement.

It is important before the signing of any contract to ensure that when the priced bills of quantities are received by the architect or quantity surveyor (the Articles of Agreement refer to the Bills being supplied to the employer) the prices should be scrutinised to see that they have been correctly written in and moneyed out, and the whole bill carefully examined to see that all is in order. This is a most important duty, and should be carried out scrupulously in every case. If any mistakes are found they must be dealt with at once; should the mistakes in moneying out, for example, be small or nullify themselves no further notice need be taken of them, but if a larger error is discovered it should at once be dealt with in accordance with Code of Procedure for Selective Tendering 1972 of which you should have a copy for reference. Quite recently I found a mistake in moneying out of £4849 against the builder; this was dealt with at once and everything put in order. Had the mistake not been discovered until the work was well in hand considerable difficulty might have arisen. A case occurred in 1914 where, owing to a mistake in the quantities such as I have been describing, a claim was made which, if given effect to, would have increased the sum of £20 352 to £133 405. I am confident that had the quantities been carefully examined the mistake would have been discovered and the matter set right before the contract was signed. This case must have been a costly one, as an action had to be brought in the Chancery Division for rectification of the contract.

I was once retained in connection with a dispute between an architect and a builder, where mistakes in the pricing and moneying out of a bill of quantities were very prominent and where the parties finally drifted into a lawsuit; therefore make a very definite note about my advice in connection with this matter.

If you are called upon to deal with small works costing say £1000.00 or less, a short form of contract may be all that is required and I have included in the *Appendix*, page 330, a short form of contract that has been in use in our own office on many occasions and has so far proved satisfactory provided the employer and the contractor have complete confidence in the architect. If you prefer a more formal contract there is the Form of Agreement designed for Minor building works or maintenance work issued by the RIBA dated June 1968 revised 1970 but this form is not appropriate for work for which a Schedule of Rates is required for valuing variations.

Now to consider the clauses of the Conditions of the Standard Form of Building Contract (1963 revised 1973). Clause 1 virtually repeats Article 1 and contains the express undertaking for the contractor to complete the works. It also, however, states that this must be done to the reasonable satisfaction of the architect. Whilst what is reasonable could be argued at great length in court, there is, however, a gentle hint that you must never be unreasonable in your demands upon the contractor. If the contractor finds a discrepancy between the contract drawings you have issued and the bills of quantities which, of course, should represent an exact measurement of the work that he has undertaken to do, then he must give you notice in writing specifying the nature of the discrepancy and then you have a duty to issue instructions to him, also in writing I recommend, as to how you intend the matter to be put right.

Clause 2 deals with architect's instructions and it is of very great importance that you fully understand the duties that fall to you under this clause of the contract. The clause contains three sub-clauses. The first deals with the compliance of the contractor with instructions issued by the architect. The second deals with the testing of the validity of an architect's instruction, and the third deals with the method by which instructions should be given.

In the first sub-clause the employer has the right to employ and pay other persons to execute any work necessary if the contractor has not, after seven days of the receipt of a written notice from you requiring compliance with an instruction you have issued, carried out the work. In the second sub-clause the contractor may ask you to specify in writing the provision of those conditions which empowers you to issue a particular instruction, and if he does not think that you are acting in accordance with the terms of the contract he may ask for the appointment of an arbitrator to give a decision.

The third sub-clause says categorically that all instructions you issue shall be issued in writing. There is a proviso for the confirming of oral instructions, but as a matter of advice in practice it is safest always to write and confirm what you have said at any meeting with the contractor as soon as you are back in the office.

Clause 3 establishes that under this particular contract the contract documents are the Articles of Agreement and the Conditions, the contract drawings and the bills of quantities as priced by the contractor when submitting his tender. The contract drawings are those from which the quantity surveyor prepared the bills of quantities, and it is my advice that you ensure that every drawing and detail is completed before the bills of quantities are finished in order that there will not be the danger of changes in later drawings which will automatically bring about variations. Whilst this may be the policy of perfection, and the contract does provide for variations as we shall see later, it is nevertheless true that most troubles on building contracts stem from the fact that the initial tender is based upon incomplete or not properly considered information and it is when decisions are taken later to correct this that is when contractors often have a very genuine cause for complaint. It is perhaps because of this that sub-clause 4 states that as and when necessary the architect shall furnish the contractor with such drawings and details as are reasonably necessary to explain or amplify the Contract drawings. You will realise I hope how necessary it is that your detail drawings show no more work than is provided for in the contract drawings and specification. I know from experience how easy it is to put more work into these than you originally intended. At first you may have wished to have only plain four-panel doors to your rooms, but when the work has commenced you feel you would like them a little more ornate, so you just add a few lines, and without thinking about extras issue the detail to the builder, who perhaps carried out the work without remark and in due course at the settlement of accounts asks for an extra, which, although you may legally refuse to allow, you do not feel you can in fairness disregard because you have yourself been the cause of it. It is easy to order work involving an extra without in the least intending to do so, and this must be guarded against. When you instruct the foreman to make what you think is only a slight alteration in the work, be sure it is made clear that this is not to be an extra. In settling builders' accounts I am constantly coming across items which are undoubtedly variations on the contract and are claimed as extras, and when I mention the matter to an architect I am told that although he certainly ordered the work, he had no idea that it was to be charged for as an extra.

The temptation to alter (and incidentally to increase) the work when detailing is very strong among architects and from a habit it easily grows to a disease, and infallibly causes trouble and anxiety. It may be thought that it is not the place of a quantity surveyor to advise the architectural profession on a matter which is certainly its own particular province, but an architect friend of mine assures me that my advice is worth giving. I will quote his own words. He said to me 'It is true that any architect worth the name will want to alter his details as the work progresses'. Most really great architecture has been produced in this way — by a careful revision of every part in the light of the revelation which comes as the building gradually takes its shape. But the practicability of doing this belongs to the past rather than to the present, and the architect who indulges himself in this way prepares a path of endless trouble. The young architect should train himself to visualise his design in all its detail. He should prepare large scale drawings, and satisfy himself that all his future requirements are fully covered. When estimates are coming in he should make another careful review of his details, and school himself to accept the design as final before the contract is signed. If he can do this, he will save himself and his client many future anxieties; he will acquire habits of decision, and his reputation will certainly not suffer.

From a business point of view there is no doubt that the constant alteration of details is bad, for it gives the builder an excuse for endless claims and invariably increases the cost of the work. I have heard of architects who have wished that, when a contract was signed, they could get a friend to see that it was carried out as planned — someone, in fact, who would save them from themselves and from the difficulties which they knew they would put in their own way.

There is also a proviso in sub-clause 5 that the contractor must keep one copy of the contract drawings and of the unpriced bills of quantities and any specification, descriptive schedules or other documents that you have issued ready and available on the works so that you may be able to refer to them at any time you visit. It specifically excludes the need to keep a copy of the priced bills or contract bills on the site since, of course, these are very private documents and the contractor must make his own decision as to how he keeps these, and who may have access to them. Sub-clauses 6 and 7 are self explanatory, but the final sub-clause 8 states that any certificate that you have to issue under these conditions shall be issued to the contractor. This differs from the local authority edition of this contract where it is stated that any certificate you issue shall be issued to the employer and you must send a copy only to the contractor.

Clause 4 deals with the by-laws and regulations of local authorities, provisions of Acts of Parliament, etc, and is very important. The architect, the surveyor, the contractor and everybody else must comply with the regulations of the local authorities, and it is well to grasp that at once and never let it escape you. It is useless to endeavour to evade the regulations, which, after all, are framed for the protection and well-being of everybody. You may find that some authorities are more insistent upon the strict letter of the regulations than others, but in all cases the local or district surveyor will insist on the spirit of the regulations being complied with. If you have strong views upon some special subjects which seem contrary to those expressed in the regulations you can, of course, endeavour to get the surveyor to adopt your point of view, but if you cannot convince him you will have no option but to do what he requires, or you will only be in difficulties. There is an important thing to remember about this clause, and that is that the contractor is definitely authorised to make any variation from the drawings and bills of quantities which may be necessary in order to conform to the regulations of the local authorities. It is true that he must first give the architect written notice of his intention, but if the architect ignores the notice the contractor is authorised to proceed with the work. This, I think, shows how necessary it is to understand the Building Regulations 1972 and to prepare the drawings to comply with them, and see that provision is made in the bills of quantities for all fees and charges legally demandable except, however, value added tax which is to be dealt with separately as I am explaining under clause 13A following. It was in the 1948 revision of the 1939 form that the question of liability for payment of rates and taxes was first introduced into the Conditions of Contract because by then local authorities had been authorised to make these charges in respect of Foreman's offices and other huts if they are considered to have a sufficient degree of permanency.

Clause 5 indicates the method to be adopted when setting out the works. You will be required to supply carefully dimensioned drawings and if a mistake is made it seems certain that your client will have to bear the cost of rectifying the error. If there are errors after the initial setting out has been done then the contractor will be held responsible. This clause will I think show you the importance of accurate surveys of sites and buildings to which I have referred in chapter VI.

Clause 6 refers to materials and workmanship which are to be, so far as procurable, of the respective kinds described in the bills of quantities. You must be sure when you write your specification that you state correctly what kind of material and workmanship you require and do not specify things that may not be obtainable. The words 'so far as procurable' first appeared in the 1931 edition to which I have referred already and as a quantity surveyor not then consulted I was of the opinion that they should be deleted because the contractor could so easily construe them to mean that certain materials and/or workmanship were unprocurable at the price he could afford to pay. These words were retained when the 1939 edition appeared and they might then in time of war have been necessary because so many things were in short supply. This clause empowers the architect to ask for proof that materials are as specified and it also allows him to instruct the contractor to open up for inspection any work covered up and so on subject, however, to the cost being added to the contract sum unless such an inspection shows that the work was not in accordance with the contract.

Sub-clause 4 gives the architect authority to order the removal of any works, materials or goods, not in accordance with the contract, while under sub-clause 5 he is empowered to issue instructions for the dismissal of any person employed upon the works. It is not infrequent for a man to be dismissed from a job following a complaint from the architect although with present day labour shortages and independence, it is to be avoided as far as possible for obvious reasons, but the dismissal of a foreman is unusual though in rare cases even this could be enforced.

Clause 7 refers to Royalties and Patent Rights and is, I think, self explanatory in that care must be exercised by the architect not to specify any patented articles etc without careful consideration of the financial implications that may be involved.

Clause 8 refers to builder's foreman. It is well to remember the importance of the foreman and to see that clear directions are given to him. The contractor is responsible for the mistakes of the foreman, and if a mistake is made it is only natural for the foreman to blame someone else, so be very careful with your instructions. It is easy to order an extra in ordinary conversation with the foreman when you have no intention whatever of doing so, but there is a safeguard in clause 2 of the 'conditions' which says that all architect's instructions to the contractor must be given in writing, and states definitely that verbal instructions must be confirmed in writing by the contractor. If this is so you will be wise to make it clear to the contractor that you intend to follow this procedure.

Clause 9 gives the architect power to inspect works in progress both in the workshops of the contractor and the sub-contractors. It is the duty of the contractor to see that all sub-contractors agree to give this access and in clause 27(a) (ix) a similar provision is made. I have never heard of a contractor refusing permission to the architect to visit his workshops; as a rule he is always pleased to welcome the architect and show him everything, and the more often such visits take place the closer is the contact between the architect and his work. The shop foreman is one of the key men of the building industry and the more he sees of the architect the better.

Clause 10 refers to the appointment of the clerk of works, and places him definitely under the architect and as an inspector of work and materials. You should instruct him to keep you advised of every difficulty that arises and of every variation that comes to his notice. You must remember that having a clerk of works does not relieve you, as architect, of your own responsibility. Note that any directions given by the clerk of works have to be confirmed in writing by the architect.

Clause 11 defines the method of dealing with variations and shows how the prices are to be ascertained. It begins by stating that no variation shall vitiate the contract. One often hears people say that a contract is broken because some variations have been made, but this clause makes it clear that this is not so. As a matter of fact, I do not think that it is at all easy to break a contract, that is, to make it invalid.

Sub-clause 3 empowers the architect to issue instructions in respect of expenditure under P.C. Sums usually by the nomination of Sub-Contractors. It is important here to note that should a nominated Sub-Contractor default or become bankrupt the Architect has a duty to make a new nomination as the main Contractor is not liable to carry out the remaining work himself although he could do so by mutual arrangement.

The person to measure and value the variations is the quantity surveyor who you will note has been appointed in the Articles of Agreement and undoubtedly this is the best person to do the work. The quantity surveyor spends so much of his time in estimating and checking builders' prices that he ought to be in the best position to undertake this work from the client's point of view. I always feel that it is scarcely fair to expect an architect to spend half his time in studying prices in order to fit himself to act under this clause, for I can assure you that it takes a very great deal of study to keep constantly up to date as regards prices of labour and materials, especially now that prices change so rapidly. In reading this clause you will realise the importance of having bills of quantities referred to in the Articles of Agreement and in clauses 1 and 3 of the Conditions properly priced out.

This is the only clause in the contract which refers to daywork. Daywork prices may be defined as follows, 'the net cost of labour and materials to which is added a percentage to cover overhead charges and profit', generally in excess of the average profit on a contract because as a rule they concern small and detached items of work. Because of this you will notice (and not be surprised) that the execution of daywork is carefully guarded as daywork prices are only to be allowed if the work cannot properly be measured and valued under the provisions of pricing laid down in sub-clause 4(a) and (b) of clause 11. There should be a definite agreement as regards daywork charges either by the contractor quoting his prices in the contract Bills or by reference to the Definition of Prime Cost of Daywork as mentioned in sub-clause 4 (c) (i) and (ii). As regards the acceptance of daywork charges you will see that the contractor has a duty to deliver vouchers detailing the labour and materials within a week following that in which the work has been executed.

You should insist on this procedure, for in modern contracts I have seen many instances of the contractor producing dozens of daywork sheets that have not reached the architect until months after the work has been done and likewise been unknown to the quantity surveyor who is trying to keep a strict cost control on the contract.

Under sub-clause 4 (d) you will read that the prices in the Contract Bills determine the valuation of items omitted but with a proviso concerning such omission affecting the general conditions of work.

In earlier editions of the RIBA Contract it was up to the architect to decide whether work could properly be measured and valued and to him also whether omitted work varied the General Conditions, but in the present contract (1963 Edition revised 1973) it is not stated by whom these decisions are to be made, thus giving the contractor a clear case for argument if he is so disposed. So you must be careful to see that decisions on these points are made as things progress and not left until the final settlement of accounts.

Sub-clause 5 states that the cost effect of variations shall be given in interim certificates, both as regards the contractor's own work and that of his sub-contractors — thus it becomes necessary for valuations to be made at regular intervals throughout the contract period. This is a relatively new clause in the contract and is a great help to the contractor, but it cannot be challenged since if the quantity surveyor is to keep a rigid cost control and advise the architect and the employer properly he must complete this process in any case.

As regards sub-clause 6 here is presented a very significant point again from the contractor's point of view. Even if all the valuing processes so carefully described in clause 4 and followed by the architect and quantity surveyor have been carried out the contractor is permitted to claim that he has incurred direct loss or expense and you as architect (or the quantity surveyor if you so direct) are called upon if the contractor makes such a written application to ascertain the amount of each loss or expense and to see that the result is included in the next following interim certificate. You must take every precaution to avoid an issue under this clause which in

effect takes the place of the third paragraph of clause 1 of the earlier edition of the contract for otherwise you may find yourself and the employer in considerable trouble.

Unfortunately in my experience many claims have arisen under this sub-clause despite all the architect's efforts to follow the letter of the Conditions not because the valuing processes under sub-clause 4 have not been done properly, but by reason of the fact that the contractor finds he is losing money or is not making the profit he expected and he therefore looks around for someone to blame and relies on this sub-clause 11(6) sometimes with complete disregard to his own fallibility in organisation on the site. So as I say be very careful indeed to get everything agreed as you go along so as to avoid the implications that can thus arise.

Clause 12 affirms that the quality and quantity of the work shall conform to that set out in the bills of quantities and also lays down that unless otherwise stated the bills shall have been prepared in accordance with the principles of the *Standard Method of Measurement* last before issued by The Royal Institution of Chartered Surveyors. The clause also contains a specially important provision that nothing contained in the bills of quantities shall 'override, modify or affect in any way whatsoever the application or interpretation of that which is contained in these conditions' and states that errors and omissions shall be treated as variations.

As regards the quality and quantity of the work, it is obvious, I think, that the provision in the contract is sound and that the bills of quantities are the correct document where these should be defined since the specification is excluded from the contract documents. The specification where bills of quantities form part of the contract, need consist of directions only as to the position of the various things given in the bills of quantities, in fact, where the bills of quantities are sufficiently clear there will be no need to mention the greater portion of the contents of the bills.

No doubt you will realise the significance of the reference to the *Standard Method of Measurement* whether imperial or metric. As a quantity surveyor I welcome this provision as in the past there have been far too many slipshod bills of quantities issued to contractors, and, unless it is otherwise expressly stated, any serious departure from the *Standard Method* will have to be treated as a variation in accordance with paragraph 2 of this clause.

When we consider the stipulation that nothing in the bills of quantities is to override, modify or affect the conditions in the form of contract we must exercise great care. In almost all important works there will be special conditions, required by the employer and accepted by the contractor, which may involve important modifications in the form of contract.

When you are drafting clauses for the specification or for use in the bills of quantities that conflict with the clauses in the form of contract you must see that they are drafted in the clearest and most definite language, and high-lighted in the tendering documents otherwise a conflict of opinion may result and litigation or what is almost as bad, the threat of litigation may arise.

The second paragraph of the clause is, I suggest, a hint that you should employ a good quantity surveyor, for I am sure no client will appreciate having to pay for errors or omissions in the bills of quantities.

Clause 13. This states that the contract sum may not be adjusted or altered, subject only to sub-clause 2 of clause 12. This emphasises the wisdom of the priced bills being carefully examined before the contract is signed as I have already said earlier in discussing the 'Articles of Agreement'.

Clause 13(A). A recent addition to the Conditions since Value Added Tax only commenced on the 1st April 1973. Clause 13A first appeared in the 1972 revision of the form and is amended in the July 1973 edition to define VAT and lay down that the Employer and Contractor must sign a supplemental agreement which appears on pages 30-32 of the conditions and explains that the influence of this Tax must be excluded from the Contract sum.

Clause 14 concerns materials or goods unfixed on or off-site and decrees that these once delivered may not be removed unless you agree. Where the value of such materials and goods has been included in an interim certificate the contractor remains responsible for loss or damage except in cases where the employer definitely accepts the risk by insurance as defined in clause 20 (B) or (C).

Sub-clause 2 refers to the value of materials and goods ready for use, but not yet delivered to the site. This empowers the Architect to include in an interim certificate the value of such materials or goods subject to clause 30 (2A) which I shall discuss later, but with the contractor being responsible while they are stored off site and when they are eventually delivered to the site except then with the same proviso as to the employer's responsibility under insurance in clause 20(B) or (C).

Clause 15 specifies that when the works in your opinion are practically completed you must issue a certificate to that effect and it is most important for you to ensure that this is done at the time. Retrospective establishing of the practical completion date is no longer permitted — indeed it was never advisable. Printed 'Certificate of Practical Completion' forms are issued by the RIBA.

As regards defects after completion, a most important phase of the architect's work, clause 15(2) puts a period to the liability of the contractor for making good materials and workmanship not in accordance with the contract. If you do not fill in the space in the appendix to the form of contract (Defects Liability Period) the period will be 6 months. This length of time is quite usual though some architects prefer 12 months in order that the building may have a whole year to settle down. The correct procedure for you to adopt under this clause is to make an inspection of the work when the period mentioned is nearing completion and prepare a complete list of all the defects you find or which are pointed out by your client. Send a copy of this to the contractor and ask him to have the defects remedied as quickly as possible. The following list of defects was recently sent to a contractor, and will form a good guide:

List of defects, shrinkages or other faults which have appeared at The
Red Building, York Road, Dorset, arising from materials or
workmanship not in accordance with the drawings and specification or
the instructions of the architect (see clause 12 of the Conditions in the
Form of Contract)

Drawing-room
Plaster near mantelpiece is discoloured and ceiling is badly cracked.
Door leading to entrance hall will not open.
Lock of cupboard door is defective.
Shrinkage has occurred in the oak flooring.

Staircase
Landing and treads are defective.
Door at top of staircase will not shut.
Enriched plaster cornice is chipped and there is a crack in plaster frieze.
Casing to radiator is loose.

Dining-room
Wall-paper at side of fireplace is defective.
Panel in door to hall is cracked.
Mitres in architraves of doors are badly made.

Own bedroom
Floor boards over hot-water pipes are loose.
Plaster cornice is cracked.
Painting to new woodwork is defective.

Bedroom No.2
Cement hearth is cracked.
Door to cupboard has twisted and will not shut.
Portion of plaster ceiling has broken away.

Generally
Joints in rain-water pipe near dining-room are defective.
Several tiles on roof are broken.
Cement paving in kitchen yard is cracked and defective in places.
Stone coping over entrance hall is chipped.
Pointing to brickwork near kitchen window is loose.
Cement pointing to hip tiles near dining-room chimney has fallen out.

The defects, shrinkages, etc or other faults, detailed above are required
to be amended and made good on or before the 1st day of July 1974.

John Brown
Architect

The preparation of a list of defects is not difficult, but it should be the result of a very thorough examination, and will be more satisfactory if you consult your client before you issue it, as during his short occupation of the premises he may have observed defects that might take time to discover during your visit. It is, however, quite another matter to get the defects dealt with satisfactorily. It is seldom that a building is erected without some reparations being necessary and although most contractors are quite ready to meet their obligations and make good any defects that may have occurred, you will occasionally have to deal with one who will require a lot of pressure before he puts things really right. You may also have to deal with a client who is unreasonable in his complaints, and who also may not wish to have the work carried out during, or shortly after the maintenance period. In the latter case some sort of compromise must be made.

You should arrange a meeting with your client and the builder at the premises and settle how and when the work is to be done. If the client does not wish to have the repairs carried out, possibly through not wanting to have his house or premises disturbed, then you can suggest a money payment, so that the client can have the repairs carried out when convenient to himself. You may have some difficulty to persuade both the client and the builder to agree an amount, for the builder will naturally underprice the repairs which he thinks he could carry out cheaply himself, whereas the client will want to cover what he thinks will be his future expense. With patience and tact, however, you should succeed, especially as the builder will be anxious to get a final settlement of his account and so be able to close his books and write off the contract as finished, while the client will be free to use the money when he pleases. Be careful to see that the schedule of repairs is properly priced, for if the sum agreed does not in fact prove sufficient to carry out the necessary work you are bound to have some complaint from your client. Should it be necessary to have defects remedied during the maintenance period you will be within your rights to call upon the contractor to carry out the work whenever agreeable to your client.

When you issue your instructions to make good defects in workmanship you will have to satisfy yourself that the measures taken to do this are effective. For instance, suppose you found there is a crack in the brickwork, it will not be sufficient to have this cut out and rebuilt if the cause of the crack, which may be a defective foundation, is not removed. Or suppose the roof has spread so as to start a movement in the parapet, a good deal of dismantling may be involved before you can be certain that the trouble is cured. Such serious structural defects will not often be met, but when they occur the builder may allege some fault in design or instructions to relieve himself of responsibility. In such cases you must be prepared to fix the responsibility where it belongs and enforce your decision.

By far the commoner types of defects will be those of cracked plaster, shrunk woodwork and discoloured decorations. You will have to decide the nature of the repair which it will be necessary to do in order to make a permanent job that will be wholly satisfactory. Cracks in plaster are often caused by shrinkage in stud or block partitions or joists, and if this is suspected you should get some promise from the builder to put right any subsequent trouble from the same cause. Cracks should be cut out in dovetail section and filled in carefully where they are serious, but it is unwise to cut out hair-cracks, since it is an unnecessary weakening of the sound plaster. These latter can be made good by redecoration. The shrinkage of woodwork presents a very large number of difficult problems, especially in these days when thoroughly seasoned timber is difficult to obtain. In all serious cases the joinery should be removed and reframed, but reasonable methods of repair short of this are allowable where the builder is genuinely anxious (and can be trusted) to make a good job. The most difficult cases are timber doors and windows, and no concession should be made which will affect the future functioning of these essential features or their perfect fit. Decorations will be the most thorny subject, because it is not always reasonable to expect the decoration on new surfaces to stand without blemish. For this reason many architects postpone the final coats to some twelve months after completion, and where this is not practicable it might be wise to make monetary provision in the contract for a certain amount of redecoration to be carried out during or at the end of the maintenance period. Your client will want the decoration to be perfect and yet that may not be a possibility until work has settled down finally.

The most satisfactory situation is when you have a builder who is always ready to remedy trouble in support of his own reputation and irrespective of legal obligation. There is no department of the architect's work where the mutual trust between a considerate client, and honourable builder and a wise architect is so much to be desired as in the period after completion when little disappointments are bound to occur and can be magnified or quickly dispelled in proportion to the goodwill of all parties concerned.

A specific provision of clause 15 is that the architect must deliver the schedule of defects to the contractor not later than 14 days after the expiration of the Defects Liability Period. Under sub-clause 6 the architect is empowered at any time during the Defects Liability Period to order the making good of defects etc if he considers it necessary to do so. One can think readily of defects, the making good of which could not reasonably be left until six or even twelve months after practical completion and the commencement of the Defects Liability Period.

Further, the architect is called upon under sub-clause 4 actually to issue a certificate as to the completion of making good whether under the final or intermediate Schedule of Defects under sub-clauses 2 and 3. The RIBA supply printed forms entitled 'Certificate of Making Good Defects' which also provide for a record being kept as to whom copies are being issued.

The contractor is relieved as under the older editions of the Contract of any responsibility for damage by frost after practical completion unless the architect certifies that such damage is due to injury which took place before that date. You must watch this point and certify according to your records although I cannot advise you that this will necessarily be the end of the matter unless very careful meteorological records provide an infallible proof.

Clause 16. This clause clarifies the circumstances concerning 'Partial possession by Employer' and it is very important in the case of large contracts though it has little or no serious meaning in the case of say a private house or any building which can only function as a complete entity. As an architect's practice grows — or if you are a 'job runner' in a large office you must of course study this clause carefully.

In earlier times where there was no such clause in the contract I used to advise the inclusion in my Bills of Quantities of a clause giving the employer the right to enter upon and use any parts of the building provided such use in the architect's opinion was not detrimental to the Contractor. As time went on and more and more large buildings — offices, flats, laboratories, halls of residence etc became the vogue, the contractors were not satisfied with the matter being left to the 'architect's opinion' and thus this clause then called 'Sectional completion' appeared, first in the 1963 edition of the contract.

It is a good addition to the conditions and in general terms it merely says that the rules about matters which normally apply to the whole contract must be taken as applying to sections thereof if taken over by the employer with the contractor's consent.

Here again there are the requirements that the architect must issue certain certificates — in writing of course — and you should follow these implicitly if you have a contract where 'Partial possession' applies.

Clause 17 prohibits the employer or the contractor from assigning the contract without the written consent of the other party. It seems unlikely that a contractor would go to considerable trouble to secure a contract and then wish to assign it to someone else, but it has happened. Likewise the employer in these days of frequent 'take-overs' may find himself with the necessity of so doing.

The clause also prohibits the contractor from subletting any portion of the works without the written consent of the architect. I believe this clause is seldom strictly adhered to. In most large contracts subletting by the contractor seems to be the rule rather than the exception, and frequently contractors do not ask for the architect's permission to sublet. You will find that excavating is sublet, carting materials, plastering, glazing, painting, joinery, plumbing — in fact, almost everything. I recently settled an account with a builder where the whole job was sublet in spite of this clause, and I found myself confronted with the sub-contractor when I set about squaring up the accounts. You should note that the architect's consent must not be unreasonably withheld; but it is I think the architect's duty to discuss the point with the contractor in the first instance and discover how much of the work he is able to carry out himself.

Clause 18 makes the contractor responsible for damage or injury to persons and property; it is of considerable importance in the client's interest. It means, for example, that if the builder, in excavating for the foundations, lets down the wall of an adjoining owner he will have to rebuild it and make good all damage at his own cost. I remember when the site of a large building in the Strand, London, was being excavated for the basement it was necessary to do some blasting of old foundations. The men had not taken sufficient precautions, and a small stone from the foundation hit a man in the face. This man, who by ill-luck happened to be a solicitor, managed to get £200 from the contractor.

It must always be remembered that, although the legal liability is on the contractor, the employer may also be involved in much trouble and anxiety should any claim for damage be occasioned, as in the event of a legal process he may have to defend an action. My advice, therefore, to an architect is to keep a vigilant watch, in the interests of the client on the precautionary measures adopted by the contractor.

There is the not unreasonable proviso here that the contractor is not responsible if the liability is due to any act or neglect of the employer or any person for whom he is responsible. An example might be where despite a notice of danger the employer walked on to the site to see how things were progressing, or sent one of his own staff who similarly ignored the warning. I recall this type of case very clearly in a hall of residence building for a university for whom I was acting. The contractor — very well known indeed — had a keen foreman or agent who displayed a notice that no one should enter upon the site or building except with the contractor's express consent, yet the bursar of the university being after all the employer, as it were, walked around and was duly ordered off. At first the bursar was most indignant, but after a little discussion was man enough to agree that the contractor was within his rights for if an accident had occurred the university (or the bursar) and not the contractor would have been responsible.

This clause naturally also exempts the contractor from liability if this works are the subject of insurance by the employer against fire, under clause 20(B) and (C). Clause 18 makes the contractor liable for indemnifying the employer but does not say that he must do this by insurance which is covered by the provisions of clause 19 following.

Clause 19 explains the position regarding insurance against injury to persons and property. In the case of personal injuries this cover is unlimited, but with damage to property the cover has to accord with the requirements of the bills of quantities.

Sub-clause (b) requires the contractor or any sub-contractor to produce evidence that these insurances are properly maintained, while sub-clause (c) enables the employer to effect the insurances should the contractor default.

Sub-clause (2) (a) calls upon the contractor to cover in the joint names of the employer and the contractor such amounts of indemnity as may be specified in the contract bills of quantities in respect of damage to any property other than the works themselves. It specifies under sub-clause (I) (II) (III) (IV) and (V) the types of circumstances involved. Of course there is provision for insurances to be placed with insurers approved by the architect and for the contractor to deposit the policies and premium receipts with him and again for the employer to himself insure if the contractor defaults in insuring or continuing to insure under this clause.

Clause 20 provides for fire insurance of the works and is divided into three alternative parts, and you must remember to strike out the two paragraphs which are not appropriate.

Paragraph (A) in sub-clause (1) relates to new work where you want the contractor to be responsible so it calls upon him to insure in the joint names of himself and the employer against all possible risks of damage as are clearly specified in the clause, for the full value of the works plus professional fees (previously taken as 8½ per cent for architects' and surveyors' fees) but now at a percentage to be entered in the Appendix to the Conditions to which I shall refer again later. All unfixed materials are to be included in the insurance, but not you will note temporary buildings and plant, tools and equipment owned by the contractor as these are normally covered by the contractor's own bulk policy.

The normal requirement of the insurers being approved by the architect is included and likewise the duty of the contractor to produce evidence of insurance as is also the procedure to be adopted should the contractor fail to insure or in continuing so to do. A facet of fire insurance introduced in the 1963 version of the Conditions covers the position if the contractor carries an overall fire insurance for all his turnover as it were, but you will only need to study this when the occasion arises, usually of course with large contractor's organisations.

Sub-clause 2 defines the procedure to be followed after fire damage and the acceptance of the claim.

Paragraph (B) is really the reverse of (A) in that in some perhaps fewer cases it may be necessary for the fire insurance of new works to be the responsibility of the employer.

Paragraph (C) deals with alterations and additions to existing buildings where it is clearly wise for the insurance to be effected by the employer. He should insure the whole of the existing structure and their contents and the works being the alterations or extensions in question with the same exclusions of contractor's plant etc.

Should the employer in this case fail to insure or to maintain such insurance the contractor may do so and of course for him to cover the existing structures and contents he must be given access to find out what their value is.

Sub-paras (b) and (c) deal with either the contract being determined, subject to agreement, of both parties and possible arbitration if necessary (b) where for example total or near total destruction has resulted from the fire or for the contractor to proceed to make good the damage (c) where the damage is only partial.

Clause 21 is generally called the *time clause*. Provision is made in the appendix to the form of contract for the insertion of the date for possession of the site and for completion of the contract, subject to the provision for extension of time discussed later under clause 23. Sub-paragraph 2 of this clause empowers the architect to postpone works, but you must remember that this can itself be a valid reason for extension of time. At a recent meeting an architect of repute said: 'The question of time should be determined at the outset by the architect in consultation with the quantity surveyor and should be stated in the bills of quantities' a principle which is confirmed in the 'Code of Procedure for Selective Tendering 1972' to which I have already referred. This is not always an easy task and if you are not sure as to the correct length of time required to carry out your designs, when you invite tenders you should ask each builder to state the length of time he will require. This will give you a guide as to the right period. You should also discuss this point with your client, who will generally be found to have decided views on the subject, and, as a rule, will expect to have the work completed in half the time it ought to take. If you try to tie down the contractor to an unreasonably short time it will generally lead to disappointment for your client whereas a reasonable period will be best for everyone.

Many circumstances affect the length of time required to carry out a contract and no hard and fast rules can be laid down. A higher price may have to be paid for works in consequence of the shortness of the periods allowed for performance and therefore as much time should be allowed as circumstances permit. If you are dealing with a small house you may have to tell your client that the drawings will take a month, and the builder will require 6 months to build the house. Your client may then retort: 'The builder who is putting up those houses in Blankshire has offered to build one for me in a month'. To this you will have to find some good reply and you might say that a house built in a month will probably collapse in less than a month. It is well to remember that, as a general rule, the more rapidly the fabric of a building is constructed the better it stands, whereas the reverse is the case with joinery and other fittings. Joinery must have sufficient time for preparation if it is to be sound and not give trouble in the future.

Should you have a contract where no time for completion has been fixed, then a reasonable time is implied and the determination of what is reasonable is a question of fact to be settled after a full consideration of all the details of the case.

It is almost as important to the architect as to the contractor that a contract should be completed to time, therefore any methods which will help to attain this object should be welcome to all parties. But it is a common feature of modern building that the time given to carry out the work is too short. Under such conditions it is most important to be able to see at a glance how the work is progressing. For this purpose a progress chart is most valuable and there is no more useful aid to expedition than this simple device. It is in reality a plan of campaign worked out to schedule, and though essential on large contracts it can also be very useful to small ones. The preparation of such a chart can be a complicated matter and should be done by the contractor in consultation with the sub-contractors and submitted to the architect for his remarks which should only be advisory for progress is the responsibility of the Contractor. I have included a copy of a progress chart used recently in the building of a new house, this should form a useful type for general guidance, although the

NEW HOUSE AT BLANKTON
VICTOR R.J. BROWN
ARCHITECT

PROGRESS CHART
CONTRACT TIME
SIX MONTHS

Nº	SERVICE	MAY	JUNE	JULY	AUGUST	SEPTEMBER	OCTOBER
1	EXCAVATION						
2	CONCRETE						
3	BRICKWORK						
4	DAMP COURSE						
5	DRAINS						
6	FRAMING FLOORS						
7	ROOF-WOODWORK						
8	SLATING						
9	PLASTERING						
10	DOORS		DETAILS	MAKING		FIXING	
11	WINDOWS		DETAILS MAKING FIXING				
12	FITMENTS		DETAILS	MAKING		FIXING	
13	PLUMBING						
14	SANITARY FITTINGS		SELECTION	DELIVERY	FIXING		
15	GRATES		SELECTION	DELIVERY	FIXING		
16	MANTEL PIECES		DETAILS	MAKING	FIXING		
17	HOT WATER						
18	ELECTRIC WIRING						
19	ELECTRIC FITTINGS		SELECTION	DELIVERY	FIXING		
20	GAS SERVICES						
21	GLAZING						
22	IRONMONGERY		SELECTION	DELIVERY	FIXING		
23	FLOORING-WOOD						
24	PAINTING-EXTERNAL						
25	PAINTING-INTERNAL						
26							
27							

Note   The estimated periods in the above chart should be filled in with red or black ink as the work proceeds, the progress of the work can thus be seen at a glance.

chart will require to be varied for each type of building, as, I think it will be obvious there cannot be a standard form to suit all structures. I have been associated with many buildings where progress charts have been used but have never seen two charts exactly alike.

Clause 22 deals with damages for non-completion to contract time and the amount of such 'Liquidated and Ascertained Damages' requires to be entered in the appendix to the contract. It is usually the amount decided on by the employer, architect and quantity surveyor and stated in the bills of quantities (or specification) upon which the contractor's tender is based, but you may find on occasion that a contractor will make some criticism of the amount at tender stage. Then the amount would require to be one agreed by mutual consent if that particular contractor is entrusted with the work.

The amount should bear some sort of relation to the size of the job. For example, £5 per week for a contract involving £10 000 would be quite as absurd as £50 a day for a contract amounting to £500, provided there were no special circumstances. I have heard of a contract with damages at £100 per day, but this, I think, is exceptional. Much will depend on the use the building is going to be put to when completed. Obviously a large block of flats or an hotel can prove considerable expense if the completion date overruns because of advance bookings, staffing, etc, whereas a public library — I hope this is a good example of the contrary — will only involve the public in inconvenience but not expense and the Local Authority in perhaps minimum staff problems.

'Liquid and Ascertained Damages' must not constitute a penalty. They must be a reasonable and genuine pre-estimate of the damage they are designed to cover. The Courts will not interfere with liquidated damages but they will not enforce the payment of a penalty. It is advisable for a record to be kept by the architect of the calculation made in arriving at the amount of Liquid and Ascertained Damages at tender stage.

You must be very careful to follow the requirements about certifying in writing when you think the work ought to have been completed and not let this vital point drift on until after practical completion. I have a case before me now where the architect only issued his certificate of non-completion to contract time (or extended time) after the issue of his final certificate, and after the passage of a great length of time the validity of this procedure has not yet reached the High Courts.

The clause states that in the event of the overrun being certified by the architect the employer may deduct the amount of damages from any money due or to become due to the contractor. This procedure does not usually meet with the contractor's approval who will put up every argument he can lay his hands to show that it is unfair. It is not the duty of the architect you should note to reduce his certificates by the amount of damages, but to the employer to deduct it after he has been notified of the architect's certificate of lateness.

Clause 23 provides for extension of time in certain cases, and it is under this clause that you will probably be asked by the contractor to extend the period of the contract. According to the strict working of the clause the contractor does not have to make this request, for his responsibility is only to notify the architect immediately any of the causes of delay occur and then it is up to the architect to make a fair and reasonable extension of time to the extent that in his opinion the reasons put forward by the Contractor have delayed or will delay the Contract Completion date. You will notice there are many things mentioned as possible causes for delay. I warn you, however, that if you have to extend the time owing to your not having given the contractor details or instructions specifically asked for by him, then you will find yourself in difficulties with your client. You may think you will have no difficulty in keeping up to time with your work, but I assure you it is a frequent source of trouble, and that it is sometimes not easy to supply the contractor punctually with all the details and directions he requires.

In a recent contract the contractor asked the architect for the whole of the details of the stonework of a very large building, and said that if he did not receive them at once he would have to ask for an extension of time for the completion of the contract. This was thought by the architect to be a most unreasonable request, as it was a practical impossibility to get all the details done so quickly as to comply with the demand and they had certainly not been prepared ready for issue when the contract was signed. As the contractor in this case was under heavy damages to complete by a given date he did his best to secure an extension of time on every occasion. You will most certainly be faced with a demand to extend the time on account of bad weather. Contractors as a rule seem to forget that this clause refers to exceptionally inclement weather and not simply to a few showers of rain. You must have a record kept of abnormally adverse weather during a contract and grant an extension of time accordingly. If a clerk of works is employed this record will be one of his duties.

This clause also deals with delay on the part of nominated sub-contractors and Suppliers and with contractors and tradesmen employed direct by the client. The contractor is under an obligation to notify the architect in writing of any cause of delay, and when you have granted an extension of time you will find it advisable to let your client know and explain to him the circumstances.

You should be very careful about granting extensions of time during the progress of the work, for to do so may lessen the efforts the contractor should make to catch up with his original programme. It is usually better to keep notes of any causes of delay (and of any methods you may have permitted the contractor to employ for speeding up the work) and decide what extension of time is proper at the end of the contract, for even if extensions of time may be granted retrospectively (but not after the final certificate has been issued) I am sure it is best in the interest of all parties not to delay your decisions about extensions of time and certainly to decide in good time for the establishment of the practical completion date referred to under clauses 15 and 30 of the Conditions.

You will observe that sub-clauses (j)(i) and (j)(ii) should be struck out if they are not to apply. I usually advise the deletion of these provisions for extension of time, for after all the contractor having been given the opportunity of tendering must decide in advance whether he can provide the requisite labour and materials. Just as the employer as his opposite number has to decide if he can provide the requisite money. Of course things could go wrong either way, but I do not associate such a circumstance with an extension of time. However in times of acute shortage of labour and materials you may find that the Contractor will not sign a contract unless these two sub-clauses are retained.

Force Majeure is as before the first reason listed for an extension of time and I have often tried to get a legal luminary to tell me what this really is. I think it must be taken in the same way as 'the field' in horse racing parlance that it is there to cover anything not covered elsewhere — an epidemic for example.

Clause 24. This is the most vital clause added to the text of the Conditions in the 1963 edition of the Contract, for it enables the contractor to make claims for extra payment despite all the other provisions of the contract. It is true that the contractor has to make written application to the architect and that the architect has also to be of the opinion as to loss and/or expense, but I can assure you that if the architect is not in agreement with the contractor's application this does not be any means — even if it should — dispose of the matter.

The formidable sub-clause (a) pre-supposes delay by the architect in supplying the contractor with the necessary instructions, drawings, details and levels for which the contractor has specifically applied in writing so you must, as I have said before, ensure that the contractor has everything necessary well in advance for carrying out the work, otherwise you will be involved in almost endless argument or arbitration or law.

Sub-clauses (b) (c) (d) and (e) are much clearer to assess, but as with (a) you will see that if the contractor's application is made in reasonable time (and you really should ensure that he has no grounds for doing so at all) and upon it becoming apparent that there is something in what he claims your duty is to ascertain (or instruct the quantity surveyor to do so) the amount of such loss and/or expense and include it in interim certificates if available, but in any case to add it to the contract sum.

As I have intimated before the employer as your client is not likely to be impressed with having to foot the bill if an extra under this clause arises (at all but certainly not if it is attributable to sub-clause (1)(a) of this clause).

Clause 25 entitled 'Determination by Employer' details the procedure to be followed should the contractor suspend the works, fail to carry them out with diligence, or refuse to comply with the architect's notices or assign the contract contrary to clause 17 of the Conditions. It also refers to bankruptcy of a contractor. It is a very unusual and risky thing for a contractor to stop a job. I do not think I have ever been engaged on a building where the work has been stopped. I have often heard the contractor say that he would stop the job if the client did not pay an amount duly certified, but that kind of threat usually ends in nothing. If a client delays payment, the contractor's remedy is provided for in clause 26 of the Conditions. In cases where an employer does not pay the certified amounts within the time specified, I think the contractor is justified in claiming interest upon the amount of the certificate.

It appears that the contractor can, under Clause 25 suspend the works for at most 14 days, when the following action should be taken. The architect must give written notice to the contractor to resume, and if the contractor does not proceed with the works the employer after ten days can in writing determine his employment. This seems to me to be a long time to have to wait and may mean a great disadvantage to your client. This period of time and what it involves might well be put before your client before the contract is signed.

It is probable that this problem has brought about the tendency for the contractor being called upon to sign a 'Performance Bond' under which he is bound with sureties to complete the work included in the contract. Alternatively if the contractor fails to complete the sureties shall satisfy and discharge the damages sustained by the employer up to the amount of the Bond.

The method of dealing with the bankruptcy of a contractor follows the procedure detailed in paragraph (3) (a) (b) (c) and (d), but such an event would have to be discussed with your client who would, no doubt, bring his solicitor to your assistance. In Government contracts provision is generally made for the termination of the contract in the event of a contractor becoming bankrupt, but I believe in practice the trustee or receiver is first given the option of completing the work in the interest of the creditors, and if he can do so, this is the simplest solution and provides a good way out from what is usually a really difficult and trying business.

Clause 26, 'Determination by Contractor' sets out the procedure to be followed if the employer does not pay the amount of any certificate within 14 days of its presentation and continues to default for a further 7 days after notification by the contractor about determination within a further 7 days. The 14 day period is now mandatory whereas in earlier editions of the contract the period has to be decided on and entered in the appendix. As a rule employers pay within a few days after receipt of the architect's certificate (passed on to him by the contractor). I have known of employers paying in advance of the architect's certificate, but this can cause difficulties, but no employer should require more than the full 28 days protection.

'Any certificate' in the wording of this clause excludes, you should note, one arising under the VAT Supplemental agreement to which I have referred under clause 13(A) above.

The contractor is also empowered under this clause to determine the contract subject to giving written notice thereof to the employer or the architect in the event of the employer interfering with or obstructing the issue of any certificate or by the carrying out of the whole or substantially the whole of the works being suspended for a continuous period of the length named in the appendix to the Conditions by reason of any of the causes mentioned in clause 23 'Extension of Time' except, (a) exceptionally inclement weather (b) local combination of workmen, strike or lock-out and (c) delay on the part of nominated sub-contractors or suppliers which the contractor has taken all reasonable steps to avoid or reduce.

Thus in a nutshell the contractor cannot determine the Contract for any of the above three circumstances (a) (b) and (c) nor can he incidentally because the architect has had to issue some instructions concerning antiquities under clause 34 of the Conditions. He can, however, not unnaturally determine the Contract in the event of the employer becoming bankrupt as referred to in sub-clause 26 (1) (d).

Sub-clause 26 (2) described the procedure to be followed upon a determination of the contract by the contractor as discussed above but I do not think you need spend much time on studying this for determination by the contractor is not a frequent occurrence and when it does happen you will have plenty of notice to enable these provisos to be studied. Both in the case of clauses 25 and 26 it is highly probable that solicitors or even Counsel will be involved and with this in mind I have included in my list of Recommended Books several covering Building Contracts.

Clause 27 is concerned with persons nominated by the architect to supply and fix materials or goods or to execute work. These nominations, of course, arise from the expenditure of prime cost sums included in the contract bills or sometimes they arise as a result of the architect's instructions as to the expenditure of provisional sums. All such specialists and others whom the architect selects are referred to as 'nominated sub-contractors' and it is stated that prime cost sums for their work include 2½% cash discount. When you call for estimates from potential sub-contractors under this clause you must instruct them to allow for this cash discount for the main contractor. It is provided in this clause that the architect shall not nominate any person as a sub-contractor against whom the contractor may make reasonable objection or who will not enter into a sub-contract which provides for one of a variety of regulations which are listed under sub-clauses (1) to (X) of clause 27. Perhaps the item of paramount importance here is that the sub-contractor must indemnify the contractor against any failure to observe the same obligations in respect of the sub-contract as those to which the contractor is liable in respect of his own contract. Payment for the sub-contractors' work shall not be due until the contractor has received the architect's certificate but at that time the contractor has 14 days in which to pay the sub-contractor. The contractor is to furnish the architect if requested with proof that the amounts included for sub-contractors in previous certificates have been paid. If the information is not automatically forthcoming you should never fail to obtain this proof, for it is not uncommon for the contractor to put off paying the sub-contractor and thus cause unnecessary inconvenience and trouble for yourself.

Printed forms for the 'appointment of a nominated Sub-contractor' are issued by the RIBA which also provide for a record being kept as to whom copies are being issued.

Should you desire to pay a sub-contractor before the general works are completed, paragraph (e) of this clause provides the method, but the sub-contractor must indemnify the contractor against latent defects, by which I understand are meant defects not visible or apparent at the time payment is made to the sub-contractor.

This clause also lays down the rules concerning extensions of time which may be granted by the Main Contractor to the sub-contractor but only with the architect's written consent and approval.

You will all be aware, no doubt, that there is such a thing as a trade discount to which I have previously referred (page 40). I think it is practically universal in the commercial world. This trade discount can be almost any percentage upon the published price of an article, and this must be allowed, not to the contractor, but to the client. When you are settling up an account, if you have no quantity surveyor, you must make a practice of seeing all the the receipted accounts, not merely the invoices, and, of course, set off the actual payments against the sums provided in the contract.

Clause 28 deals with specialists, tradesmen or others who supply materials to be fixed by the contractor and are referred to as 'nominated suppliers'. It lays down that a cash discount of 5 per cent shall be allowed to the contractor, and that payments shall be in full within 30 days of the end of the month during which delivery is made. When you call for prices for such things as ironmongery, sanitary fittings, etc, you must notify the merchants that their estimates must include 5% cash discount.

Clause 29 requires no explanation; it simply provides that the contractor shall permit the execution of work by anyone the client likes to send on the job, but as the contractor will not be liable for personal injury to any artists or tradesmen engaged by the employer you should notify your client of this, so that he may know the risk, if he proposes to send workmen on to the job during the progress of the works.

Clause 30 generally called the *Payment Clause* must be examined with care for you will find in the appendix to the form of Contract that there are several matters to attend to as consideration of the various sub-clauses will reveal.

Sub-clause 1 describes interim certificates and makes it mandatory that the contractor is entitled to payment within 14 days from the presentation of the certificate. In earlier editions of the ccontract this period was subject to an entry in the appendix to the conditions and thus could vary according to the circumstances but this is no longer the case. This sub-clause explains that interim certificates before Practical Completion have to be issued at regular intervals according to the Period of Interim certificates specified in the appendix which if none other is stated is to be one month which is in most cases the period most convenient to both parties to the contract.

Interim certificates can be issued after Practical Completion when further amounts are found to be due to the contractor but not at intervals of less than one month.

Sub-clause 2 describes how interim certificates are to be valued and says that they should only include materials and goods not yet incorporated in the work provided they are reasonably properly and not prematurely brought to the site and then only if properly protected. But this point is qualified again in sub-clause 2A which permits the architect in his own discretion to include other materials not on the site which are intended for use in the work as defined in sub-clause 2A (a) to (h). It is most important that such materials which are then the property of the Employer, are properly set aside and adequately labelled so that in the event of a liquidation by the manufacturer or supplier, the Liquidator or Receiver knows to whom they belong.

Sub-clause 3 refers to the 'Retention Percentage' now limited to 5% (earlier it could have been 10%) or even a lower rate if agreed between the parties and, you will note, specified in the appendix. There is a footnote to the effect that if at tender stage the employer estimates the Contract sum at or over £250 000 the percentages should not exceed three per cent. After Practical Completion an interim certificate must only credit half the retention (b) while sub-clause 3 (c) naturally reduces the amount the employer may retain by reason of partial possession (16 (f)) and/or the early release of balances to nominated sub-contractors (27 (e)).

Sub-clause 4 lays down certain rules concerning amounts retained. We have already seen that under clauses 15 and 16 and now we see again in this clause 30 (4) (c) that the Defects Liability Period has to be entered in the appendix.

A most important provision particularly from the quantity surveyor's point of view perhaps appears in sub-clause 5 which stipulates that the measurement and valuation of the work shall be completed in a pre-determined time which is called the *Period of Final Measurement and Valuation*. This is to be entered in the appendix where you will observe it says that if no entry is made it is to be taken as 6 months from the date of Practical Completion. In earlier editions of the Contract this period, if none other was stated, was only 3 months so the current form of contract does to this extent realise the problem confronting the quantity surveyor and the contractor if the job is a large and complicated one with many variations.

You might well say that there ought not to be so many variations as to upset the completion of the accounts within the six months period and I would certainly agree on a small Contract, say for a house, or even a block of flats, but in the case of a large scientific building, for example, many variations can occur as the work proceeds for it would be ridiculous for the employer not to be able to take advantage of day to day inventions and improvements so that his building after say a two or three year building contract is already out-of-date when he takes it over. In such a case I would prefer the more sensible entry in the appendix of the words 'as soon as reasonably practicable' or if this is criticised as being too indeterminate at least a period not less than the maintenance period itself which in this case would no doubt be twelve months as I have suggested under clause 15 (2) earlier.

Sub-clause 6 defines the procedure concerning the architects final certificate which according to the printed word should be issued before the expiration of 3 months from the end of the Defects Liability Period or from completion of making good of defects (which period if there is the not unusual argument as to what is or what is not a 'defect' can greatly exceed 3 months) or from the receipt by the architect of the documents so necessary for the settlement of the accounts (see sub-clause 5 (c) of clause 30). Furthermore if the contractor is making claims under the various clauses we have already discussed the issue of the final certificate may well be delayed for even a year or more, but we must remember that this provision for a final certificate within the 3 months period — however desirable — savours of Utopia.

You will see in sub-clause 7 that save as therein qualified the Final Certificate is to be taken as conclusive evidence that the works have been properly carried out and completed except for three possible points which could make it erroneous — see sub-clause 7 (a) (b) and (c). A final but important point is made in sub-clause (8) that no certificate other than the final certificate (with three possibilities of error) shall of themselves be considered evidence that works, materials or goods to which they relate are in accordance with the contract. Thus the contractor cannot say as regards interim certificates you included such and such in certificate No. 6 and therefore that is proof that you were satisfied with it. Naturally you would not include in any interim certificate the value of works, etc which you knew were unsatisfactory, but you may not discover this until later on and the Conditions provide the necessary remedy if such should be the case. The final certificate, however, does discharge the contractor from all his liabilities save as noted above.

Always remember that you must be absolutely conscientious in your certificates, and certify what you really believe is the correct amount, quite irrespective of what either your client or the contractor may say. You will be aware that you can always have a valuation made of the works by the quantity surveyor before you issue any certificate, so that there should be very little risk of over or under certifying. You will realise that, with the exception only of your right under the contract to defer the issue of a certificate until you have received proofs that all nominated sub-contractors have been paid, you must issue your certificates as they become due, and if your client wishes you to act otherwise (not an unusual thing) you discuss the matter with the contractor before the certificate is acutally due and try to come to some arrangement for delayed or instalment payments or whatever your client has in mind. If you cannot make any such arrangements on your client's behalf before the date for certifying then you must issue your certificate and leave the matter to be settled between your client and the contractor.

Should your client wish to pay by instalments of fixed value or the contractor require, on account of his financial standing, to have certificates at a less frequent intervals than one month, you must first agree these amounts and dates with your client and the contractor. It is very seldom that a contract of any size can be carried out without instalments, therefore this clause must be amended to suit the new requirements and what are called *Stage* payments must be arranged for. You can make a rough calculation of the amount likely to be required by the contractor, say once a month, and then insert this sum as the amount of the instalments. For example, if the contract amount is £5000 and the length of time given to carry out the work is five months, the sum of £1000 less percentage for retention might be a suitable amount if certificates were to be issued once a month. Of course you must satisfy yourself before issuing a certificate that the amount you certify complies with the contract in respect to the correct amount and you must remember that the amounts must not be more than the value of the works executed and of materials and goods delivered upon the site for use in the works up to and including a date not more than seven days before the date of certificate. You will see a reference to the possibility of 'Stage payments' in clause 30 of the Conditions sub-clause 2.

Some architects keep a graph showing the relationship between their certificate valuations and the contractors completion programme. If the work is going smoothly the graph will be 'S' shaped with the expenditure starting slowly and increasing substantially after about one third of the contract period, should this not be so then at this time the Architect should make approaches to the contractor concerning his progress otherwise the contract will in all probability not finish on time.

Clause 31, 'Fluctuations', is set out in five parts A, B, C, D and E and either A or B requires to be deleted. We used to speak of 'Fixed Price' or 'Fluctuating' contracts meaning that the former involved the contractor when tendering taking a chance on increases in labour and materials — by estimating a suitable figure to cover his anticipation of the future during the length of the particular job — or that in the latter case he tendered at rates of labour and prices of materials at the date of tender (being defined now as 10 days prior to the date for the receipt of tenders by the employer) and being paid the net cost of all agreed increases in labour and materials (or debited with any decreases). In reality of course there never was a 'Fixed Price' as most of your clients would wish to understand, for sums for contingencies and pc and provisional sums were always subject to adjustment even if there were no variations.

In the 1963 (revised 1973) edition of the Contract which we are now considering, however, both clause 31A and 31B envisage fluctuations with the difference that 31A, permits increases (or decreases) in wages and cost of materials to be paid to the contractor in addition to the contract sum, whereas 31B only permits such an addition or deduction which is also allowable under 31A in respect of types and rates of contribution, levy and tax or duty as the case may be. To this extent only therefore can a contract retaining clause 31B as opposed to clause 31A be described as 'Fixed'.

Sub-clauses 31C calls upon the contractor to ensure that in any sub-contract he shall incorporate similar conditions either 31A or 31B as are part of his own contract.

Sub-clause 31D explains the general procedure in dealing with Fluctuations with the requirement of the contractor giving written notices to the

Architect and lists certain definitions. There is a proviso as before that no addition to or subtraction from the Contract sum made as a result of fluctuations shall in any way alter the contractor's profit.

Whereas up to June 1973 costs under clauses 31A and 31B were paid to or allowed by the contractor 'net' there is now in the July 1973 edition of the Contract, provision under a new clause 31E for a percentage to be applied to the addition or allowance and the contractor should be given the opportunity of quoting his percentages at tender stage so that, if accepted by the employer, the amounts can be entered in the appendix on page 29 of the Conditions.

Clause 32 deals with outbreaks of hostilities and clause 33 with war damage. At the date of this sixth edition of *Architectural Practice and Procedure* these two clauses carry no particular significance, but you should, of course, study them carefully should occasion arise.

Clause 34 covers the position with regard to antiquities and you will I am sure be fully aware of the importance of this for there have been so many cases in recent times where, for example, Roman remains have been discovered, the preservation of which is of great public interest. I could recall perhaps as a very good example the Temple of Mithras in the City of London, the establishment of which for all time must have been the subject of considerable expense to the contractor (not to mention the public spirited employer) and to have delayed the work so as to qualify for the additional payment and an extention of time to the contractor as defined in sub-clauses 34 (3) and 23 (k) respectively.

Clause 35 is the arbitration clause and does not require much explanation. The two parties can normally agree mutually to an arbitrator, but if they cannot do so then that person will have to be someone appointed by the President or a Vice President of the RIBA. You will note that except where otherwise specifically provided the actual hearing of the arbitration can only take place after practical completion of the works or the abandonment of the works, unless with the written consent of the parties.

The matters which can be referred to arbitration during the course of the contract are those relating to the appointments of the architect or quantity surveyor in the event of either of them ceasing to be architect or quantity surveyor under the contract, the question as to whether or not the issue of an instruction is empowered by the Conditions, clause 2(2), whether or not a certificate has been improperly withheld or is not in accordance with the Conditions, or any dispute or difference concerning hostilities and war damage, clauses 32 and 33. It will be seen that all these matters affect the carrying out of the work and it would make things difficult if arbitration had to be postponed until the contract was completed, in fact it would be almost impossible to complete the works unless the questions in dispute were decided forthwith.

It should be noted that this arbitration clause does not apply to any dispute arising under the VAT agreement to which I have referred under clause 13A above.

I think you should always bear in mind that the conditions of contract should aim at protecting both the employer and the contractor and should be so framed that, as often as possible, differences of opinion which might arise during the course of the work should be settled by the architect. Although it might be assumed that the employer, the architect, the quantity surveyor and the contractor were all equally capable, straight-forward and conscientious this has not always been the case. I think, however, that it is safe to say that the architect, with his intimate knowledge of the details of the contract, is the right person to give the final decision.

The Appendix to the form of contract has been devised in schedule form so as to bring to your notice at a glance the various items that have to be filled in. It thus avoids the necessity of going through the clauses in the Conditions every time you have to fill a contract form. It seems unnecessary to remind you that the information required should be properly given, otherwise you may be faced with conditions other than those you expect. My remarks under the various clauses, together with those that follow here, will, I hope, assist you in doing this.

Defects Liability Period, clauses 15, 16 and 30. If the space provided is left blank this period will be 6 months. I have made some reference to this period under clause 15. You may consider six months too short a period in a large job, but you should discuss the matter with your client before you put in the period decided upon, which must appear in the specification or bills or quantities upon which the contractor has agreed to tender.

Percentage to cover professional fees, clause 20A. This entry concerns the reinstatement of damage caused by fire, etc. In the case of a simple house 15 per cent for architects and quantity surveyors fees may be adequate, but where a very complicated scientific building is seriously damaged not only architects, quantity surveyors and legal fees will be involved, but also structural engineers and electrical and mechanical consultants fees will have to be met and 15 per cent will again be appropriate because fees are chargeable at lower rates on larger contracts.

Dates for Possession and Completion (clause 21) — These two dates must be filled in as they are of vital importance.

Liquidated and Ascertained Damages, clause 22. The rate and period, although initially entered on the tendering documents when decided upon by both employer and contractor, must be filled in. If you wish to have a 'bonus' for earlier completion this should also be added although I normally recommend that the question of a bonus should not be considered seriously unless and until the contractor is quite clearly falling back on his programme and the employers interests are seen to be in jeopardy.

Period of delay, clause 26. This concerns determination by the contractor and it is quite usual to make no special entries leaving the periods to be as printed, ie 3 months under (i) and one month under (ii).

Prime Cost sums for which the contractor desires to tender, clause 27(g). This clause gives the contractor an opportunity of stating whether he wishes to tender for any work that is covered in the bills of quantities by pc sums. You will, as a rule, have obtained prices for all work usually carried out by sub-contractors, and have a desire to employ these particular firms. Under this clause, however, the contractor, if you agree, shall be permitted to tender for such work without prejudice to the employer's right to reject the lowest or any tender. If you are dealing with a large and respectable firm of contractors it may be of advantage to your client for them to carry out as much of the work as possible subject, however, to their not sub-letting it without your consent.

Period of interim certificates, clause 30(i). This is usually agreed as one month.

Retention percentage. Usually five per cent, but variable as I have already stated under clause 30(3) earlier.

Period of final measurement, clause 30(5). Usually 6 months but variable as I have discussed under clause 30(5) earlier.

Percentage additions, clause 31E, I have referred to these in relation to fluctuations under clause 31E earlier and the appropriate percentages should be entered here.

The Supplemental Agreement (the VAT agreement) follows on pages 30-32 of the Conditions and it provides for the employer paying the contractor any tax properly chargeable on the supply of goods and services by the contractor to the employer under the contract. There are certain provisions regarding assessments, statements and receipts and the agreement lays down that any disagreements are not subject to arbitration but are referrable to the Commissioners of Custom and Excise.

I have now completed the examination of the Standard (1963 revised 1973) form of contract and advise you to get a copy and study it carefully, making notes as to any points which are not clear and endeavouring thoroughly to understand the form. You can also refer with advantage to the Practice Notes on the Standard forms of contract issued by the Joint Contracts Tribunal. No doubt you will have realised the difficulty of appreciating the full effect of some of the clauses, and perhaps the following remarks may help when you are faced with matters coming within a specially difficult clause. Try to eliminate all the legal phraseology, and get down to the framework, as it were, upon which the clause is built. To show you what I mean, let us take clause 26. I think you will find it easier to understand if it is written like this: (If the employer does not pay to the contractor the amount due or obstructs the issue of any certificate or commits bankruptcy or if the whole or substantially the whole of the works is delayed the contractor may determine this contract). When you have thoroughly grasped the shortened clause you will, I think, have no difficulty in understanding that given in the legal document.

Now let us examine the reasons for the issue of two forms of contract by the RIBA, the one where quantities form part of the contract and the other where they do not. In the latter case a clause is inserted in the Conditions stating that 'any bills of quantities or other statements as to quantities of work supplied to the contractor shall not be deemed to form part of this contract', and therefore, if there are any mistakes in the quantities, either deficiencies or excesses, no claim can be made either by the contractor or the employer. In the former case, where quantities form part of the contract all discrepancies in the quantities can be adjusted, and the builder is thus certain to be paid for the right amount of work, but although it is not so stated in words it seems quite clear that no rectification of errors as they affect the contractor's prices and calculations can be made, but only errors in descriptions or in the quantities.

It will thus be seen that the two forms have been produced to meet the views of two schools of thought, and, personally, I have no hesitation in recommending that quantities should form part of the contract.

The contract need not be stamped unless it is under seal when it must be stamped with a 50p revenue stamp as a Deed and this can be done while you wait on presenting the document at the Inland Revenue Office, Bush House,Strand, in London or at certain provincial stamp offices. There are also facilities for stamping through the Post Office, but this takes a few days. A contract requiring an impressed stamp must be presented for stamping within thirty days of its date. A contract is often made with one or more copies so that each party can have a signed copy. In such cases only one copy is stamped 50p but, if presented at the same time the other copies can be stamped 25p as duplicates. Heavy penalties can be imposed if documents are insufficiently stamped or presented for stamping out of time and strict adherence to the above rules is advised, as a Court may not take notice of a document unless it is properly stamped. The above stamp duty is only for contracts of the kind discussed in this work and should not be taken as applicable to the stamping of documents generally.

A contract can usually be under hand but in dealing with limited companies, corporations, charities, etc, the authority of the person signing should be checked. Local authorities have Standing Orders relating to contracts and although you are not always concerned to see that such orders have been complied with it is as well to make yourself familiar with them. Caution should also be exercised in dealing with clubs on which legal advice should always be taken wherever possible. Without advice, never accept a club as a contracting party unless it is incorporated as a limited liability company. In other cases some substantial individual should enter into the contract personally.

It is now desirable to consider briefly forms of contract other than the one we have been studying. It may happen that you will be instructed to carry out some work on a prime cost basis; that is to say, the builder is to be paid the actual cost of the work plus an amount for profit. In practice, as we shall see, the substance of this contract is threefold, the charges being divided into three parts, (a) the prime cost of the work, (b) establishment charges, and (c) builder's profit. This method should be always avoided in entirely new work, where it should be possible to proceed on the normal lines already described, since, however, good and well intentioned your builder may be, he has, under it, no personal incentive towards expedition or economy. But it may be the only practicable method. Its great drawback from the client's point of view is that it is seldom possible to forecast the ultimate cost of the work and I always advise against its use. I have included in the *Appendix*, page 333 a form for prime cost contracts.

There are several considerations which must be borne in mind when a prime cost contract is being negotiated, the chief being the actual (ie prime) cost of the work, how it is to be arrived at, and what is really means. I cannot explain this better than by saying that, as a rule, prime cost means (a) the amount of wages paid, in accordance with the current Working Rule Agreement, also the amounts paid under any Act of Parliament by way of Employers' Contributions and for holiday stamps and (b) the net cost of all materials, after deducting all trade, cash or other discounts; (c) plants consumable stores and services and (d) any sub-contractor's and sub-let work. It does not include establishment charges and it is therefore of great importance to define what these charges (which are also called *trade expenses*, 'overhead charges', etc) really are, but it is not easy to lay down a definite rule. The list I have given in the form of contract (see *Appendix* page 334) contains the items which I consider should be included under this heading, but I am quite aware that there may be considerable divergence of opinion on the subject. A similar list has, however, been included in several important contracts, and has worked well. Its merit is that it is quite definite, and there should be no room for dispute as to what the builder must carry out under the percentage included in the contract.

The RIBA have issued a Fixed Fee form of Prime Cost contract dated 1972 where the prime cost is payable as before plus a fee which has been agreed beforehand so that there is an incentive to the contractor to keep the cost low so that his fee represents a better relation to turnover.

What makes a prime cost so onerous to the architect or his surveyor is the checking of the contractor's books in order to certify the correct amount, and this checking must be done in a very thorough manner. It is important to insist upon the contractor keeping separate cost books for each job and having separate receipts for all materials required for the work. You will probably find that the contractor will wish you to accept invoices for goods supplied and will not be able to show you the actual receipts. The materials supplied for your job may have been included in accounts for material required for other work, and further, most contractors pay for goods on a monthly account, thus making it difficult to be quite certain that you are paying only for goods supplied to your job. You must therefore be firm in your insistence on the documents relating to your contract being kept entirely separate and complete. It is sometimes advisable further to ask the contractor to keep a separate banking account for the contract.

A careful check must be instituted at the job itself, and if no clerk of works is employed it should be made clear that you will require the foreman to check into the job all goods supplied and also all surplus materials which are returned to the builder's yard. You will, of course, check all the foreman's returns with the invoices or accounts, but you should also, when you visit the job, see that the foreman is really checking the material as it is delivered. Should there by any question as to the quality of material supplied it may be necessary to measure the work upon completion. It is extraordinary how materials can disappear from a job, and as the contractor under a prime cost contract knows that he will be paid for all materials supplied, there is not the incentive to look after this matter which is present in the case of a lump sum contract.

It is a good plan to obtain from the contractor a monthly statement of the cost, and to check this statement and the prime cost books as soon after its receipt as possible. It is much more satisfactory to get the checking done once a month than to wait until the contract is finished.

In connection with the preparation of a prime cost contract it is necessary to agree with the contractor the percentage to be added for (a) establishment charges and (b) profit. If you desire competition in the matter it can easily be obtained by sending your form of contract with the list of items included in establishment charges to a number of builders and letting them state the percentage they require. If your client has already decided to employ a certain builder, the question of the percentage for establishemnt charges can generally be settled by asking the builder to supply evidence of the cost to him of such charges, and the rate of percentage for profit can generally be agreed at an amount not exceeding, say, 10 per cent.

Another form of prime cost contract which is sometimes adopted makes the actual wages paid to the workmen and the cost of materials the basis as before, but excludes everything else. The percentage added for profit and all other services is at the same time increased. The result is that the checking of the costs, becomes rather easier than under the more usual form, and there can be no dispute as to what constitutes establishment charges or other services rendered by the contractor.

A further variant to this form of contract is to have the total amount to be paid to the builder for establishment charges and profit stated at the commencement of the job, and to have it laid down that no additional amount will be paid whatever the cost of the job may eventually be, provided that no additional work is ordered. You can get very good competition under this form of contract by asking the builders to estimate the value of the proposed work and to state the amount they require to be paid for establishment charges and profit. As an incentive to get the work carried out cheaply, an agreement can be made under which the builder shares a portion of any amount saved on his estimate. As the builder gets no financial advantage if the job costs more than estimated, he has every incentive to keep down the expense. You should have no difficulty in varying the fixed fee form of contract or the form given in the appendix to suit this case.

A favourite form of contract used by Government departments and some local authorities is the Schedule of Prices or Measure and Value contract. In this case a document is prepared, something like a bill of quantities in which all the quantities are approximate but rates for every item have been given, the whole monied out and a total secured before issue to the contractors. A bill of preliminaries is also given to enable the contractor to make specific provision for such services as water for the works, temporary lighting, temporary roads, damage to roads and property, watching and lighting, etc, and also to give the contractor the opportunity to state the rate of commission he would require on all sub-contractors' works. The contractor is asked to tender for the work by stating whether he will agree to the printed rates or whether he requires more or will agree to less than the rates. I have described the form in detail in the chapter on *Schedule of Prices*. The quantities given in the schedule are approximate to the amount of work required, and the work so carried out is measured and priced out as the work proceeds. Thus it is considered that a tender which will be somewhere near the total cost of the work, can be more quickly obtained and so the client will get a fairly definite idea of his complete expenditure and be able to have the work commenced at an earlier date than if the more usual bills of quantities were prepared.

Mention should be made of one other method of carrying out work, although it does not quite come under the heading of contracts. I mean when the employer appoints a man to act for him as clerk of works, to buy all materials direct from the merchants, to engage the men and pay the wages, thus eliminating the builder. There may be exceptions where the works have been carried out satisfactorily under thoroughly competent direction, but I have formed the opinion that it is about the most expensive manner in which building work can be done. For this reason it is seldom likely to commend itself, either to the client or to the architect.

I had almost forgotten to mention the verbal form of contract. A contract to be legal need not necessarily be in writing, although it is almost inconceivable that any matter connected with building should be dealt with in any other way. I remember being called in some years ago by a solicitor, to help settle a dispute in connection with a small house at Harrogate. A builder, who had erected many houses in the locality, had agreed, verbally, to erect a house similar to one of the others already built. It was amazing to find how many difficulties had been brought about by this unusual, but not entirely unknown, form of contract. Agreement could not be secured even as to the identity of the sample house referred to and in the matter of detail the divergence of opinion was almost beyond belief.

A special form of contract concerns minor building works for which a grant under the Housing Act 1969 will be made. It is entitled *Agreement for Improvement Grant Works* dated December 1970 and copies can be obtained from the RIBA.

You may sooner or later be concerned with a 'package deal' form of contract under which the contractor provides the whole of the services required — design, cost control and construction — so that independent architects, consultants and quantity surveyors are not appointed. Frequently however the employer prefers to have the advice of his own quantity surveyor in such a case. Also mention should be made briefly of consortia whether in the building and construction industry or even among professional offices. These are sometimes advantageous in completing large works or in economy in administrative expenses but you are unlikely to come across such arrangements in the early days of your own practice. The principle of a consortium should, however, be borne in mind in case you are employed in a large office.

A form of Contract for use in connection with works of civil engineering construction is another to which I should draw attention. The current edition is dated June 1973 and copies can be obtained from, *inter alia*, The Institution of Civil Engineers. It is complete with a form of tender, form of agreement and Performance Bond and you should study this document in case you are engaged in architectural work associated with civil engineering contracts.

I do not think there are any forms of building contract in general use other than those I have referred to, but I am of opinion that none of them is as satisfactory to the client as the usual 'Lump Sum Contract' based on properly prepared drawings and bills of quantities, and although it is sometimes claimed that time is saved by getting on with the work at the earliest possible moment and before all the necessary particulars have been prepared, I cannot remember a case where this method has really proved satisfactory as regards both expenditure and expedition.

I emphasised at the beginning of this chapter the great importance of mastering the subject of contracts, on the intricacies of which many books have been published. One work of this kind is that issued by the Ministry of Works with the title *The Placing and Management of Contracts for Building and Civil Engineering Work*. It is a report by a Committee appointed by The Ministry of Public Building and Works dated 1964 and well worthy of careful study as is also the report dated 1967 of the Economic Development Committee entitled 'Action on the Banwell Report'. You will find that these documents confirm the advice I have endeavoured to give in this book.

Chapter XIV
Inspection of works in progress

It will be one of your duties to inspect buildings in course of erection. I do not think it is necessary for me to impress upon you the importance of this. In chapter XXIV I shall tell you something about the responsibilities of architects and I may say, in passing, that these are very great. Careless inspections of work in progress may lead to very great trouble, even to the marring of an architect's reputation. I have often heard architects say, after an inspection by one of their assistants, that they were no wiser than before he had visited the building. In other words, the assistant had not taken sufficiently definite particulars of all that was going on.

Now, the chief object of inspecting work in progress is to see that the work is being carried out in accordance with the drawings and specification. Do not forget to check the leading measurements of the buildings when the excavations are finished, as discrepancies found at the commencement are easy to rectify. If your contract is the standard form (1963, revised 1973), you will find that under clause 5 you are required to furnish the contractor with carefully dimensioned drawings to enable the contractor to set the works out, so that should any mistakes be made, it seems clear that your client will have to bear the cost of rectifying the error unless the contractor is himself in error in setting out. Your reputation will be greatly affected should such a thing occur, but for your consolation I may say that I have never had to deal with such a catastrophe, but I have been associated with a case recently where the contractor was in error and as a result had to buy some adjacent land to accommodate the garages of the scheme. You must have not only a thorough acquaintance with the drawings and specification, but also a sound knowledge of materials and a ready method of testing them, otherwise you will be unable to tell whether the work is being carried out properly.

I advise you all, somehow or other, to learn simple methods of testing materials. For example, sand. How are you to tell good sand from bad? The following tests will be sufficient for your purpose: take a handful and rub it between your hands or on a sheet of white paper; if no deposit of clay or loam is left, this will indicate that the sand is sufficiently clean. Put some sand in a glass jar and fill the jar with water; stir it, and the sand will settle at the bottom and any clay will rise to the top. Examine the sand to see if it is sharp. A good pit sand should be sharp, and you can easily see the difference if you compare it with the usual kind of sand on the sea-shore. Taste the sand to see if it is fresh as it is important that there should be no salt in it.

You must satisfy yourself that the bricks are of the quality and make specified, and also that they are good bricks, suitable for the purpose and the position where they are to be used. Good bricks should ring true when struck together. Bricks that do not ring are soft, shaky, or underburnt, and should be rejected. When broken the fracture should show evenness of texture and there should be no cracks.

You will have to decide the depth at which your foundations must be laid. This is of the utmost importance, and, although you may get (and should expect) assistance from the foreman, especially if he is a local man, you must omit no precaution to assure yourself that you have really reached a 'solid bottom'. The surveyor to the local authority will inspect the trenches before the concrete is laid but you should not proceed on his approval only but make up your own mind that all is well. If you have arranged to have trial holes sunk before you completed your drawings, this will have enabled the quantity surveyor to take out the quantities accurately but only a site inspection can finally determine the actual depth of excavation needed. In having trial holes dug it is a good plan to excavate them about $3'.0''$ square and to a depth of say $3'.0''$. In the centre of the trial hole a further depth of $12''$ can easily be obtained by digging out a small portion of the bottom; and then, if an iron bar is sunk as far as possible, you can tell definitely what sort of foundation you have to a depth of something like $5'.0''$ or $6'.0''$ which is sufficient for all ordinary cases. Foundations in clay are affected by atmospheric changes to a depth of about $3'.0''$ below the surface, but where funds are short I am afraid the risk is often taken of putting them in less deep than this and this is one of the most frequent causes of settlement.

While you are young you should, on your inspections, ask the builder's foreman to explain any points on which you are in doubt; you will usually find him very willing to help you. As you get older it will be more difficult for you to do this. You will be expected to know all there is to be known about building, and so must not display your ignorance. Therefore, make the most of your opportunities now, and get all the information you can.

I remember, some years ago, inspecting some work at a house in Sussex, I noticed that the concrete for the floors was very weak, and on investigation found that the boxes or frames used for measuring the proportions — 1 part of cement to 4 parts of aggregate — were incorrect with the result that the concrete was being put in far too weak. All the concrete already in position had to come out; it would in any case have fallen down if the formwork had been removed. You must therefore take special notice of this matter of measuring proportions. In some cases, although the frames may be of the correct dimensions, you will find that the workmen fill that for the aggregate too full; then they throw the frame for the cement — which has no bottom — hard down upon the aggregate, with the result that the aggregate fills part of this frame also, and there is not sufficient space left for the proper quantity of cement. They should be made to use a straight-edge on the aggregate frame, and a threat to have a bottom put to the cement frame usually suffices. One of my friends, on inspecting some foundations a little time ago, noticed that the top of the concrete was finished off very smooth. This aroused his suspicions, and so he had some of the top scraped off. He was considerably surprised to find that there was no concrete at all, but only broken brick and stones with a screeding of cement on the surface.

Watch the mixing of concrete very carefully whether by hand or machine, and see that it is carried out as specified. One of the usual defects is that the aggregate does not contain sufficient small stuff or sand to fill the interstices. Ordinary concrete should have no holes in it, and, on the other hand, the small stuff should not be in excess, or the cement will have a greater surface to cover than is intended. There are special forms of concrete that do contain voids such as 'no-fines', foamed slag or aerated concrete and these have their special uses and of course must also be carefully mixed.

Similar difficulties will meet you in connection with the mixing of cement mortar. The desire to save a little on the cost of cement seems to be an incurable disease from which some builders suffer. If they are discovered their suffering is intensified.

Examine the brickwork carefully. You will often find that there is plenty of mortar on the outside edge of the bricks and none anywhere else. This will be a chance for a few carefully chosen remarks to the foreman, who will no doubt see in future that the brickwork is properly carried out. Such a fault is as prevalent today as it ever was and only as recently as June 1970 a well-known architect wrote to the builder engaged upon a large and important contract in London calling attention to the fact that the bricklayers were omitting to fill the centre of the brickwork with mortar.

You will at first find some difficulty in satisfying yourself as to the quality of the timber. If you obtain a book of timber brands, you may be able to tell the quality by reference to the marks at the end of the joists, rafters, etc, but it is very difficult. Good timber looks bright and clean. If well grown the ends show a clean cut. A woolly and open grain between the rings indicates a weak, soft wood. The sides also should be fairly smooth and bright, not dull, rough and woolly. There should, of course, be little sapwood, none at all of a green or blue tint, no shakes, and no dead black knots. These are a few simple hints, but a good deal of experience is necessary to enable you to judge timber; therefore take every opportunity to increase your knowledge in this difficult subject, and do not hesitate to ask the foreman or a good carpenter to help you. A carpenter knows good timber by the feel of it under the plane or saw.

There are many qualities of glass, and if you specify Selected glazing quality, you may get Ordinary glazing quality unless you are very smart. You must expect to get 3 mm glass if you specify 4 mm, so be on the look-out. The weight of glass can be tested approximately by a gauge but you will not have to do this if you have taken the precaution of specifying that the glass is to be delivered to the site in the makers original packages. See that the glass is put in the sashes the right way. If one side is rough it should be on the outside.

Paint is difficult to test. You should either specify the use of a well-known brand or that the builder is to supply samples for testing. If you are in doubt and the job is specially important the sample should be sent to a specialist. If you specify five coats of paint you will be lucky if you get four, unless you are very watchful. Pure white lead is perfectly smooth between the fingers; it contains no sign of grit. Paint, when dry, should be tried with the fingers spread out and drawn down it. It should neither be too 'tacky' nor too dry. One means too much oil and the other too much turpentine.

Keep your eye on the asphalt. Some architects will pass anything that is black. The best plan is to specify that it is to be laid by a firm upon whom you can rely and that the asphalt is to comply with either the appropriate British Standard Specification or the specification of the Natural Asphalt Mine-Owners and Manufacturers Council from whom you can obtain advice upon asphalting matters at any time.

In selecting a good slate you must see that it does not absorb water. Stand a slate in a bucket of water and leave it there for 24 hours. There should be little or no sign of moisture above the water-line. A good slate has a metallic ring when struck, and should be hard and tough, but not brittle. Tiles are tested in much the same way, but, of course, absorb water more freely.

For stone a good plan is to visit the quarry and examine the old buildings in the neighbourhood. If the stone is a good weather stone there will be no signs of decay upon the face. A good stone should absorb only a small quantity of water. Try this with one of the blocks sent for use in the work. Immerse it in water for twenty-four hours and note the weight of water absorbed. See that the stones are laid upon their natural quarry bed. You will find it very difficult to decide this point when it is worked, especially with stone like Bath stone. Just as the joiner knows which way the tree grew by planing a piece of timber, so the mason knows which is the quarry bed by working a piece of stone; some judicious questions to the mason will therefore help you. The quarry owner usually has a mark put upon the block of stone to indicate the bed, and if a similar mark is put upon each piece of stone as it is cut from the block as supplied there will be no doubt as to the actual bed of the stone when used.

Specify 'British Standard' stoneware drain pipes 'Tested' for soil drainage and see that you get them. If you are in doubt about your lime or cement, the best plan will be to send a sample to a specialist for analysis, but as a rule there is no difficulty in this, as the builder is quite as anxious as you are that his lime and cement should be good.

Keep your eyes open for light weight lead. If 6 lb weight is specified, it seems natural that 5 lb weight should be used — of course, quite by mistake! If you have any suspicion, get the foreman to cut off a square foot and then weigh it for yourself. You can use a gauge, but if you do, be careful where you try it; one part of the lead may be thicker than another. The simplest way of testing lead pipes is to have a $12''$ length cut off and weighed. The following list will, I think, be of assistance to you in your inspections:

1   Ask for samples of all materials called for in the specification such as sand, bricks, aggregate, cement, tiles, etc, this demand should be made as soon as the contract is signed.

2   Arrange for a meeting with the sub-contractors on the job in order to have everything properly co-ordinated.

3   Satisfy yourself that the builder has obtained all the necessary approvals of local authorities, etc.

4   Notify the builder that you require the fire insurance policy at once. There should be no delay in getting the building insured.

5   Remind foreman to obtain the steel required for joists, reinforcement to lintels, etc.

6   See that the work is progressing at a proper rate, and if not, notify the contractor.

7   As soon as trenches are excavated inspect them to see that a good bottom has been obtained, and that the trenches are kept free from water. Allow no concrete to be laid until the trenches have been approved.

8   Note the method for measuring materials for concrete, and see that the right gauge-boxes and proportions are being used.

9   See that the mortar has been mixed in the proportions specified and proper measures used.

10   Note that the drain-pipes are of the quality specified, British Standard pipes must all be marked 'British Standard' or 'British Standard Tested'.

11   Decide position of damp-proof course.

12   Take special notice of the brickwork, and see that all joints are filled up solid with mortar. Brickwork is often left full of cavities.

13   Insist on having the bricks thoroughly wetted before being used.

14   See that the damp courses in cavity walls are divided, ie a separate damp course to each portion of the wall. It is essential that the cavity should be formed at least one course lower than the inner damp course; unless this is done there is great risk of damp penetrating to the inner wall.

15   See to provision of vertical damp courses or other precautions where the solid floors adjoin boarded floors, or in cases where adjoining floors are at different levels.

16   Settle the firm to lay asphalt, and obtain a written guarantee from the builder that the material is of the make and quality specified.

17   Settle positions of air bricks under floors.

18   See that holes are left in sleeper walls and through internal walls to allow free circulation of air under floors.

19   Warn the foreman not to take down formwork to concrete floors until you have been consulted.

20   The pointing of brickwork is often badly done. The raking out and filling in are equally important, and need much care. All joints should be raked out at least ¾"

21   Arrange that proper precautions are taken to prevent mortar dropping into cavity walls. It is almost impossible to clear out the cavity after the walls are built, and where (as is usual) cavity walls are built in cement mortar, the mortar hardens very rapidly and cannot be raked out. It is a

very simple matter to arrange long battens, with supporting wires, which can be lifted as the wall rises, but bricklayers are very apt to neglect this.

22 See that the iron ties in cavity walls are cleared of mortar. This is often neglected, and leads to damp getting through the walls.

23 See that cavity walls are properly closed each side of window and door frames with a vertical damp course of slate, etc, and that lead aprons under sills, where specified, are not omitted.

24 Cavity walls should be formed into solid walls at the top by means of oversailing courses (generally two courses) to carry the wall plate for rafters. This is important as ensuring that the weight of roof is borne by both walls instead of by the inner wall only.

25 See that cement is cleared off tile or stone pavings, or they will be permanently stained.

26 Note the fixing bricks are built into walls in order to save plugging with wood plugs, and arrange with the foreman as to their positions.

27 Satisfy yourself that all stone is laid on its natural quarry bed.

28 See that lead or other damp course is inserted in cavity walls above window or door frames.

29 Arrange the position of damp courses to chimney-stacks. They should be as near the roof-line as possible.

30 Get your client's approval to the type of cooker you propose to use, and also of any other fittings proposed.

31 Settle the sizes of the grates and mantels in order that the fireplaces can be built to correct sizes. It is often better to build the fireplaces larger than shown on the drawings, as cutting a fireplace wider than built is more expensive than making it narrower.

32 Warn the foreman to get full particulars of all chases and recesses required by sub-contractors for pipes, etc.

33 See that the work is not being delayed by any action on the part of a sub-contractor.

34 Check gauge of tiling or slating to roofs and ascertain that courses are nailed as specified.

35 Do not allow wood plates to be built into walls to take ends of joists. Wrought iron $2'' \times \frac{1}{4}''$ bearing bar galvanised or tarred, should be used instead, on a cement screed.

36 Check the distances apart of joists, rafters, etc.

37 Before floor boards are nailed down see that all rubbish, shavings, etc, are cleared out.

38 Satisfy yourself as to the quality of the timber immediately the first load is delivered, and also that subsequent deliveries are equal to approved.

39 Decide where rows of herring-bone strutting are to be placed.

40 Warn foreman that joinery must be delivered on the site un-primed.

41 See that trimming joists are tusk-tenoned and not stub-tenoned as sometimes may be observed in inferior work.

42 See that roof timbers are properly framed and securely nailed together and to wall plates.

43 Examine woodwork around chimney-stacks and flues to ensure that none is fixed within $9''$ of any flue.

44   In fixing wood mantelpieces see that no fixing plugs are driven into flues.

45   See that floors are protected when laid, also stairs. Staircases are sometimes damaged by use during the building operations. Good builders keep the works and the surroundings swept clear of rubbish at regular intervals.

46   Look for the iron water bar in wood window-sills; it is sometimes omitted.

47   Settle height of all shelves. Slate shelves are better fixed ½" clear of walls for easy cleaning.

48   See that wide boards in panels, shelves, etc, are properly cross-tongued. This is frequently not done.

49   See that all fittings are properly protected, both before and after fixing.

50   The height of sinks and lavatory basins should not be left to the discretion of the workmen. They are better too high than too low. For sinks 3' 0" and for lavatory basins 2' 9" to top is a useful rule.

51   Do not accept any test of drains, plumbing, hot water, etc unless either you are present at the test or you have a trusted representative.

52   Allow no pipes to be run in the internal angles of walls. Always keep them well clear of the angle and not buried in plaster.

53   Iron gutters are often insufficiently fixed. See that all screw-holes are occupied with proper size screws and cast-iron stop-ends provided. The backs of gutters should be painted before being used.

54   Arrange for sufficient stop cocks on hot and cold water services in order to facilitate repairs.

55   Stop cocks on pipes should be labelled to prevent careless handling. See that there is a proper safety-valve to hot-water service, and that the expansion pipe delivers over cold-water cistern.

56   See that pipes exposed to frost in draughty roofs are covered with felt wired on, or other approved lagging, and that the water cistern, if in the roof, is also protected from frost.

57   Arrange that all water taps are same pattern; it frequently happens that hot-water taps are of different pattern from cold.

58   See that there are draw-in boxes in electric light tubes at all accessible angles.

59   Arrange for the positions of electric light and bell points, and agree the various circuits of the wiring, also settle the exact position of all switches.

60   Arrange with the plumber and hot-water fitter the exact runs of their pipes, and in cutting joists do not permit them to run pipes down the centre of rooms.

61   See that you have the correct lap with lead coverings, especially to the rolls.

62   Settle the position of the cold-water cistern and pipes, and endeavour to keep the cistern as far away as possible from the bedrooms, and the pipes as far inside the building as possible.

63   See that the roof tiles or slates proposed to be used are satisfactory

and of the quality specified.

64   See that the plaster is in bags as specified and properly stored on the site under cover.

65   See that metal lathing for plaster is well secured and braced.

66   If you are using plasterboard for ceilings see that the heads of clout nails are well home and that joints are filled with plaster before being covered with scrim.

67   Note that the window and door frames against brick jambs, etc, are painted.

68   See that 'knotting' is not forgotten, and that it is efficient.

69   Note the number of coats of paint. Insist upon each coat being of a distinct tint for the purpose of checking, and see that the work is well rubbed down between the coats.

70   Note that the undersides and tops of doors, backs of eaves, fascia and similar items are painted.

71   Do not allow the use of sandpaper on woodwork which is to be varnished.

72   See that the varnish is of the quality specified.

I think you will realise from the foregoing remarks that there is plenty to do when inspecting works in progress. I advise you to make careful notes of your inspections and to write a short report after each visit, giving the number of men engaged, the exact state of the work, and any other information of interest.

The following copy of a report will serve as a guide:

Report upon progress of work at
New House, Blankton

Date . . . .

1   I visited the above house on Friday last, the 20 June and report as follows:

(a) The walls of the house are built up to the level of the first floor.

(b) The walls of the outbuildings are built up to damp-proof course level.

(c) Slate damp-proof course is laid to the walls of out-buildings. New damp course slates have been used as specified.

(d) The joists to ground and first floors are fixed, and timber for the roof is on the site.

(e) The sand previously condemned had been carted away.

(f) Trenches had been dug and a portion of the drains laid. The connection to the public sewer had been made by the workmen of the local council.

(g) Door frames had been delivered and some fixed. The frames had been primed before delivery, and I instructed the foreman to see that no further joinery was primed before delivery on the site.

2   The number of men actually at work during my visit, including the foreman, was ten.

3   The foreman stated that one day last week (17th) was so wet that

work ceased on that day and the job was closed down.

4   Details are urgently required for bay window in drawing-room and fittings in kitchen.

5   I attach a small photograph showing the building.

I have often been asked to give my opinion as to the number of times an architect should visit the job during progress of the work. It is laid down in the Conditions of Engagement of the RIBA that 'The architect shall make such periodic visits to the site as he considers necessary to inspect generally the progress and quality of the work but he shall not be required to make exhaustive or continuous inspections . . . '. This seems to me to leave the matter very much in the architect's hands, and I think the number of visits should depend upon the character of the job itself. If you have a reliable contractor and foreman you will not need to inspect the works, to see that proper materials are being used and satisfactory workmanship is being performed, as often as if you are unfortunate enough to have people to deal with whom you cannot trust. Then, again, some clients are much more exacting than others, and are never happy unless the architect is almost always on the job. If you have a good clerk of works the matter becomes easier; you can be satisfied with paying fewer visits. If the work is situated near your office you will naturally visit it more frequently than if it is many miles away. The matter must, I think be left to your own discretion. A fortnight between each visit is quite long enough to enable the builder to do a number of things which you would wish to have undone. It is a good plan not to arrive at the job at meal-times if it can be avoided. The foreman always like to be about when the architect arrives; and although surprise visits are quite legitimate and indeed advisable, it is better that they should not take place when all the men are away.

Chapter XV
Certificates

One of the responsible duties of the architect is to issue certificates for payments due to the contractor who is carrying out work under his supervision. In chapter XIII the position of the architect as regards the issuing of certificates has already been touched upon. It will be obvious to you that in a large contract the contractor must be provided with instalments of money to enable him to finance the work, and the payment of these sums by the employer is regulated by the architect, whose duty it is to certify from time to time what amount is due for payment.

In issuing interim certificates the architect must be careful to satisfy himself that they are for the proper amount due. It is unfair to the contractor during the progress of the work to pay him less than he is entitled to, and it is unwise to pay him more than the correct amount. If you certify overpayments to the contractor during the progress of a contract, even though there be sufficient margin left to enable the matter to be adjusted in the final certificate, it is an extremely unwise action, which may land you in trouble should any difficulties arise, such as the bankruptcy of the contractor. Should you over-certify and the contractor fails in business your client may have to incur additional expense in order to complete the work, and in such a case you may find yourself liable to make good the loss sustained by your client. I therefore advise you to be very careful with your interim certificates. In my own practice I endeavour to assist the architect by making up a statement of the value of the work actually carried out, and in this way we seldom receive complaints from the contractor that he is being underpaid, and, of course, the employer is being protected against any overpayment. This method is provided for in the standard form of building contract (1963, revised 1973), where in clause 30 it is laid down that valuations for interim certificates shall be made whenever the architect considers them necessary. My advice to you is that you should always consider them necessary. I must warn you that as a rule contractors, in their desire to be paid as much as ever they can obtain, are adepts in the preparation of plausible financial statements, and these should be very closely scrutinised. These statements are often based on the actual cost of the works to the contractors, which does not necessarily bear any relationship to the amount due under the contract, and therefore should be taken with reserve. The following example will show you the kind of statement as prepared by a quantity surveyor:

NEW OFFICES, LONDON

Statement for Certificate 12

Queen's Gate
Westminster
4 November 1972

To
Messrs Jones and Robinson
Architects

£

Notices to district surveyor	10.00
Templates	20.00
Clerk of works insurance	10.00
Fire Insurance	25.00
Clerk of works office	20.00
Liability and National insurances	150.00
Watching and lighting	25.00
Cover up and protect	20.00
Gantry	75.00
Hoarding	20.00
Street paving	20.00
Water	25.00
Sheds for cement, etc	15.00
Conveniences	5.00
Dayworks	120.00
Work below lower basement floor	228.00
Strong rooms	1000.00
Hardcore	60.00
Layer of concrete 150 mm thick	250.00
Layer of concrete 225 mm thick	350.00
Brickwork	4500.00
Glazed facings	900.00
Cast-iron drains, manholes, etc	75.00
Reinforced concrete work	2000.00
Steelwork for air ducts, etc	100.00
Portland stone	10625.00
Granite	350.00
Special platform	30.00
Asphalt	430.00
Grillage and work to adjoining premises	225.00
Sundry small works	350.00
Sub-contractors, etc	
Carving and models	300.00
Lifts	332.00
Strong room doors	600.00

Continued £23265.00

Continued £23265.00

Testing materials 68.00
Patent floors 1250.00
Steelwork 15650.00
Steel windows 375.00
Sanitary plumbing 250.00
Drainage 300.00
Hot-water work 350.00

£41508.00

Less retention (5% say)   2000.00

£39508.00

Amount previously certified (Certificates
  Nos 1 to 11)   33000.00

£6508.00

NOTE   This statement is approximate, and is
prepared only for the purpose of an
interim certificate.

William Smith
Surveyor

The quantity surveyor would not normally send you a fully detailed statement but would either write a letter or send you the formal Royal Institution of Chartered Surveyors recommendation setting out the amount to be certified to the contractor and giving details of the amounts included in the certificate for payment by the contractor to nominated sub-contractors. Before, however, issuing any certificate you will be wise to ask the contractor for proof under clause 27(c) of the Conditions of Contract, that all amounts for nominated sub-contractors included in previous certificates have been paid as I have mentioned already on page 126.

The issue of final certificates presents another aspect of the case. Before you issue one, it is necessary to satisfy yourself that the contractor has paid all accounts due to sub-contractors or to other persons for services covered by prime cost sums. In my specifications I always include a clause to the effect that the final certificate will not be issued until the actual receipted accounts for all services dealt with under prime cost sums have been seen. This is the only safe way, and should always be carried out. In order to illustrate this point I may mention a case that occurred a few years ago in my own practice. A firm of contractors in London were carrying out some alterations to a house in the country and the time for the issue of the final certificate had arrived. The architect told me that he proposed to issue this, as he wanted to get the whole matter settled up. I advised him to wait until I had inspected the receipted accounts for sub-contracts, but he considered this quite unnecessary, as the firm was so well established. However, I felt very strongly upon the subject and wrote to the architect pointing out the danger of his proposed action should the

FORM OF CERTIFICATE

Certificate No. . . . . . .   19 Queen Anne's Gate
                                                            Westminster, SW 1
                                                            . . . . .19 . .

I hereby certify that the sum of . . . .
. . . . . . is due to . . . . .of . . . .
on account of . . . .

	£
Amount previously certified	£
Amount as per this certificate	£
Total amount certified	£

. . . .
Architect

Counterfoil

Certificate No. . . . . . .   19 Queen Anne's Gate
                                                            Westminster, SW 1
                                                            . . . . .19 . .

I hereby certify that the sum of . . . .
. . . . . . is due to . . . . .of . . . .
on account of . . . .

	£
Amount previously certified	£
Amount as per this certificate	£
Total amount certified	£

. . . .
Architect

Certificate

---

contractor not have paid all the accounts. This caused him to wait, and in due time I inspected all the receipts. The final certificate was then issued, three weeks later the firm went into liquidation. The architect was thus saved from what might have been a very embarrassing and difficult situation.

Another point to make a note of is to endeavour to get your client's concurrence in the issue of the final certificate and also to the amount to be certified, although you will understand, as I have already pointed out in chapter XIII on Contracts, you must not allow yourself to be influenced either by client or contractor as to the amount of, or date when you issue, your certificates. In order to do this the accounts of the job must have been prepared and agreed between yourselves and the contractor, and you must be ready to show your client full details of the cost of every portion of the work. Should you have any difficulty in explaining the accounts you will find the services of your quantity surveyor useful. I have often had this task to perform, and I have never failed to make the client understand where the money has gone, though possibly I have not always succeeded in satisfying him that he has received value for his money, especially as in some cases he may have had no warning that 'extras' were being incurred.

The example above illustrates a page from a certificate book and shows the form which I suggest you should use. You will see that the form and counterfoil are identical, and each should be filled in. The form is then detached and sent to the builder or client. You will thus have in your possession an identical copy of your certificate which can be referred to at any time, and would enable you to provide an actual copy should it be necessary. As you are probably aware the RIBA issue pads of standard certificate forms set out in a similar way to the RICS recommendation forms, and the use of these is becoming increasingly more popular.

You may be in doubt as to whether your certificate should be sent to the contractor or to the employer. I have noticed that architects vary in their practice in this matter, but if the standard form of building contract (1963, revised 1973) is used (see clause 3(8)) your interim and final certificates should be sent to the contractor. When you send a certificate to the contractor, you should, of course, at the same time notify your client. It is a wise plan to let your client know a little time before you issue a certificate that you are proposing to do so, in order that he may make any necessary arrangement for payment within the stipulated period. He may have to sell stock or get money transferred from deposit to current account, for which a little notice will be required.

Chapter XVI

Variations

I think it may be accepted as a fact that no contract of any magnitude is ever carried out without variations, which may be either additions to or omissions from the contract. It is, of course, most desirable that the net result of such variations should not be an addition to the amount of the contract, but I am well aware that circumstances often seem to conspire together to make this impracticable. Nevertheless, an architect will do well to endeavour to build up a reputation on his ability not only to produce suitable plans and good designs, but also to carry out his schemes for the amount of the tender. Nothing annoys a client more than to be faced with a substantial bill of extras, and whatever may have been the cause, should this occur, the architect's reputation is bound to suffer. I would suggest therefore certain precautions which, if taken, will make for a result more satisfactory both to the client and to the architect than when they are neglected.

Variations may be made either on the definite order of the client or by the architect on his own responsibility. As regards the former, the architect should always safeguard himself by acquainting the client in writing, before the variation is proceeded with, as to the financial effect involved. There can then be no room for dispute or blame when the final account is presented. As regards the latter, the first precaution should be to provide a certain amount in the contract for contingencies and unforseen circumstances arising out of the contract to be expended only upon the written authority of the architect, and then never to exceed this amount without the client's approval. A sum equal to about 5% upon the estimated cost is generally considered a suitable provision, but in works of alteration as much as 10% may be advisable. This amount for contingencies must never be used for works not originally contemplated, otherwise it will defeat its own object. A further precaution sometimes adopted is to provide a small amount of provisional quantities to be used for necessary work within the scope of the contract, the extent of which it was not possible to ascertain before the tender was accepted.

It is when the further drawings and details mentioned in clause 3 of the Conditions of the standard form of building contract (1963, revised 1973) are being prepared that the architect is tempted to put more work into them than was originally contemplated. When inspecting the work in progress, also, it is a very easy thing to suggest improvements without fully realising their financial effect. A strict curb must be placed on all such natural desires if worry and trouble are to be avoided later. In chapter

XIII, I have already discussed the question of variations at some length, but the matter is so important that I propose to emphasise certain points at the risk of repeating myself.

Often an architect will give the foreman a verbal order for something which he has no idea will involve additional expense, and he is surprised to find, when the accounts are being examined, that the builder claims an extra for this. A few years ago I had to square up an account in which the builder claimed an extra on all the doors, etc, which were of pitch-pine instead of deal, as specified. The architect was very indignant at the charge, and professed to have understood that there would be no difference in the cost. The only safe plan is to be very careful in making any departure from the drawings and specification, and unless you are absolutely sure that you are not incurring an extra, the builder should be consulted before you order the variation, and a record made of the consultation.

It should be remembered that a variation can be proved, not only by a written order, but also by any drawing signed by the architect. It is quite clear from Clause 11 of the standard form of building contract (1963, revised 1973) that if the contractor is of opinion that any drawing or direction involves an extra, he is to give notice to that effect before proceeding. If the contractor's special attention were drawn to this at the start of a job the responsibility of the architect would be greatly lessened, but I am afraid that this condition is often not insisted on as strictly as it should be.

I strongly advise you to adopt a regular system of variation orders, and never to order anything except in writing and on a proper form. It is unnecessary to have a form printed. You can use your own printed note-paper and commence by heading the first order 'Variation Order No.1', and continue in the same way all through the job. You can then instruct your quantity surveyor not to treat anything as a variation unless it is supported by a properly signed variation order. It is, however, clear from clause 11 of the standard form of building contract (1963, revised 1973) that only variations that are authorised by the architect in writing should be measured.

Whenever a new contract is started with a contractor whom I have not known previously I invariably inform him in writing that no variations upon the contract will be recognised by me unless he is able to produce a variation order signed by the architect. Circumstances may make it difficult to carry this into effect, but as a rule it makes the matter more simple.

The following is an example of a variation order:

VARIATION ORDER 6

Queen's Gate
Westminster SW1
6 April 1960

Contract, New residence at Marlow.

M . . . . are hereby authorised, according to the Conditions of Contract, to perform the following work, viz:

1   Carry out the bay window to drawing-room in accordance with drawing No. 27.

2   Cut new opening in east wall of dining-room as directed on the site.

3   Omit the stone coping to yard wall.

4   Substitute $2''$ thick red facing bricks for the $3''$ bricks specified at a total extra cost of £14.

5   Construct the rain-water tank as shown on drawing No. 29, the price to be agreed with the quantity surveyor.

6   Order the grates and mantels from Messrs Blank & Blank in accordance with their estimate of £52, dated 3 April 1960.

Peter K. Robinson
Architect

As an alternative, and a very good one, you can use the printed 'Architect's Instruction' forms provided by the Royal Institute of British Architects. In this way your variation order becomes an architect's instruction serial numbered 1 onwards. The form makes provision for a record being kept as to whom you are issuing copies.

You may perhaps be in doubt as to how far you can go in ordering extra work at contract rates without being unfair to the builder. For example, you may be building a house for a client who desires to add an extra room. You are certainly entitled to order this to be done by the builder at contract rates, but if your client wants an entirely new building erected − such as a garage, with workshops, etc, you are then on doubtful ground. If the builder is making a profit upon the house he will not object to erect the garage, etc, but if he is making a loss he will strongly object; in such a case a fair increase in rates should be agreed, as it is unreasonable to expect a builder to carry out new work at a loss.

Chapter XVII

Prime cost sums and sub-contractors

I have bracketed these two subjects together, as they are generally associated in the carrying out of a contract. A prime cost sum is included in the specification for work which is usually carried out by a sub-contractor, that is, a person employed by the general contractor on the instructions of the architect.

When an architect is designing a new building it very often happens that he has no time adequately to deal with such matters as heating, hot-water supply, electric wiring, ventilating, sanitary plumbing, etc. In order to avoid delay, therefore, he provides in the specification lump sums of money for these services. These sums are included by the contractor in his tender, and they form part of the amount of the contract. When the work commences the architect begins to think out the details of the work for which the prime cost sums have been included, and probably he will obtain estimates from several firms for the special works required. Should you have a general contractor who is accustomed to carry out contracts of considerable size he will expect to be allowed to give a tender also for the special items, and it is usual to allow him to do so; in fact, if you are using the Standard Form of Building Contract (1963, revised 1973), you will find that clause 27(g) states that the contractor shall be permitted to tender for works for which prime cost sums are included in the bills of quantities if the architect is prepared to receive them. As a rule tenders for works for which prime cost sums are provided have been invited and received before a contractor is selected and a contract signed, so that it can make things a little difficult and even unsatisfactory if tenders are invited at a later date. This matter is also referred to in page 131.

There are several things to remember about sub-contractors. Clause 27 of the Standard Form declares that all specialists or others who have been nominated or selected by the architect to supply and fix materials or to execute work on the site are sub-contractors employed by the general contractor; you must therefore exercise a good deal of care in your dealings with them. You must never order anything direct from them, but instruct the general contractor to do so, and it must be made quite clear that the general contractor is acting for himself and not as the agent of the client when he orders work from a sub-contractor. This position appears quite clear in clause 27(g) of the Standard Form, but you may not always use this form, so that it is well to keep this point in mind.

Many architects nominate the same sub-contractors over and over again. They get used to the architect's work and methods, and this makes things work very smoothly. These particular sub-contractors are not always put into competition with other firms, but it is wise occasionally to have a competition in order to prevent the special sub-contractors from gradually increasing their prices.

When you ask specialists to give a price for certain work you must be careful to let them know that the firm whose tender is accepted will be a sub-contractor to the general contractor, and will be required to enter into a contract with him in terms consistent with the principal contract; a special sub-contract form for this purpose is issued by the National Federation of Building Trades Employers and the Federation of Associations of Specialists and Sub-Contractors. It is also important to point out to a potential sub-contractor that he must include for a cash discount of 2.5%. When you ask firms to quote for supplying only materials to be fixed by the contractor the cash discount to be allowed will be 5%.

So important is it considered by architects and quantity surveyors that estimates and quotations from specialist firms shall be prepared on fair and proper lines that special forms have been published and are available from the Royal Institute of British Architects and the Royal Institution of Chartered Surveyors to cover this point. One form is the Standard Form of Tender for Nominated Sub-Contractors and another a Standard Form for Nomination of Sub-Contractors. Similar forms are available dealing with nominated suppliers.

The first of these forms, in addition to the Form of Tender itself, recites the conditions of tender and if the various entries are properly completed there can be no doubt that the sub-contractor's tender is submitted on proper lines and based upon accurate information concerning the contractor's Head Contract.

The second one covers the acceptance by the architect of the sub-contractor's estimate, by the process of nominating him to the main contractor and draws attention to the Standard Form of Sub-Contract for their use. It also provides for a record being kept of those parties to whom copies have been issued.

Except in very small or simple cases I strongly advise the use of these forms, for by doing so it is virtually impossible for any vital point concerning sub-contractors' nominations to be overlooked.

There is also a special Employer/Sub-Contractor form issued by the RIBA which provides for the nominated Sub-Contractor or Supplier to give an independent guarantee to the Employer covering design and workmanship. This form of warranty should be considered in every case where the Sub-Contractor's work includes substantial design elements.

In addition to the sub-contractors recognised by the architect to carry out work in respect of prime cost sums there may, on a large job, be many sub-contractors employed by the general contractor to carry out work which as a rule he himself has no facilities to perform, for example, plastering. It is usual for the general contractor to sublet this work to a specialist firm, and the same thing may apply to many other services. I know some firms who seem to be financial agents rather than builders; they sublet excavating, brickwork, stonework, joinery, slating, plumbing, plastering, glazing and painting — in fact, it is sometimes difficult to find any work that the general contractor actually does himself. Contractors are often indignant if a large part of their contract is given to special firms to carry out. A contractor of considerable experience is reported to have said that a builder could consider himself fortunate if as a result of competitive tendering he received 45% of the actual work, the remainder going to sub-contractors, whereas, in civil engineering work a contractor would compete for probably 95%. I cannot vouch for these figures but, if it is so, a builder's indignation would carry more weight if he did not so frequently sublet some of the work mentioned above.

If the general contractor gives you notice that he proposes to sublet any of the work you should give the matter very careful consideration. If you have a first-class London builder it may be an unwise thing to allow him to sublet, for example, the joinery, as in all probability he will let it to a firm whose work will not be anything like as good as that turned out in his own workshops; therefore do not give permission for such subletting unless you are satisfied that your client's interests will not suffer. It is, of course, often to the advantage of the client that work should be sublet; plastering is one of the items which I think is always done better by a good firm who specialise solely in this work.

You will find it a very wise proceeding to make early arrangements with sub-contractors, so that their work can be commenced immediately the contractor requires them. A little staff work in this respect at the commencement of a job will often avoid much delay during the progress of the work. I suggest, therefore, that as soon as you have received your client's approval to the sketch plans, you should select the specialists you propose to employ and instruct them to prepare their schemes, so that their proposals can be incorporated in your own working drawings. Thus the frequent alterations to the plans which occur, even after the contract has been signed and the actual work commenced, will be avoided. Where the job involves the spending of public money you will nearly always have to obtain competitive estimates for sub-contractors' work so that it will be essential for you to warn the specialist whom you consult that he will have to tender later in competition with others.

You should also make a special effort to see that the work of the sub-contractors is progressing at a proper rate. If you arrange occasional meetings between the contractor, sub-contractors and yourself, you will find this a great help to everyone concerned. This will probably overcome any slight difficulties which, if not dealt with as they arise, will cause much trouble and delay in the completion of the work.

'Provisional sums' as distinct from 'prime cost sums' are sums provided in the specification or bills of quantities for work or for costs which cannot be entirely foreseen, defined or detailed at the time the tendering documents are issued. When the architect is able to decide in detail upon such matters estimates can be obtained from the contractor as required and it may well be that these may involve the employment of nominated sub-contractors. It will be seen therefore that in certain cases 'prime cost sums' can arise out of 'provisional sums', which procedure is covered by clauses 11(3) and 27(g) of the Standard Form of Contract.

Chapter XVIII

The quantity surveyor and his work

The quantity surveyor is a man who has received a thorough and severely practical training in all matters relating to building — a training quite as extensive in its way as that of the architect. His chief work is the preparation of bills of quantities. As soon as the architect has finished the drawings and specification for a building — except in small cases — it is necessary that the builders who are to be invited to tender for the work should each be supplied with an accurate and complete document called a *bill*, containing in detail the quantities, sizes and descriptions of all the various materials and workmanship required in each trade. It is obvious, therefore, that the quantity surveyor must not only possess a full knowledge of the materials and workmanship which he is called upon to measure, but also that he must be able to grasp clearly the intentions of the architect as delineated on the drawings. He must know all the stages through which work has to pass before it is finished; and, of course, he must have a mind for detail coupled with an aptitude and a liking for figures and orderly methods.

There are, however, many duties other than the preparation of bills of quantities which fall to the lot of the quantity surveyor — duties intimately connected with the quantities on which the work is based. Some of these are as follows:

(a) Prepare schedules of prices.

(b) Prepare estimates of variations as the work proceeds.

(c) Measure and value variations as the work proceeds.

(d) Prepare statements for interim certificates and advise as to the amount of the instalments to be paid.

(e) Prepare final statements of builders' accounts.

(f) Explain details of final accounts to clients.

(g) Examine and check builders' prime cost accounts.

(h) Advise architects as to the relative value of alternative materials and forms of construction.

(j) Prepare approximate estimates from sketch plans and provide a cost planning service.

(k) Prepare statements of account in connection with arbitrations or actions at law and estimates for dilapidations, etc.

(l) Prepare Time and Progress Schedules and Charts in connection with the rapid progress of building.

(m) Control the cost of a project throughout its construction period.

I have already dealt in detail (chapter IX) with bills of quantities. With regard to schedules of prices (a), these will occur, as I have explained in chapter X, where bills of quantities are inapplicable. As an illustration I remember a case in which some large timber structures had to be removed from a site in England to the Isle of Man and re-erected there. The ordinary quantities could not be given, and therefore a schedule was prepared; that is, a detailed list of materials and workmanship. This list, together with the original plans, was sufficient to enable builders to add the prices or rates at which they were ready to execute the various items of work. On completion the whole of the work was measured up and priced at the agreed rates. The whole of this work, as will readily be seen, belongs to the province of the quantity surveyor, just as much as if there had been bills of quantities.

As regards variations (b), the important service that you may confidently ask your quantity surveyor to perform is to see that a strict record is kept of the extra cost — or saving — of each variation as it arises, and notify your client, at any rate, of all extra expenditure; so that when the final statement is presented it will show only authorised items. If the work you are engaged upon does not need the services of a quantity surveyor you should ask the builder to make a statement showing the financial effect of any variation before you order it. Remember that you may make a variation without realising that it involves an extra, and this should make you more careful than ever.

In cases where the value of variations has not been agreed as they arise (c) — and I am afraid such cases are very numerous in large schemes — it is the duty of the quantity surveyor to measure and adjust all omissions or additions. If you read clause 1 of the conditions of contract in the standard form of building contract (1963, revised 1973) you will see that all variations authorised by the architect or subsequently sanctioned by him are to be measured and valued by the quantity surveyor. There are obvious reasons why an architect should prefer this task to be undertaken by his quantity surveyor rather than by himself, and, moreover, no one can be better qualified to interpret the bills of quantities and to deal with the variations than the man who prepared them. I believe it is absolutely true to say that no single building or work of any size has been carried out without variations upon the contract. There are always additions and omissions, and the financial success of your work will often depend upon the ability and acuteness of your surveyor.

The issue of certificates for payments on account (d) (in connection with which the reader is referred to chapter XV) is a duty performed by the architect, but in all important and many small operations he will find the quantity surveyor's assistance of great value. Where there is no quantity surveyor it is a usual practice to get the builder to prepare a statement showing the approximate value of the work done, but when you have a quantity surveyor it is a safer plan to let him do this. If an architect inadvertently certifies more than is due to a builder his client's confidence is likely to receive a shock if he knows about it.

The preparation of the final statement of accounts for building works (e), is perhaps one of the most important duties of the quantity surveyor. The building work has been duly carried out to the satisfaction of everybody concerned, and there remains only the final payment to be made. Naturally the client will require a statement showing how the money has been spent. If the contract amount has not been exceeded the

NEW HOUSE, OXFORD
Statement of account of Messrs Smith and Son's work in
connection with the erection of a new house at Oxford for
John Williams Esq

		Messrs Robinson and Son
Date		Architects
		£
To amount of Contract dated		22 560.00
To amount of authorised additional estimates as follows:		
	£	
(a) Oak parquet floor to drawing-room	223.00	
(b) Special cornice in lounge hall	110.18	
(c) Oak doors to entrance instead of soft wood	111.15	
(d) Motor-pit in garage	112.50	
(e) Oak entrance gates	71.12	627.95
		23 187.95
By amount of omissions as follows:		
(a) Provision for contingencies	1 000.00	
(b) Gravel paths to front entrance	62.22	
(c) Saving on provision for hot-water supply	5.38	
(d) Saving on provision for sanitary fittings	7.15	1 074.75
Total amount of account		22 113.20
Amount already certified		2 250.00
Balance remaining to be certified		£863.20

The work in connection with the above account has
been measured and valued by me in accordance with the
contract and the figures have been agreed to by the
Contractors.

John Brown
Chartered Surveyor

matter is very simple, but this unfortunately is very seldom the case. Alterations will have been made in the original proposals, additional work may have been carried out and omissions made; but, if, during the carrying out of the contract, the variations have been properly measured and brought into account by the quantity surveyor and the client has been informed, as I have already suggested, there should be little difficulty over the final account, which should, of course, show the amount of the contract and also the cost of the various additions and omissions. If the client is not in possession of all these particulars a fair and informative statement is necessary, and your surveyor will be useful to you in making this document a reasonable and convincing one. The statement of account on page 160 will, I think, form a good basis for your on statements.

It is not at all unusual for the quantity surveyor to be asked to explain to the client the final accounts in detail (f), and if he has prepared these I think it is a very good plan. Many of my accounts run into hundreds of pages, and the architect not being entirely familiar with all the details might find some difficulty in interpreting a number of the items. I think the plan usually adopted by the architect is to send to the client a short statement of account, and to say in a letter that full details are available if he should wish to see them.

An important duty of the quantity surveyor is to examine and check builders' actual costs (g). A large quantity of work has in recent years been carried out upon the basis of prime − or actual − cost, plus profit, and under this system it is absolutely necessary to have every item of expenditure checked. This work should never be undertaken by an architect, and, indeed I know of no single architect who is also an artist, who has any desire to check builders' accounts. It is obviously the work of the quantity surveyor, who is specially fitted by his training for this class of work, and who will be able to satisfy the client not only that the charges for materials and time are correct, but that the quantity of materials used and the time expended in carrying out the work are also correct. I remember checking the prime cost of a large building carried out by one of the big London firms, and in the course of my examination of the accounts I asked the builder's accountant whether, in the event of his being a client and having a house built upon the prime cost plus profit basis, he would think it necessary and worth while to have the builder's accounts checked by a quantity surveyor. He said he would certainly have the accounts checked, and he felt almost inclined to say that it would be worth the cost of having them checked even twice. This, I think, well illustrates the importance of the quantity surveyor's work in this respect.

The quantity surveyor is always prepared to advise as to the most economical materials to use and the cheapest form of construction to adopt (h), so that where cost is a consideration this help should be very useful and tend towards smoothness in the carrying out of building work. I do not wish to imply in any sense that the architect cannot do these things himself, but only to point out that the quantity surveyor, from the nature of his work, should be in a better position to advise on such matters. An architect consulted me recently in the case of a flat roof, and asked which was the cheaper plan; to lay concrete to the necessary slopes to run off rain with a suspended level ceiling below, or to lay the concrete with a level soffite and to form the necessary slopes or falls with fine concrete in addition. As this form of construction was to apply to a large building it was most important to know the relative cost of the two schemes.

In the preparation of approximate estimates and cost plans (j) the quantity surveyor should be very useful, as he makes a speciality of this work. He is much more likely to be accurate than the architect, whose time is very fully occupied in studying the requirements of his client and the details of his own particular work.

Should you be engaged in an arbitration case or an action at law (k), you will find it essential to be supported by a quantity surveyor, who will prepare all the necessary statements of account. Provided your surveyor has adopted an impartial and correct attitude, his estimates will be treated with respect and your position greatly strengthened. A surveyor's estimate in connection with dilapidations will also prove most useful, and in practice is more likely to be accepted than an architect's.

Time and Progress Schedules and Charts (l) and Critical Path analyses, are now frequently used, and the quantity surveyor, owing to the diversity of his practice, must necessarily come into contact with many such forms. He will, therefore, be able to advise and assist you in their application. A simple form of progress chart is given on page 120.

The quantity surveyor is expected to control the cost of the work throughout the construction period (m) and to prepare periodic financial statements for the architect and the client.

There is another duty of the quantity surveyor which I should like to mention. This is the adjustment of the Fluctuations clause of a contract which enables the contractor in certain circumstances to recover any increases in the cost of labour and materials which have taken place since his tender was submitted. Likewise the client can have the benefit of any reductions although these are rare at the present time. Now the calculation of these rises and falls is a very difficult matter. It is generally fairly easy to get some sort of statement from the builder when there is a rise, but it is not quite so easy when there is a fall and you should ensure that the contractor provides you with a schedule of basic prices upon which his tender is based before a contract is signed. You should rely upon your quantity surveyor to do this work and to ascertain the correct amounts. I can assure you that his job is not one to be envied.

The quantity surveyor is prepared to assist the architect in many ways. He will write your specifications for you, survey the sites, measure up buildings, visit works in progress, and generally make himself useful. If he is a really good man you will find his services of very great help. I believe that only a few years ago a very eminent architect publicly acknowledged the services which his quantity surveyor had rendered to him; so you will realise that I am not claiming for him more than is right.

As soon as your working drawings are sufficiently advanced you should explain to your client that quantities will now be required and he should be asked to agree to the appointment of a quantity surveyor. It is important that the client should understand the necessity of employing a quantity surveyor, what duties he will perform, the amount of his fees, and the way these fees are paid. There should be no mystery about the appointment of a quantity surveyor, otherwise you may have to face a very difficult situation.

Some few years ago I prepared quantities for alterations to a large house in London. The architect had not notified his client that a quantity surveyor was to be employed. He had given his client an approximate estimate of the cost of the work, and when tenders were received the lowest estimate was very much in excess of the architect's figure. The client refused to proceed with the work or to pay the architect or quantity surveyor. This case, I think, makes it clear how important it is that a client should know about the quantity surveyor and his work; and if, when you are in practice for yourself, you prepare quantities in your own office, then it is more important than ever that the client should know what is being done. You must always be prepared for work falling through even after the receipt of tenders based on full quantities. I warn you that a certain type of client will not readily pay for abandoned work; you will thus see that, if he is ignorant of the usual procedure, the fees of the quantity surveyor, as well as your own, will be involved.

Besides the respective spheres of the architect and the quantity surveyor, there are many duties which are common to both professions, in which — not being the pleasantest of duties — they may be said to share one another's burdens; I refer to the preparation of schedules of dilapidations, reports on houses and property, and party wall awards. In these matters the young architect will find his surveyor a valued counsellor and friend.

Chapter XIX
The client

My remarks about the client will be somewhat brief. An architect is in a better position than I am to discourse feelingly on this subject, but as it is said that the onlooker often sees most of the game, perhaps a few remarks of mine may be useful.

It is unnecessary for me to say that when you are in practice yourself you must manage somehow or other to obtain a client. What I would like to impress upon you is that, if you wish to succeed, it must be your chief business to lay yourself out to please him. It takes a very great man to succeed by pleasing himself and disregarding his clients. Some clients are much more easy to get on with than others, and you must be prepared for all sorts. You may be blessed with one who gives you no trouble at all and is pleased with everything you do; but, on the other hand, you may be unfortunate and have one who does not know his own mind, is difficult to satisfy, and who expects to be waited upon hand and foot. He will be constantly on the telephone, and will expect you to meet him on the job almost every day. A client of this disposition is very trying and occupies a great deal of your time, but, believe me, he provides a golden opportunity for your education in one of the vital parts of your professional life. It is not only true that the noblest study of mankind is man; it is also no less a fact that the architect who wishes to succeed in life must lose no opportunity of studying the idiosyncrasies of his clients, until he is able to adapt himself with ease to their various moods. Do not therefore brood over troubles and worries, but take a keen interest in this study of character and determine so to act that difficult clients will return to you and will recommend others perhaps of a more pleasant type.

One of your most important rules should be to endeavour to give a client what he wants. He pays the piper and therefore he ought to call the tune. Many architects, however, seem to think that the client need not be given what he wants, but what they wish to design, and there is no surer way of losing his work. Therefore, if your client wants a house built — well, build him a house and do not endeavour to persuade him that what he really requires is a swimming-bath. You will say that this is an absurdity, and so it is, but so also is the idea that you have any business to force your views down a client's throat. It is no doubt often the case that a client has but a dim notion as to how his ideas can be carried out, and it is then an architect's privilege to guide him with expert advice. Perhaps you may be asked by such a client to add a games room to his house. You will make your survey of the premises, and the client will probably say where he thinks the games room should be built. Your duty, clearly, is to take note of all the circumstances of the case, and if you see a better site you might prepare two sketch designs, one showing the addition in what you consider is the best position and the other where your client asked for it. If, when you show him the two schemes, he still prefers his own, it is your business, with a good grace, to do the very best you can to make that scheme successful.

Never disdain the client who only requires a small amount of work done. I remember hearing of an architect who was asked to make a very unimportant addition to a wealthy man's house. Evidently this architect was an expert in the study I am asking you to take up, for this case ended in the client spending something like £100 000. Although, in amount, this is, I think, an exceptional instance, small work may often lead to larger.

Should you be fortunate enough to win a competition, or be employed in a case where your client is a corporation, public body, or a limited liability company, be sure to obtain a formal letter of appointment. It is legally necessary that this should bear the seal of the corporation or company. I believe many architects in the past have found themselves in difficulties owing to the omission of this formality, and I warn you to be careful in such circumstances.

I understand that in America the employment of an architect forms the subject of a written agreement between the client and the architect. It would be wise at times to have some such agreement in this country and, indeed, the RIBA publish a short form of agreement for general use between a building owner and an architect, but, as a rule, an architect hardly cares to suggest this. Perhaps the nearest the architect can get to a formal agreement is to write a letter confirming the instructions of his client, and it might be a good plan to mention at the same time that your charges will be in accordance with the RIBA scale. Some little time ago a firm of estate agents was in correspondence with me and I noticed at the top of their note-paper was printed the words, *Terms in accordance with the scale of the Royal Institution of Chartered Surveyors.* I am not suggesting that you follow this example, but evidently the firm referred to had suffered from not having their fees previously agreed and wanted to insure against such a thing happening again. The client usually instructs the architect verbally to prepare plans, and the matter then drifts in a comfortable sort of way until in due course the contract is signed and the work is carried out. Occasionally, however, trouble arises; perhaps the tenders received are far above the architect's approximate estimate, or some unforeseen circumstances cause delay. In such cases the work may be put off or perhaps abandoned, and the client may not be too willing to make what is called in the Civil Service a *nugatory payment.* It is very seldom that a client altogether repudiates his architect, but you must be prepared for trouble if the tenders come out higher than your approximate estimate, and if your client refuses to pay your fees on this account the best plan is, I think, to grin and bear it, not because you have no legal claim, but because it is generally the best policy. I have every sympathy with a client who tells his architect definitely that he wishes to spend not more than a certain sum, and then when the tenders come in finds that the lowest is double the amount of the estimate. If he is reluctant to pay the architect his fees how can one blame him?

More trouble arises on this point than on any other, and I will therefore conclude this chapter by giving you a piece of advice which, if you adopt it, will save you many sleepless nights. Be always quite candid and straightforward with your clients. If they ask for more accommodation in a building than can be given for the money they wish to spend, do not proceed with your designs knowing all the time that more money will have to be found. Have the matter thrashed out at a very early date. Get your own view of the cost supported by that of your quantity surveyor, and thus place all the responsibility on the client if he still decides to go on and have the work put out to tender. There is really no need for half the anxiety which many architects give themselves owing to their diffidence in advising a client at once that his schemes are too extensive for the means at his disposal. The time has to come for this disclosure, and every week's delay makes it more difficult. Never underestimate in any circumstances. Nothing pleases a client more than to receive satisfactory tenders, and nothing is more annoying all round than tenders which are too high, involving the cutting down and spoiling of a scheme which leaves the client dissatisfied with both you and it. Always remember that your clients lack technical knowledge and find a real difficulty in reading plans — circumstances which demand the utmost tact and perseverance on your part in the interpretation of your schemes.

The difficulty which most people find in understanding plans can be overcome in some degree by the preparation of a a model. Models need not be large or expensive to achieve their object, which is to give the client a greater insight into the meaning of the drawings than he possesses. A model has as much charm as a drawing has mystery to the average person, and you will no doubt gain earlier appreciation and remove the risk of great disappointment if you have recourse to a model whenever you are in difficulty.

Chapter XX
The clerk of works

A clerk of works is a person appointed by the employer to watch over and superintend on his behalf the progress of building works and to see that the provisions of a contract, as regards materials and labour, are properly carried out. Although his salary is paid by the employer, the clerk of works is generally nominated by the architect. I have, however, known cases where the architect paid the salary and received the money in due course from the employer, but I believe this is exceptional at the present time. Before appointing a clerk of works, therefore, the architect should obtain the consent of his client both to the appointment and to the rate of pay.

When you require a clerk of works, if you do not yourself know one, your best plan will be to consult any of your fellow architects, and if this fails your quantity surveyor may be able to suggest a suitable man. You can apply to the Institute of Clerks of Works and another approach is to insert an advertisement in the technical press.

The best clerk of works is one who has worked at a trade and has afterwards gained a good experience on works as a builder's foreman. Such a man will usually be well acquainted not only with all the details of the work, but also with the tricks of the trade, and he should have gained a useful knowledge of the handling of men. I think the best clerks of works have generally been either carpenters, masons, or bricklayers, and in the selection of a suitable person you should take into consideration the character of the work to be carried out. Should the most important part of the work be stonework, then obviously a mason would have the most practical knowledge, but if joinery predominates a carpenter should be selected, provided that other qualifications are equal.

It is important that you should have a really reliable, competent and honest clerk of works, for if you have one who lacks any of these qualities you would be far better without his services. Remember, however, that the fact of having a clerk of works on the building will not relieve you of your responsibilities as architect for the quality of the workmanship and materials. It will be useless to plead that, because there was a man expressly appointed for the purpose of checking the materials, examining the workmanship and seeing that the specification was properly carried out, you are not responsible if bad work had been executed. This seems a little unfair, but I believe I am right in what I say.

Now in order to obtain a good clerk of works you must offer him a salary sufficient for his position. Some architects and clients expect to obtain a man at a salary very little higher than the wages paid to an ordinary workman, but this is neither sufficient nor satisfactory. The clerk of works has as many temptations as other people, and he should therefore be given no cause to be slack in his duties or to accept a commission from an unscrupulous builder to make up for the smallness of his pay. Bear in mind that if you want a really first-class clerk of works you must pay him a first-class salary.

Sometimes one clerk of works is able to look after two buildings at one time. Generally, however, this is not a good plan, unless the works are very small and close together. In such a case his salary and expenses would be apportioned to the two works.

The duties of a clerk of works consist in looking after the actual work as it proceeds; they may be enumerated as follows:

(a) Examine all materials proposed to be used in the building in order to see that they are in accordance with the specification.

(b) Watch the progress of the work, and see that it is carried out in accordance with the specification and plans.

(c) Make a careful record of all work that is carried out as day-work. Sign the day-work sheets as a correct record of the time spent and materials used for any particular piece of work. Sign the day-work sheets as a correct record of the time spent and materials used for any particular piece of work.

(d) Survey small portions of the building, making any necessary sketch plans to assist the architect in getting out details, etc.

(e) Make rough working drawings and details for any trade, to submit to the architect.

(f) Keep careful notes of all variations upon the contract, to enable the quantity surveyor to obtain a correct measurement of the work as carried out.

(g) Visit contractor's workshop and yards to examine work in process of construction.

(h) Write careful and accurate reports of the state of the work for the consideration of the architect.

(j) Assist the architect with advice, when requested, as to foundations, alternative materials, etc.

In order to enable the clerk of works to carry out his duties he must possess certain qualifications, of which the following appear to me to be the more important:

(a) He must be honest, reliable and competent.

(b) He must be temperate in all things.

(c) He must have a thorough knowledge of all the usual building materials and of the manner in which building operations are carried out.

(d) He must be punctual and assiduous in his work.

(e) He must be able to make a simple survey of either land or buildings.

(f) He must have a sound knowledge of building construction and be able to make working drawings and details in any trade.

(g) He must be methodical in his work of keeping notes, making reports, etc.

(h) He must possess a considerable amount of tact to enable him to adopt the correct attitude towards the client, quantity surveyor, builder, foreman, and other men with whom he will come in contact.

(j) He must have a general knowledge of the value of work and of the leading items of each trade.

(k) He should be able to use a dumpy level and to set out a building.

(l) He should have a good knowledge of builders' quantities and of the way in which work is usually measured by the quantity surveyor.

(m) He should be a man of definite views, able to make up his mind at once, and capable of defending his position if necessary.

The clerk of works should receive all his instructions from the architect, who should supply him with a complete copy of the contract particulars and the bills of quantities, and also a copy of all drawings, details and variation orders that are made during the progress of the work. The clerk of works usually obtains a supply of the necessary stationery, measuring-rods, etc, and charges their cost to the employer, but drawing-boards, tee-squares, etc, are usually supplied by the builder.

As a rule the clerk of works furnishes the architect with a weekly report, keeping a copy for himself also, as to the state of the works, the number of men employed in each trade, the amount and quality of the materials delivered upon the job, the detail and other drawings required by the builder, the names of visitors during the week, the state of the weather, the time of cessation of work, how long the job is stopped and the causes, etc. Architects have a special form printed for the use of the clerk of works. These forms when filled regularly make a very fine record of the progress of the work, and form a good method of communication between the architect and the clerk of works.

The form which is printed on the next page, which I have compiled from various forms in use, may be found useful, and will, I think, suffice for all purposes. It can, of course, be increased in size to suit any particular contract.

The clerk of works has no power to alter or modify the provisions of a contract, and in the case of an over-zealous or self-important man it is occasionally necessary to have this distinctly understood at the first opportunity. For example, if second quality bricks are specified, he has no power to insist upon first quality, and if the finest workmanship is specified, he will not be faithfully carrying out his duties if he agrees to second-rate workmanship.

It is very necessary that the architect should do nothing to impair the position or authority of the clerk of works. Disagreements will naturally arise between the clerk of works and the foreman touching the quality of materials or the manner of carrying out work, and in these cases the settlement of the disagreement will rest with the architect. The clerk of

CONTRACT ....

Clerk of Works Report　　　　　　　　　　　　　Report No ....

Week ending .... 19 ......

To Messrs. .... *Chartered Architects, Bedford Square, W.C.1.*

Workmen employed	Sat	Mon	Tues	Wed	Thurs	Fri	State of Works
Contractor's Men							
General Labourers							
Bricklayers							
Masons							
Slaters or tilers							
Carpenters							
Joiners							
Smiths							
Plasterers							
Plumbers							
Glaziers							
Painters							
Foreman							
Timekeepers							
Sub-Contractors' Men							
Total number of men							

Days	State of the weather	Names of visitors	Time lost
Saturday			
Monday			
Tuesday			
Wednesday			
Thursday			
Friday			

Materials on ground	Queries and drawings required

works should be upheld if this is reasonably practicable, but even if otherwise, tact should be exercised in order to 'save his face'. Sometimes you will find that the foreman is a smarter man than the clerk of works, and in such a case it is a great temptation to the architect to give orders to the smarter man, but I wish to impress upon you the importance of never passing over the clerk of works. It is done sometimes, but I am sure it is a most unwise and, in fact, unjust thing to do.

The clerk of works should be furnished with copies of all documents relating to the works, including copies of all specialists' contracts and specifications, in order that he may have first-hand knowledge and receive his instructions direct from you.

Never hesitate to consult your clerk of works. Make a friend of him. You will find that, as a rule, he knows a lot more about the practical side of building than you do; and if you are frank with him he is generally very ready to help you in any way he can, so consult him. If you are in any doubt as to your full-size details, show them to the clerk of works before you issue them to the builder. It is a good plan to arrange for him to call at your office at stated periods and to let him see the drawings while they are being prepared.

Chapter XXIII
Fees

Although the subject of fees and charges is, of necessity, an important one to everyone concerned in building, the true architect will never regard the acquisition of wealth as the main object of his practice. There is often, however, a great temptation to make an estimate of the probable amount of your fees as soon as you get a job, but it is a bad habit to get into. Always remember that your work is the first thing — your fees should take care of themselves.

As regards fees paid to architects, these are regulated by the Conditions of Engagement and scale of fees published by the Royal Institute of British Architects. The scale is a minimum one and you may therefore safely adopt it for all work coming within its limits. If you should desire to charge more than the scale rates, you may experience considerable difficulty in enforcing your claim should your client object to the charges and refuse to pay. The scale is generally accepted in the Law Courts as evidence of the customary charges of architects, but unless you have a definite agreement with your client you may find some difficulty in recovering your full fees.

An architect is, however, called upon to render many services to which the scale is not strictly applicable, and I suggest that if at any time you are in doubt as the proper sum to charge, or cannot infer the rate from some item in the scale, the best thing you can do is to ask the secretary of the Institute or one of your brother architects for his opinion. It will often be found that they have had similar experiences.

It sometimes happens that a client desires to know at a preliminary stage what amount he will have to pay his architect, and he will ask you to state an inclusive fee or lump sum. You are within your rights as a member of the Institute in doing this and you should arrive at the figure by taking your approximate estimate of the work as a basis and applying the rate given in the scale. In naming the figure you should, of course, make it plain that if material alterations are subsequently made in the scheme the additional work will have to be charged for.

There are many architects who work for public bodies and commercial firms, and are paid by way of a fixed salary. As such an employee you will not come into daily contact with fees, but it is important that you understand the basis of their calculations and keep abreast of any changes. You will find that as your practice increases many problems relating to fees will arise, such as the amounts to be charged for abandoned schemes, sketch plans, etc, but a reference to the scale of fees contained in the manner consistent with economy.

(e) If there is no clerk of works, make rough working drawings and details for any trade to submit to the architect.

(f) Keep careful notes of all variations upon the contract to enable his employer to obtain the necessary written orders from the architect and (if there is no clerk of works) to enable the quantity surveyor to obtain correct measurements of the work as carried out.

(g) Assist the architect with advice upon practical questions when requested.

(h) Must be constantly on the job during all working hours.

In order to enable the foreman of building works to carry out his duties, he must possess certain qualifications which are to a great extent similar to those already mentioned in chapter XX, but which are here enumerated in full for the convenience of the reader:

(a) He must be honest, reliable and competent.

(b) He must be temperate in all things.

(c) He must have a thorough and complete knowledge of all the usual building materials and of the manner in which building operations are carried out.

(d) He must be punctual and assiduous in his work.

(e) He must be able to make a simple survey of either land or buildings.

(f) He must have a sound knowledge of building construction and be able to make working drawings and detairls of any trades, and, in fact, be a sort of Admirable Crichton in his work.

(g) He must be methodical in his work of keeping notes, making up accounts, time-sheets, etc, and able to write clearly.

(h) He must possess a considerable amount of tact and patience to enable him to deal with, and sometimes even 'put up with' the architect, client, quantity surveyor, builder, sub-contractors, clerk of works, and workmen.

(j) He must have a general knowledge of the value of work and of the leading items of each trade.

(k) He should be able to use a dumpy level and to set out a building.

(l) He should have a good knowledge of builders' quantities and the way in which work is usually measured by the quantity surveyor.

(m) He must be able to grasp quickly the meaning of the drawings and specification, be fairly well educated, and be pleasant in his manner.

It is of the utmost importance that the foreman and the clerk of works should be on terms of mutual respect, in order that no hitch may occur in the progress of the works, but that everything may proceed smoothly and to the real benefit of everyone concerned. The foreman has a position of authority to maintain, and this should be respected and fostered by the architect and the clerk of works. To him alone should all orders or directions be given, and never to individual workmen. It is the duty of the foreman to look ahead, and to see that all materials are ordered well in advance and delivered on the works by the time they are actually needed.

If this duty is not punctually performed much time is lost and unnecessary expense incurred. The architect and the clerk of works can assist him in this matter by letting him know as early as possible of any proposed variation. Every detail drawing should be checked on the works by the foreman and the measurements verified, so that any discrepancy can be notified to the architect before the work is put in hand. This is especially important in the case of joinery and fittings.

On larger works the Contractor is normally represented by an agent who has under him trade foremen (bricklayer, carpenter, etc) while the firm controls the job from Head Office through a Contract's Manager. At site meetings which are held at regular intervals on any large contract one of the functions of the Contracts Manager is to take the chair and generally co-ordinate matters unless, as sometimes happens, the architect prefers to do this himself.

Chapter XXII
The builder and the workmen

I have not very much to say on this subject, but, as the amicable relationship which should exist between all parties engaged in carrying out a contract depends to a great extent on the attitude adopted by the architect, it is not a matter to be lightly passed over. The views I hold are the result of experience, gained partly in accompanying architects on their visits of inspection and noting the different ways in which they proceed.

In law everyone is presumed to be innocent until he is proved otherwise, and this is as applicable to the builder as to any other class of men. I find that as a rule architects treat him as honestly trying to do his best to carry out the contract and to meet their wishes, and this is, without doubt, the correct attitude. My experience is that, although builders are keen business men, the proportion of black sheep in the flock is by no means abnormally large.

At the same time, you will not be so simple as to imagine that the builder is on the job to act as a philanthropist. It is his business to make the contract pay. With his wide knowledge of materials and their cost, the builder can occasionally make useful suggestions as to variations from the specification. These may be *bona fide* and should be carefully considered, but you should be on your guard, or you may sometimes find you have agreed to the substitution, without deduction, of some material which will cost the builder less than that specified. If you have carefully thought out your specification, there should as a rule be little need to vary it.

I have sometimes been accused of being a little too harsh in my remarks about the average builder and his methods, but if a builder works to the specification, drawings and quantities upon which his estimate has been based, and tries honestly to fulfil all the obligations of his contract, then he has nothing to fear from either the architect or surveyor. It is my good fortune to know many builders who always carry out their contracts with credit to themselves and to all others concerned.

Although your relations with the builder should, if possible, be of a friendly nature, it is perhaps hardly necessary to add that, having regard to the judicial position you occupy, this friendship should never become intimate. This advice is given without any intention of casting a slur on the character either of the architect or the builder; it is simply a precautionary measure based on a knowledge of human nature, and most builders quite understand the position.

An important matter in the relation of architect to builder is the question of responsibility. The Standard Form of Building Contract (1963, revised 1973) omits any specific reference on the subject although in clause 1 of the conditions attached to the form of contract as referred to on page 106, the contractor undertakes to carry out and complete the works in accordance with the directions and to the reasonable satisfaction of the architect. This may be sufficient in most cases in defining the contractor's responsibility, but in special circumstances it may be wise to establish by the insertion of a clause in the bills of quantities or specification or by correspondence or otherwise, that the contractor is to be absolutely responsible for the proper construction and carrying out of the works. I deal in chapter XXIV with the architect's responsibilities. It is most important for the contractor to have a full sense of his duty not only in carrying out the architect's directions faithfully and completely, but also in bringing to his notice all deebatable points both as regards materials and construction. All builders of repute show a full understanding of their responsibility for the simple reason that it is essential for their own reputation. But the architect should be careful not to give directions which override the builder's judgment unless he is perfectly sure that he can accept the full consequences of his own policy.

In cases where you have a clerk of works, it is desirable, when you are inspecting a job, that any directions you find it necessary to give to the builder's foreman should be issued through the clerk of works. Where there is no clerk of works, however, you will, I think, find that the foreman, if he is a capable man, is always anxious to do everything to carry out your wishes; he can often assist you materially, if you are not above giving him a sign that his help is welcome. Often under a rough exterior the foreman hides a very sensitive soul, and a condescending attitude on the part of the architect will shut him up like an oyster. It is most desirable, especially while you are gaining practical experience, that you should make a friend of the foreman. Make no secret of your ignorance on any point of difficulty, and you will find not only that you will obtain much practical assistance, but also that he will not think less of you because you have asked for his advice.

Always take notice of the foreman when you are making your inspections. Nothing annoys him more than being ignored by the architect.

It is quite a mistaken idea that the attitude of the architect is unimportant so far as the workmen are concerned. They are very quick to size up a man, both as regards his ability and his deportment. If an architect comes on to a job and assumes an air of importance and at the same time cannot hide his ignorance, he is not likely to gain the respect of the workmen. Some of you may think it does not matter; but, after all, it is the workmen who convert your designs into actual building, and they will certainly turn out better work if they have friendly feelings towards the architect.

The workmen are quick to resent any irregular interference. In the army an order to a private is seldom given direct by the officer issuing it, and I am sure that, so far as it is practicable, it is best for an architect's directions to reach the workmen by way of the clerk of works and the builder's foreman. It is no doubt very annoying for an architect to find a workman making a bad job of some special bit of work, but even so, it is a mistake to express displeasure direct to the workmen, and worse still to convey it in unparliamentary language. The foreman is generally quite competent to undertake this duty and to employ words such as the workmen understand. Although from a competent and friendly architect the workmen will take almost anything, they prefer to be dealt with in the proper way. You must be prepared for wide differences in building practice, and even language, in various parts of the country, and information regarding these matters can be obtained in no other way than from the workmen themselves. A friendly interest in the men and in their local methods and materials will save you from many blunders and let you into many secrets which will prove invaluable.

Chapter XXI
The builder's foreman

A foreman in the building trade is a man appointed by a builder to take charge, under his orders, of building works, to see that they are properly and efficiently carried out, not only to his employer's satisfaction and profit, but also to the satisfaction of the architect and client.

The foreman is paid by the builder, who has to include in his estimate for the services of a foreman as well as for providing him with a suitable office on the works. As architect you will have no control over the salary paid to the foreman, though you should be asked to sanction this if you are carrying out a prime cost job. A good foreman can command a salary of £3000 per annum or more.

Before appointing a foreman the builder frequently discusses the proposed appointment with the architect; in fact, I know of many cases where the architect has taken the initiative and expressed a desire that a certain man should be appointed. This is the case when an architect gets to know a man well and is satisfied with the way in which he has already conducted one of his works.

It is important to the builder and everyone else concerned that the foreman should be a really reliable, competent and experienced man. As a rule he is one who by steady perseverance, intelligence and study has raised himself above the ordinary level of a first-class workman.

The foreman is paid as a rule an inclusive salary, and not at a rate per hour (or per week) as the ordinary workmen are paid; and his hours of work are apt to be much longer than those of the workmen. Frequently, in addition to his salary, the builder offers to his foreman a payment, by way of bonus, upon the financially successful completion of the job, and this provides an additional incentive to the foreman to use his best endeavours to carry out the work well and economically.

The duties of a foreman of building works consist in arranging for the carrying out of the actual work on a building, and may be enumerated as follows:

(a) Set out the whole of the works in full detail from the plans supplied by the architect.

(b) Order the whole of the materials and engage the necessary labour required to carry out the work.

(c) Direct the whole of the men under his control, in order to obtain the very best advantage out of their work.

(d) See that all the work is executed in the right and best possible

RIBA Conditions of Engagement will generally enable you to decide the correct charges and it also gives guidance as to when fees become due.

For quantities there is also a scale published by the Royal Institution of Chartered Surveyors and this varies from 2.5 to 3% upon the amount of the accepted tender, in proportion to the nature and extent of the work performed. Fees for the preparation of quantities can be charged in

No. 3 Messrs John Williams and Co. Ltd

18 Blank Street, SW1

VAT Registration No. . . . .

Date . . . . .

Tax Point . . . . .

Invoice No. . . .

To William Smith
Architect

	£
To Architect's Commission of 6% on account of Works at Century Works, Brighton, and on amount of certificate to Messrs Brown & Sons, dated 20 July 1973 for £500	300.00
Less 4% already received	200.00
	£100.00
Paid Travelling and Incidental Expenses on account	15.00
Paid Clerk of Works' Salary	
	£115.00
Add Value Added Tax at 10%.	11.50
	£126.50

addition to your fees as architect. Fees for measuring and adjusting variations upon the contract are also governed by RICS scales and should be charged separately.

Where a professional quantity surveyor is appointed it is usual for his fees to be paid by the client direct.

There are three ways of dealing with consultants' fees (steelwork and reinforced concrete, heating, hot water, electrical, etc). One is to include a sum of money in the quantities and let the contractor pay upon the architect's certificate. This procedure would need the consent of your client, though this, in my experience is seldom obtained. The second is for the architect to pay the fees himself: and the third is to follow the procedure laid down in the RIBA Conditions of Engagement and nominate or approve the consultants in agreement with the client and the payment of their fees shall be a matter of arrangement bettwween the consultants and client. Undoubtedly the last mentioned way is the most satisfactory to the architect, though it involves the client in the payment of the consultant's as well as the architect's fees, or something like 11 to 12%, upon the electric light installation or the constructional steelwork, or any other work for which a consultant is employed.

District surveyor's fees are somewhat different from those already

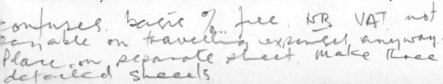

mentioned. A clause is usually put in the specification and/or quantities to the effect that the contractor must pay all fees to local authorities, etc, and the district surveyor's fees would come under this clause and be paid by the contractor. If, however, you find it necessary in any particular case to check his fees, this can best be done by referring to the district surveyor who can explain that the fees are based on the cost of the work coming under his control as defined in the appropriate GLC General Powers Act.

You may wish to know the right way for an architect to present his account, and the form given here has been made up from one in actual use for interim payments.

In letting me see the form which my friend always uses, he gave me the following advice, which I think is so admirable that I give it exactly as he told me. 'I think all architects should make it a definite practice to state clearly in their accounts what they are charging for. The commission should be given clearly — that is, the full rate of commission should be shown and any proportion received at the beginning should be credited (see form). Travelling and incidental expenses must be the actual amounts expended, and should not include the cost of additional copies of plans, etc, which it is best to charge in the final account.'

Value Added Tax at the current rate must, of course, be added to the total charge of both fees and expenses for any work carried out after the 1 April 1973 and you will find a reference to this in the RIBA Conditions of Engagement.

The final account presented to the client when the work has been completed and the contractor's accounts have been agreed should show the total charges. There are many services in the course of important works that justify fees over and above the fixed commission, and these must be set forth quite clearly with, wherever possible, the date of the client's instructions. It is wise to make your final account as brief and concise as possible, and to avoid bringing in a number of small services which though strictly outside the implied terms of your engagement are such as might reasonably be included in the scale fees.

It would be unnecessary if my book reached members of the profession alone to add that in no circumstances does an architect receive any monetary consideration from anyone but his client. But there are people so ignorant of professional etiquette as to imagine that an architect makes money in various ways from the transactions which he has to undertake. To these people it should be explained that an architect's work is to protect his client's interests, not only in planning and ensuring good buildings, but in selecting materials and fittings which give proper value for their cost. Such professional services cannot be given unless the architect is free of all obligations to a third party, and it is only necessary to quote from the Code of Professional Conduct of the RIBA clauses 2 and 3, to show how important this matter is considered. The clauses read as follows: 'A member or student is remunerated solely by his professional fees payable by his client or by a salary payable by his employer. He is debarred from any other source of remuneration in connection with the works and duties entrusted to him. . . . A member or student must not accept any work which involves the giving or receiving of discounts or commissions, nor must he accept any discount, gift or commission from contractors or tradesmen, whether employed upon his works or not'. In the case of a registered architect who is not a member of the RIBA the Code of Professional Conduct issued by The Architects Registration Council of the United Kingdom applies and it contains similar provisions.

All trade discounts are passed on to the client, and if any tradesmen or contractor ventures to suggest that any discount, commission or other consideration be paid to the architect he should immediately be made to understand that such a proposal disqualifies him from doing any future business.

Chapter XXIV
Responsibility of architects

It is absolutely essential that an architect should possess a knowledge of the legal side of his practice, including not only the conditions of contract and other formal documents relating to building work, but also the decisions of the Courts on various typical cases relating to the responsibility of the architect and the legal position of the client, the quantity surveyor, and the contractor. If you are wise you will study this subject by consulting some book of reference and noting the cases which have been before the Courts; for those who learn by experience usually purchase their experience dearly. The architect, however, is under no obligation to understand and expound legal documents, and where difficulties occur in the elucidation of such documents he is entitled to call upon his client's legal adviser, after obtaining the consent of his client.

The architect is employed by the building owner to look after his interests and becomes his general agent for all purposes relating to designing, obtaining tenders for and superintending the building of work upon which he is employed. You will understand that, acting as the agent of your client, you must be very careful not to commit him in any way which may cause trouble. If you are not sure of your authority, say in regard to the ordering of additional work, it is always advisable to consult your client, and thus make him responsible.

There are, of course, many things in connection with the carrying out of a contract where the architect has complete power. He has authority to make alterations in his details, or to vary the materials to be used, provided that the alterations do not affect the carrying out of the work in accordance with his client's instructions. For example, he is at liberty to alter the detail or size of mouldings, or to change one material for another, such as square red floor tiles for oblong tiles, but he has no authority to make radical alterations, and this is a point you must be very careful about. Possibly in a certain case you may not have had sufficient time to design your building to your complete satisfaction; but during the execution of the work you may have a brain-wave and desire to make a rather extensive alteration in your plans. This is what I mean by a radical alteration, and if you find yourself in this position your duty is to put the whole matter before your client, leaving him to decide whether or not the alteration shall be made. Remember that your drawings and specifications must be adhered to once approved and if you afterwards discover an omission without which the work cannot be completed, or that for some reason the work is impracticable, you are not empowered, without your *[handwritten marginal note at top: "An administrator of the contract according to the terms of the contract)"]*

[handwritten note: "No!"]

client's authority, to order extras to put the matter right.

We have seen that under the usual contract the architect occupies a very important position, and becomes in many instances an arbitrator with very great powers. These powers he must exercise honestly and impartially, otherwise he may find himself in a very difficult position.

There are many other questions which are liable to arise if an architect is not fully equipped with professional knowledge or is negligent in the performance of his duties. For instance, if structural defects arise, and it can be shown that these are due to faulty design, or if, through lack of supervision or negligence, defective workmanship is permitted, the client may decide to claim damages against the architect. He is also responsible if he certifies the payment of a larger amount than is actually due. In short, it is no light matter to accept a commission. It is assumed that an architect who does so is fully capable, and any failure on his part may bring upon him much trouble, although, legally, it appears to be somewhat difficult to proceed against him with success unless great negligence or carelessness can be proved. It should be remembered that although the contractor's liability to make good defects in his work is limited to the period mentioned in his contract agreement the liability of the architect to the client for negligence only terminates under the Limitation Act 1939 at the end of six years from the date when damage occurs as a result of the act of negligence. *[handwritten note: "is discovered!"]*

In all your work it is of the highest importance that you should always feel the grave responsibility attaching to your position as architect, and that you should always have before your mind the serious consequences which are bound to attend any lack of vigilance on your part. Legal responsibility is a difficult matter to define, and, in order to save your own reputation, you must not rely absolutely on the clause in your specification which allocates responsibility to the contractor. It is only reasonable that the contractor should accept in his agreement the full responsibility for the work, seeing that he is employed in actual construction; the architect is, however, by the nature of things limited to inspection at stated intervals. It is held in some quarters that, as a professional man, the architect advises his client to the best of his ability, and that, other things being equal, he should not be penalised because his advice proves to have been not the best possible in the circumstances, provided always that his bona fides are not questioned. The argument is that building works involve a financial outlay altogether out of proportion to a professional man's means, and no architect could engage in business if he could be mulcted financially for every error of judgment or omission to discover defects. On the other hand, the client must have some legal remedy when an architect is at fault, and if he can prove negligence, he can obtain heavy damages.

It is fair to say that in ordinary business the architect need not fear serious evasion of responsibility by the builder, or unreasonable retaliation on the part of his client, but since in life the unexpected so often happens, it behoves the young architect to be constantly on his guard, and to assure himself that the advice that he gives is sound, that his plans and details are in every case proper for their purpose, and that no work is carried out without his full knowledge and approval. If he ever has to face any trouble he will find that his best defence will be to produce the jackets referred to in chapter IV or his letter file or diary showing that he has spared no pains to attend to the interests of his client.

No doubt you are all well aware that under Section 1 of the Architects Registration Act 1938 a person must not practise or carry on business under any name, style or title containing the word 'Architect' unless he is registered under the Architects Registration Act 1931, although a person may use the title although it is provided that nothing in Section 1 shall affect the use of the designation Naval architect, Landscape architect or Golf-course architect.

It is, of course, desirable that all architects should be members of the Royal Institute of British Architects, and essential that they should observe the various rules, etc, which have been laid down for governing the professional conduct and practice of architects. I strongly advise you all to read these rules most carefully and endeavour to make your practice conform to them, though I expect there are times when some of the regulations will be difficult to carry out. You may be sure, however, that your responsibilities will be lessened if you abide by the rules, and you will always be able to seek the advice and assistance of the Institute whenever you are in any difficulty. If you ignore the regulations, however, your position will become more difficult, and you will be unable successfully to call upon your Institute for counsel and advice.

You may be interested to know that a scheme of insurance exists whereby architects can cover themselves against all claims based on alleged neglect, default, omission, or error on their part or on the part of their assistants. I believe there is no fixed rate of premiums such as obtains in an ordinary insurance, but each case is considered by the Insurers and the premium quoted before the indemnity policy is entered into. This 'Architects' indemnity insurance' was introduced in 1922 immediately following the decision of the Council of the Royal Institute of British Architects not to proceed with the Defence Union proposals. The Secretary of the Architects' Benevolent Society will, no doubt, be pleased to supply all necessary particulars.

An important subject to which you must give attention is that of Architectural Copyright. It is important because you should know how to protect your own rights and how to avoid infringing the rights of others. Those of you who have studied architecture will be familiar with the fact that in all the great periods there has been a marked consistency of style and detail, in fact architects have seen a virtue in following one another's lead in considering the elements of design as common property. I may therefore seem strange at first sight that there should be copyright in architecture. But a little reflection will show that, if one architect, after great labour and trouble, has arrived at a certain solution of a particular problem, whether it be a country cottage or the business premises of a company, he should have some protection from its being lightly copied or reproduced by someone who has been to no pains at all in solving the problem himself. Under the Copyright Act of 1956 the author has the exclusive right to produce or reproduce the work or any substantial part thereof in any material form whatsoever, and this copyright lies in every original artistic work, a term that includes works of architecture being either buildings, which term includes any structure, or models for buildings. The copyright is deemed to be infringed by any person who, without the consent of the owner of the copyright, does anything, the exclusive right to do which is conferred by the Act on the owner of the copyright.

It is clear that no architect, who has any self respect, will wish to obtain advantage for himself by making use of another architect's designs without the latter's consent. This is not to say that an excellent discovery which should benefit everyone need be denied to other practitioners, but that the author of the discovery should not be robbed of the reward of his skill. The question of what constitutes infringement of copyright and what does not is by no means a simple matter in so multifarious an art as architecture, and it may be that this difficulty will be reflected in the verdicts given by Courts of Law in the future. It is also quite clear, I think, that copyright in architects' drawings is absolute whether they have, or have not, artistic merit, whereas it would only be an infringement to copy a building (without reference to drawings) if the building had artistic merit.

I will take two cases as illustrations of the points that are likely to arise. The case of *Kenneth Dalgliesh v The Sandown Urban District Council* occurred in 1926, a report of which may be seen in the *Builder* of 9 April 1926. Mr Dalgliesh had been commissioned to design a bungalow, which was erected in 1923. In 1925, without any reference to the architect, the Council caused a similar bungalow to be erected which was found to be an exact copy (with the exception only of a few minor details) of the building designed by Mr Dalgliesh. In this case it is interesting to note that not only the chairman and members of the Council were sued but also the surveyor to the Council and the builder. Before the case came into Court the Urban District Council admitted the infringement and damages were duly awarded to the architect. This was a clear case of the improper use of a specific design without the consent of the architect.

The case of *Meikle v Maufe*, which is reported in the *Builder* of 8 August 1941, and also in the RIBA *Journal* of August 1941, was an entirely different one. It concerned the extension of an existing building and the virtual reproduction of the original front on the extended portion. The defence, in so far as the reproduction was admitted, was that this reproduction was necessary in the interest of architectural design, both as a duty to the owners of the building and to the public. This defence was, however, deemed to be insufficient and the case is worth reading in detail to ascertain how precisely the law works upon this matter between architect and architect.

You will be wise to give your client an opportunity of knowing that the copyright of your original drawing remains with you as their author and you cannot do this better than by giving him a copy of the RIBA Conditions of Engagement, which expressly state that 'Copyright in all drawings and in the work executed from them, except drawings and works for the Crown, will remain the property of the architect unless otherwise agreed'.

There are certain safeguards against the misuse of litigation which might make the copyright law a constant menace to architects. One of these is the necessity for the complainant to prove that his design was known to the architect who is accused of reproducing it. It is not at all impossible that two designers might arrive independently at practically the same solution of a simple problem and clause 17(2) of the Act provides for this contingency by stating that the plaintiff is not entitled to any remedy other than an injunction, if the defendant proves that he was not aware that copyright existed, and so the latter will not be liable to pay damages but may have to account for profits in respect of the infringement. Further, clause 17(4) of the Act avoids a whole series of responsibilities of a financial character or otherwise by stating that where the construction of a building, which if completed, would infringe the copyright, has been commenced, the owner of the copyright shall not be entitled to obtain an injunction to stop erection or to order the demolition of the building. In other words, the question at issue will be one of compensation only. Under the Limitation Act 1939 normally any action for infringement may not be commenced after the expiration of six years from the date of the infringement.

The term for which copyright exists is defined as the life of the author and a period of fifty years from the end of the calendar year in which he died.

You will also have to deal with *Town and Country Planning and Compulsory Purchase* and I would advise you to read a recent book on the subject by A J Lomnicki which I have included in the list of technical books which you will find in the *Appendix* page 240.

Chapter XXV
Testing drains

You must, of course, be prepared to inspect and test drains. Very little practice is required to enable you to do this, and it is desirable to learn the business before you actually have a case of your own. Take the first opportunity to visit a new building where a good but simple drainage system has been carried out, and carefully watch the test which will be made either by the sanitary engineer employed or by the surveyor to the local authority. Tests are made by water, smoke, air and odour.

You will find that the apparatus required for the water test is simple. Two or three drain plugs or pneumatic bags of different sizes, say, for 4" (100 mm) and 6" (150 mm) diameter pipes, and one or two short lengths of rubber tubing to insert in gully traps to let the air out of the pipes when you turn on the water. Commence your test by opening up all the manholes, putting a plug into the drain in the manhole nearest the sewer, and carefully securing it to prevent any possibility of a leakage of water. Then turn on all the taps that are available, and fill up the whole system with water, not forgetting to let the air out of the pipes by means of the rubber tubes inserted right through the water seal of the gully traps. When you have managed to get the drains and manholes full of water you must carefully note the exact height of water in the manholes. This can be done by sticking a small piece of stamp-paper at the actual level of the water. Then leave the water in the drains while you proceed with some other part of your work, such as inspecting the sanitary fittings, etc. If after a reasonable lapse of time, say an hour, the water is still at the same level you may be satisfied that your drains are all right, but be on the look-out that no one adds a little water whilst you are busy elsewhere, thus keeping up the level of water in a leaky drain or manhole.

Obviously in any but a simple system it will be wise to apply the test section by section, for otherwise you may find there is a leak somewhere but not be able to locate it. In these cases you should start at the top of the system so that the water can be used again by flowing down from manhole to manhole. New drains should be tested first before the trenches are filled in, but you must always apply a final test as described above and, whether the drains be new or old be sure that the manhole covers are properly bedded and sealed afterwards.

In one of my building alterations I had to order the drains to be relaid no less than three times before they would hold water. You must be adamant on this subject, and not rest content or pass the drains unless they are perfectly watertight. I have heard of some authorities who insist on the drains holding water for three days before they will pass them, but this, of course, is absurd.

Before you finish your test you should look through the drains to see whether the drainlayer has cleared all the cement from the inside of the pipes. This can easily be done by holding a small mirror in the manhole and looking into it. If the length of drain is long and you cannot see right to the end, then an electric light or an electric flash-lamp placed in the manhole next above the one in which you are holding the mirror, and casting its light down the drain towards the mirror, will often help. If you see bits of cement at the joints you must insist upon having them removed, and must see for yourself that this is done.

The mirror is also useful to show whether the undersides of the joints in the drain pipes have been properly and carefully made, and whether the invert of the drain has been laid true — that is, without any steps in it at the joints, which, if allowed to remain, would have the effect of holding up paper and similar obstructions and ultimately lead to the choking of the drain. When the drainlayer sees that you are taking such care in testing the drains, you may be certain that he will take special care to make a good job of them. You will find that a good workman really takes a pride in doing his work well. The portion of the joint in a drain which is out of sight should be as neatly finished off as the upper part which is in full view, but often this is not done.

Test the drains in your own way. Do not let the builder tell you how to do it; and always include the manholes as well as the drains, as it is quite as important that the manholes should be as watertight as the drains themselves. In cases where a clerk of works is employed on the building I expect you will let him do the testing for you, but it is always wise for the architect to be present at the test. Then, again, the surveyor to the local authority will want to test the drains, and this test is often accepted by the architect. I do not, however, advise this, because, although the local surveyor and his inspectors have no doubt a large experience in this way, they are not infallible, and, after all, you, as architect, will be held responsible should any defect appear after the work is finished and the building occupied. So make up your mind to do your own testing, at any rate until you can employ someone whom you can trust. If there is no clerk of works you will find the foreman is always ready and willing to help you, and will provide all the necessary plugs, etc.

I remember a case of an alteration to a house in Kent where some new drains were added to an existing system. The surveyor of the local authority tested the new portion, but took no notice of the old. When I went to test the drains the foreman told me that there was no need to do this, as the local surveyor had passed them. However, I insisted on testing the old as well as the new drains, and found to my surprise that, although the new drains were watertight, the system as a whole was leaky. Naturally, I complained to the local surveyor, who informed me that he had only tested the new drains, as he had no authority to test the old ones. I subsequently found that the surveyor was correct, and that under the Public Health Act 1936, he had no power to apply a water test under pressure to old drains.

In the case of existing drains the same test should be employed as for new, but, of course, you will not be able to see the outside joints of the pipes. The mirror will, however, still prove of use in the manholes. If you find any leakage of water in the drains under or quite near the house, you must condemn the system and advise your client to have it put right, either by having the system relaid or the pipes and manholes treated in such a way as to render them watertight. Then will be the time to discuss the matter with a good sanitary engineer or plumber who is acquainted with testing and repairing old drains. When the drains are laid from the house to some distant point at a lower level than the house, say across a field, and discharge into a cesspit, if the pipes will not stand the water test, if may be unnecessary to condemn them merely on that account. Full consideration should be given to this in order to save your client expense. You may have to examine some drainage which discharges into a disposal system consisting of open jointed pipes laid some way below the surface of the ground. If there are defects in some of the pipes leading to the disposal system there is not likely to be much danger to health, and they can probably be left untouched, provided that the pipes are not too leaky to allow all the flushing water to escape, leaving no means for carrying on the solids and paper to the cesspool or other points of discharge. You will have to decide such cases for yourself. I believe that opinion varies very much as to the advisability of applying the water test to old drains, for few systems of stoneware drains that have been in existence for any considerable length of time will pass such a test satisfactorily, although in operation the drains may give no trouble. Therefore you may have to be content with a smoke test, provided no major defects are apparent and the drains are satisfactory in other respects and have a suitable fall (shown by the velocity of sewage passing through). I believe it is for this reason that local authorities will pass drains that show no defects under a smoke test, provided they are properly trapped and ventilated. In any circumstances I should be reluctant to apply a water test to old stoneware drains without first obtaining consent of the owner, after pointing out to him the possibility of causing damage to the system from the pressure applied, and making the position as regards liability for damage quite clear. You must bear this point in mind should you have to give instructions to test old drains. The liability will become greater if you are concerned with a 'combined' system of drainage.

The odour test is useful where a drain or soil pipe cannot be sealed off or put out of use for the time necessary to apply a smoke or water test. This test consists of passing into the drain or pipe an essence or composition of chemicals which, on contact with water, give off a distinctive smell. The odour thus generated quickly fills the drain or pipe and, should there be a defect the odour will quickly make itself apparent through the defect. The method of applying this test is to use the chemical composition placed in a hinged metal container, kept closed by a cord wrapped around the outside. The free end of the cord must be attached to some fixed object near a wc pan or gully trap and the container placed in the pan or trap, which must then be flushed with water into the pipe or drain. The cord, unwinding as the container passes through the trap, causes it to open and water coming into contact with the chemical generates the gas. The position of the leak, should there be one, may be detected by the smell of distinctive odour of the gas in the vicinity of the defect. I have used this test on one occasion only and found it satisfactory, but I believe many sanitary engineers regard it as inconclusive and expect to have to make further tests to locate tthe position of the defect.

I believe the local sanitary authorities have power to test drainage systems by the smoke test, when application has been made to them by tenants of houses. The smoke test, with a machine of reputable make, is important, but is not nearly as reliable as the water test, as it cannot be expected that smoke will find its way through some thickness of dense clay which may overlay the drains. However, it will often find defects at the higher levels to which the water will not reach and in cases where the drains are not accessible by manholes. In the case of soil pipes this method is very useful. The smoke machine should be attached to a gully trap or air inlet. The vent pipes should not be stopped up until the smoke is seen to escape from them. This may seem unimportant, but I know of one case at least where the bend at the foot of a vent pipe (not a soil pipe) was fully choked with rest, etc.

Before commencing a test you should get some idea of the gradient of the drains. If they are of stoneware and the gradient is very steep, you may find, on filling the drains and manholes with water, that you have forced open the joints with the pressure put upon them. A $5'\ 0''$ head of water is, I think, about the limit for stoneware drains, but iron ones will stand a head of water up to $30'\ 0''$ or $40'\ 0''$. If you want to get a head of water in a very flat section of drain, this can easily be obtained by having a bend and a length of straight pipe fixed with joints, made in clay or plaster of paris, on the upper end of the drain.

The air test is rarely applied to drains, as the water test is much more convenient and reliable. A stoneware pipe drain may be perfectly water-tight, but it may not be airtight if any considerable pressure of air is applied, as the air under pressure may percolate through the cement joints when water would not do so. An air test under any considerable pressure may therefore be regarded as unfair to apply to a stoneware pipe drain, as, after all, it is mainly water with which the drains have to deal.

The apparatus consists of some rubber discs of various sizes to fit the tops of the soil and vent pipes having screwed connections in the centre; also a U-shaped glass gauge and tube fixed to stand and having a scale marked on each leg in parts of inches. When testing soil and vent pipes with air, the lower end is fitted with a stopper, and about a gallon or so of water is poured down the pipe on to the stopper in order that the latter shall be airtight. The disc is then placed in the upper end of the pipe, and the tube attached to the gauge is connected to the centre of the disc. The tube is then slipped off the gauge and the pipe blown into or air pumped into it through a small pipe. The end of the tube nearest the gauge is then pinched between the finger and thumb to retain the air in the pipe whilst the tube is being re-connected to the gauge. The result is that the air-pressure now in the vent pipe will force the water with which the gauge is charged up one leg of the glass tube. If the vent pipe is sound the water will remain at this level, but if the slightest leak exists it will fall until it is again level in both legs of the gauge. As a rule the air test is applied without interfering with the traps to the wcs, and it is therefore not possible to apply more pressure than the seal of the trap will withstand.

Although the air test quickly indicates any leakage, it is often difficult to discover where this is occurring, and in this respect the smoke test becomes useful, as this test, applied by means of a good machine, will more often than not locate the exact point of leakage. It will not always do so, however, and in that case it would be wise to call in a sanitary engineer of experience, who has a variety of methods and appliances at his disposal for his daily work of locating defects.

In the case of small tests, such as a single-soil pipe, smoke rockets if you can obtain them are effective, and may be used with advantage.

Chapter XXVI
The London building acts

[handwritten annotation: Std ref is by Pitt + Dufton see Bibliography.]

Revised with the assistance of J. Dufton *FRICS, C.Eng, MIStructE.*
District Surveyor for Westminster

With the object of securing the sound and hygienic construction of buildings, the diminution of danger arising from fire, the provision of sufficient light, air and space and generally of protecting the interests of the public, various Acts of Parliament have been passed and powers given to local authorities to make by-laws and regulations and to control building operations. Until 1966 the somewhat complicated arrangement of local authorities having their own set of rules obtained but since then, all local authorities (except Inner London — the former London County Council Area) operate under Building Regulations made by the Central Government and you should always have a copy of these Regulations at hand for reference whenever your practice concerns work outside Inner London, for you must always design your buildings and write your specifications in conformity with the Regulations. It is interesting to note that the number of local authorities will be much reduced under the forthcoming reorganisation of Local Government.

In Inner London — the old LCC area — controlled by the London Building Acts, by-laws are still made under the enabling powers of these Acts by the Greater London Council since it was formed in 1965. I understand, however, that it is the Government's ultimate aim to have a National Building Act and Regulations applicable throughout England and Wales including London although it may be some years before this is achieved.

You must understand that I am not going to try to explain all the intricacies of the Acts. It would not be fitting in this book even were I competent to do so. I want to give you, as it were, an introduction to the London Building Acts, and then leave you to make use of this in order to get a good working knowledge of the subject.

I can quite imagine that to many of you the subject will seem an extremely dry one, and, perhaps you may think it is too difficult for you to master and so may be tempted to leave it alone, but the point to remember is that it will not leave you alone. I believe you will find my hints for dealing with the Acts of assistance, and that they will help you to thread your way through them as far as it is necessary for you to do so. You may be troubled by the legal phraseology, and it will require quite a lot of experience to enable you to separate the unimportant matter from that which is essential. At first you will be unable to do this quickly, but experience and study should eventually overcome this difficulty.

In dealing with difficult subjects there are always two ways, the one to make light of the difficulties and minimise the troubles as much as possible — and the other to make difficulties and imagine more troubles than really exist. I will follow the first way, and treat the London Building Acts in as simple a manner as possible, trying to show you how to get out of certain difficulties that may arise.

There are three main Acts for us to consider:

(a) The London Building Act 1930
(b) The London Building Act (Amendment) Act 1935
(c) The London Building Acts (Amendment) Act 1939

and subsequently other important Acts such as the London Government Act 1963, the Offices, Shops and Railway Premises Act 1963 and the Fire Precautions Act 1971.

The 1963 Act brought into being the Greater London Council and repeated Parts II and III and Sections 51-53 of the London Building Act 1930, together with certain sections of the London Building Acts (Amendment) Act 1939. The major provisions of the latter however still remain in force. The second and third of the above Acts override many of the Building Act provisions for means of escape in case of fire thus confirming the trend towards common standards applicable over the whole Country. You will, of course, not find it necessary to learn off by heart all the clauses of the Acts, etc., but you will want to know sufficient to be able to steer your client safely through them and to avoid landing him in a law suit. It is more important to your client to have his building erected quickly and without unnecessary trouble and expense than to have a finely designed facade. What I mean is, your reputation will not suffer, so far as he is concerned, nearly as much on account of a faulty design as it will if you let him in for a law suit.

No two cases are ever quite alike, and the actual text of the Acts, by-laws and regulations must nearly always be consulted. No architect with a good practice can devote enough time to the study of the Acts, etc, to enable him to know them in full detail; nor is this necessary. If we can examine them sufficiently to enable you to know what sections to study and which to leave alone, we shall have made some progress.

I must explain that the London Building Acts 1930 to 1939 formed the basis of the government of London as regards building. The Act of 1930 was passed in order to consolidate the enactments relating to streets and buildings in London and was almost entirely repealed by the Acts of 1935 and 1939, as will be seen from the statement of repealed enactments given in the third schedule attached to the 1939 Act. We shall consider the Parts of the 1930 Act still in force in due course. The Act of 1935 was passed in order to revise certain provisions of the 1930 Act relative to the construction of buildings and structures and to give the Council power to effect alterations in certain of the matters concerned with such construction by means of by-laws. This is a much more simple method than having to obtain a new Act or the amendment of an existing Act every time an alteration is desired. Another important matter dealt with in the 1935 Act is that of modification or waiver of by-laws. It is possible in certain circumstances to obtain permission to construct a building or a part of a building that is not strictly in accordance with the by-laws and Section 9 of the Act outlines the procedure for obtaining a waiver.

The Act of 1939 came into operation on the first day of January 1940, and was passed in order to amend the Act of 1930, to repeal and re-enact other provisions and to bring the building law of London up to date. It is divided into twelve parts as follows:

Part		
	I	Introductory
	II	Naming and numbering of streets, buildings, etc
	III	Construction of buildings
	IV	Special and temporary buildings and structures
	V	Means of escape in case of fire
	VI	Rights, etc, of building and adjoining owners
	VII	Dangerous and neglected structures
	VIII	Sky signs (since repealed)
	IX	Superintending architect, district surveyors and fees
	X	By-laws
	XI	Legal proceedings
	XII	Miscellaneous

The Act of 1939 is the most important one, and I advise you all to study it.

Part I of the Act of 1939 deals almost exclusively with definitions. Now definitions of any kind are important, but specially so when given in an Act of Parliament relating to building. Therefore be careful to ascertain whether the definition in the Act coincides with the meaning you are accustomed to attach to the term. You may find that, under the London Building Acts, the terms mean something different from what you may have supposed.

I have made a note of several terms in the Acts; for example, what is a public building? What is an external wall, a party wall, a party fence wall, a dwelling-house, a domestic building? I am not going to reply to these questions, because you can find the answers in the text of the Acts, though you must remember that the definitions given in the 1939 Act must be considered in conjunction with the definitions in the 1930 Act, some of which have not been repealed. There are two other definitions which you will often meet with *viz* the 'building owner' and the 'adjoining owner'. When building in London you will have quite a lot to do with the adjoining owner; you will find a definition of this term in the 1930 Act, and you must know exactly what the term means.

Part II of the Act deals with the naming and numbering of streets, buildings, etc, and can be left alone, though it is interesting to note the great care which must be given to the wording of an Act when we find a clause such as this. 'For the purpose of subsection (1) of this section a number followed by a letter or a fraction shall be deemed to be a number'. You may like to know the system employed in London for numbering houses in streets. St Paul's Cathedral is recognised as a central point, and the numbering begins at the end or entrance of the street nearest to that building, except where a street leads from a main thorough-fare. Taking the sides of a street as left and right (assuming that the back is towards St Paul's or towards the main thoroughfare, as the case may be) the odd numbers are assigned to the left-hand side, and the even numbers to the right-hand side.

Part III relates to the construction of buildings and gives directions as to alterations to party walls, bay windows and turrets, roof drainage, total height of buildings, construction of public buildings, etc. You must study this part of the Act, Part VI of the 1930 Act, which has now been repealed, contained detailed directions as to the thickness of walls, the necessary information being given in the second schedule to the Act. It also contained provisions with respect to buildings of metal skeleton construction and reinforced concrete; it defined the heights of rooms and of party walls above the roof, together with many other important matters which are now dealt with in the London Building (Constructional) By-laws 1972, made by the GLC in pursuance of the London Building Acts 1930-1939, to which reference will be made later.

Part IV concerns special and temporary buildings and structures which may be erected under certain conditions, and generally after obtaining a licence from the Greater London Council.

Part V deals with the means of escape from buildings in case of fire and must be carefully considered. Some further definitions are given and must be taken into consideration when dealing with this Part of the Act. A separate publication has been issued giving principles for the guidance of applicants in the preparation of proposals to be submitted for the Council's approval under this section of the Act, and it is recommended that you obtain a copy of this booklet which will help you to understand these requirements and enable you to obtain approval to your designs so much quicker. You must also have careful regard to the Fire Precautions Act 1963 to which I have already referred.

Part VI, referring to the rights, etc, of building and adjoining owners, is most important, and must be studied very carefully. I advise you to give a good deal of attention to this Part, and to make a careful precis of all sections and really try to understand it, for you will constantly be coming in contact with this Part of the Act when you build in London. I think the best way to explain this Part will be to examine shortly the case of a building in London with which I was concerned as surveyor. In order to help us to understand the position I have prepared a rough diagram or block plan, and I propose to relate exactly what took place. It was proposed to remodel the interior of an existing building at 971 Blank Street, for use as offices, leaving the front elevation as before. It commenced simply as an alteration job, and the architect, having no idea at all that the work would be infringing the rights of the adjoining owners, designed the alterations, wrote the specification, allowed his client to enter into a contract, and the work was proceeded with. The first thing to disturb the serenity of the proceedings was a letter from the surveyor to the owners of the property marked C saying that it was assumed, from the knocking that was going on, that building operations were in progress, and that the party wall was being interfered with. He asked for plans to be submitted,and a party structure notice to be served. I soon found out that this surveyor represented only one very small interest in the building. He was inclined to make a great deal of fuss, and I came to the conclusion

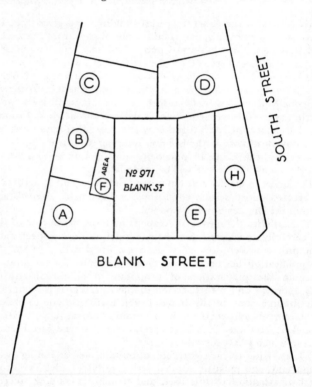

that he was anxious for a job. In reply to his letter the architect said he would be pleased to show the plans, but that as he was doing nothing to the party wall he had no intention of serving any party structure notice. This ended the matter, for the moment, as far as the property marked C was concerned.

Before proceeding further, you may like to hear something about a party structure notice. Under this Part of the Act it is laid down that a building owner shall not, except with the consent of the adjoining owner, exercise any of his rights under the Act in respect of a party wall unless at least two months before doing so he has served on the adjoining owner a party structure notice stating the nature and particulars of the proposed work, the time at which it will be begun and, if it is proposed to construct special foundations, plans, sections and details must be sent. 'Special foundations' are stated to mean in this Part of the Act 'Foundations in which an assemblage of steel beams or rods is employed for the purpose of distributing any load'. You can obtain a form of party structure notice published by the RIBA, and this form can be filled in to suit your particular case. There are also several other forms which may be used in connection with party structures which should be consulted. Whenever you have anything to do with a party wall, however small, say cutting a few holes to take the ends of steel joists — be sure you see the adjoining owner and let him know exactly what you are proposing to do. It may not be necessary to go through all the formalities of a party structure notice and award, as he may give you permission at once without appointing a surveyor to look after his interests. You must remember that the adjoining owner can demand the two months' notice, and this delay may be a serious thing for your client. I was recently interested in a case where delay in building involved considerable daily loss to my client. Therefore, see the adjoining owner at the earliest opportunity and be open and frank with him; you will find it the best plan in the long run.

But, to proceed with our case. You will notice that No 971 is almost surrounded by other buildings. The portion marked F is an area common to three different buildings. After the work was actually commenced the scheme was revised, and now involved the raising of a portion of the external wall of No. 971 on one side of the area. The first thing to be done was to find out who was the owner of the property marked A, and it was discovered that it belonged to a large corporation, that they had leased the building to a society, that the ground floor was underleased to a tradesman, and that all the upper floors were leased to various professional people and used as offices. To get this information took quite a long time and much patience. Now, under the London Building Acts it is necessary to serve a party structure notice upon practically everyone concerned — I understand that yearly tenants are about the only persons who can be ignored — so we had to find out the names of all the persons who had been granted leases of the rooms on every floor adjoining our premises, and as the building marked A was of many storeys this was a most formidable proceeding. However, in due time this was done and party structure notices duly served. It is extraordinary how important occupiers of offices, etc, feel when there is any question of an adjoining building being altered. Each of the parties concerned was entitled to appoint his own surveyor to act, but fortunately in the case of building A we had only two surveyors to deal with, and this made things much easier. Many meetings took place between the surveyors and myself, and after much discussion an award was agreed upon.

The award is, of course, a very important document, and determines what work is to be done, the time and manner of doing it, and generally any other matter arising out of or incidental to the proposal. I have included a copy of a party structure award in the *Appendix*, page 340 and it is well worth careful study. You will see that where there are many adjoining owners and occupiers in a building it may mean many awards, and therefore it is important to the architect of the building to get all the awards as much alike as possible. In the Act it is provided that the costs incurred in making the award shall be paid by such party as the surveyors determine, and this is usually done by inserting in the award the amount of the fees to be paid. I think it is the usual custom for the building owner to pay all the costs in connection with party structure awards, so that if there are many interests involved the matter may become very expensive.

We found that the occupier of the building marked B was also the owner, and this simplified matters. As it happened, the surveyor who he appointed was a retired district surveyor who, naturally, knew his business well, and did not try to gain an unfair advantage as not infrequently happens.

Now we come again to building marked C. The surveyor to the adjoining owner, you will remember, had been told that no work to the party structure was proposed, and he had to a certain extent been snubbed. I believe he thought that he now saw his chance of getting even with us. The first thing he did quite properly, was to ask to have his fees paid by the building owner. This was agreed to on the understanding that the matter was proceeded with and an award duly made. A party structure notice was then served, and a meeting took place. The surveyor, however, made himself so objectionable, and demanded so large a sum of money for a concession — which in point of fact, was no concession at all — that the architect advised his client not to proceed with the portion of work affecting the building marked C.

Let me inpress upon you the need for tact, judgment, and the spirit of compromise in dealing with party wall cases. When you are dealing with some surveyors your patience will also be severely tried, but if you make a practice of acting straight-forwardly in all dealings such as I have described, I believe you will come through all right.

We have now to consider the building marked D. Here, again, we were fortunate, as the owner and the occupier were one and the same firm, and the surveyor appointed to act was a most considerate and capable man. The notice was served, the award duly made, and no difficulties of any kind occurred. As regards the building marked E, no action was necessary, as there was no interference with the party wall.

In the case of a building in the west end of London, recently finished, where I acted as surveyor for one of the adjoining owners, there were twenty-four different interests to deal with. The surveyor to the building owner had a most difficult job, as can be imagined, in getting all the awards made.

I hope what I have said with reference to this Part of the Act will make you alive to the importance of losing no time, as soon as a scheme is sufficiently matured, in obtaining information as to the interests of the adjoining owners and putting in hand the necessary negotiations. You will be wise to ascertain from your client immediately you receive a commission whether the adjoining owner has any rights of water, light, air, etc or other easements, or whether there are any reservations or obligations in the deeds relating to the property, as the omission to obtain these particulars may very seriously affect the work and cause unnecessary delay for which a client may hold you responsible.

As regards the cost of carrying out building work to party walls, the provisions in Section 56 of this Part of the Act must be studied. Section 58 lays down the procedure to be followed as regards the account of expenses and is specially important in defining the rates and prices for the work, which are to be 'estimated and valued at fair average rates and prices according to the nature of the work, the locality and the cost of labour and materials prevailing at the time when the work is executed'. This seems clear that, so far as concerns work to be carried out as the result of an award, the prices ruling when the work is actually executed must be allowed. In connection with prices for building work which had been carried out at a date much earlier than when the award was made and when prices were much lower, a judgment was given in 1926 to the effect that the prices to be allowed were to be those in force when the work was actually executed and not the prices at the time of the award. In an award made in 1919 by the superintending architect to the London County Council he stipulated that the building owners were to be at liberty to use the existing party wall upon first making payment to the adjoining owners of a moiety of the costs and expenses of the erection of such portion of the wall as the building owner desired to use, such moiety to be ascertained by measurement and valued upon the basis of the actual expense incurred by the adjoining owner at the time the wall was erected. This question of the cost to be paid for the use of an existing party wall is of great importance to the building owner at the present time, when prices are so much higher than they were a few years ago, for if prices for the work were to be computed at present-day rates the amount to be paid could easily be three times the actual cost of the wall when built. Provision is made in this clause to deal with the situation where the adjoining owner makes use of a new party structure additional to the use made by him at the time the work commenced. In these circumstances whether the adjoining owner makes use of the party structure during its execution or at a later date, a proportion of the expense actually incurred by the building owner must be borne by the adjoining owner, regard being had to the extent of his additional use of the party structure.

Part VII deals with dangerous and neglected structures. The expression 'Structure' is given a special definition in this Part, and includes 'any building or wall or other structure and anything affixed to or projecting from any building or wall or other structure'. One of the duties of the district surveyor is to make known to the London City or Borough Council any information he may receive to the effect that any structure is in a dangerous state, and to take steps to remove any immediate danger. Notice must be served by the Council upon the owner or occupier of the structure, requiring him forthwith to take down, repair or otherwise secure it, as the case may require, and if the owner of the structure disputes the necessity of any of the requirements comprised in a notice he may serve on the Council a written requirement that the dispute shall be referred to arbitration.

Part IX is important as dealing with the superintending architect and the district surveyors. These officials are appointed by the Greater London Council, and have very definite duties to perform. You will probably not come into contact very often with the superintending architect. With the district surveyors, however, it is quite different; you will very frequently come into contact with them, and you will find the district surveyors are most helpful. Should you be in difficulty at any time in regard to points in the Acts concerning your building, do not hesitate to go to the district surveyor and consult him. It is useless to try to get the better of him, because he is, as a rule, quite as clever as you are, and probably knows a great deal more about the Acts and regulations than you do or are ever likely to do. Go to the Council or the district surveyor, show that you are desirous of complying with the regulations and not trying to avoid them, and you will find they are willing and pleased to afford you all the assistance they can.

Inner London is divided into twenty eight districts, including the City of London, for the purposes of the Acts, and each district is placed under the supervision of a district surveyor with a deputy and staff to assist him as necessary. To become a district surveyor it is necessary to possess one of the qualifications mentioned in Section 76 of the 1939 Act, which states that 'No person shall be qualified to hold the office of district surveyor unless he —

    (a) possesses a certificate either
        (i) of proficiency to perform the duties of the said office granted by the board constituted under Section 77 (Examination of candidates for office of district surveyor) of this Act; or
        (ii) of competency to perform the duties of the said office granted before the commencement of this Act by the Royal Institute of British Architects; or
    (b) has been examined by the Council (the GLC) and found by them competent to perform the duties of the said office; or
    (c) has filled the office of district surveyor'.

It is also necessary to be qualified as an Architect, Engineer or Surveyor.

Part X deals with the powers of the Greater London Council to make by-laws. I shall have something to say about by-laws a little later.

Part XI concerns legal proceedings and the appointment of the Tribunal of Appeal. Avoid legal proceedings whenever possible. They rarely end satisfactorily for either party, and the very fact that they have been resorted to is, I think, usually an indication that the spirit of compromise has been absent from the negotiations. The Tribunal of Appeal consists of a panel of six persons, one person being appointed by each of the following:

The Secretary of State.

The Royal Institute of British Architects.

The Royal Institution of Chartered Surveyors.

The Institute of Civil Engineers.

The Institute of Structural Engineers.

The London Region of the National Federation of Building Trades Employers.

The Tribunal has power to hear and determine appeals referred to them under the London Building Acts or any by-laws made in pursuance of these Acts.

Part XII is headed 'Miscellaneous'. Amongst other things it deals with penalties which may be incurred by persons who commit offences against the Acts, etc. It also states what buildings etc, are exempt from parts of the Acts. You should read this Part carefully. Attached to the Act are three schedules which you must consider. The first schedule details the fees payable to the Council in respect of dangerous structures. The second schedule gives the fees payable in respect of services rendered by the district surveyors and also sundry rules in connection with their services. The scale of fees was amended by the GLC (General Powers) Act 1965 and is now based on the basic cost of the work subject to the supervision of the district surveyor. The third schedule gives the list of enactments which have been repealed wholly or in part by the Act of 1939 and certain other Acts.

We must now consider Parts V, XI and XII of the 1930 Act, which are still in operation.

Part V, treating of open spaces about buildings and the height of buildings, is very important to the architect, and must be carefully studied. It chiefly concerns buildings of the domestic class, and does not include those to be used wholly or principally as offices. (Note: Sections 51-53 are repealed)

Part XI deals with dangerous and noxious businesses, and can be left alone until the unlikely event of your having such a case presents itself.

Part XII concerns dwelling-houses on low-lying land, and gives the council power to make regulations, which they have done. If you are building near the river — say at Rotherhithe — you will certainly have to go carefully into this matter, as there are many important matters to be observed. Any information in connection with this section of the Act can be obtained from the Council's Engineer at County Hall, Westminster Bridge, SE1.

We have now finished our brief consideration of the London Building Acts, and must now deal with the by-laws and regulations.

By-laws for the construction and conversion of buildings, etc., were made by the London County Council, and first came into force on the 1 January 1938. These have since been revised and the by-laws now in force are the London Building (Constructional) By-laws 1972. These have been referred to already on page 197. You can obtain a copy of these by-laws, which are published by the Greater London Council from County Hall, SE1. These by-laws are much too extensive for me to go into detail, but you would be wise to obtain a copy and make a précis of every section, with diagrams showing exactly what you are empowered to do, and thus obtain a good working knowledge of its many provisions. As in the 1939 Act there are many expressions which have particular meanings assigned to them and these definitions must always be observed. The by-laws are divided into fourteen parts and three Schedules:

Part	
I	Definitions
II	General
III	Dead, imposed and wind loads
IV	Materials of construction
V	Sites and foundations, etc
VI	Roofs, enclosures and cladding
VII	Walls and piers
VIII	The structural use of steel
IX	Structural use of concrete
X	Timber
XI	Fire resistance
XII	Flues, chimneys, hearths, ducts and chimney shafts
XIII	Oil burning appliances
XIV	Lighting and ventilation and height of rooms

You will find in these by-laws definitions of the terms used in the by-laws, references to British Standard Codes of Practice (CP), and directions as to plans, sections and calculations which must be submitted to the district surveyor with the building notice. A clause to the effect that every person who contravenes or fails to comply with the by-laws will be liable to a penalty not exceeding £50, and in addition a daily penalty not exceeding £10, is a reminder of the serious importance of obtaining a thorough working knowledge of the Acts and by-laws.

Part III will be found to contain directions as to the construction of buildings so that they may be capable of safely sustaining and transmitting all the loads likely to come upon them. There is also a form of permanent notice, which must be exhibited in a conspicuous position, stating the maximum permitted load on floors not used for residential purposes.

Part IV contains specifications of requirements for the following materials: aggregate, cement and sand for concrete, with correct proportions, structural steel, reinforcement for concrete, lime mortar, stone, bricks and blocks, slates, roofing tiles, asbestos cement sheeting, sheet steel roofing, lathing and plastering, and structural timber, and tables showing required strengths of various grades of concrete.

Part V gives directions as to foundations of buildings, covering sites with concrete and maximum pressures permissible on the various grades of concrete.

Part VII refers to walls and piers, including construction and materials, minimum thicknesses, cavity walls, damp proof courses, etc. This Part also lays down regulations as to recesses and openings in walls, a most important matter where space is of so great value as in London, and gives rules as to chases in party walls. In connection with this point I was called in to inspect some work that had been carried out at a house in Westminster. The building owner had cut many chases in the party walls, and his so doing had drawn the attention of the adjoining owner to the work. The adjoining owner had quite rightly complained to the building owner, who then asked me to act for him. I found not only that the work had been carried out quite contrary to the London Building Acts, but also that it could not be defended from a constructional point of view. I therefore advised that the adjoining owner should be pacified and met as far as possible. In the result my client had to build up all the chases he had cut, which meant a considerable expenditure of time and money, the whole of which would have been saved had he, or his builder, been cognisant of and complied with the Acts and by-laws.

Part VIII deals with the use of structural steel in foundations, steel skeleton frame buildings, steel columns, bolts, rivets and riveting, grillage beams, etc by reference to BS 449, etc.

Part IX is concerned with reinforced concrete and relates to CP 114, 115 and 116.

Part X concerns structural timber and relates to CP 112.

Part XI details the provisions for fire resistance of constructional elements with a table showing the periods of fire resistance required in various types and sizes of buildings. There are limits as to floor areas in certain types of buildings and instructions regarding the construction of party walls, staircases, and landings, etc. This is a most important section and should be carefully studied as the rules contained herein seriously affect both construction and design.

Part XII deals with the construction of flues, chimneys, hearths and chimney shafts, and states that a chimney shaft may be square, circular or any regular polygonal shape, so that here you have considerable scope for your designing abilities.

Part VI refers to many different matters, such as roof coverings, projections from buildings, lighting and ventilation and arches over public ways. You must have noticed the regularity of the mansard slopes of roofs in new buildings in London. This is on account of this Part of the by-laws, which prescribes that the plane of the surface of the roof shall not incline from the wall upwards at a greater angle than $75°$, and as space is so valuable, naturally many architects avail themselves of the steepest slope they can get.

A further publication that is well worth studying is the Code of Practice entitled 'Buildings of excess height and/or Additional Cubical Extent Requiring Approval under Section 20 of the London Building Acts (Amendment) Act 1939'. This gives particulars for the guidance of applicants in the preparation of proposals to be submitted for the Council's consideration and information as to the conditions that may be imposed by the Council when approving proposals. All the relative sections of the 1939 Act are collected together here, thus enabling you to see much more clearly exactly what you may or may not do when faced with the problem of constructing a large building in London. In addition, the manner in which applications for approval are to be made is given.

These documents should be consulted whenever occasion arises, but it may well be that revisions are being considered even while this book is being printed, so that you must keep yourselves up to date in these matters by obtaining and studying copies of the latest by-laws, regulations, etc.

You must expect to be required to follow very strictly the regulations of the London Building Acts and by-laws, which we have been considering, but you may count upon the courtesy of the officials who administer them, as they are generally men of wide experience who can, and will, assist you in reconciling your requirements to the regulations. The same may be said of the large provincial towns.

Beware of delaying your negotiations with the local authorities. As soon as your sketch plans have been agreed with your client you can, in London, discuss the project with the GLC or, in the country, with the surveyor to the local authority, when you will generally find out any matters to which exception may be made and be advised, at an early date, of any requirements which you may not have satisfied, which will save you the trouble of varying the contract after it is signed.

Chapter XXVII
Ancient lights and rights of way

An architect engaged in building schemes, in the congested parts of London or other large towns, not infrequently finds that windows in the adjoining properties overlook the site upon which it is proposed to build. As the existence of such windows may very seriously affect his designs, one of the first things the architect should do is carefully to consider the position of the windows and to ascertain definitely whether any or all of them are entitled to be called *ancient lights*. This may be a little difficult to do. As a rule, the owners of properties containing ancient lights are fully alive to their rights and interests, and not only will there be little chance for you to overlook them, but it may be a matter involving a good deal of investigation to satisfy yourself as to whether a claim is well founded or not.

Generally speaking, the right to an ancient light is acquired when the access of light to it has been actually enjoyed for 27 years without interruption, but in view of the fact that no action taken to interrupt the enjoyment is legally effective until the expiration of twelve months, even if it is submitted to, it follows that the right can really be acquired in a little over 26 years.

The law on the subject of ancient lights is not always easy to follow, and is, I am convinced, one of the most, if not the most, difficult subject that an architect or surveyor has to deal with, for it seems to admit of so many and various interpretations. It often happens also that the case in which one is interested presents points which do not seem to have been before the Courts previously. Thus the case must be treated entirely on its own merits, and this requires a good deal of judgment. Should a question of ancient lights be taken into Court for settlement, the owner of the alleged ancient lights will, of course, have to prove that he or his predecessors have enjoyed the right for at least 27 years, and he will no doubt try also to prove that any diminution of light will seriously affect his business. This latter point must be taken carefully into consideration, and it is one on which there is usually much uncertainty. For, although there may be no shadow of doubt about the windows being ancient lights, the mere assertion of the fact may not in itself be sufficient to debar you from obstructing a good deal of the light previously enjoyed.

My advice to you is to use every endeavour to come to an agreement with an owner of ancient lights rather than go to law with him. In the first place, prepare your plans, showing exactly what you wish to do, of course having regard to any ancient lights which overlook your site; take the plans to the owner of the property containing ancient lights, and have a friendly discussion with him. You may thus find the case much simplified, especially if you are able to convince him that your proposals will not seriously affect his rights. It may be that the windows affected give light only to, say, a staircase, where a little less light would not be detrimental, and in that case an arrangement should easily be arrived at. If, on the other hand, the windows illuminate a jeweller's workshop, any diminution of light would be a serious matter. In such a case, if no compromise can be suggested, it is well to accept the position and to modify your design accordingly. You may find that your proposed new building will obstruct, say half the light to a bedroom window, but that the amount of light still remaining will be quite sufficient for illuminating the room. In a case such as this you may have good grounds for objecting to any curtailment of your design, and, by the exercise of a little tact, it should be possible to induce a reasonable owner to accept your point of view. Unfortunately, you are likely to meet with owners whose 'points of view' are as immovable as ancient lights themselves, and here again I advise you that it is as a rule expedient to give way to some extent rather than ask your client to face the uncertainties, not to mention the cost, of a law case.

Should you have a case of ancient lights soon after you have commenced practice it will be a real help to you to have a surveyor at hand who has had experience in this subject.

The question of the law relating to the 'right of air' is rather outside the scope of this book (not to say, my experience), but I wish to point out to you that there is such a thing, and that you may possibly be called upon, in the course of your practice, to consider it. Although I have often had to deal with ancient lights, I have as yet had no case relating only to the loss or restriction of air.

You will infer from the foregoing remarks that it is important to prevent an owner of premises adjoining any property in which you are interested from acquiring the right to ancient lights. You should be very careful to object to any lights which have not been in existence for at least 26 years.

Under the Rights of Light Act 1959, the period of 20 years laid down by the Prescription Act 1832, is extended to 27 years for the purposes of any proceedings for determination of whether a person is entitled to an absolute and indefeasible right to the access and use of light to and for a dwellinghouse, workshop or other building. The same Act also provides machinery for registration of a notice with the local authority the effect of which is that the access of light is treated as obstructed to the same extent and with the like consequence as if an opaque structure of dimensions specified in the Notice had on the date of registration been erected by the applicant. The Notice must be in the prescribed form and accompanied by a certificate issued by the Lands Tribunal certifying that adequate notice has been given to persons concerned. The procedure under this Act is complicated, and it is sufficient here to note that these provisions exist.

Prior to the 1959 Act in the absence of agreement the only way to prevent time running out was to erect an opaque structure on the boundary. This was always expensive and sometimes impossible, as where new lights are opened many storeys up. A 1959 Act notice is effective up to whatever height the notice states.

Here I would caution you that in any case in which you may have to alter or rebuild a wall containing ancient lights a very accurate survey must be made defining the position and exact sizes of the openings. To preserve the right it is necessary, in the rebuilding, to keep the openings substantially in the same relative positions and to the same sizes as before.

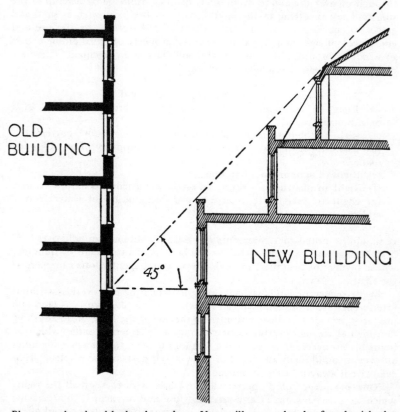

OLD BUILDING

NEW BUILDING

45°

Photographs should also be taken. You will some day be faced with the question 'How near can I build to certain ancient lights without infringing the rights of the owner?' and the matter may be difficult to determine. There is, however, a rough standard to go by, and that is the angle of 45°. Although I do not think there is anything very definite about this rule, yet it does give a guide. From the bottom of the lowest ancient light an angle of 45° is set up and the new building should be kept within this angle. This should leave sufficient light for the old windows, and the existence of the rule can at any rate be used as an argument with the owner. I had a case of this kind in the City, where the adjoining owner accepted my proposals based on the angle of 45°. You will see clearly from the diagram how great a restriction upon building the existence of ancient lights entails, and how important it is that such rights are not acquired against your client's interests.

Earlier in this chapter I used the word 'easement'. As this is a very important word I will say something more about it. An easement may be defined as a liberty, advantage, or privilege which one proprietor has through or over the estate of another, distinct from the ownership of the soil, and not involving taking anything out of the land, such as sand and gravel, or cutting peat, turf, etc. The right, therefore, to the use and enjoyment of light and air passing over the property of an adjoining owner to windows in a building close to the boundary is an easement. There are many other forms of easements, such as:

(a) Rights of way across an adjoining owner's land.
(b) Right to maintain water or drain pipes through the land of a neighbouring owner.
(c) Right to the passage of rainwater through a neighbour's gutter.
(d) Right to draw water from a well on the property of an adjoining owner.
(e) Right of support to a building.
(f) Right to obstruct a stream and divert water from its natural course.
(g) Right to take more than a reasonable amount of water from a stream.

It should be noted that easements can only be obtained or held over land or buildings and can only exist for the benefit of other land or buildings whose owners or occupiers or their servants and agents alone can exercise the right.

Every owner of land has certain rights which he can exercise without interference from anyone. He can do whatever he likes with his land and property provided he does not infringe the law of the land, or do anything detrimental to his neighbours or contrary to the terms under which he holds his property. If he owns the freehold he can, for instance, dig holes all over it, build walls all round or over it, sell parts or the whole of it, or even give it away if he feels so disposed.

Now the owner of property will obviously wish to keep all the rights which he possesses, or, at any rate, not lose any of them without having some say in the matter. This is where easements come in. If we think of an estate on which there has been no encroachment of any sort it will be clear that the acquistion of any easement — such, for example, as a right of way — will lessen the value of the property, and therefore the owner must make it his business to see that no such right is acquired, at any rate without receiving a satisfactory *quid pro quo*.

We may now consider how easements are acquired, and what should be done to prevent their wrongful acquisition.

An easement can be acquired in several ways, but the method of which we must take particular notice is, by prescription — in other words, by uninterrupted use for a certain number of years. This is the cause of nearly all the cases which arise.

To obtain an easement by prescription means to gain a right or title to use something, say a right of way over another man's property, by reason of the fact that the right has been exercised, for a certain number of years, and that during such period the right has not been interrupted by the owner. Practically it means that the possessor of the easement has obtained something for nothing — something which often costs a large sum of money to extinguish.

Here we must consider the Prescription Act 1832 and The Rights of Light Act 1959 which have a very important bearing on the subject. You should read them carefully, and especially study the clauses, which give the number of years during which an easement must be used for the right to become absolute and indefeasible. The Highways Act 1959 (sections 28, 34, 110 and 111) deals with the erection, dedication by prescription, stopping up and diversion of Public Rights of Way.

I have dealt fairly fully in the first part of this chapter with the rights of light and air to a building, so that I need now only refer to the periods necessary to establish a right to other forms of easements.

Perhaps the easiest one to understand is the ordinary right of way. Forty years' enjoyment of a way over the property of another owner gives an absolute and indefeasible right, but twenty years' enjoyment of the easement gives a *prima facie* right, which is practically all that is necessary; so that twenty years would seem to be the period to be specially noted.

You must therefore be very careful in all your dealings to remember this twenty years, and always advise a client to interrupt the enjoyment of an easement or public right of way in order that no right may be established. The acquisition of a public or private right of way across your client's land can be safeguarded by frequently closing the way to traffic for definite periods, which should be duly notified to the person likely to claim an easement.

There is another form of easement to be considered, *viz* an easement of necessity. If a man buys a plot of land entirely surrounded by another person's property, and with no outlet to a public road, he is entitled to a 'way of necessity', even though nothing has been said in the deeds relating to the purchase. It would, of course, be an unwise thing to allow a client to buy such a plot of land without first arranging for proper access to it, but such things have been known to occur. I remember one such case several years ago, in which a public authority bought a plot of land without any mention being made of a right of way to it. The vendor was, however, eventually forced to give the right. This way of necessity may also apply to pipes for conveying water or to drains, etc.

I will not attempt to discuss all the questions that can arise over easements, as it is seldom that any two cases are alike. You should obtain a good book on this subject and put in a few hours' study in order to get a better knowledge of it. I will content myself with giving a short list of some of the more important points:

(a) The owner of the land over which a private right of way exists is not necessarily bound to repair it, but the owner of land adjoining or making use of a public right of way can be made to contribute towards the cost of making it up including the necessary drains and channels.

(b) An interruption of a right of light must be continuous or the notice under The Rights of Light Act 1959 effective for at least one year.

(c) To prevent the public acquiring a right of way, the road, etc, should be closed at least on one day in each year.

(d) An owner is entitled to the support of an adjoining owner's land or walls.

(e) An existing well can be sunk deeper, if desired, even if by doing so water is drained away from adjoining wells. I remember a case of this kind in Sussex where I had to deepen a well 10' 0" in order to get a better supply of water. This affected the adjoining wells, but their owners' only remedy was to deepen their own wells.

(f) An owner is entitled to take a reasonable amount of water from a stream, but must not decrease to any material extent the normal flow.

(g) No owner may pollute a stream of water flowing through his land, and if the water is already polluted he must not add to the pollution.

(h) If the use of an easement is varied it may be lost, eg if you have a vehicular right of way to a garden, and you wish to turn the garden into a brickyard, you are not entitled to use the roadway for the purposes of the brickyard.

(j) If your client possesses a building with ancient lights, and the adjoining owner is erecting a building which is likely to interfere with the lights, you should at once advise an application for an injunction to stop him from going on with his building.

(k) If you are proposing to interfere with an alleged ancient light on the property of an adjoining owner, and after receipt of notice you still proceed with your building, you may find that the Courts will force you to pull it down. You must therefore resist any temptation to chance your client's luck — seldom does it pay.

Chapter XXVIII
Dilapidations

Some day, in the course of your practice, you will be called upon to survey a house for dilapidations and to prepare a Schedule of Dilapidations. It is, of course, very necessary to understand what is meant by the term *dilapidations*, and I think the following statement will explain it in a general way:

> *Dilapidation* is the result of the failure of a tenant in temporary occupation to keep the premises let to him in repair, and the word expresses this state of disrepair. *Waste,* which is closely allied to dilapidation, is the word used to describe destruction or injury done to the premises to the prejudice of the owner, and may be what is called *voluntary waste* (that is pulling down any part of the buildings, cutting down trees, etc), or *permissive waste* (that is, neglecting to keep the premises in repair, allowing parts of the buildings to decay for want of paint, etc).

A schedule of dilapidations, therefore, is a document which sets out in detail the various parts of the buildings which are out of repair and in what way they are out of repair, but does not profess to give the manner in which the repairs should be carried out; it is therefore quite unlike the ordinary building specification or bill of quantities. Although the schedule does not specify the method of repair, you must be prepared with an idea of the work involved for the purposes of the estimates mentioned later on. I propose to exclude altogether ecclesiastical dilapidations, which are rather different from the ordinary dilapidations with which you are likely to have to deal.

Generally speaking, questions of dilapidation arise at the expiration of a term of years' occupation of premises, though they can also arise at stated periods during the occupation. For example, a person desires to take a lease of a house, the owner desires to let the property, and terms are agreed. If the lease is for a number of years, the person taking the property — the *lessee* — generally covenants to keep it in good repair, and if he fails to keep this covenant, a claim for dilapidations is made by the owner — the *lessor*.

In preparing a schedule of dilapidations, the first thing to be done is to consult the lease, which is the document that contains all the various covenants entered into and is signed by both parties to the arrangement. You will find in it what is generally called the *repairing clause*, which sets out — of course in a legal way — the extent of the lessee's obligations. It is in connection with this clause as a rule that all the trouble arises.

It will be your duty to go to the premises and examine in full detail every part of the property to see whether it is in the condition and state of repair required under the lease. This means, of course, that you must understand the precise effect of the repairing clause and be able to form an opinion as to what items you are to include in your schedule. The following example of a repairing clause is from a lease under which I prepared a schedule of dilapidations the typical portions of which are given in the *Appendix*, page 344. This will, I think, explain the matter better than a lengthy description:

'And will during the said term at his own expense without being thereunto required to do so well and sufficiently repair uphold support sustain maintain point pave cleanse glaze tile amend and keep the said premises with all fixtures and additions thereto and the drains manholes soil and other pipes and sanitary and water apparatus thereof and all party and other walls rails fences pales hedges ditches and gates thereto belonging in good substantial and tenantable repair and will once in every third year during the said term paint with two coats at least of good oil paint in a workmanlike manner all the outside wood stone cement stucco ironwork and such other work of or belonging to the exterior of the said premises as are usually or ought to be painted and will once in every seventh year during the said term paint in like manner all the inside wood and ironwork and other parts of the property usually painted and wash stop whiten colour paper with suitable paper of as good quality as that in use at the commencement of the lease all parts of the said premises as are now or usually whitened coloured or papered and will at the expiration or sooner determination of the term deliver up to the lessor in good substantial decorative and tenantable repair and condition the said premises together with all buildings erections and fixtures now or hereafter to be erected thereon.'

You must not think that the preparation of a schedule of dilapidations is a simple matter, for this is by no means the case. The covenants to repair are worded in various ways in different leases, and the liability of the lessee depends to a great extent on such wording. Before you are in a position to deal with dilapidations, therefore, it is necessary that you should study the subject. The best way to gain a good working knowledge of the law relating to dilapidations is to obtain a good textbook and go through it carefully. You will find it most interesting, if at the same time a little complicated. You must acquire a knowledge of the legal terms, and become familiar with the effect of the various clauses — I mean the extent to which they affect the liability to repair. Although in case of doubt you must consult the solicitor who is acting in the matter, it should be remembered that his business ends in interpreting the legal phraseology of the lease. Its effect on the practical question of dilapidations is a matter on which an experienced surveyor is more competent to advise.

When you are studying this subject you will find that the question of 'fixtures' is of much importance. There are landlord's fixtures and tenant's fixtures, and they must be treated in a different way in dealing with dilapidations. For example, the occupier of the premises will have to hand over the landlord's fixtures in a proper state of repair, but the tenant's fixtures he will be able to remove from the premises. Therefore you must know the difference between the two kinds of fixtures. Landlord's fixtures are, shortly, such things as cannot be removed without injury to the freehold, and tenant's fixtures are things which have been fixed by a tenant and can be removed by him during his tenancy provided that no serious damage is caused to the freehold. I think an ordinary kitchen dresser is a good example of a landlord's fixture, and blinds a good example of tenant's fixtures.

When a schedule of dilapidations has been prepared it will be necessary to serve it upon the lessee, and this can be done either by the solicitor or the surveyor. If you have to do this, it will be wise to consult the solicitor as to the form of the notice. The following form may be of assistance:

> High Street
> Westminster
> Date . . . .

To
 A Blank Esq

I hereby give you notice on behalf of Mr John B Williams, of Red Court, Blanksbridge, that you have committed breaches in the covenants to repair contained in the lease of New Court, Blanksbridge, dated 25 August 19—, and I hereby require you to remedy the said breaches by forthwith executing and carrying out the repairs, etc, specified in the Schedule of Dilapidations hereto annexed and to do all other acts requisite to put the premises into repair in accordance with the covenants in that behalf.

> WILLIAM THOMAS
> Surveyor and Agent for Mr John B Williams

You will now wish to hear how to proceed in getting the necessary particulars for the schedule. The procedure is quite simple. Take a notebook and a measuring rod and go to the premises, having previously made an appointment with the occupier. You must keep to a definite order of working. I always commence inside the house at the top; and while there I get all the information I can about the roof; then work my way down, leaving the exterior until the end. Proceed to examine everything in order — for example, floor, walls, ceiling, doors, windows, fireplace, etc — and make the necessary notes in your book, putting your estimate of the cost of making good the wants of repair against each item. Be very careful to call the rooms by their right names, so that anyone other than yourself will have no difficulty in understanding to which room you are referring.

You must bear in mind, moreover, that a surveyor must be prepared to give an estimate of the cost of making good the dilapidations. In cases where a schedule is accepted by the lessee, and he proceeds to carry out the work, no estimate is required, but the matter is frequently settled by a money payment. In cases, however, of disagreement the matter may have to be settled in court, and a surveyor's estimate is then essential. The best way to make an accurate estimate is to value the items as you take notes of them, and this requires a good deal of experience. If you do not feel capable of doing this, you should turn the work over to your quantity surveyor, or at any rate ask him to assist you with the estimate.

I suggest a good exercise is to experiment with the house in which you live. You must get practice somehow or other before you can undertake a dilapidation case. Go through your house in full detail and note every item requiring repair. Try to assess the cost of putting it right, and see how far you can go with your work. You should find it interesting and you will learn a good deal, perhaps enough to show you how careful you will have to be when you get a dilapidation commission.

I have already referred to the possibility that a dispute between the lessor and the lessee at the termination of a lease may lead to its being taken into Court. Should this occur you will be required to give evidence to support the schedule of dilapidations and the estimate you have prepared for the lessor. It is also possible, however, though this is far less frequent, that you may be required to give evidence on behalf of a lessee, if the lessor is seeking to prove an excessively heavy schedule. In order that Counsel may be fully acquainted with what you are ready to say the solicitors will require you to produce what is called *A Proof of Evidence*. I hope the example given in the *Appendix* page 377, will be of some assistance and also enable you to realise that, although most cases of dilapidations are settled out of Court, you should always bear in mind that this may not be so and, therefore, in making your schedule you must be absolutely fair to both sides and ready to give evidence in a clear and convincing manner, always consistent with the terms of the lease, which you must assume has been understood by both parties when the lease was signed. You must appreciate that although you give the solicitors a Proof of Evidence in the form of a consecutive statement, your evidence in Court will be given in the form of question and answer. It is from the Proof that Counsel decides what questions to ask, and it will be your function to answer those questions, whether they be asked by Counsel for your own client or for the other side.

If you are asked to advise a client who is about to enter into a lease for a long term, you should realise that under an ordinary full repairing lease, not only will your client have to keep the premises in repair but to put them into repair, if this is necessary, and the state of repair that will be required to satisfy the provisions of the lease will probably be affected by the age and locality of the premises; it is advisable, therefore, in the case of a long lease, that the property should be surveyed and a schedule of condition prepared, such as I have given in the *Appendix* page 357. This schedule should, of course, be signed both by the landlord and the tenant and a copy kept with the lease. It should be pointed out that there are certain provisions in the Landlord and Tenant Act as regards dilapidations and I think the most important points for us are the following: 'Damages for a breach of covenant or agreement to keep or put premises in repair during the currency of a lease, or to leave or put the premises in repair at the termination of a lease, whether such covenant or agreement is expressed or implied, and whether general or specific, shall in no case exceed the amount (if any) by which the value of the reversion (whether immediate or not), in the premises is diminished owing to the breach of such covenant or agreement as aforesaid, and in particular no damage shall be recovered for a breach of any such covenant or agreement to leave or put premises in repair at the termination of a lease if it is shown that the premises, in whatever state of repair they might be, would at or shortly after the termination of a tenancy have been or be pulled down, or such structural alteration made therein as would render valueless the repairs covered by the covenant or agreement'.

You will find many different expressions in leases referring to the condition of property, such as, tenantable repair, good repair, habitable repair, necessary repair, sufficient repair, substantial repair, etc and you must consider carefully what these terms mean. As far as my experience goes they all mean very much the same thing, which is, that a building must be kept in such repair as, having regard to the age, character and locality of the premises would render it reasonably fit for occupation by a reasonably-minded tenant of the class who would be likely to take it.

A term which frequently occurs when dealing with leases and agreements in connection with property, is 'fair wear and tear excepted'. It has often been said that this term relieves the tenant from the responsibility of keeping the premises in repair and to a certain extent I think this is correct, but it cannot be taken for granted but must be considered in conjunction with the wording of the lease or agreement. If, for example, the document states that the tenant must 'deliver up at the expiration or sooner determination of the lease the messuage in as good state of repair and condition as it now is in, reasonable fair wear and tear excepted', the words would, I think, mean the premises must be handed over in as good condition as when the lease was signed, except that no repairs due to ordinary use could be required. I am sure that the words do not mean that a tenant need not look after the property nor do small immediate repairs which are required to keep the premises weatherproof, nor to replace tiles or panes of glass, etc.

Before leaving this Section I would draw your attention to important Acts of Parliament relating to Landlord and Tenants rights and obligations in respect of security of tenure, rent and repair. They are The Landlord and Tenant Act 1954 (as amended by the Rent Act 1957, the Leasehold Reform Act 1967, Rent Act 1968 and the Housing Finance Act 1972) and the Housing Act 1957, and the Housing Act 1961 (as amended by the Housing Acts 1964 and 1969). It is impossible for me to discuss these enactments in detail here, but you should make yourself familiar with their provisions and I recommend that you obtain from HM Stationery Office copies of the various standing orders, explanatory pamphlets and booklets which are issued in connection with these measures.

The Landlord and Tenant Act 1954 (*inter alia*) extends the principle of protection to provide security of tenure for occupying tenants under certain leases of residential property at low rents, known as ground rents, and for occupying sub-tenants of tenants under such leases. In the absence of agreement the Courts have to fix the terms upon which the tenant is to remain in occupation, and may in connection therewith have to make certain provisions as to repairs, and such repairs are referred to in the Act as 'initial repairs'. The type of tenancy affected by this Act is one where a dwelling-house has been held under a lease granted, for example, at Christmas 1875 for, say 99 years at a ground rent of £5 per annum. Such a lease would contain covenants which impose on the tenant a liability to maintain the dwelling-house in the same state of repair and condition as it was when it was first erected in the case of our example in 1875. When such a lease expires, if it were not for the provisions of this Act, the tenant's covenant to repair could be very onerous, particularly where there has been a change for the worse in the character of the neighbourhood. In addition to insisting on these repairs, the landlord could, if not controlled, demand a high rent and impose other conditions if the tenant wished to remain in the house.

The Rent Act 1968, as read in conjunction with the Housing Finance Act 1972, makes provision for phasing increases of rent up to the registered rent in two sets of circumstances; (1) after conversion from a controlled to a regulated tenancy, and (2) after an improvement for which an improvement or standard grant has been given and first registration of a rent.

It should be noted that in the Landlord and Tenant Act 1954, it is required to bring the dwelling-house into 'good repair', and the expression 'good repair' means good repair as respects both structure and decoration, having regard to the age, character and locality of the dwelling-house.

Whereas the Housing Act 1957, as amended, provides for a dwelling-house to be fit for human habitation, and in determining whether a dwelling-house is fit for human habitation regard shall be had to its condition in respect of the following matters: (a) repairs; (b) stability; (c) freedom from damp; (d) internal arrangement; (e) natural lighting; (f) ventilation; (g) water supply; (h) drainage and sanitary conveniences; (i) facilities for preparation and cooking of food and for the disposal of waste water.

The Housing Act 1961 (sections 32 and 33) makes statutory provision for the first time for the distribution of repairing burdens between landlord and tenant in short tenancies of dwelling-houses. This has the effect of imposing implied burdens on landlords where there are no specific repairing obligations on either side and also seeks to prevent the practice of imposing extensive repairing obligations on tenants under short tenancies. Section 32 makes landlords liable for structural and external repairs and for the maintenance of the main sanitary, water, electricity and gas fittings and renders ineffective any provision in a tenancy which seeks to place these burdens on the tenant.

In determining the 'standard of repair' required by the lessor's repairing covenant regard shall be had to the age, character and prospective life of the dwelling-house and the locality in which it is situated.

Covenants which purport to impose on lessees obligations which by the Housing Acts are imposed on the lessor notwithstanding any contract to the contrary are to the extent that they conflict with the statute null and void. If the premises are residential and section 32 of the Housing Act 1961 applies, then a tenant's repairing covenant is of no effect so far as it relates to obligations imposed on the landlord by that section, unless the county court judge has authorised the inclusion of the clause in the lease or agreement. If section 6 of the Housing Act 1957, applies, the statutory condition and undertaking of fitness for human habitation can only be excluded if the letting be for a term of not less than three years upon the terms that the house be put by the lessee into a condition reasonably fit for human habitation, without any option to either party to determine before the expiration of three years.

Finally, I recommend that you make yourself acquainted with the Housing Act 1969, and the Government circulars issued in connection therewith. This Act makes further provision for grants by local authorities towards the cost of providing dwellings by conversion or of improving dwellings and houses. You should warn your clients to make full enquiries about the procedure before commencing any work as otherwise it may not be possible for the local authority to give assistance.

Chapter XXIX

Reports on property to be purchased

The architect or surveyor is often called upon to inspect property proposed to be purchased or taken on lease. His services are required because of his special knowledge of building in all its branches, and the cost of construction. The client, having visited, say, a house, and made up his mind to acquire the property, being a wise man, as a client sometimes is, desires to have an expert opinion before he actually commits himself. Your duty, therefore, must be to write a report containing all the necessary technical information, and also a clear and definite recommendation in order to enable your client to arrive at a decision.

I have prepared the following form, a copy of which I suggest you should take with you to the property to be inspected. This list of items will give you a good guide as to the things you should take into consideration.

FORM FOR REPORT ON PROPERTY

Report upon ....
Particulars of property taken ....

---

1   Make a rough plan of the house, starting with the ground floor.

2   Make a list of all rooms in the house, with the sizes and heights.

3   Describe any special features of the rooms, such as, kind of grate, bay windows, cracked ceilings, cornices, floors, etc.

4   Describe all sanitary fittings, such as baths, sinks, wc apparatus, lavatory basins, etc.

5   Examine the hot-water supply and describe the apparatus as simply as possible. State if boiler is in kitchen range and hot-water tank in bathroom or elsewhere, or independent boiler and cylinder, etc. Measure tank or cylinder and give capacity. If house is occupied, find out whether system is efficient, *viz* how many baths at one

time, etc. Is there a safety valve on the boiler or
circulating pipes?

6   Note the cold-water supply, whether from company's
main or any other source, well, etc, and describe any
special features, such as the distance of well from house,
etc.

7   Note how rain-water is disposed of, whether in tanks
or into drains.

8   Examine cisterns, generally to be found in roof space;
measure size and give correct capacity (6¼ gallons to cubic
foot). Will it be necessary to have cisterns cleaned out?
Note Cistern—open at top.
        Tank—closed receptacle.
Is there a lead tray to the cold-water cisterns and a waste
pipe to the tray?

9   Describe wc apparatus.
Wash-down pedestal pan.
Wash-out pedestal pan.
Long hopper.
Syphonic closet.
Valve closet.
    Examine flushing cisterns and note if properly fitted
with overflows and if they work properly.

10   Note if wc apparatus is clean, and if not, recommend
the use of spirits of salts for cleaning. Soil in pan is a
frequent source of unpleasant smell.

11   Make special note of any unusual features of wc
apartment. Is it well ventilated, with a window in outside
wall, or is it situated inside the building with a borrowed
light into a passage, etc?

12   Note the kind of bath and whether in good
condition. Are the taps in good condition? Is there a puff
or ventilation pipe to the trap?

13   What make and size of lavatory basin? Is the waste
properly trapped and is there a puff or ventilation pipe?
Does the waste discharge into a rain-water head?

14   What kind of sink is there in the scullery?
If an old-fashioned stone sink, recommend its removal. Is
the waste pipe properly trapped and does it discharge over
a gully outside?

15   Examine the system of drains. If there are manholes, take up the covers, and if the manholes are well constructed it will give a guide to what may be expected of the drains.

16   Note if there is a ventilation pipe and also a fresh-air inlet to the manhole nearest the sewer.

17   See if drains discharge into a public sewer or into a cesspit. If into a cesspit, note distance from house and condition, also if properly ventilated.

18   If satisfied that the drains are all right, say so in your report, but state that your remarks are from surface examination only, and recommend that the drains be tested if house is to be purchased.

19   Take particulars of the gas, electric light and bell services and report as to their efficiency.

20   Make a list of all the fixtures in the house.

21   Note if external painting is required.

22   Examine roof by looking at the condition of slates or tiles, etc and noting, approximately, number of new slates or tiles required.

23   Carefully examine ceilings in upper floors to see if any damp has come through roof; this will help to give idea of state of roof.

24   Examine carefully the wood floors, skirting, etc, to see if there is any dry-rot, and if there is, make a special note in your report. This is a most important matter.

25   Note construction of roof and if boarded, etc, and size of rafters.

26   Note condition of chimneystacks, pots, and any lead flashings, eaves gutters, rain-water pipes, etc.

27   Is there a damp-proof course to the house? Examine the walls for signs of fracture. If there are cracks disappearing into the foundations consider the nature of the soil. Should the soil be clay and the foundations not deep enough, shrinkage of the clay during very dry weather may have caused settlement in parts of the foundations and consequent fractures in the walls. Excessive water caused by

a broken drain or the presence of large trees in the
vicinity may also cause fractures.

28   What is the price asked for the property?

29   Note whether the property is freehold or leasehold.

30   If freehold, find out whether there are any
restrictions.

31   If leasehold, find out term of years, when term
commenced, what restrictions are imposed and amount of
ground rent.

32   Make a rough plan of the site showing the approach
and any special features, such as tennis courts, garden
houses, conservatories, etc.

33   If possible, note the ownership of the various
fences to the property and note the state of their repair.

34   State if garden is in good condition or otherwise,
paths in repair, and remark generally upon condition of
things outside the house.

35   What is the probable age of the buildings?

36   Note the class of property near the house you are
inspecting, as this may have an effect upon the valuation.

37   If you recommend the acquisition of the property,
state the amount of your valuation and the price to be
offered.

38   Make a definite recommendation so that your client
will be assisted in making up his mind.

39   Give an approximate estimate of cost to put the
house in decorative repair or to bring it up to date.

You will, of course, amplify this list to suit any particular case you are
dealing with, but if you get all the information indicated upon my list you
will not go far wrong. I have given in the *Appendix*, page 351, a report of
an actual survey made some while ago, but with the name of the property
altered. You should study it carefully and use it as a type for your own
reports. I do not claim that the way in which I frame my reports is the
only right way, but I do consider that they contain a full and accurate
description of the property, and give my clients the kind of information

and assistance they require. You should make a careful study of the report and notes, and then prepare a similar report on the house you live in. You will thus gain a good deal of experience, and when you receive a commission of the nature referred to in this chapter you will have acquired quite a lot of useful knowledge which will enable you to execute it with confidence.

It does not take an experienced man very long to obtain the necessary information for making his report. In the case of the report referred to above, the whole of the information was obtained in less than 3 hours, and this included taking the necessary measurements for making the sketch plan of the house and garden, drains, etc. Naturally you will at first take a little longer, but with practice you will find that the work becomes easy, and you will experience great pleasure in the knowledge that you have acquired the ability to make a really satisfactory and workmanlike report, one which is of real help and assistance to your client, and is also worth the money that he will have to pay for it.

I should perhaps at this point remind you to be extremely careful when reporting on defects in timber for it is impossible for anyone examining an existing building to say that he has inspected all the timber, because so much of it is hidden or covered by paint, carpets, furniture, etc. If you are wise and take out a professional indemnity insurance policy you will find that your premium is fairly high if you make structural reports and most insurance companies insist on special wording being incorporated in your report covering your examination of timber. In my own office the following wording is used in the reports we prepare:

'It has not been possible for us to make a detailed examination of floor joists, wall plates, roofing timbers, underside of floor boards or other timbers in the premises. No guarantee or assurance can therefore be given that any timbers are free from rot, wood worm or other infestation. Arrangements can be made for a detailed examination and report to be carried out by specialists if required.'

These reports, and all similar ones, must be prepared in a thorough manner, because your client will certainly hold you responsible for any omissions. You should, however, display a little practical wisdom in the method of presenting your report. For instance, you may be asked by someone to report on a property to which he has taken a fancy, and yet for certain reasons you may feel bound to condemn it. If, as a consequence, he lets it go, he may find nothing else he likes so well, or a friend of his may like it, convert it into an attractive dwelling, and you will bear the blame for his loss. You can always present your report in a formal business fashion, not making too much or too little of defects, etc, nor going out of your way to express an opinion. Then, when your client questions you further, you can discuss it with him, and gauge how far the personal element weighs with him. Remember that the value of a place is more to one person than to another, and always try to show your client the easiest and most economical way of remedying defects in a property, if indeed there is a remedy. Other clients, far from wanting you to be lenient, will desire you to spare nothing in your severity, but you must not overstep the mark of justice and fairness to the vendor as well as to the intending purchaser.

You may be asked to advise a client as to the desirability of taking a house or other property on lease, and find that one of the clauses in the proposed agreement is to the effect that the property is to be given up at the end of the term in a condition similar to that when taken. In a case like this you should visit the house and make a very careful and detailed report as to the condition of the property, and what defects you find, in order that at the termination of the lease there can be no dispute as to the condition the property was in when the lease was signed. You will find in the *Appendix*, page 357, a report on the condition of a house which a client of mine proposed to take upon a 14 years' lease. This will, I hope, help you to make your own report in a workmanlike manner. You should take special care to identify the various rooms referred to in the report. When dealing with a large property it is advisable to attach a plan and to number all the rooms on the plan. One of my recent reports concerned a hotel in London, in which, in addition to the usual reception rooms, offices, kitchen quarters, etc, there were 42 numbered bedrooms. I marked upon the plans the numbers of the bedrooms so that they tallied with the numbers painted on the bedroom doors, and these numbers were, of course, used for reference in the report. It should, however, be borne in mind that in the years to come room numbers may be altered, or a bedroom for instance, may be put to another purpose and become an unnumbered room. In this and other ways future identification may be made difficult if not impossible. I advise you therefore to make the references to your plan clear and so make identification certain.

As regards the value of the property referred to in items 37 and 38 on page 223 although you may well be able to give a valuation for a small house you will be unwise to attempt to do so for any larger property. Today many outside factors have to be considered when assessing the value of a property, such matters as the future development of the area, the possibility of the compulsory purchase of all or a part of the land by a Government department and of course whether any statutory restrictions will prevent full use of the premises for your client's purpose, and a valuer must make searching enquiries before he can accurately express an opinion. Therefore, unless you happen to be qualified to give this advice you should request your client to obtain the services of a valuer.

Chapter XXX
Arbitrations

In the chapter on contracts you will remember that I referred several times to the arbitration clause. I think it is of importance that you should understand what arbitrations are and how they are conducted. Although I have had personal experience of several arbitrations, I remember only one that was called into existence under the arbitration clause in the RIBA form of contract (now the Standard Form of Building Contract). I think this goes to show that as a rule builders, architects, and their clients are reasonable people who are prepared to carry out building contracts in a spirit of compromise.

Under the 1963 Edition (July 1973 Revision) of the standard form of contract everything can be made the subject of arbitration except disagreements under the VAT Supplemental Agreement as already explained in chapter XII. If, as architect, you should give a decision which is not agreed to by the builder, and you refuse to alter it, he can always call in the arbitrator, though as I have already said, he seldom does so.

It should be noted that arbitration proceedings shall not be opened until after practical completion or alleged practical completion or termination or alleged termination of the contractors employment or abandonment of the works. There are, however, four cases when arbitration can take place during the progress of the works:

(i) in the event of a dispute arising in regard to the appointment of a new architect or quantity surveyor under Articles 3 or 4 of the Articles of Agreement.

(ii) in the event of a dispute as to the validity of an instruction.

(iii) in the event of a dispute whether a certificate has been improperly withheld or is not in accordance with the conditions.

(iv) in the event of a dispute under clauses 32 and 33 (outbreak of hostilities and war damage)

It may assist you if I endeavour to define a few of the terms which are of common use in connection with arbitrations. An *arbitration* may be defined as the means whereby a dispute between two or more parties can be settled by a person — called the *arbitrator* — to whom the contending parties mutually consent to submit their differences. An *arbitrator* is the person appointed to settle disputes between contending parties, who might otherwise resort to litigation. An *umpire* is a person appointed to decide differences that may arise between two arbitrators and the two arbitrators must appoint an umpire immediately after they themselves are appointed.

A submission or *arbitration agreement* is a written agreement to submit present or future differences to arbitration. A *reference* is the actual hearing of the case by the arbitrator, and the *award* is the decision or judgment given by the arbitrator after a careful inquiry into the case submitted to him. The award is as a rule final and binding on all parties. The costs of the reference and the award are left to the discretion of the arbitrator, who may direct by whom, to whom, and in what manner the costs are to be paid.

Arbitration usually results from a dispute between two parties on matters capable of being looked at from more than one point of view. The parties decide, therefore, to submit the case to arbitration, and they agree upon the terms to be submitted, which are embodied in the document called the *Submission* or *Arbitration Agreement.* The authority of the arbitrator to act is contained in the submission, and generally the reference is entirely governed by the Arbitration Act 1950. This Act I think you would be well advised to read.

An arbitration is by far the best method of settling differences where the disputes involve technical questions, and when the points in dispute can be stated in the submission in a simple way. Where you are dealing with a contract which is not to be governed by English law then you must ensure that appropriate amendments are made to the Arbitration clause.

An arbitration should be much less costly to the parties than an action at law, though if intricate legal questions are involved an arbitration may prove to be a more expensive and lengthy business. Indeed, in several cases in which I have been interested, I feel sure that had they been decided in the Law Courts, instead of by arbitration, the costs would have been less and the result more satisfactory to all parties.

It is very seldom that either side to an arbitration is satisfied with the result. If you are an interested party it is very difficult to look impartially at both sides of the case. You will be biased in favour of your own view, to the detriment of that of your opponent, and thus, when the result of the arbitration is known, you are likely to be disappointed. In nine cases out of ten I think it will be found that the arbitrator steers a middle course, and this would appear to indicate that a submission might usually be avoided if the disputing parties gave closer attention to each other's arguments and reasons.

There are several things to be noted in connection with arbitrations. When you find, say, in connection with one of your contracts that disputes are arising which you as architect have no authority to deal with, then you must begin to think of what will happen if the disputes go to arbitration, as provided for in the contract. It is always wise to get the points in dispute reduced in number as far as possible, settle everything you possibly can, and give the arbitrator direct and definite points to decide. If you do this you may sometimes find that the need for arbitration has vanished as a result of 'give and take'.

When the points to be arbitrated upon have been settled, the arbitrator must be appointed, and it is quite usual for the parties to meet and agree to a person satisfactory to all; but, failing agreement, if the dispute is in connection with any matter referred to in the Standard form of building contract, the arbitrator will be appointed by the President or a Vice-President of the RIBA. When the arbitrator has agreed to act, the matter will be no longer in your hands, but will be conducted by the arbitrator who will decide where the reference shall take place and the date.

A submission is as a rule made in writing, and sets forth the whole of the matters to be arbitrated upon. It is generally signed by both parties, and in the case of an arbitration under the Standard form of contract it would be signed by the builder and the client. It is most important that the submission should contain every point which it is desired to submit to the arbitrator, and therefore it must be framed with great care. A solicitor is often invited to assist in its preparation. A submission is often silent as regards the costs of the arbitration and this I think is a pity, for, as I have already pointed out, an arbitration may be, as a rule, less costly than an action at law, yet it still is often much more costly than is contemplated and therefore if the arbitrator's fees can be settled before the arbitration the only charges that remain will be the costs of the reference including those of expert witnesses, legal advice, etc. Of course, apart from the amount of the fees and costs, there is always the question of who pays them. Under the Act of 1950, in the absence of agreement between the parties, the arbitrator has a discretion to direct to and by whom and in what manner the fees and costs or any part thereof shall be paid.

At the reference the following procedure is usually adopted. The arbitrator invites the claimant to put his case and to call any witnesses in support of it; then the respondent replies, calls his witnesses and sums up his case; the claimant then replies, and the hearing is closed. There may, of course, be several sittings and also visits to sites, buildings, etc.

When the arbitrator has prepared his award he usually notifies both parties, and informs them that it can be 'taken up' upon payment of his fees. This always appears to me a very 'canny' arrangement. No one likes to pay for an unpleasant decision, and as the award is, as I have already said, usually unsatisfying to both parties, it is really a wise precaution on the part of an arbitrator to make sure of his fees before making known his decision, but it would be unwise for him to make unreasonable charges, as an arbitrator's or umpire's fees can be taxed by a taxing officer of the Courts, and this would ensure that no excessive charges were allowed.

Chapter XXXI

Fire insurance

Revised in 1973 with the assistance of Mr D H G Forrest, Principal of Gladstone Forrest & Co., Insurance Brokers.

An architect when designing new buildings, or alterations and additions to old ones, must arrange for the protection of the new buildings during erection against damage by fire, and also see that the existing buildings are covered against extra risk during building operations. This duty is properly discharged by inserting a clause in the specification, or conditions of contract, placing the responsibility upon the contractor and seeing that he actually insures the property with an approved office and forwards the policy to the architect for inspection and safe custody. This aspect of fire insurance is dealt with in chapter XIII, but it may not be out of place here to remind architects that the Fire Offices Committee have issued rules for buildings of fire resisting construction and if these rules are followed in designing new buildings a lower rate is actually charged. Furthermore, if the premises on erection are provided with an automatic sprinkler installation a big saving in the premium will result, and smaller discounts will be allowed if other extinguishing appliances are installed. Should you be commissioned to design a large building you should consult an insurance company which has a staff of surveyors always available and ready to give advice on the latest developments of fire resisting construction and the special matters which, if complied with, will enable the company to reduce the ordinary premium.

Another duty of the architect is to value an existing property with a view to insurance, and to advise as to the form in which the policy should be prepared. It is necessary, therefore, to understand the general principles which govern fire insurance, and the following brief remarks may help you in this respect. The subject is, of course, a large one and involves many questions too intricate to be dealt with here. For a fuller treatment of the subject the reader is referred to standard works on fire insurance.

The valuation of a property is a matter of considerable importance. It is a favourite argument that it is unlikely that a building will be totally destroyed in the event of a fire and, at any rate, the foundations (if any) will not be affected. You should in making your valuation include everything that would be required to reinstate the property as existing at the time of your valuation and the insurance company should be notified that you have done this. A sum should also be included for the removal of debris.

When an owner of property desires to effect an insurance against damage or destruction by fire he usually requests the agent of an insurance company, or an insurance broker, to insure the property for a certain amount, which in the case of large properties is arrived at as the result of a survey and valuation. The company will give a covering note of insurance pending ,the issue of the formal policy. The policy is the formal contract between the insurance company (the insurers) and the property owner (the insured), and this, being a very important document, should be carefully examined by the insured in order to satisfy himself that everything is covered in the manner he desires. I think people are inclined to be lax in this respect and to leave the details to the insurers or their agent on the assumption that the policy is bound to be right. If you have to effect an insurance for a client I advise you to satisfy yourself that the wording of the policy both as regards the enumeration of the various items and the description and identification of buildings or other property is in order and that you have covered, as far as possible, all the points which may be likely to arise in case a fire occurs. You should also warn your client that the valuation should be reconsidered at suitable intervals to keep in line with the level of building costs.

There are many points about the policy which must be considered. It should be realised that a policy of fire insurance is a contract of indemnity against loss by fire. It follows, therefore, that, although the insurers may be called upon to pay the cost of reinstating the destroyed property, their real liability (subject to sufficiency of insurance) is to pay the actual value of the property damaged up to the amount insured, the underlying principle of fire insurance being, in every case, the reimbursement for loss sustained by the insured within the limit expressed in the policy, the sum insured being the limit of the amount which the insured is entitled to receive and not the measure of the loss.

It will be well when you are advising upon the drawing up of a proposed policy to bear in mind the question of the fees and expenses of the architect and surveyor which will be incurred in dealing with the reinstatement of the property should a loss occur. This will be referred to later, but in passing it may be stated that it is important to have these fees and expenses expressly covered in the policy, and it should be noted that the insurers will not pay fees for the preparation of a claim. The usual clause to cover these fees is 'on architects, surveyors and legal fees for plans, estimates, specifications, quantities and supervision necessarily incurred in reinstatement following destruction of, or damage to, the said buildings by any peril hereby insured against, a percentage in accordance with the scales of the Royal Institute of British Architects, the Royal Institution of Chartered Surveyors and the Law Society, but not such fees in connection with the preparation of any claim hereunder'.

Should there be any intricate matters in connection with an insurance you would be wise to consult an insurance broker whose primary business is to protect the insured.

As I have already shown, in an ordinary policy the insurers are responsible for the actual loss caused by the fire up to the amount for which the property is insured, or at their option for the reinstatement of the premises to a condition similar to that in which they stood immediately before the fire, subject to the same limit of the sum insured. For instance, if a building is worth £5000 at the time of the fire and is insured for £5000 the insurers will be liable, in the event of the property being totally destroyed, for the full £5000, but if damage to the amount of only £2500 is done, that amount only will be the sum to be paid.

Where the sum insured is very large or the hazard of fire is deemed to be abnormal, it is usual for the insurance to be under-written by two or more offices. As a rule, on the occurrence of a fire the companies appoint one assessor to deal with the whole matter, and one of his duties will be to apportion the loss between the insurers, therefore this matter need not trouble us here. The office bearing the largest amount of insurance will usually take the lead in dealing with the settlement, and the other offices generally follow without active participation in the discussion of details.

It is important that the description of the property to be insured should be carefully and accurately drawn as the insurers' liability is limited to the extent of the contract contained in the policy. This description is not difficult to draft in the case of ordinary houses, but may be more complicated when a large number of buildings of various kinds are included under one policy. It is always desirable, though seldom done in the case of small property on account of the cost, to have careful plans, elevations and sections prepared and notes made of all fittings, decorations, etc. This is especially the case when old property having special features of stone, oak, slates, plaster, etc, is being considered, as, unless this is made quite clear in the policy, the insurers may endeavour to meet the claim, after total destruction by fire, by payment of the cost of rebuilding the house in modern materials without reproducing the beautiful features of the old building. Any variations that may be made to the property or changes in occupation during the currency of a policy should be reported at once to the insurers, who will have the document endorsed and the matter will then be in order. This is of much importance and should always be impressed upon a client, for if the insurers have not been notified and given the opportunity to consider the changed nature of the risk their liability may cease to apply, and would in fact do so if the risk was increased.

A further duty of the architect is to prepare a claim on behalf of the insured and negotiate a settlement with the insurers' assessor in the case of damage or destruction by fire of property that has been insured. This is a subject of which all architects should at least have a working knowledge, for it requires considerable experience to deal with satisfactorily. If a fire occurs in a building in course of erection the matter is somewhat simpler than in the case of an old building. In the former case there will be a builder on the job, and if a proper contract has been entered into, including bills of quantities, etc, there should be little difficulty in arriving at a correct valuation of the loss. When, however, the fire occurs in an old building there are many problems to be considered.

We will now assume that a fire has occurred in an existing building which is insured and that you have been commissioned by the owner to act on his behalf. The first thing to be done is to give notice to the insurers that a fire has occurred, letting them know roughly the extent of the fire. If it is a serious one they will at once instruct their assessor to inspect the property and report. There is invariably a clause in the policy referring to this early giving of notice; there should therefore be no delay as to this. You should also at once go to the scene of the fire and inspect the damage; no time should be lost in this respect, in fact an assessor for the insurers is often on the spot before the fire is extinguished.

Many questions will arise and must be dealt with at once. You should request your client to let you have the insurance policy immediately, as your course of action must be determined by its terms. Arrange for a meeting with the insurers' assessor at the earliest possible date. Get him to agree to have the building cleared as far as possible and all dangerous walls, chimney-stacks, portions of roofs, floors, etc, removed. If necessary propose to him that a temporary roof should be erected over the whole of the building to facilitate reinstatement when the claim has been agreed. Should you be dealing with the damaged and destroyed contents of a house, obtain approval of the insurers' assessor to have the damaged article, (the salvage) such as carpets, bed-clothing, curtains, blinds, etc, collected and sent for drying, cleaning, etc. This will probably save a good deal of money in the long run and the cost can be brought into account and included in the claim. You must then set about preparing the claim, and remember that in most insurance policies a period is named within which the claim must be delivered, thirty days is usual, but this period can be extended by permission of the insurers if the fire is a serious one and difficulties arise in preparing the claim.

Each case must be treated upon its merits, but it will generally be found that in cases of serious fires complete plans will be required showing the building as it was left immediately after the fire. If the fire has destroyed practically the whole building it may be very difficult to prepare plans for its reinstatement, unless there are in existence some old plans or records which will give you a sufficient guide. Under one of the conditions of most insurance policies the insured is under the obligation to supply all necessary particulars of the destroyed property to the insurers should they decide to exercise their right under the policy to reinstate, and therefore this is an important matter. Reinstatement by the insurers, however, is now very rarely resorted to.

An estimate of the cost of reinstatement will then be required and the best plan is to have a proper bill of quantities prepared by a quantity surveyor, who will also price out the bill in detail and give you the estimated cost. This will form the basis of your claim, though not of necessity the measure of the loss.

You will probably find a clause in the policy to the effect that 'If the claim be in any respect fraudulent or if any fraudulent means or devices be used by the insured or anyone acting on his behalf to obtain any benefit under this policy or if any destruction or damage be occasioned by the wilful act or with the connivance of the insured all benefit under this policy shall be forfeited'.

This does not, of course, mean that a claim which is too high or not strictly accurate in all respects can be challenged as fraudulent or can be used to debar the insured from obtaining the correct amount for reinstatement, but the clause must be borne in mind and the claim must be bona fide.

A short priced abstract of the bill of quantities will probably be all that is required to satisfy the assessor of a first-class insurance company, but you may find yourself dealing with a company whose financial position is such that it is imperative for them that their loss ratio be kept down at all costs and who will therefore do their utmost to endeavour to water down your claim. If, however, you are sure that your claim is accurate, as it ought to be, you should refuse to accept anything less than the amount asked for.

You will find that all this work takes a substantial amount of time. First there is the time taken in getting the necessary measurements and preparing the plans, then the quantity surveyor will require time to prepare and price a bill of quantities, and finally the negotiations with the insurers' assessor will probably be prolonged much more than you at first expect. If is therefore a wise plan to let your client know that a considerable period may elapse, according to the extent of the fire, before the reinstatement of the damage will be complete. A fire claim for about £14 000 which I recently settled took exactly four months; another case for about £21 000 in which I was interested took over nine months, and a further case involving a claim for £4000 took only a fortnight. If, therefore, your client expects the claim in connection with a serious fire to be settled in a few weeks he is likely to be disappointed and you will do well to give him a hint at an early stage.

The damaged property previously referred to as 'salvage' must be taken into account in the settlement of the claim. You will not infrequently find that the insurers will act generously with you at the settlement and leave the salvage in your hands for you to dispose of as you think fit, but it must be remembered that if the insurers have agreed to pay the full value of any damaged property the salvage belongs to them and they can sell it or dispose of it in any way they think best.

You will be certain to be faced with the question as to which of the parties to the policy is to bear the cost of the architect's and surveyor's services in connection with the reinstatement of the work. Many of the existing policies do not mention either the architect or surveyor, but as the services of these professional men will be required it seems only right that in a policy of indemnity the insurers should bear the charges. I have not been able to find a law case that gives any help in this matter, but I am of opinion that it is a liability of the insurers and advise that a claim should be made for these fees in all cases where an architect or surveyor is employed. Many insurance companies will, if the sum insured is adequate to cover fees in addition to the property specified pay a reasonable sum, but they usually like to make it a kind of 'ex-gratia' payment, whereas it seems to me that as the insured will be bound to employ professional assistance in the reinstatement of his property it is only right that these fees should be treated as a loss strictly incidental to the loss of a building.

If, however, you wish to avoid any dispute as to this it will be well specifically to insure for these fees.

You may receive a demand from a private fire brigade for expenses incurred in extinguishing the fire. This should be sent at once to the insurer's assessor, and it will be found that the insurers will usually pay all reasonable charges. There will no doubt be claims from other persons who assisted in the work and who will ask to be paid the actual cost of clothes, etc, damaged whilst either assisting in putting out the fire or in salvaging the contents. These claims should be sent at once to the insurer's assessor, who will deal with them. The claims for the loss of servants' clothes and belongings should be included under the insurance of the contents of the house, and care should be taken to see that the wording of the policy covers these items.

On the occurrence of a fire it is important to take precautions to see that nothing is lost by theft during or after the fire. The police will assist in the matter and you should call for their services at once. I think the insurers will pay the value of any goods stolen during the fire provided there is no specific clause in the policy exempting them from this liability.

A fire claim in connection with a building in course of erection should be dealt with in a manner similar to that applying to an existing building, but there may be some special items to remember; for example, the unfixed materials lying in the building or upon the ground outside. If, as is usual, such materials are the property of the insured they will be covered by the policy, but if they belong to the contractor the matter might be quite different. In any case not only should the policy cover the building in course of erection but also prepared work in connection with the contract which, although in or about the premises, has not been incorporated in the actual construction.

It should be remembered that insurers are only bound, and rightly so, by the conditions of the policy. It is therefore important to see that all prospective losses of a consequential character, such as rent, rates and taxes, fees, etc, are properly insured and detailed in the policy. This can be done quite easily if the Home protection or comprehensive form of policy is used. This form includes cover, amongst other things, for the buildings, and contents, loss of rent, claims by the public, burglary, housebreaking, larceny and theft, employers' legal liability, bursting or overflowing of water tanks, apparatus and pipes, aircraft and articles dropped therefrom, riot and civil commotion and malicious damage etc, and a condition is usually made that the total sum insured represents not less than the full value.

In practically all insurance policies the right is reserved to the insurers to reinstate the property if they desire to do so, but no provision is made for the insured to require the insurers to reinstate and it will be found that they very rarely wish to exercise this right and much prefer to settle the claim by a money payment. This latter alternative is generally the one also preferred by the insured, as it obviates all questions as to how the reinstatement shall be carried out. You will find that, as a rule, an owner of property after a fire will wish to take the opportunity of effecting some alterations and improvements, and it is clear that if the insurers insisted on reinstatement the matter in such a case would become very complicated, although it could of course be arranged. It is, however, preferable to negotiate a money settlement.

It is always desirable to ascertain the cause of a fire, and this should be stated when sending in a claim. It is of little importance to the insured how the fire was caused as the insurers are liable to make good loss up to the amount stated in the policy however the fire was caused, unless of course it is from a cause specially exempted in the policy.

In making up the claim, damage by water and smoke can be included, as the insurers are liable for all damage to the property insured caused by the fire, and the question whether the water is used to extinguish the fire or to protect adjoining property does not affect the matter.

Should you be unable to effect the settlement of a fire claim you will probably be faced by arbitration. This is the method generally provided for in the policy in case a settlement cannot be reached. Provided your claim is reasonable and a fair one you should have no hesitation in suggesting arbitration. It will be found, however, that some policies do not provide for arbitration and then the dispute must be taken to the law courts for decision. In chapter XXX I have given the procedure which must be followed in an arbitration case.

All fire policies covering trade risks contain an 'Average' clause and we must now consider what this means. The usual condition of 'average' is expressed as follows:

'Whenever a sum insured is declared to be subject to average, if the property covered thereby shall at the breaking out of any fire, or at the commencement of any destruction of or damage to such property by any other peril hereby insured against, be collectively of greater value than such sum insured, then the insured shall be considered as being his own insurer for the difference and shall bear a rateable share of the loss accordingly'.

This condition of 'average' means that, if a property is under-insured at the time of the fire, the cost of making good any loss that may occur will be proportioned between the insurers and the insured in the relation existing between the actual value of the property and the sum insured. For example, if the value of the property is £10 000 and it is insured for only £5000, should damage by fire occur to the extent of say £5000 the company will be liable to pay only one half, viz £2500. It will be assumed that the insured acted as his own insurer for the difference between the amount of his insurance with the company and the full value of the property in the event of a loss, and thus will contribute towards the amount of the loss by a proportionate abatement of his claim upon the insurers. This will show how necessary it is that the sum insured should represent the full value of the property, for if such is the case the 'average' clause becomes inoperative.

I have already referred to the question of the 'contents' of a house. It may be said that the insurance of furniture, wearing apparel and personal belongings have nothing to do with the practice of an architect. To this I cannot agree, as it is not an infrequent matter for an architect's advice on this subject to be sought and therefore he should be acquainted with the elementary principles of this important branch of insurance and be able to give his client useful and correct advice. I am sure that a client will appreciate his architect's services far more if he is able to explain this subject than if the only thing he can do is to advise that the insurance of 'contents' is a matter for an insurance broker rather than for an architect.

It can be assumed that a large number of insured give little thought to the correct value of their furniture and effects, and even less thought to a correct valuation of their wearing apparel, but make a guess at an amount (which is generally far below its true value) and, should a fire occur, trust to the generosity of the insurers to make good the loss, at any rate, up to the extent of the amount of the insurance. But, insurance of furniture and wearing apparel is not quite as simple as this, and, unless the matter is considered more carefully than is usually the case, much disappointment awaits the insured should he be so unfortunate as to have a serious fire, and the insurers decide to stand by the strict legal interpretation of the policy.

I think it is absolutely necessary that some kind of estimate should always be made and, now that values are changing so rapidly, it is more important than ever that the insured should have a record of his furniture and effects. In order to help you prepare such a record I have included in the *Appendix*, page 370, some typical portions of an inventory and valuation made by me in 1964. The estimated value of the contents included in this inventory when taken was £3750, the present-day value, however, will probably be four or five times as much. It will be appreciated that the value of furniture fluctuates considerably so that it will be wise to have your valuation reconsidered from time to time. Should it not be possible to have a proper inventory prepared possibly on account of the expense, and your client will consider the second best is good enough for him, then you should advise him to make as careful and accurate an estimate as possible before taking out a policy.

It must be remembered that whatever the sum for which you insure you cannot recover more than the value of your property at the time of the loss and that when making a claim it will be necessary to convince the insurers that you were in actual possession of the furniture, etc, and that the amount you claim is the correct value at the time of the loss and not necessarily the amount of money you paid for it.

Should a fire occur it will be a great help if the insured can produce accounts and receipts for the goods destroyed, but the best thing is to be able to produce an inventory, prepared by a qualified valuer. This inventory can be submitted to the Insurance Company before the policy is completed and will almost always be accepted by them as evidence that the goods were in your possession at the date when it was prepared; they will also accept the valuation as reasonable evidence of the values of the items detailed at the date of the compilation of the inventory, and as a basis for the settlement of the loss. They will probably wish to have a copy of the inventory to place with the policy, but it must be remembered that the recognition of an inventory by an insurance company even when mentioned in the policy does not constitute a contract to pay a fixed sum in the event of a loss, regardless of the value of the property at the time of a fire.

You may wish to have some information as to the insurance of your drawings and papers. It will be obvious, I think, that original drawings and papers of which no copies exist cannot be replaced, and therefore the insurance against damage by fire can only be paid as compensation for the loss. As a rule the insurance companies will undertake a risk of this sort, and will quote a special premium to suit each case. A usual clause in an insurance policy is 'It is hereby declared that the Company's liability in respect of plans, drawings and designs shall extend only to the value of the materials and labour necessarily bestowed thereon to reproduce the same, but in no case shall the Company's liability in respect of any one plan, drawing or design, exceed £ . . . .'.

There is also a scheme under which you can insure against additional expenditure of carrying on your practice following a fire at your office and against loss of income. The policy is called a Consequential Fire Loss Policy and details are readily obtainable from any broker or insurance company.

Appendix

LIST OF TECHNICAL BOOKS RECOMMENDED

Chapter	Title	Author or Editor	Publisher
III	Handbook of Archi- tectural Practice and Management		RIBA Publications
	Architects Guide to Running a Job	Ronald Green	Architectural Press
	Architects Guide to Site Management	Ronald Green	Architectural Press
	The Architect in Practice	A J Willis and W N B George	Crosby Lockwood
V	Libraries for Professional Practice	Patrick Calderhead	Architectural Press
VI	Practical Surveying	G W Usill	Technical Press
VII	A J Metric Handbook	Leslie Fairweather and Jan A Sliwa	Architectural Press
VIII	Specification Metric Edition 1 & 2	Dex Harrison	Architectural Press
	Specification Writing	A J Willis	Crosby Lockwood
X	Schedule of Rates for Building Works (Metric Edition) 1969		HM Stationery Office
XI	Elements of Estimating	David S M Hall	Batsford

Chapter	Title	Author or Editor	Publisher
	Architects' and Builders' Price Book	Davis, Belfield and Everest	Spon
	Mechanical and Electrical Services Price Book	Davis, Belfield and Everest	Spon
	Laxtons Building Price Book	W R Wheatley	Kelly's Directories
XIII	The Standard Form of Building Contract	Derek Walker-Smith and Howard Close	Charles Knight
	Building Contracts and Practice	Emden & Gill	Butterworth
	The Placing and Management of Building Contracts	Banwell Report	HM Stationery Office
	Law and Practice of Building Contracts	D Keating	Sweet and Maxwell
	Hudson's Building and Engineering Contracts	I N Duncan Wallace	Sweet and Maxwell
	A J Legal Handbook	Freeth and Davey	Architectural Press
	Critical Path Analysis	D W Lang	Teach Yourself Books
XIV	Mitchell's Building Construction		
	Structure and Fabric	Jack Foster	Batsford
	Materials	Alan Everett	Batsford
	Components and Finishes	Harold King and Alan Everett	Batsford
	Environment and Services	Peter Burberry	Batsford
	Problems in Building Construction and Tutors' Guide	J Trill and J T Bowyer	Architectural Press

Chapter	Title	Author or Edited by	Publisher
XXIV	The Law relating to the Architect	E J Rimmer	Stevens & Sons
	A J Legal Handbook	Evelyn Freeth and Peter Davey	Architectural Press
	A Summary of Town and Country Planning Law and the Law of Compulsory Purchase and Compensation	A J Lomnicki	Batsford
XXV	Mitchell's Building Construction: Environment and Services	Peter Burberry	Batsford
XXVI	The Building Regulations 1972		HM Stationery Office
	Guide to the Building Regulations 1972	A J Elder	Architectural Press
	Guide to the London Building (Constructional) By-Laws and Building Acts	P H Pitt and J Dufton	Architectural Press
XXVIII	Law of Dilapidations	B W Adkin	The Estates Gazette
XXIX	Guide to Domestic Building Surveys	Jack Bowyer	Architectural Press
XXX	Elements & Procedure in Arbitration,	William H Gill	Sweet and Maxwell
	Arbitrations and Awards	John P H Soper	The Estates Gazette

SPECIFICATION

Note   The following specification is of the fully detailed type that will be needed where quantities do not form part of the contract, and the specification does. Where quantities form part of the contract, the specification, being no longer a contract document as noted on page 104 usually takes the form of a series of schedules of windows, doors and finishings similar to those shown on pages 62, 63, and 64, together with a number of clauses giving descriptions of items of work which are not self-specifying by reference to the drawings and bills of quantities.

The accommodation in the house for which the following specification was written was as follows:

Ground floor	*First floor*
Living-room	Four bedrooms
Dining-room	Two bathrooms
Entrance hall	WC
Cloakroom	Linen store
Lobby	Dressing-room
Porch	
Office	
Kitchen	
Scullery	
Larder	
Boiler-room	
Coal store	
Coke and Wood store	
Servants' wc	
Enclosed yard	
Sun porch	
Garage	

Most of the ordinary materials used in building have now been made the subject of a British Standard and you should obtain a copy of the sectional list of British Standards *Building* published by the British Standards Institution, 2 Park Street, London W1 which will enable you to see exactly what materials are covered in this way.

It is not sufficient just to specify that a certain material is to conform to its particular British Standard, however, unless you have read the Standard in question and have ascertained that there are no alternative sections, parts, etc. To obtain the benefit from these publications you must refer to them accurately and state exactly what you require. You will see many references to British Standards in the following specification, which is referred to in chapter VIII page 56.

𝕾𝖕𝖊𝖈𝖎𝖋𝖎𝖈𝖆𝖙𝖎𝖔𝖓 of work required to be done and materials to be used in the erection and completion of a house and outbuildings at Haywards Heath, Sussex, for Robert Z Blank Esq

Victor R J Brown Esq, FRIBA
Chartered Architect
Westminster, SW1

January 1974

Preliminaries
Conditions of Contract
1   The Agreement and Schedule of Conditions of Building Contract to be used will be based upon the form issued under the sanction of the Royal Institute of British Architects, the National Federation of Building Trades Employers and the Royal Institution of Chartered Surveyors dated 1963, Private Edition (July 1973 Revision) so far as applicable and except as provided hereafter, and Quantities will not form part of the Contract.

Site of buildings
2   The site of the buildings is believed to consist of turf and vegetable earth about 225 mm thick overlaying gravel, but no responsibility is accepted in respect of the nature of the material to be excavated. A trial hole has been sunk on the site of the new building and can be inspected by the Contractor.

Work included in the Contract
3   The work included in the contract consists of the erection and finishing complete of the house together with external pavings, entrance drive, forecourt, etc.

Drawings
4   The drawings referred to in the specification are as follows, and consist of:

No.1 Plans, elevations and sections. ⎫
No.2 Foundations and roof plan.   ⎬   1:100 scale
No.3 Site works and drainage plan.   ⎭
No.4 Joinery details.   1:20   scale

Order of proceeding with work
5   The whole of the works must be proceeded with in such sections and at such times as ordered by the Architect.

Drawings and Specifications, etc

6   The Contractor shall furnish to the Architect on the signing of this contract a schedule of rates upon which the Contractor's estimate has been based, unless such schedule has already been furnished. The contract drawings and the said specification and the said schedule of rates shall remain in the custody of the Architect so as to be available at all reasonable times for the inspection of the Employer or the Contractor. The Architect without charge to the Contractor shall on the signing of this contract furnish him with two copies of the contract drawings and of the specification, and shall within a reasonable time also furnish him with such further drawings as are reasonably necessary to enable him to carry out all Architect's instructions and with any further details which in the opinion of the Architect are necessary for the execution of any part of the work. If any bills of quantities are provided, nothing contained therein shall confer any rights or impose any obligations beyond those conferred or imposed by the contract documents, namely, by the contract drawings, specification and conditions referred to in the articles of agreement. The Contractor shall keep one copy of the contract drawings and the specification on the works so as to be available to the Architect or his representative at all reasonable times. Upon receiving final payment the Contractor shall forthwith return to the Architect all drawings and specifications bearing his name.

None of the documents hereinbefore mentioned shall be used by either of the parties hereto for any purpose other than this contract, and neither the Employer, the Architect nor the Surveyor shall divulge or use except for the purposes of this contract any information contained in the said schedule of rates.

Contractor to provide and do everything necessary

7   The Contractor shall provide everything necessary for the proper execution of the works, according to the true intent and meaning of the drawings and specification taken together, whether the same may or may not be particularly shown on the drawings or described in the specification, provided that the same is reasonably to be inferred therefrom; and if the Contractor finds any discrepancy in the drawings, or between the drawings and specification, he shall immediately refer the same to the Architect, who shall decide the procedure. Figured dimensions to be followed in preference to scale dimensions, and all dimensions and particulars to be taken from the actual work. It must be distinctly understood that the whole of the conditions of the specification are intended to be strictly enforced, and that no extra charges in respect of extra works will be allowed unless they are clearly outside the spirit and meaning of the specification nor unless such works shall have been ordered in writing by the Architect. Any instructions given verbally shall be deemed as instructions for the proper execution of the works not involving extra charges.

Expedition of works

8   Possession of the site will be given to the Contractor immediately the contract is signed. The works must be carried out with due diligence and expedition, and the whole of the works, including all extra and additional works ordered by the Architect must be completed, subject to any extension of time, by the date mentioned in the Contract.

Local and other authorities' notices and fees

9   (a) The Contractor shall comply with and give all notices required by any Act of Parliament or by any regulation or by-law of any local authority who have any jurisdiction with regard to the Works or with whose systems the same are or will be connected and he shall pay and indemnify the Employer against any fees or charges (including any rates and taxes other than Value Added Tax) legally demandable under such Act of Parliament, regulation or by-law in respect of the works.

(b) The Contractor before making any variations from the Contract Drawings or Specification necessitated by such compliance shall give to the Architect written notice specifying and giving the reason for such variation and applying for instructions in reference thereto.

(c) If the Contractor within seven days of having applied for the same does not receive such instructions, he shall proceed with the work conforming to the provision, regulation or by-law in question and any variation thereby necessitated shall be deemed to be a variation under clause 11 of the Conditions of Contract attached to the Articles of Agreement.

(d) The Contractor must provide for and pay all fees and charges under the above clause.

Setting out of works

10   The Architect shall furnish to the Contractor, either by way of carefully dimensioned drawings or by personal supervision at the time of setting out the works, such information as shall enable the Contractor to set out the enclosing walls of the building at ground level after which the Contractor shall be responsible and shall at his own cost amend any errors arising from his own inaccurate setting out, unless the Architect shall otherwise direct. The Contractor shall provide at his own cost all planking, gangways, etc, necessary for affording access to every part of the works, and all assistance or attendance required by the Quantity Surveyor to enable him to ascertain the particulars, and obtain the measurements of the work done.

Materials and workmanship to conform to description

11   All materials and workmanship shall be of the respective kinds described in the Specification and the Contractor shall upon the request of the Architect furnish him with vouchers to prove that the materials comply therewith. The Contractor shall arrange for and/or carry out any test of any materials which the Architect may in writing require and the cost thereof shall be added to the Contract sum unless provided

for in the Specification or unless the test shows that the said materials are not in accordance with this contract. Samples of all materials to be used must be submitted to the Architect.

Contractor to obtain his own information

12   The Contractor to visit and examine the site, and satisfy himself as to the nature of the existing roads or other means of communication, the character of the soil and of the excavations, the correct dimensions of the work, and the facilities for obtaining the special articles, and shall obtain generally his own information on all matters affecting the execution of the works. No extra charge made in consequence of any misunderstanding, or incorrect information on any of these points, or on the ground of insufficient description will be allowed.

Foreman

13   The Contractor must keep on the works during all working hours a competent General Foreman who shall be empowered to receive and act upon the instructions given by the Architect, and any such instructions, directions or explanations given to the Foreman shall be held to have been given to the Contractor. The Foreman to be provided with a proper office as necessary for the work and to which the Architect, Quantity Surveyor and their representatives shall have access at all times.

Misconduct of workmen

14   The Contractor shall, on the request of the Architect, immediately dismiss from the works any person employed thereon by him who may, in the opinion of the Architect, be incompetent or misconduct himself, and such person shall not be again employed on the works without the permission of the Architect.

Access for Architect to works

15   The Architect and his representatives shall at all reasonable times have access to the works and/or the workshops or other places of the Contractor where work is being prepared for the contract, and in so far as work in virtue of any sub-contract is to be so prepared in workshops or other places of a sub-contractor (whether or not a nominated Sub-contractor as defined in clause 27 of the Conditions of Contract) the Contractor shall also by a term in the sub-contract so far as possible secure a similar right of access to those workshops or places for the Architect and his representatives and shall do all things reasonably necessary, to make such right effective.

Clerk of Works

16   The Employer shall be entitled to appoint a Clerk of Works whose duty shall be to act solely as Inspector on behalf of the Employer under the directions of the Architect and the Contractor shall afford every facility for the performance of that duty.

Office for Clerk of Works

17 The Contractor to erect and keep in repair a proper office on the premises for the use of the Clerk of Works, in which all drawings and specifications must be kept with care, and to which the Architect, the Clerk of Works and their representatives shall have full access at all times; the walls and ceiling to be lined throughout with 13 mm insulating boarding and the office to have ample windows and one external door fitted with a lock. The office to be fitted up by the Contractor with desk on one side with large drawers for drawings, and small drawers for papers, etc, and with locks and keys, and with large table and chairs and two AOa drawing-boards with tee-squares, etc, and all other necessary conveniences for keeping and preparing drawings as well as for writing. The Contractor to provide suitable heating and lighting for the office, and to keep it clean and in good order at all times. Any removal of the Clerk of Works' office, fittings, etc, from the original position to any portion of the new buildings during construction of the works must be carried out by the Contractor at his own expense. If a Clerk of Works is not employed the cost of providing and maintaining the office will be deducted.

Telephone

18 The Contractor shall provide a telephone on the PO service in the Clerk of Works' office and be responsible for and pay all charges in connection with its installation and for keeping it in good order during the Contract. A Provisional sum of £25 is to be included to pay the PO charges for calls and all other expenses to be borne by the Contractor. Should the Contractor require a telephone in the Foreman's office he must make allowance for and pay all charges in connection therewith.

Ascertainment of prices for variations

19 No variation shall vitiate this contract. All variations authorised by the Architect or subsequently sanctioned by him in writing shall be measured and valued by the Quantity Surveyor who shall give to the Contractor an opportunity of being present at the time of such measurement and of taking such notes and measurements as the Contractor may require. The Contractor shall be supplied with a copy of the priced bills of variations not later than the end of the Period of Final Measurement stated in the *Appendix* to the Conditions and before the date of the Architect's certificate in respect of such variations, and the valuation thereof unless previously or otherwise agreed shall be made in accordance with the following rules:

(a) The Schedule of Rates mentioned in clause 3 of the Conditions shall determine the valuation of extra work of similar character executed under similar conditions as work priced therein:

(b)), the said rates, where extra work is not of a similar character or executed under similar conditions as aforesaid, shall be the basis of prices for the same so far as may be reasonable, failing which a fair valuation thereof shall be made:

(c) Where extra work cannot properly be measured and valued the Contractor shall be allowed day-work prices at rates calculated in accordance with the 'Definition of Prime Cost of Daywork carried out under a Building Contract' issued by the Royal Institution of Chartered Surveyors and the National Federation of Building Trades Employers, together with percentage additions as set out in the contract Schedule of Rates, or where a definition has been agreed between the said Institution and the appropriate body representing any sub-contracting trade at rates calculated in accordance therewith (whether in the last mentioned case the work be done by the Contractor or by a sub-contractor):

Provided that in any case vouchers specifying the time daily spent upon the work (and if required by the Architect the workmen's names) and the materials employed shall be delivered for verification to the Architect or his authorised representative not later than the end of the week following that in which the work has been executed;

(d) The prices in the above mentioned Schedule of Rates shall determine the valuation of items omitted; provided that if omissions substantially vary the conditions under which any remaining items of work are carried out the prices for such remaining items shall be valued under rule (b) of this clause.

The measurement and valuation of the works shall be completed within the Period of Final Measurement stated in the appendix and if no other period is so stated then within 6 months from the practical completion of the works and effect shall be given to the measurement and valuation of variations by adjustment of the Contract Sum.

Bad workmanship

20   The Architect shall, during the progress of the works, have power to order in writing from time to time the removal from the works, within such reasonable time or times as may be specified in the order, of any materials which in the opinion of the Architect are not in accordance with the specification or the instructions of the Architect, the substitution of proper materials, and the removal and proper re-execution of any work executed with the materials or workmanship not in accordance with the drawings and specification and instructions; and the Contractor shall forthwith carry out such order at his own cost. In case of default on the part of the Contractor to carry out such order, the Employer shall have power to employ and pay other persons to carry out the same; and all expenses consequent thereon or incidental thereto shall be borne by the Contractor, and shall be recoverable from him by the Employer, or may be deducted by the Employer from any moneys due or that may become due to the Contractor.

Defects after completion

21   Any defects, shrinkage or other faults which shall appear within the Defects Liability Period stated in the appendix to the Conditions

and shall be due to materials or workmanship not in accordance with this contract or to frost occurring before completion of the works, shall within a reasonable time after receipt of the Architect's written instructions in that behalf be made good by the Contractor and (unless the Architect shall otherwise direct) at his own cost; provided that the Contractor shall not be required to make good at his own cost any damage by frost which may appear after completion, unless the Architect shall decide that such damage is due to injury which took place before completion. In the case of default the Employer may employ and pay other persons to amend and make good such defects, shrinkage or other faults or damage, and all expenses consequent thereon or incidental thereto shall be borne by the Contractor and shall be recoverable from him by the Employer, or may be deducted by the Employer from any moneys due or that may become due to the Contractor. Should any defective work have been done or material supplied by any Sub-Contractor employed on the works who has been nominated or approved by the Architect, the Contractor shall be liable to make good in the same manner as if such work or material had been done or supplied by the Contractor.

Work to be opened up at the request of Architect
22   The Contractor shall, at the request of the Architect, within such time as the Architect shall name, open for inspection any work covered up; and should the Contractor refuse or neglect to comply with such request, the Architect may employ other workmen to open up the same. If the said work has been covered up in contravention of the Architect's instructions, or if on being opened up it be found not in accordance with the drawings and specification or the instructions of the Architect, the expenses of the opening and covering it up again, whether done by the Contractor or such other workmen, shall be borne by, and be recoverable from, the Contractor, or may be deducted as aforesaid. If the work has not been covered up in contravention of such instructions, and be found in accordance with the said drawings and specification or instructions, then the expenses aforesaid shall be borne by the Employer and be added to the contract sum; provided always that in the case of any urgent work so opened up and requiring immediate attention the Architect shall, within a reasonable time after receipt of notice from the Contractor that the work has been so opened, make or cause the inspection thereof to be made, and at the expiration of such time, if such inspection shall not have been made, the Contractor may cover up the same, and shall not be required to open it up again for inspection except at the expense of the Employer.

Assignment or sub-letting
23   The Contractor shall not, without the written consent of the Architect, assign this contract or sublet any portion of the works; provided that such consent shall not be unreasonably withheld to the prejudice of the Contractor.

Sub-Contractors and Suppliers

24   Where prime cost or provisional sums are included in the specification for persons to be nominated or selected by the Architect to supply and fix materials, or to execute work on the site, they are to be regarded as nominated sub-contractors to whom the terms of clause 27 of the Conditions of Contract apply. Where prime cost or provisional sums are included in the specification in respect of any materials or goods to be fixed by the contractors, the suppliers are to be regarded as nominated suppliers to whom the terms of clause 28 of the Conditions of Contract apply.

Injury to Persons and Property

25   Injury to persons. The Contractor shall be solely liable for and shall indemnify the Employers in respect of any liability, loss, claim or proceedings whatsoever arising under any statute or at common law in respect of personal injury to or the death of any person whomsoever arising out of or in the course of or caused by the execution of the work unless due to any act or neglect of the Employers or of any person for whom the Employers are responsible.

Injury to property. The Contractor shall be liable for and shall indemnify the Employers against any loss, liability, claim or proceeding in respect of any injury or damage whatsoever to any property real or personal in so far as such injury or damage arises out of or in the course of or by reason of the execution of the works and provided always that the same is due to any negligence, omission or default of the Contractor, his servants or agents or of any Sub-contractor.

Policies of insurance. The Contractor shall secure the due performance of these indemnities by entering into proper and sufficient policies of insurance.

Insurance

26   The Contractor shall in the joint names of the Employer and Contractor insure against loss and damage by fire for the full value thereof (plus 15% to cover Architect's and Surveyor's fees) all work executed and all unfixed materials and goods upon the site but excluding plant, tools and equipment and shall keep such works, materials and goods so insured until the works are delivered up; such insurance shall be with a company or companies approved by the Architect and the Contractor shall deposit with him the policies and premium receipts; should the Contractor make default the Employer may insure as aforesaid and deduct the premiums paid from any monies due or to become due to the Contractor.

The Contractor shall upon settlement of any claim under the policies aforesaid proceed with due diligence to rebuild or repair the works and replace or repair the materials or goods destroyed or injured. All moneys received under such policies (less the said 15%) are to be paid to the Contractor by instalments under certificates of the Architect and the Contractor shall not be entitled to any payment in respect of the rebuilding or repair of the works or the replacement or repair of the materials or goods destroyed or injured other than the moneys received under the said policies.

Time for completion
27   The whole of the works, together with all minor additional works (if any) ordered by the Architect, shall be completed within twelve months from the date of possession of the site, subject, nevertheless, to the provisions contained in the contract for extension of time.

Damage for non-completion and bonus
28   If the Contractor fails to complete the works by the date mentioned in the Contract, or within any extended time, the Contractor shall pay or allow to the Employer the sum of £40 as liquidated and ascertained damages for each week which shall elapse between the prescribed date and the date on which the works are certified by the Architect as complete. Moreover, the Employer shall pay to the Contractor by way of bonus the sum of £40 for each week the building is handed over for occupation by the Employer before the date of completion.

Receipted accounts
29   The receipted vouchers for all articles or work for which prime cost amounts or provisional sums are given in the Specification must be produced at the final settlement of accounts and before the final certificate is issued. The Contractor shall also produce to the Architects or the Surveyors the receipts for all such payments as may have been included in the preceding certificate when applying for a further certificate in his own favour.

Payment
30   Payment will be made at the rate of 95 per cent of the value of the work actually done and fixed in the building. The balance of 5 per cent will be retained by the Employer until the works are certified as complete, when one half of this sum will be paid; the other half, together with any further sum due to the Contractor at the final adjustment of accounts, will be paid on the expiration of the period of maintenance. Applications for certificates to be accompanied by detailed approximate statements showing the amount of work executed.

Sub-contractors requirements
31   The Contractor is requested to obtain from the various Sub-contractors, for whom provisions are made in this specification, a statement showing what their requirements are as regards recesses, chases, etc, so that they may be built correctly in the first place and no alterations needed afterwards. If the Contractor fails to do this the onus of the alterations must fall upon him, and he will be required to carry

out the necessary work at his own expense.

Facilities
32   The Contractor to afford facilities to any other parties employed upon the building, so that their work may proceed during the progress of the building, and, unless otherwise specified, to provide for such parties proper, sufficient, and, if necessary, special scaffolding, hoisting, and ladders, and supply them with water and lighting.

Watching and lighting
33   The Contractor from the time of being placed in possession, must watch, light, and protect the works, the site and the surrounding property by day, by night, and at week-ends. All artificial light required for the works and to enable the Contractor and Sub-contractors to complete the works in the specified time including for the workmen of any Sub-contractor or Special Tradesmen, must be provided by the Contractor at his own cost.

Scaffolding and plant
34   The Contractor to provide the whole of the necessary plant, scaffolding, tackle, cartage, and labour necessary for the prompt and efficient execution of the works, and remove same at the completion of the work.

Water
35   The whole of the water required for the works, including that required by Special Tradesmen and Sub-contractors, must be provided by the Contractor, and must be clean, fresh water. The Contractor must execute any temporary plumbing required at his own expense, and pay all fees and charges.

Sheds and workshops
36   The Contractor to provide all necessary workshops and sheds for the use of workmen, and storage of materials, and maintain and keep the same in order to the satisfaction of the Architect, and remove them at completion.

Temporary conveniences
37   The Contractor to provide all temporary conveniences for the use of the men. The same to be kept disinfected and clean at all times during the progress of the works, and cleared away at completion, and the ground made good after. The position of these sheds, etc, must be carefully selected, and the approval of the Architect obtained before erection.

Area for work
38   The area which the Contractor will have for his use in carrying out this contract is shown coloured green on the block plan, and the

Contractor must keep his workmen strictly within these limits.

Hoarding
39   The Contractor to obtain licences, and pay fees for, and to provide, erect, maintain, and afterwards remove all hoardings necessary, with all gates and fastenings, etc, to the satisfaction of the Architect and the Local Authorities.

Advertising on hoarding
40   The advertising rights on any hoarding or scaffolding will be reserved to the Employer and the Contractor must keep them free from bills or advertisements until they are let or otherwise dealt with. No notice boards, except the Contractor's own name board will be permitted to be exhibited upon the hoarding or scaffolding unless specially sanctioned by the Architect.

Cartage of materials
41   The Contractor's attention is drawn to the question of cartage of materials to the site by motor-lorries, or other vehicles, in case any special regulations are imposed, or special arrangements required, by the Local Authorities, or any question of payment for making good damage to roads is raised by them. He is to include in his tender for any payment, or for any work necessary as no responsibility in this matter can be accepted by the Employer.

Loading and unloading materials
42   The Contractor to take care, in loading and unloading materials for the works, that the streets, roads and footpaths are not obstructed or the traffic impeded, and he must conform with the police regulations for carting, loading and unloading all materials, plant, earth, debris, etc, to or from the building.

Cover up and protect
43   The Contractor must cover up and protect from injury from any cause all new work. He must also supply all temporary doors, protection to windows, and any other requisite protection for the whole of the works executed, whether by himself or Special Tradesmen or Sub-contractors, and any damage caused must be made good by the Contractor at his own expense.

Protect fences, etc
44   The whole of the fences, paths, trees, shrubs, greens, and other surfaces about the buildings or approaches thereto, which are required to be maintained, must be protected and kept free from damage due to the operations in connection with the works.

Temporary road-making
45   The Contractor to provide such temporary road-making on the

site as may be necessary for the proper performance of the contract, and for his own convenience, but not otherwise.

Frost
46 No concrete work or setting of masonry to be executed during frosty weather without the written approval of the Architect being first obtained. This approval, if obtained, shall not exonerate the Contractor from having to reinstate in an efficient manner, and to the satisfaction of the Architect, any work which may be damaged by frost, inclement weather, etc.

Removal of water
47 The Contractor to be responsible for all pumping that may be required to keep the several works dry down to the level of the bottom of the excavations, and to carry out the other requirements of this specification, and he is to remove the hole of the water finding its way into the same from rain, springs, or any other sources from which it may come, as no accumulation of water will be permitted at any time during the execution of the contract.

Articles of value
48 All articles of value and of antiquarian or archaeological interest that may be found in the excavations, or on the property of the Employer, shall be handed over to the Architect.

Attendance
49 The Contractor to attend upon, cut away for, and make good after, all trades mentioned in this specification.

Cart away rubbish
50 All rubbish as it accumulates from time to time during the progress of the works, and at completion, including that of Sub-contractors and Special Tradesmen to be cleared and carted away, and all materials condemned by the Architect to be removed.

Contingencies
51 The provisional sum of £1000 to be provided for contingencies and unforeseen works and expended only as the Architect may direct, and to be deducted in whole or in part, if not required.

Marginal notes
52 The marginal notes in this specification are for the convenience of reference only, and are not to affect the construction of the clauses.

Cleaning on completion
53 All floors, pavings, staircases, etc, to be scrubbed; all glass to be cleaned on both sides to windows, screens, doors, skylights, rooflights, etc, all gullies, gutters, pipe heads, etc, to be cleared out, and the premises left clean, perfect, and watertight upon completion.

Appendix to the Conditions
54   The *Appendix* given on page 29 of the Conditions annexed to the
Articles of Agreement will be filled in as follows:

Clause	Marginal description
15, 16 and 30	Defects liability period (six months)
20A	Percentage to cover professional fees (15%)
21	Date for possession (the date agreed upon and as will be stated in the Contract; or alternatively a pre-determined date if this can be specified)
21	Time for completion (twelve months from the date of possession)
22	Liquidated and ascertained damages (£40.00 per week with a corresponding bonus for earlier completion)
26	Period of delay: (i) by reason of loss or damage caused by any one of the contingencies referred to in clause 20(A) or clause 20(B) (if applicable) (three months) (ii) for any other reason (one month)
27(g)	Prime cost or Provisional Sums for which the Contractor desires to tender (A letter should be attached to the Form of Tender giving a list of these items)
30(1)	Period of interim certificates (One certificate per month)
30(3)	Retention percentage (5%)
30(5)	Period of Final Measurement and Valuation (6 months)
31E	Percentage addition (The percentage stated by the Architect at tender stage in relation to clause 31B only as clause 31A is to be deleted)

Conditions of Contract
55   The attention of the Contractor is directed to the Conditions
annexed to the Articles of Agreement and he is to allow in his tender
for any sum or sums that he may consider necessary for the items given
below in tabulated form. All the clauses in the Conditions other than
those set out below have been referred to previously in this Specification. Where the Conditions set out in this Specification vary from
those set out in the Contract, the Conditions in the Contract are to
prevail.

Supplemental Agreement (the VAT Agreement)
(This agreement which is to be signed by the Employer and the Contractor at the same time as the Contract provides for the Employer paying the Contractor for any tax properly chargeable by the Commissioners of Customs and Excise on the Contractor for goods and

services supplied by him to the Employer. The Contractor is obliged to make certain assessments and to prepare interim and final statements of tax and if necessary to appeal to the Commissioners in the event of the Employer's disagreement with the figures.)

Lowest tender
56 The Employer does not bind himself to accept the lowest or any tender.

Excavator and Concretor

Surface soil
57 The site of the building and yard to be cleared of turf and vegetable soil to a depth of 225 mm or as may be directed, and the same wheeled to spoil in a convenient spot not exceeding 200 m distance and afterwards spread over positions as directed as top dressing, any surplus not required to be carted away.

Sand and gravel in excavations
58 Should suitable sand or gravel be found in the excavations, and the Contractor is allowed to use the same in the work, he will be required to pay the Employer the full market value. Any sand or gravel taken from the excavations will remain the property of the Employer, and in the event of it not being allowed to be used in the work, the subject of this contract, the Employer reserves the right to dispose of it in any way he wishes, or to direct the Contractor to cart it away as ordinary excavated materials.

Excavations
59 The area of site, and foundations of walls, pipe trenches, surfaces under floors, and other work indicated on the drawings, to be excavated to the lengths and widths shown, and to the depths as directed by the Architect on the site, according to the nature of the subsoil, and to ensure that the bottoms of the trenches are sufficiently solid for a good foundation. All surplus excavated material to be spread on the site or carted away as directed.

Planking and strutting
60 The sides of the excavations to be timbered and shored in such a way as may be sufficient to secure them from falling in, and the timbers to be maintained as long as necessary.

Level, fill and ram
61 All trenches for foundations to be levelled and rammed, if so directed, and all trenches for drains and pipes to be formed, graded, and rammed. The trenches around foundations and walls, and around and over pipes, to be filled in and rammed in 300 mm layers. All

excavations for foundations to be inspected and approved by the Architect or his representative before any concrete is laid therein.

Variations in excavations
62   All variations from the drawings in respect of the excavations will be measured from time to time, as they occur, by the Quantity Surveyor, and the Contractor must not fill in the earth, etc, until the measurements of such variations have been agreed to.

Make up ground
63   The ground within and around the buildings to be made up with hardcore, levelled, and graded as shown on the drawings, rammed and consolidated as necessary.

Hardcore
64   Hardcore to be formed of well broken brick, stone or other approved dry material that will pass in all directions through a 50 mm ring, well rolled, rammed and consolidated.

Portland cement
65   Cement throughout the whole of the work to be ordinary Portland cement to comply in all respects with the requirements of BS 12. The cement to be stored in a watertight shed with boarded floor raised at least 150 mm above the ground and must be used as far as possible in the order in which it has been stored.

Aggregates
66   Aggregates for concrete shall comply with the requirements of BS 882 and 1201. Coarse aggregates for plain concrete to be 38 mm — 5 mm nominal size and for reinforced concrete to be 19 mm — 5 mm nominal size. Fine aggregate shall be natural sand or crushed gravel sand Grading Zone 1. All-in aggregate to be 38 mm maximum size.

Water
67   Water for mixing concrete, etc, shall be clean and free from acids, vegetable matter, etc. Only water fit for drinking will be considered fit for use.

Materials and mixing of concrete
68   The materials for the concrete to be carefully measured in proper proportions, measuring boxes of suitable sizes being made and used for the purpose. The mixing of the concrete to be done by power-driven batch mixers of a type approved by the Architect. The mixers shall be suitably protected from the wind to prevent loss of cement. The aggregates and cement shall first be mixed dry and then after the addition of water. The concrete must be mixed for not less than two minutes and until it is of even colour and of uniform consistency throughout. The machine mixers and all handling plant must be

thoroughly washed out when mixing ceases and also when recommencing the mixing. The batch sizes shall be such that only whole bags of cement are used. If permission for mixing by hand is given the materials are to be mixed on a clean boarded platform and turned over at least three times in a dry state, once while water is added through a rose headed jet and once when wet and then wheeled to the site where it is to be deposited.

Traffic over concrete
69   No traffic of any kind to be allowed over any concrete until it is thoroughly hard.

Stale concrete
70   No stale concrete which has commenced to set to be used or mixed with any other concrete, but shall only be used as hard core.

Concrete
71   The concrete except where otherwise described to be composed of one part of Portland cement by volume, two parts of fine aggregate and four parts of coarse aggregate all measured and mixed as previously described and carefully deposited and rammed.

Concrete in foundations
72   The foundations to walls to be formed of concrete, composed of 1 part of Portland cement to 6 parts of 'All-in' aggregate, well rammed to required levels to receive brickwork. The concrete is to be laid to the dimensions given on the drawings and is to fill the whole of the trenches as dug. The thickness may be increased by the Architect after inspection of the trenches, but all additional concrete will be paid for as an extra.

Concrete under floors and pavings
73   The ground surface below all floors and pavings to be covered with a 150 mm thick bed of Portland cement concrete (1:2:4 38 mm aggregate). The concrete to be properly levelled and finished with a spade face under floors.
Concrete under pavings to be laid and finished to falls and currents.

Concrete lintels
74   The lintels to windows and door openings to be composed of concrete 1:2:4 19 mm aggregate. The lintels to be reinforced by steel rods 12 mm diameter for openings up to 1200 mm wide, 20 mm diameter for openings above 1200 mm wide, one rod for every half-brick in thickness of the wall carried. The lintels to be 150 mm deep for all openings up to 1200 mm in the clear width, and 25 mm deeper for each 300 mm beyond 1200 mm. The lintels to bear 112 mm on the walls at each end, and to have the surfaces hacked to take plaster.

Concrete to steps
75   Concrete to steps to be 150 mm thick (1.6) finished ready to take brick and tile coverings.

Concrete blocks
76   Concrete blocks for posts, stay bars and intermediate supports of fencing, scrapers, etc, to be composed of concrete as for foundations.

Gravel paths
77   The paths coloured brown on plans to be excavated for and formed with 100 mm bed of hardcore covered with 50 mm of coarse gravel, watered and well rolled to firm and even surfaces, and to falls and currents.

Entrance drive
78   The entrance drive and paths coloured grey on plans to have a 150 mm layer of hardcore, with a camber or fall from the centre or crown at the rate of 25 mm in every 750 mm of breadth and to be rolled with a six-ton roller and then covered with 75 mm tarmacadam paving in two courses, the base course 56 mm thick with 38 mm granite aggregate and tar and asphaltic bitumen binder, the wearing course to be 19 mm thick medium textured and laid warm with 9 mm granite aggregate and binder as before. The whole of the paving to be manufactured and laid in accordance with the requirements of BS 802.

Bricklayer

Cement
79   The cement to be as described in Concretor.

Lime
80   The hydrated semi-hydraulic lime is to conform to BS 890, and to be stored as described for Portland cement.

Water
81   The water to be as described in Concretor.

Bricks
82   The ordinary building bricks are to be hard, sound, square first quality 'Phorpres' Flettons, grooved where required for plastering. No soft or place bricks will be allowed to be used and bats are only to be used where necessary to ensure the proper bond. The facing bricks are to be 65 mm hand-made sand-faced bricks for facing £45 net per 1000 delivered to site in full lorry loads. The Contractor is to unload the bricks at the site and stack in convenient positions as required.

Gauged mortar
83   The mortar for all external brickwork unless otherwise described to be composed of half part white cement, half part Portland cement, two parts hydrated semi-hydraulic lime and six parts of sand of an approved colour. The mortar for internal brickwork to be composed of one part of Portland cement, two parts of hydrated semi-hydraulic lime and nine parts of sand.

Cement mortar
84   The cement mortar, unless otherwise specified, to be composed of one part of Portland cement to three parts of sand.

Mixing mortar
85   The materials to be accurately and separately measured in suitable boxes and the ingredients to be first thoroughly mixed by being turned over twice in a dry state after which the water to be added and the whole mixed by being again turned over twice to the proper consistency for use. No more water to be added after the mortar has once been mixed. Mortar to be mixed only in small quantities and none will be permitted to be used which has been mixed more than two hours or which has previously set.

Brickwork
86   The whole of the walls to be built in cement mortar up to damp-proof course, all internal half brick walls to be built in cement mortar, all other brickwork to be built in gauged mortar as described. The brickwork to be executed in strict accordance with the drawings and in English bond. The external half brick skin of hollow walls are to have snapped headers to preserve bond. The bricks to be well bedded and all cross and back joints filled up solid with mortar and to be grouted every course with stiff liquid mortar. The bricks to be well wetted before use by being dipped in a tub of water or continually watered with a hose, and no false headers to be used except where absolutely necessary. Walls specified to be rendered on the outside to have the joints raked out at least 12 mm deep and the face of the brickwork is to be hacked, or grooved bricks are to be used to form a good key.

Hollow brick walls
87   Hollow walls to be formed by leaving a cavity 62 mm wide at a distance of 112 mm from the outer face of the wall, and the two walls to be bonded together with galvanised mild steel vertical twist strip wall ties to conform to the requirements of BS 1243; type A placed chequerwise every metre horizontally and every fifth course vertically, both ends bedded in mortar. The cavity to commence one course below the damp-proof course and to be kept and left clear of all droppings by using battens in the cavity, and the wall ties in all cases to be carefully cleared of mortar as the work proceeds and as soon as the battens are

shifted. Openings to be left at intervals in the brickwork at the bottom of the cavities, and the rubbish cleared out with rods, the openings afterwards to be built up.

Sample panels of facings
88   Include for erecting and afterwards demolishing and carting away four sample panels of facing bricks each 900 mm x 600 mm to show methods of pointing, colour of mortar, etc.

Facings
89   All external walls (except where covered by rough cast or cement rendering) and chimney-stacks to be faced with hand-made, sand-faced bricks as described.

Pointing
90   All external joints of walls built in facing bricks are to be raked out not less than 18 mm deep as the work proceeds and are to be pointed on completion with external quality gauged mortar as described finished with a hollowed horizontal joint and a flush perpend.

Cleaning down brickwork
91   On no account whatever must any cleaning down be done to the brickwork until definite instructions have been received from the Architect, and care to be taken to protect the walls from scaffold splash. Cleaning down must be finished before pointing is commenced.

Height of courses
92   No four courses of brickwork to gauge in height 25 mm more than the thickness of the bricks themselves.

Regularity of erection
93   The brickwork to be carried up in a uniform manner, no portion being raised more than scaffold height above any adjoining work, the whole to be carried up with true and level beds and perpendicular faces.

Sundry labours
94   All cutting to rakes, splays, indents, birdsmouths, squints, etc, to be performed, and all openings and rough relieving arches to be formed, as may be necessary. All joiner's frames for windows and doors to be built in. All beams, sleepers, plates and other similar items set in the brickwork to be bedded in cement mortar.

Brick arches
95   The brick on end flat arches to windows and doors to be constructed with facing bricks as described, and with radiating joints, the soffites to be formed with 12 mm camber.

External sills
96   External window sills to be formed with facing bricks on edge with two courses of roofing tiles as described laid flat, the whole bedded and pointed in cement mortar.

Internal tile sills
97   The 225 mm wide internal sills to Kitchen, Garage, Larder, and Boiler Room to be formed with 225 mm x 225 mm thick red quarry tiles to BS 1286 with rounded nosing bedded in cement mortar and pointed in coloured mortar and notched at ends to reveal.

Projecting bands, etc
98   Projecting bands of brickwork and oversailing courses to chimneys to be built with facing bricks as described.

Copings
99   Coping to walls to be formed with one course of facing bricks on edge, set and pointed in cement mortar, and with two courses of plain tile creasing in cement mortar. Proper plain gunmental or delta bronze coping irons to be inserted to end courses of coping

Brick steps
100   Brick steps, where shown, to be formed with facing bricks on edge with two courses of ordinary roofing tiles under, the whole set in cement mortar upon a 150 mm bed of cement concrete, as specified for foundations. Steps circular-on-plan to have a plain roofing tile inserted in the joints, the whole to be pointed in cement mortar.

Fireplaces
101   All fireplaces to be constructed in the usual manner with brick jambs, and in all cases where the backs are less than one brick thick they must be rendered with cement mortar 25 mm thick. Proper segmental brick rough arches to be turned over fireplace openings upon 62 mm x 12 mm wrought iron chimney bars cambered and with split ends turned up and down, the bars to be at least 450 mm longer than the openings. Concrete lintels, formed as before specified, may be used instead of brick arches, and the chimney bar dispensed with.

Suspended hearths
102   Hearths to be concrete (1:2:4 18 mm aggregate) 75 mm thick formed upon proper fillets nailed to joists, filled in upon centering and reinforced with steel fabric to BS 4483 Ref A142, weighing 2.22 kg per m^2.

Tile and briquette hearths
103   The hearths to all bedrooms to have glazed tiles, which will be supplied under the provisional sum for grates. Tiles to be bedded and

pointed in cement. The hearth to the living-room to be formed in briquettes also supplied under the provisional sum and to be laid upon and including Portland cement and sand screed 18 mm thick, the briquettes to be bedded and jointed in cement mortar and pointed in coloured mortar.

Flues, etc
104   The necessary corbelling over for the breasts and stacks to be built, and all chimney flues formed of the sizes shown, which are in no case to be less than 225 mm x 225 mm with as easy bends and turns as possible. Flues to be parged with mortar composed of one part cement, three parts hydrated non-hydraulic lime and ten parts sand by volume and cored at completion, and tested by passing a sweep's brush through the flues. Flues to be gathered over the fireplaces as quickly as possible.

Chimney-pots
105   The chimney-stacks to have plain, red, terracotta chimney-pots, to conform to BS 1181, Type 4D with square base and 0.75 m long, set and well flaunched up with cement mortar, and to project 75 mm above the flaunching.

Grates and mantels
106   The following grates and mantels to be included for and obtained from a supplier nominated by the architect:
Living-room: steel grate with briquette surround and hearth, slate and hardwood panels and capping, etc, and fire brick interior, pc £100.00
Bedrooms 1, 2 and 3: steel grate with tiled surround, hearth, and wood mantel-piece and fire-brick interior, pc £60 each.

Setting grates, etc
107   All grates, hearths and mantelpieces to be set and fixed in the most careful and approved manner, with all necessary fire-brick and fire-clay, copper cramps, and wire, the spaces at back of grates being built up solid.

Beam filling
108   Beam filling to all eaves to be of brickwork in gauged mortar.

Rough rendering
109   Where smoke flues pass through floors, ceilings, and in roof spaces, the faces of brickwork to be roughly rendered with cement mortar.

Damp-proof course
110   The damp-proof course to all walls to be formed of two courses of stout new Welsh damp-course slates laid to break joint and bedded and flushed over in cement mortar.

Air bricks
111 Terracotta air bricks 225 mm x 75 mm of approved pattern to be built in where shown and flues formed for same rendered all round with cement mortar. Flues where they occur through hollow walls to be constructed with stout slates across the cavity.

Pointing flashings, etc
112 Joints in brickwork to be raked out for the top edge of flashings, and the flashings to be wedged with lead wedges, and pointed in cement mortar. The damp-proof course also to be pointed with cement mortar where showing on external walls.

Holes through walls
113 Holes through walls to be left, or cut for all pipes, etc and made good after with brickwork in cement mortar.

Spaces between joists
114 The spaces in walls between joists to be filled in with brick filling in gauged mortar.

Corbel out
115 Corbels to be formed for roof timbers, and the ends of all timbers, etc to be cut and pinned to walls and made good to facings, etc.

Fixing bricks
116 Fixing bricks where used are to conform to BS 1180, Part Two, with clinker aggregate.

Brick pavings
117 The floors to the porch to be laid with hard red paving bricks, to approval, laid to pattern indicated upon drawings. The bricks to be laid and pointed in cement mortar.

Bed frames, etc
118 All solid window and door frames, etc, to be bedded in cement mortar, and frames to be pointed with an approved mastic.

Slate shelves
119 One tier of slate shelves 35 mm thick to be fitted up in larder, set in cement upon dwarf half-brick walls, the top of shelves to be 600 mm above level of floor.

Bases for rainwater butts
120 Brick platforms as bases for rainwater butts to be 675 mm x 675 mm x 300 mm high above level of ground adjoining, built in red facing bricks in cement mortar upon concrete foundation 300 mm thick.

Garage walls, etc
121   The internal walls of garage, boiler house, and fuel store to be finished fair, with flush struck joints.

Stone paving
122   The areas, as shown on drawing, to be paved with 50 mm thick random York stone, set with open joints upon a 150 mm bed of hard core.

Drainlayer

Stoneware drains
123   The stoneware drains, junctions, bends, etc, to comply in all respects with the requirements of BS 65 and 540 and to be 'British Standard Surface Water' for rainwater drains and 'British Standard' for soil drains.

Jointing stoneware pipes
124   The stoneware pipes are to be laid dry, the joints to be made by inserting one or more rings of rope yarn so as not to occupy more than one-quarter the socket depth and then completely filling the socket with cement mortar (1:1) finishing with a fillet of cement mortar (1:1) outside trowelled smooth. The joint inside to be struck off with a dolly or scraper and on no account is any cement to be left on the inside of the pipe.

Iron drain pipes
125   The cast iron drain pipes to be the best quality with spigot and socket joints and must comply in all respects with the requirements of BS 437.

Jointing iron drain pipes
126   Joints in iron socket pipes to be made with best quality lead wire of proper thickness to go twice round the pipe, and to be tightly caulked in the socket, the joints to be then run in with soft blue English pig lead and caulked down flush with the socket.

Sizes of pipes
127   The specified sizes of all pipes to be understood as the internal diameter or bore.

Pipe trenches
128   The trenches for the drain pipes to be carefully excavated to true hanging lines according to the inclination and depths so that the pipes shall have a fair bearing throughout their full lengths. The trenches to be carefully filled in after the drains are laid and tested and great care to be exercised so as not to disturb the drains. The whole to be consolidated and rammed and any depressions in the finished surface over drains to be made up.

Falls in drains
129   The drains to be laid to falls of not less than 75 mm in 3 m.

Bed of concrete for drains
130   All soil drains to have a cement concrete bed 450 mm wide and 150 mm thick below the sockets of pipes, mixed in the proportions specified for foundations, and flaunched up after the pipes have been tested, to the top of the pipes. Hollows are to be left for the socket of the pipe to enable the barrel of the pipe to rest for its whole length on the concrete bed. Any holes that may be formed by accident in the bottom of the trenches by removing too much ground or caused by made-up ground under the drain or otherwise, must be filled with cement concrete, and rammed to proper level at the Contractor's expense. There will be no concrete bed to the rain-water drains.

Joints in drains covered with concrete
131   Where vertical pipes drop into a socket of drain pipe the concrete under the bend to be carried up in a block so as to cover the joint to a depth of 100 mm after the drains have been tested and approved.

Concrete cover to drains
132   Wherever pipes pass under buildings they must be covered with cement concrete at least 150 mm thick above the tops of sockets and 300 mm wide.

Gully traps
133   Gully traps to be fixed where shown, on a bed of cement concrete 150 mm thick, and to be of stoneware of approved make, with 150 mm square, heavy, galvanised-iron grating. Proper connection to be made to drains. Channels at side of gullies to take waste pipes to be 100 mm salt-glazed open channels 600 mm long, discharging over gullies and set in concrete 150 mm thick.

Rain-water shoes
134   Stoneware rain-water shoes or trapless gullies with square galvanised iron gratings to be fixed upon a bed of concrete 150 mm thick at the foot of all rain-water pipes properly connected to drains. Connections of iron rain-water pipes to stoneware shoes to be made with perforated lead discs fitted into sockets of shoes.

Manholes
135   The manholes to be constructed in the positions shown and as follows:
Internal dimensions: 787 mm x 675 mm or as shown on plans.
Bottom: 150 mm thick cement concrete.

Walls: One brick thick local stock brickwork in cement mortar.

Cover: 100 mm thick cast cement concrete 1050 mm x 900 mm perforated, rebated for, and fitted with, a strong galvanised cast-iron, single-seal, air-tight cover 610 mm x 457 mm to BS 497, Grade C, Table 6, weighing 37 kg bedded in cement mortar.

Sides: Sides of manholes to be rendered with cement and sand in equal proportions, finished with a polished face.

Channels: White glazed channels (half section for main channels and three-quarter section for branches discharging over main channels) fixed in 150 mm of cement concrete trowelled to a fine face with cement and sand (1:1) and with sides steeply sloped up to the sides of manhole. The benching to be taken up 75 mm vertically above the centre channel before commencing the sloping part.

Disconnecting trap

136   A glazed stoneware disconnecting trap, of approved make and conforming to the requirements of BS 539, with cleansing arm and stopper to be built into the side of manhole nearest the sewer. The stopper to be bedded in cart-grease and sand, and to have galvanised-iron lever and chain, the chain fixed with a stout staple to wall of manhole immediately under the cover. The trap to be packed with cement concrete round wall of manhole and properly connected to drain.

Water test for drains

137   Before the trenches are filled in, the water test to be applied to every section of the drains and manholes by the Contractor at his own expense, and a certificate to the effect that the drains are in proper order to be obtained from the local Sanitary Inspector and forwarded to the Architect. A final test may be made by the Architect after the ground is filled in, and all defects must be made good before the drains will be accepted.

Fill in drain trenches

138   The trenches to be carefully filled in after drains are laid and tested, and great care to be exercised so as not to disturb the drains, the finest and best of the excavated material being used for packing round the pipes. The whole to be thoroughly consolidated and rammed and any depressions in the finished surface over drains made up.

Fresh-air inlet

139   Fresh-air inlet to manhole having disconnecting trap to be formed with 100 mm drain connected to the manhole about 150 mm below level of cover and finished with a 2 m length of 100 mm coated, cast-iron pipe and mica flap valve fixed to a 175 mm x 100 mm softwood post, rounded on the top, and let 1 metre into ground, the post to be treated with a preservative liquid before being fixed and set in a block of concrete.

Connection to sewer

140   The drain from the manhole to the public sewer to be in stoneware pipes, as before specified, properly connected to the sewer, and any necessary work to be carried out to the satisfaction of the Surveyor to the Local Authority and left perfect.

Soak-away pits

141   Soak-away pits to be formed where shown on plan of the size and depth necessary, but not less than one cubic metre, and as decided upon the site. The pits to be built to conform in every way to the requirements of the Local Authority filled with dry material, and covered with a slab of cement concrete finishing about 300 mm below finished surface of ground.

Rain-water tank

142   The rain-water tank to be circular-on-plan, the size shown on drawings, on 300 mm thick dished, concrete bottom, as described for foundations, but the proportions to be 1:6 and the surface, before setting, to be finished smooth with Portland cement and sand in equal parts 19 mm thick. The walls to be one and a half bricks thick, of hard bricks, moulded to radius, built in cement mortar. Well-tempered clay 300 mm thick to be well puddled all round the back of walls. The inside of walls to be rendered 19 mm thick with Portland cement and sand, in equal proportions, finished at bottom with quadrant fillet 75 mm radius. The top to be formed of concrete 225 mm thick composed of granite siftings of approved size and Portland cement in the proportion of 4:1, on temporary boarding strutted up from the bottom, and to have two 127 mm x 76 mm x 13.36 Kg/m rolled steel joists completely inserted in the concrete. A manhole in the concrete top to be formed 450 mm square, with four courses of half brick wall in cement mortar around the same, covered with 75 mm thick York stone 750 mm square tooled all round and with two galvanised wrought iron rings bolted through the stone. In the upper course four 225 mm x 75 mm strong galvanised iron air inlets for ventilation and overflow to be built in. The tank to be filled with water and tested in the presence of the Architect, and the tank must stand the test before it will be accepted.

Roofer

Tiles

143   The tiles are to be 267 mm x 164 mm hand-made sand-faced tiles holed and nibbed and will be delivered to the site in full lorry loads at the pc prices stated below. The contractor is to allow for taking delivery, unloading and stacking in convenient positions.

Plain tiles	pc £42 net per thousand
Eaves and top edge tiles	pc £42 net per thousand
Verge tiles	pc £84 net per thousand
Ridge tiles	pc £4 net per dozen
Valley tiles	pc £4 net per dozen
Bonnet hip tiles	pc £4 net per dozen

Roof tiling
144   The whole of the roofs to be covered with plain tiles as described. Each tile to be laid to a 75 mm lap and every fourth course nailed with two galvanised-iron nails 50 mm long.

Eaves
145   Eaves to have double courses of tiles, the undercourse to be proper eaves tiles nailed with two nails to each tile as before specified.

Verges of tiling
146   All verges of tiling to have tile and half with an undercourse of tiles laid flat, the whole to be bedded and pointed in cement mortar. Verge tiles to be tilted up to prevent water dripping from eaves.

Valley tiles
147   Valleys to be formed with proper valley tiles to suit the pitch of roof, and to course and bond with the tiling, and to have tile and half if necessary.

Hip tiles
148   Hips to be covered with ordinary bonnet-shaped hip tiles secured with long galvanised-iron nails, the end of each tile filled in with cement cut back from edge of tile. The hip tiles to course and bond with the tiling and hips to have tile and half if necessary.

Tile ridges
149   Ridges to be covered with half round ridge tiles bedded in lime mortar, and pointed in cement. The two top courses of tiles on either side of ridge to be set in lime mortar. Ends of ridge tiles to verges to have the spaces filled in with small pieces of tile bedded and pointed in cement.

Cuttings etc, to roof tiles
150   All cutting to tiling to suit special slopes to be performed, and tile and half to be used wherever necessary to avoid the use of small pieces of tile.

Make good roof tiling
151   Any damaged or defective tiles to be taken out and reinstated with new. All gutters to be cleaned out, and all roof and other tiling left perfect and watertight on completion.

Glass tiles and fix soakers
152   Two sets, each containing thirteen 265 mm x 165 mm *Armour-cast* twice drilled glass tiles, 10 mm thick, to be fixed in roof to course and bond with the ordinary tiles. Each glass tile to be secured to the battens with two copper screws and the roof boarding cut through as necessary. All lead soakers to be fixed where necessary with two copper nails to each.

Hip irons
153   Ends of all hips to have plain 25 mm x 6 mm hip irons, each out of 900 mm of metal twisted and with shaped ends, the irons screwed to wood hip with three stout steel screws.

Vertical title hanging
154   The vertical tiles to walls where shown to be similar to the roof tiles, each hung to a 38 mm lap and fixed with two 38 mm stout screws. The eaves to have double course bedded and pointed in cement mortar.

Carpenter, Joiner and Ironmonger

Timber
155   The timber for carpenter's work to be sound, bright, square-edged unsorted Swedish, unsorted Finnish or merchantable Douglas Fir. The timber for joiner's work to be unsorted Kara Sea or prime clear Douglas Fir. The timber for floorings and matchings to be unsorted Swedish or unsorted Finnish. All timbers to be sound and well conditioned, clean, free frame wanes, injurious open shakes, large, loose or dead knots, and cut square and straight, all to be thoroughly seasoned and with only a very small proportion of bright sap and no discoloured sap whatever. The whole of the timber to be cut into the required scantlings at least three months before being framed.

Preparation of timber
156   The preparation of timber to commence simultaneously with the beginning of the work, and proceed continuously till all the woodwork is stacked upon the site and protected from the weather.

Floor boards
157   The whole of the floor boards to be stacked on the site, face downwards, within a month of the commencement of the work and protected from the weather.

Framing
158   Framed doors, etc to be prepared as soon as practicable after commencing the work, laid aside, and not glued up until required for

fixing. In all cases panels must be primed or stained before work is glued up.

Sizes of timbers
159   All timber and framings, unless otherwise specified, to hold the full dimensions figured on the drawings or specified, allowing 3 mm for planing on each wrought face. All sizes given for mouldings, etc, are the finished sizes.

Priming Woodwork
160   All woodwork to be delivered on the site and approved by the Architect before it is primed. The bottom edges of all doors and the backs of external door frames to be primed and painted one coat just previous to fixing.

Timber near flues
161   No timber or woodwork of any description built into walls to be left within 225 mm of any flue.

Centering, etc
162   All centering and turning pieces, plugs, slips, brackets, firings, fillets, blockings, etc to be provided and fixed where ordered or necessary for properly carrying out the work.

Wrought iron plates and other ironwork
163   Wall plates under ends of floor joists to be 50 mm x 7 mm tarred and sanded wrought iron, built into walls in continuous lengths and bedded in cement mortar. All other ironwork, spikes, nails, bolts, etc, to be provided.

Spacing of timbers
164   All rafters, floor and ceiling joists to be fixed not more than 300 mm apart in the clear, except where otherwise shown.

Wall plates, purlins, etc
165   Wall plates, ridge pieces, and purlins to be in long lengths, halved, spiked, and framed as shown. Scarfs to be placed at the points of supports so as to weaken the timbers as little as possible.

Protect floors
166   All floors to be protected, as soon as laid, with sawdust, to be renewed when required, and cleared away on completion.

Plugging walls
167   The walls to be plugged where required for fixing joinery.

Machine planing
168   Machine planing and moulding to be finished off smooth by hand.

Pellating
169 Wherever the word 'pellated' is used in the specification it is intended that the work to be performed shall consist of covering the heads of screws, bolts, nails, etc, with grain blocks let in and glued.

Glazing beads
170 Wherever 'movable or glazing beads or fillets' are specified they must be hardwood, secured with brass screws in cups, the screws placed about 25 mm from angles, and average 150 mm apart.

Backings, blocks, nails, screws, etc
171 Joiner's work to be fixed upon proper backings, blocks, fillets, tilting fillets, firrings, bearers, or trimming pieces as may be requisite, finished with the necessary fillets, beads and stops, to render the whole perfect and complete. The work also to be fixed with the necessary nails, screws, concealed and slotted screws, holdfasts, wall hooks, or other ironmongery of sufficient length and strength.

Cross-tongued joints
172 All widths in joiner's work exceeding 225 mm to have properly glued and cross-tongued joints.

Deal edging to paths
173 Gravel paths to be finished both sides with 150 mm x 38 mm rough timber edging, secured every 900 mm to 50 mm x 50 mm pegs 600 mm long driven into the ground, the whole to be creosoted under pressure before being fixed.

Roofs
174 The roofs to be constructed as shown with timbers of the following scantlings, all strongly framed together and well nailed to wall plates and ceiling joists:

Wall plates	112 mm x 75 mm
Rafters	112 mm x 50 mm
Ridges	225 mm x 38 mm
Valley rafters	275 mm x 50 mm
Hip rafters	275 mm x 50 mm
Struts	112 mm x 75 mm
Purlins	175 mm x 100 mm
Collar ties	125 mm x 50 mm
Ceiling joists	125 mm x 50 mm
Sprocket pieces	50 mm thick

Ridges and purlins to be properly scarfed together where necessary and secured with 12 mm diameter wrought iron bolts. Ceiling joists to be fixed against flues upon 38 mm x 9 mm galvanised wrought iron holdfasts. Wall plates to be given a coat of preservative liquid before being fixed.

Trim for stacks, etc
175   Roof and ceiling joists to be trimmed for chimney-stacks, trap door, etc, with timbers 25 mm thicker than ordinary timbers.

Half-timber work
176   The whole of the half-timber work to be constructed with well-seasoned English oak, with adzed face. The timbers to be the thickness shown on details and to be grooved or rebated as required for rough cast, put together in white lead, and pinned with oak pins left to project 19 mm. The whole to be framed, morticed and tenoned together in the best possible manner. The oak must not be treated in any way, but left in its natural state. Struts, etc, to be formed with natural-shaped pieces of timber.

Beams to bays
177   Beams to bay windows to be formed with two 225 mm x 75 mm softwood members blocked apart and bolted together, the ends resting upon concrete templates.

Floor joists
178   The wood floors to be constructed with 112 mm x 75 mm fir joists to ground floor and 225 mm x 50 mm to upper floors, the joists fixed not more than 300 mm apart. All joists to be securely nailed to the wall plates. Properly trim for all fireplaces, stairs, etc, with trimming joists 25 mm thicker than the ordinary floor joists. Small fillets to be put round hearth trimmings to receive concrete hearths. Where joists cut into rafters of roof the timbers to be strongly spiked together.

Herring-bone strutting
179   Floors of bedroom to have one row of 50 mm x 38 mm softwood herring-bone strutting well spiked to the floor joists.

Eaves fascia, etc
180   All eaves to have 175 mm x 31 mm wrought, rebated and moulded fascia boards, nailed to the feet of rafters to serve as tilter for the tiling. The projecting eaves to be formed with 100 mm x 50 mm joists fixed to ends of rafters with ends built into walls and bedded in cement mortar and 75 mm x 50 mm wall pieces. The underside of eaves to be lined with 18 mm match-boarding, and to have 50 mm x 25 mm moulding under, nailed to plugs driven into walls, match-boarding to be tongued into eaves fascia.

Tiling battens
181   Tiling battens to be 38 mm x 25 mm securely nailed to the roof boarding, properly spaced to take tiling, the batten nearest eaves to be double. Battens for vertical tiling to be plugged to walls.

Tilting fillets
182   All necessary tilting fillets to be fixed wherever required.

Gutter boards
183   Gutter boards to be 31 mm thick, with edges shot, fixed upon strong framed bearers with all necessary gusset ends, 50 mm rebated drips not more than 3 m apart and 38 mm rounded rolls, etc. Gutters to have a fall of at least 38 mm in 3 m.

Cesspools in gutters
184   Cesspools in gutters to be formed of 25 mm wrought softwood dovetailed at angles, and perforated for outlet pipe, the cesspools to be not less than 225 mm square and 150 mm deep internal dimensions.

Roofing felt
185   The whole of the roof to be covered with self-finished bitumen asbestos felt to conform to BS 747, Class 2, Type 2B' and weighing 16 kg/10 m^2, securely fixed with galvanised clout nails to rafters and lapped 150 mm in all directions.

Oak fences
186   Enclose the site on North and East sides with close weather-boarded oak fencing 1½ m high with 125 mm x 100 mm posts at 3 m centres, arris nails ex 75 mm x 75 mm, 150 mm x 25 mm gravel boards and 50 mm x 25 mm counter rails all framed together and 62 mm x 38 mm bevelled capping to run over posts filled in with 100 mm sawn oak feather edged palings nailed with galvanised fencing nails. The posts are to be let 600 mm into the ground and set in concrete and to be creosoted before fixing. On completion the whole of the fencing is to be given two coats of creosote.

Floors
187   The floors of sitting- and dining-rooms to be laid with 31 mm softwood grooved and tongued flooring, in 112 mm widths, secretely nailed. All other floors, including walking-way in roof (5m^2), but excepting scullery, boiler-house, garage, coal, coke, and wood stores, to be laid with 25 mm softwood, straight joint flooring boards of ordinary width, well jointed and securely fixed to each joist with two 57 mm brads to each board, well punched in. All the flooring to be well cleaned off and protected with sawdust until the plastering is completed.

Wood block floor
188   The whole of the hall to be laid with best quality oak blocks, tongued, grooved, and inter-locking, 225 mm x 75 mm x 31 mm thick, laid herring-bone pattern, with a plain margin, 150 mm wide, tongued and grooved together. The blocks and margin to be laid in bitumen with the joints as fine as possible, the whole carefully cleaned off to a

perfectly true and level surface ready for polishing. The work to be carried out by a firm approved by the Architect, and the floor to be stained and wax polished.

Cuttings and notchings

189 All circular cutting, scribing and fitting to wood blocks up to stone or other floors, notching underside of blocks for electric light or other tubes and pipes; and notchings round pipes, where required, to be carried out.

Cleaning off wood block floors

190 Immediately the oak block floors are laid they must be covered with a thick layer of sawdust, which must be maintained until instructions are received from the Architect to proceed with the work of cleaning off and scraping; this latter work must not be done until such instructions are given, and not as soon as the floors are laid.

Traps in floors

191 Traps to be formed in all floors where shown or necessary to give access to electric light and bell wires.

Skirtings

192 All bedrooms and the kitchen to have 125 mm x 18 mm moulded softwood skirting fixed upon proper splayed grounds, and mitred at angles. Skirting to the hall to be 125 mm x 18 mm moulded oak. Plastering to be continued at back of skirtings.

Stud or quarter partitions

193 Stud or quarter partitions to be constructed with 100 mm x 75 mm heads, sills and posts, 100 mm x 50 mm interties, quarters and diagonals, all framed and braced together and to be as self-supporting as possible. Nogging pieces, placed not more than 1 m apart, to be 100 mm x 38 mm. Bridging-pieces to take the sills of partitions where the partitions run in the same direction as the joists, to be framed in between the floor joists and spaced not more than 1 m apart.

Ashlaring

194 The ashlaring to rooms in the roof to be formed with 75 mm x 50 mm heads, sills, posts, braces, studs, etc all as specified for stud and quarter partitions, with bridging-pieces, etc, as described in the last clause.

Window surrounds

195 The surrounds to metal windows to be 87 mm x 63 mm wrought framed rebated splayed and rounded oak with 125 mm x 75 mm framed rebated weathered rounded and throated oak sill. The frames to be fixed in the brick openings with galvanised holdfasts as described and bedded in cement mortar and pointed with mastic.

Dormer windows
196   Framing to form dormer windows to have 100 mm x 100 mm
softwood posts, 100 mm x 75 mm heads and sills, 100 mm x 50 mm
studs, 138 mm x 50 mm joists to flats, firred to falls, which are to be
from the outside of the dormer to the roof. Cover the tops of dormers
with 25 mm rough boarding with edges shot, 38 mm rounded rolls and
a 50 mm x 25 mm arris fillet all round outside for lead. Cornice to be
formed with 75 mm x 38 mm softwood moulding, mitred at angles.
The cheeks of dormers to be covered with 31 mm boarding to take
lead. Angles of dormers to have 125 mm x 31 mm deal angle casing to
cover joint of lead, the casing tongued together and to cover window
frame. Flats and cheeks of dormers to be covered with roofing felt as
previously described before the lead is laid. Surrounds to metal
windows to be formed with 100 mm x 67 mm solid, moulded, rebated
softwood frames and heads, 100 mm x 75 mm solid, twice moulded
and twice rebated mullion, where shown, and 150 mm x 75 mm oak
sills, as described in last item, the frames finished round on the outside
with 50 mm x 25 mm moulded deal scribing fillet, and on the inside
with 25 mm x 25 mm cover mould.

Iron water bars
197   All window-sills to have 25 mm x 3 mm galvanised-iron tongues,
bedded in white lead in grooves in wood or stone, and the sills to be
bedded in white lead.

Window boards
198   Windows to have 25 mm thick oak window boards with rounded
edge, grooved on the underside for plaster and tongued on back edge to
oak sill. The window boards to be screwed to fir bearers plugged to
brickwork and the heads of the screws are to be let in and grain
pellated. Internal window sills to Kitchen, Garage, Larder and Boiler
Room are to be tiled as specified in Bricklayer.

Larder window
199   Larder window to have softwood frames 25 mm thick, to slide,
the frames covered with stout galvanised-wire gauze nailed on.

Louvre shutters
200   Louvre shutters to windows, where shown, to be 50 mm thick
softwood, formed in panels, with frames rebated and moulded, and
having 75 mm x 12 mm louvres fixed in grooves cut diagonally, the
lower panels of all shutters to have wrought and rebated frames hinged
to the main frames with 50 mm steel butt hinges, and fitted with
suitable opening fittings, pc £1 per frame. Hang the louvre shutters with
suitable iron parliament hinges, and fit each shutter with wrought iron
catch to hold shutter open and 12 mm wrought iron bolt to go through
window frame fitted with brass butterfly nut. Wrought iron continuous
strap hinges to be supplied, all as detail, to all louvre shutters where to
be hung in sets.

Architraves to windows
201 Architraves to windows of wcs, bathroom and scullery to be 75 mm x 25 mm softwood moulded, elsewhere windows to have 112 mm x 25 mm oak moulded architraves, all to be fixed to wrought and splayed softwood grounds, plugged to walls.

Front door
202 Front door to be 50 mm two-panel oak, bolection moulded both sides, with raised and fielded panels on outside only, hung to 125 mm x 112 mm solid, wrought, framed, rebated, grooved, and moulded oak frame, with 100 mm brass butt hinges, and fitted with two 200 mm brass barrel bolts, brass door chain, 150 mm mortice dead lock, brass *Yale* rim latch with six keys, brass knocker, pc £5 and brass letter plate, pc £5. Frame on outside to be finished round with 50 mm x 38 mm moulded oak scribing fillet.

Back door
203 Back door to be 50 mm softwood three-panel door, the lower two panels bead flush both sides, the upper panel glazed with 6 mm polished Georgian wired glass. The glass panel to be glazed with beads bradded in and the edges to be bedded in wash-leather. Hang the door to 75 mm rebated and moulded softwood frame, with 100 mm brass butt hinges and fitted with rim lock and furniture, pc £3, two 200 mm iron barrel bolts, and iron door-chain. Outside of frame to be finished round with 25 mm x 25 mm softwood scribing fillet. Bottom of door to have 125 mm x 50 mm weather fillet, tongued to door, and screwed on from the back with steel screws. Iron weather bar to door to be 38 mm x 6 mm bedded with cement in groove in step.

Yard door
204 Yard door to be 50 mm softwood, framed and braced, filled in with 18 mm V-jointed match-boarding in narrow widths, with segmental head and hung to 112 mm x 75 mm solid, wrought, rebated and moulded softwood frame, with 100 mm wrought iron butt hinges and fitted with strong *Norfolk* latch and 200 mm iron barrel bolt.

Small door to garage
205 Small door to garage to be 50 mm softwood, two-panel flush moulded both sides, hung to 112 mm x 75 mm solid, wrought, rebated and moulded sofwood frame, with 100 mm brass butt hinges, and fitted with *Yale* lock and three keys. Frame to be finished round on the outside with 25 mm x 25 mm softwood moulded scribing fillet.

Garage doors
206 Large doors to garage to be 62 mm softwood framed and braced, filled in with 25 mm V-jointed match-boarding in narrow widths and having rebated and beaded meeting stiles, the doors hung with *Collinge's* galvanised-iron hinges of suitable size to 175 mm x 100

mm solid wrought, rebated and moulded softwood frames, and fitted with two 300 mm iron barrel bolts, 50 mm x 9 mm wrought iron locking bar and staples, and rebated mortice dead lock, pc £5.

Internal doors
207 All internal doors to be 43 mm solid core flush doors faced both sides with 5 mm plywood for painting and with solid hardwood lipped edges, hung with 100 mm steel butt hinges to 38 mm rebated softwood linings, and fitted with 150 mm mortice locks and furniture, pc £3 per set. Doors to wcs and bathroom to be fitted with 150 mm brass barrel bolts in addition.

Dowels for door frames
208 All solid frames to have 12 mm diameter, galvanised steel dowels, 150 mm long let into frames and into steps or concrete.

Trap-door
209 Trap-door in ceiling of landing to be formed with 175 mm x 31 mm wrought, rebated, softwood curb, finished round on ceiling side with 75 mm x 12 mm plain softwood architrave, and fitted with 38 mm softwood square-panelled door.

Fixing frames
210 All door frames and window surrounds to have 25 mm x 3 mm galvanised wrought iron fixing cramps 300 mm long, one end drilled and screwed to back of frame, the other end split and built into brickwork, two cramps to each side of frame. The cramps to large doors of garage to be 75 mm x 12 mm metal, four to each side of frame.

Architraves to doors
211 Architraves to doors to scullery, kitchen, servants' wc, larder, pantry, coke and coal stores to be 75 mm x 25 mm softwood, splayed, elsewhere 112 mm x 25 mm fixed to wrought and splayed softwood grounds, plugged to walls.

Coal and coke boards
212 Coal and coke boards to doors of fuel store to be 31 mm thick softwood, wrought all round, 1 m high, each board 225 mm wide with two hand holes, and having softwood fillets fixed to door frame to form slides.

Picture rails
213 Sitting-room, dining-room, hall, and all bedrooms to have 50 mm x 31 mm softwood wrought grooved and splayed, properly mitred picture rail, fixed to softwood wrought and twice splayed grounds, plugged to walls.

Pipe casing
214 Pipe chases in plastered walls to be covered with 18 mm wrought

softwood beaded casings, secured with brass screws in cups to 25 mm rebated and framed softwood grounds, plugged to walls.

Chair rail
215   Kitchen to have 75 mm x 31 mm wrought and moulded softwood chair rail properly mitred and fixed to softwood wrought and twice splayed grounds, plugged to walls.

Staircase
216   The staircase to be constructed of softwood with 31 mm treads, having rounded nosings with small moulding under, and 25 mm risers, all rebated and grooved together, glued, blocked, and bracketed, and on strong fir carriages. Each tread to be screwed to riser with three long steel screws. Strings to be 38 mm thick, plain softwood wrought and beaded, the outer string finished with 75 mm x 38 mm thick moulded capping tongued on. Nosing to form top step to be 31 mm. Balusters to be 25 mm square turned, three to each tread, fixed square and diagonally alternatively. Newels to be 87 mm x 87 mm plain square, with edges rubbed off, and finished with 112 mm x 112 mm moulded square oak caps, 75 mm thick, dowelled on. Handrails to be 62 mm x 50 mm oak, housed into caps of newels: wall rails to be 50 mm x 50 mm softwood, fixed upon iron brackets. Apron linings to be 25 mm thick, beaded on lower edge, and having capping as for top of outer strings. Handrails and caps to newels to be polished. Spandril under stairs to be formed with softwood panelling 38 mm thick to match room doors.

Dresser
217   Deal dresser for kitchen to be 1.5 m long, with lower portion 525 mm deep, with 38 mm sides and 50 mm cross-tongued whitewood table top. The bottom part to be formed into cupboards, with 38 mm panelled doors, and three dovetailed drawers over, with 12 mm bottoms, 19 mm sides and 25 mm fronts, all glued and blocked together, and with hardwood runners and two brass drop handles to each drawer with nuts, 38 mm cut and shaped ends, four tiers of 31 mm shelves, arris grooved for plates, and having four dozen brass cup hooks of various sizes, 19 mm fascia, 25 mm top, with 38 mm x 25 mm moulding as cornice, 19 mm matched and beaded back. Each cupboard to have one 275 mm shelf.

Cupboard in kitchen
218   Cupboard at side of dresser to be of clean softwood having the lower part formed with 31 mm wrought frame, with square panelled doors to form cupboard, hung with 50 mm iron butt hinges, and fitted with brass butterfly turnbuckle and staple. Cupboards to have 150 mm x 19 mm plain wrought softwood skirting, with one shelf the full width fixed in each, and the doors to have two 25 mm diameter holes drilled in each for ventilation. Drawers over cupboards to be 175 mm deep,

having 25 mm beaded fronts, 19 mm rims, dovetailed together, and 19 mm bottoms, on proper oak runners, the drawers fitted with brass drop handles. Divisions between cupboards and drawers to be 19 mm thick. Table top to be 31 mm thick cross-tongued whitewood, with rounded corners where shown, and moulded edge. Upper part to have 31 mm wrought frame filled in with sash doors, having rebated sash bars with movable deal fillets, hung with 62 mm wrought iron butt hinges, and fitted with brass butterfly turnbuckle and staple. Divisions to cupboards to be 19 mm thick, and each cupboard to be provided with three 25 mm softwood shelves upon proper bearers. Top of cupboards to have 19 mm boarding, finished round with 50 mm x 25 mm softwood moulded cornice. Six dozen assorted brass cup hooks to be fixed and backs of upper cupboards to be formed with 19 mm match-boarding.

Cupboard in dining-room
219   Cupboard in dining-room to be formed with 38 mm cupboard front and door to match room door, the whole finished round with softwood architraves, as before specified. Six shelves to be fitted up the full depth of cupboard and 25 mm thick upon proper bearers, as before specified. Door to be hung with 100 mm butt hinges and fitted with rim lock and furniture.

Shelves, etc, in larder
220   Larder to have two tiers of clean softwood shelves, 25 mm thick, 275 mm wide, fixed upon cast iron brackets built into walls, the shelves fixed 12 mm from walls. Slate shelves are specified in Bricklayer. A small cupboard to be fitted up under slate shelves at window end, formed with panelled doors and frame, and shelves all similar to that specified for cupboards in kitchen.

Shelves in pantry
221   Pantry to have two tiers of shelves, as specified for larder, 25 mm thick, 275 mm wide.

Shelves in scullery
222   Scullery to have two tiers of 275 mm x 25 mm clean softwood shelves, fixed upon 75 mm x 31 mm wrought and chamfered softwood bearers on stamped steel brackets, the bearers plugged and screwed as required.

Seat in sitting-room
223   Sitting-room to have clean softwood window seat, 38 mm thick, with moulded front edge, and 38 mm shaped brackets under.

Shelf for meters
224   Shelf for gas and electric light meters to be 25 mm thick upon strong steel brackets, fixed where directed.

Serving hatch
225   Serving hatch to be formed with two 25 mm solid cored flush doors with plywood both sides for painting and with 22 mm oak twice rebated lipping tongued in all round, each hung with pair of 75 mm brass butt hinges to 38 mm rebated linings, the door on dining-room side fitted with brass mortice lock, and each door having brass Bale's catches and knobs. Shelf at bottom of hatch to be 31 mm thick, 675 mm wide, with small moulding under, the shelf projecting 175 mm into kitchen and having two 125 mm x 100 mm shaped softwood brackets under. Architraves to be 75 mm x 25 mm moulded having 100 mm x 25 mm moulded shelf at top with small moulding under and two 150 mm x 75 mm moulded brackets. Shelf in serving hatch to be 25 mm thick.

Linen store shelves
226   Linen store to have five rows of open softwood shelves, formed with 75 mm x 25 mm all round slats, 12 mm apart, upon wrought and chamfered bearers and 50 mm x 50 mm wrought posts. All slats to be screwed on to bearers from the underside.

Luggage rack in boxroom
227   Luggage rack in boxroom to be formed with 75 mm x 31 mm softwood slats, spaced 25 mm apart, upon wrought and chamfered bearers and 50 mm x 50 mm softwood posts.

Cupboard under stairs
228   Cupboard under stairs to have two 225 mm x 25 mm clean softwood shelves, upon proper bearers and brackets, as before described.

Flap table in scullery
229   Flap table in scullery to be in softwood 1800 mm x 600 mm x 31 mm thick, fixed in position directed, the flap hung with 75 mm brass butt hinges to 75 mm x 31 mm fillet plugged to wall, and to have framed leg bracket hinged to similar bearer with 50 mm wrought iron butt hinges.

Bench, etc, in garage
230   Bench in garage to be formed with three 225 mm x 75 mm wrought softwood members grooved and tongued together and supported upon four 50 mm x 50 mm bent angle irons, and end built into wall and the other let into concrete floor, the angle irons to be drilled, and the top secured with three steel screws to each member. Skirting to back and ends of bench to be 225 mm x 25 mm wrought softwood plugged to walls. Shelf in garage to be 275 mm x 31 mm wrought softwood, the full length of bench, supported upon strong steel brackets plugged and screwed to wall.

Enclosure to cisterns
231   Enclosure to cold-water cisterns in cistern-room to be formed with 19 mm match-boarding, with match-boarded covers to lift off. The space between cisterns and enclosure to be filled in with slag wool. Floor to cisterns to be finished with 75 mm x 38 mm softwood curb, all ready to receive lead tray. Suitable softwood bearers to be provided for cisterns inside the lead tray.

Back boards to flushing cisterns
232   Back boards for flushing cisterns to be 25 mm softwood about 450 mm x 225 mm plugged to walls.

Hooks in larder
233   Six strong, bright steel hooks to be fixed in ceiling of larder.

Draining boards
234   Draining boards of teak 31 mm thick, grooved in the usual way, to be put to sinks in kitchen, pantry and housemaids' closet, the boards fixed level upon wrought softwood bearers and iron cantilever brackets built into wall. Back of draining boards and sink to be finished round with 150 mm x 19 mm plain wrought teak skirting upon proper grounds.

Water butts
235   Two 180 litre casks, twice tarred externally, to be set upon bases previously specified, as water butts, fitted with 25 mm softwood ledged covers, twice tarred and perforated for inlets and to have wood butt cocks. Overflow pipe of 38 mm lead to be put to each butt to discharge over gullies.

Attend upon
236   The Contractor to attend upon, cut away for, and make good as necessary after plumber to the pedestal closets with flushing cisterns, bath, lavatory basins, sinks, water cisterns, gas cooker, etc.

Wall eyes for creepers
237   Where walls are covered externally with cement or stucco, galvanised-iron eyes 50 mm long, with split ends, to be fixed in the joints of the brickwork before the cement or stucco work is done, the eyes to be fixed 1 m apart horizontally and 0.6 m vertically.

Oil locks, etc
238   All locks, hinges and other ironmongery with moving parts to be well oiled.

Steel and Ironworker
Scrapers
239   Wrought iron scraper of approved pattern, pc £5 to be put to

back doorway and fixed in block of concrete 600 mm x 600 mm x 300 mm.

Ironwork in roof
240   All the iron straps and plates for bolting roof timbers together, and all bolts, nuts and washers, as indicated on detail drawings, to be supplied.

Hip irons
241   Hip irons to be 25 mm x 6 mm wrought iron, 900 mm long, screwed to wood hips and with shaped ends.

Railings and gates
242   The pc sum of £500 to be provided for wrought iron railings and entrance gates to be erected complete by a sub-contractor to be nominated by the Architect.

Chain link fences
243   Enclose the West and South sides of the site as shown with galvanised chain link fencing consisting of 50 mm mesh 2.50 mm diameter chain link 1350 mm high complete with three straining wires fixed to and including 38 mm x 38 mm x 5 mm angle iron standards 2 m long, pointed and driven 600 mm into the ground at 2.5 m intervals. Corner posts to be 50 mm x 50 mm x 6 mm angle 2 m long set in concrete complete with stays and straining fittings.

Metal windows
244   Include the pc sum of £800 for metal windows to be supplied, delivered and fixed complete by a sub-contractor to be nominated by the Architect. Unload on site and unpack the metal windows, get in and hoist to their required position for fixing on various levels and attend upon the firm supplying and fixing the windows and give assistance in taking sizes and giving instructions so that no mistakes may be made, and provide all ladders, scaffolding and plant and erect special scaffolding if required and give them all facilities for doing their work.

Plasterer
Lime
245   The lime for plastering to be well burnt stone or chalk lime, and to be run into putty at least one month before use.

Cement
246   The Portland cement to be as previously described.

Sand
247   The sand for plastering to be in accordance with BS 1198

Hair
248   Ox hair only to be used, and to be long, strong, dried and perfectly clean. It is to be free from grease and other impurities and well beaten.

Cement floating
249   The cement floating to concrete for wood blocks or other floors to be 19 mm thick, composed of 1 part of Portland cement to 3 parts sand.

Ordinary plastering
250   The plaster to be an anhydrous gypsum plaster and to conform to the requirements of BS 1191, Class C. The first and second coats of plaster are to be composed of two volumes of anhydrous gypsum undercoat plaster mixed with one volume of lime putty and six volumes of sand. The setting coat is to be anhydrous gypsum finishing plaster used neat.

Workmanship
251   The standard of workmanship to be of the very best quality and the whole of the plastering is to be carried out in the best possible manner in accordance with the recommendations of the British Standard Code of Practice 211 'Internal Plastering'.

Leave plaster perfect
252   The plastering to be left perfectly free from blisters, rust, or copper stains.

Screeds
253   Screeds to be used throughout, and the whole of the plasterer's work finished to a perfectly true and even surface.

Metal lathing
254   The expanded metal lathing to be 24 gauge BB 252 quality expanded metal lathing painted with black asphaltum and fixed with galvanised staples.

Repair plastering
255   All broken or damaged rough cast and plaster work to be repaired after all the other Tradesmen have left, all plastering to be made good where small pieces have been cut away for Electricians, Plumbers, or Engineers.

Plaster walls
256   All walls specified to have white glazed tiles, to be rendered, floated and set, the walls of bathroom and wcs finished for paint and elsewhere for emulsion paint, or paper.

Plaster ceilings
257   All ceilings to be covered with gypsum base-board 9.5 mm thick to BS 1230, fixed with galvanised nails to fir joists. The joints between boards to be filled with neat anhydrous gypsum plaster and covered with jute scrim dressed into the plaster and the whole finished with an approved board plaster not less than 3 mm thick.

Plaster studding
258   All ashlaring or studding to be covered with expanded metal lathing securely fixed and plastered with three coats. The base coat to be of metal lathing quality.

External rendering
259   The whole of the external walls, where left uncoloured on drawings and to half-timber work, to have rough cast executed as follows: the walls must first be rendered with 5 parts of sand and 2 parts of Portland cement, and while still green a second and final coat to be applied, consisting of 5 parts of sand and 2 parts of Portland cement and 1 part of lime. The face of the plaster to be worked with a wood float.

Point flashings
260   Lead flashings, etc, to be neatly pointed with cement and sand (1:1).

Wall tiling
261   The walls of kitchen and bathrooms and wcs to be covered for a height of 1500 mm with 152 mm x 152 mm x 6 mm standard quality white glazed wall tiles to comply in all respects with BS 1281, bedded and jointed with straight joints in cement and sand on a 12 mm screed of Portland cement and sand (1:3) and pointed in white cement and with all necessary rounded edge tiles. Walls of larder to have similar tiles 1200 mm in height above slate shelf, all window sills and reveals where occurring in wall tiled areas to be covered in similar tiles and all arrises and top edges to be formed with rounded edge tiles.

External Plumber
Lead
262   The lead used to be the best milled lead and of the full weight specified and to comply with BS 1178.

Solder, etc
263   No solder to be used in laying the lead work, except where quite unavoidable, and no continuous strip of lead to be more than 2.4 m long, laps to cover 75 mm and to be welted where necessary to make good work.

Gutters
264   Gutters behind chimney-stacks, and where required, to be covered with Code 6 lead, turned up 225 mm under tiles over fillets, and 150 mm against walls, finished with Code 5 lead flashings, 150 mm wide, let 19 mm into the joints of brickwork, and not less than 150 mm wide on sole at narrowest part.

Lead flats
265   All flats to be covered with Code 6 lead having all necessary drips, rolls, etc, the cheeks of dormers to be covered with Code 5 lead, secured with proper dots, and having soakers and flashings to tiles.

Lead dots
266   Solder dots to be formed by counter-sinking the boarding, dressing the lead well in, securing with pairs of inclined screws, and filling the hollows with solder neatly finished.

Chimney aprons
267   Aprons to lower sides of chimney-stacks to be Code 5 lead, let 19 mm into the joints of brickwork, and brought not less than 75 mm down the chimney side, to lie 150 mm on the tiles, well worked round the returns of the stacks, and then covered with the flashings.

Lead soakers
268   In all cases where the raking line of tiling meets brickwork, Code 4 lead soakers to be fixed, one to each tile, turned up 75 mm against walls, and lying 125 mm on the tiles, and to be 75 mm longer than the full gauge of the tiling.

Lead flashings
269   Lead soakers to be covered with Code 5 stepped flashings 200 mm wide, turned 19 mm into the joints of brickwork. Other flashings to be Code 5 lead, 175 mm wide.

Lead wedges
270   All flashings to be secured with lead wedges, and where stepped flashings occur one wedge to every other step must be provided.

Lead to sills
271   All oak window-sills to have Code 6 lead flashing, copper nailed at 50 mm centres to sills, and bedded in red lead to brick or tile sills.

Lead work in hollow walls
272   Heads of sash and door frames, built into hollow walls, to be protected by flashing of Code 5 lead, turned up against inner face of lintel and 38 mm over top and carried outwards over the cavity and dressed over outer face of heads, the flashing to project 50 mm over either end of frame.

Copper nails
273   All aprons, flashings, soakers, and other lead work to be fixed with copper nails where required.

Lead damp courses
274   Damp courses to chimney-stacks to be of Code 5 lead in one piece to each stack, perforated for flues. The lead to be inserted as near down to the roof as possible, and to project 12 mm from external face, except where it can act as flashings, when it is to be turned down same depth as ordinary flashings. The lead in the flues to be dressed up close against brickwork, so as to throw the water outwards.

Eaves gutters
275   Eaves gutters to be cast-iron 127 mm diameter half-round pattern to comply in all respects with BS 460, bolted and fixed on galvanised wrought iron fascia brackets, two to each 6 ft 0 in. length, with all requisite cast angles, stopped ends, and outlets with short nozzles cast on. The outlets to be fitted with galvanised-wire domical gratings. All joints in gutters to be made in red lead cement.

Rain-water pipes
276   Rain-water pipes to be 3 in. nominal diameter cast-iron pattern to comply in all respects with BS 460 with projecting ears cast on jointed in red lead cement and fixed 38 mm clear of walls with 75 mm galvanised rose-headed pipe nails and galvanised tube distance pieces to hardwood plugs let into face of walls, provide all requisite swannecks, shoes, bends, etc.

Internal Plumber
Water supply
Water pipes
277   All water pipes to be of lead to conform to BS 602. All joints in pipes to be wiped.

Water fittings
278   All fittings to be for high-pressure service, and approved, if necessary, by the local water company.

Water pipes in ground
279   All pipes in ground to be laid at a depth of not less than 750 mm.

Water company's requirements
280   The Contractor is to satisfy himself as to the requirements of the local water company, and provide for compliance with the same in all respects, and pay all official fees and charges.

Bib cocks
281   Bib cocks and stop cocks are to conform to the requirements of BS 1010.

Wall hooks
282   Wall hooks for fixing pipes to be galvanised iron, and all pipes to be supported on bearers where possible.

Water service
283   Water service to be laid on from the company's main with 19 mm lead pipe, in accordance with the local regulations, and proper connection to be made to the company's main or the company to be paid for so doing.

Stop cocks
284   A 19 mm brass stop cock to be fixed in brick box with iron cover immediately inside boundary fence, a further stop cock, easy of access, inside the house, is to be fixed where directed, and one on the down service immediately below the cold-water cistern.

Bib cocks to sinks
285   Chromium plated brass bib cocks, lettered 'Hot' and 'Cold' to be put to each sink.

Cold-water cistern
286   The 19 mm lead rising main to be laid on to a 125 gallon, (nominal) galvanised, mild steel cistern to conform to BS 417, Grade A, BS size number SC 125, fixed in the roof on strong fir bearers, and with 19 mm Portsmouth ballvalve and union.

Lead safes
287   Lead safes of Code 5 lead to be fixed under the cold-water cistern, and to have 75 mm x 38 mm softwood fillets all round, the lead being dressed up and over the same, and copper nailed; 50 mm lead overflow pipes to be provided to lead safes discharging through roof, and having cast brass hinged flaps on outside. Proper flashings to be put to tiles around pipes.

Down water services
288   The cistern to be drilled for 19 mm brass boiler screw unions with fly nuts and lead washers, and a 19 mm down service to be taken to bath with 12 mm services to all other fittings, and proper connections to be made to all taps and cisterns.

Overflow pipes
289   19 mm overflow pipes to be put to flushing cisterns, and 31 mm overflow pipes to water cisterns, with brass unions and nuts as necessary. The overflow pipes to be taken into the open air and finished with cast brass hinged flaps. Proper lead flashings to be put to pipes where required.

Water supply to boilers
290   The cistern to be drilled for 19 mm brass screw unions with fly nuts and lead washers, and 19 mm lead supply pipes to be run to both heating boilers and proper connections made.

Sanitary Fittings
Sinks
291   The pc sum of £200 to be provided for sink units in kitchen and scullery which must be fixed in position; 38 mm lead waste pipes to be put to sinks with drawn lead 'P' traps to conform to BS 504; the waste pipes taken through walls to discharge into glazed channels.

Lavatory basins
292   The pc sum of £60 to be provided for three lavatory basins, and the same to be fixed in position. 31 mm lead wastes and traps to be fixed all as described for sinks and hot-and-cold-water services connected to taps. The water from first floor sinks to discharge into hopper heads.

Baths
293   The pc sum of £150 to be provided for two baths, and the same to be fixed in position. 38 mm lead wastes to be fixed all as described for sinks, and hot-and-cold-water services connected to the taps.

Wcs
294   The pc sum of £120 to be provided for four high level wcs, including apparatus, seats, flushing cisterns with brackets and chain pulls. The closets to be fixed in positions shown, proper connections to be made to drains and to soil pipes. Flushing pipes to be 31 mm lead, fixed with lead clips to walls, and rubber cones to pans. Wcs on upper floors to have 87 mm lead branch pipes of Code 7 lead, connected with brass sleeves to iron soil pipe, other pans to be connected direct to drain. Overflow pipes with beaded and wired ends to discharge outside building.

Protect sanitary fittings
295   All baths, sinks, closets and other sanitary fittings to be covered up and protected as directed until the completion of the contract.

Soil and ventilating pipes
296   The soil and ventilating pipes to be 100 mm diameter heavy

cast-iron coated pipes to conform to BS 416; jointed with tarred gasket, and run with metallic lead caulked in, the pipes fixed 50 mm from walls with galvanised pipe nails driven into hardwood plugs through short lengths of galvanised iron pipes. The ventilating pipes to be carried up at least 600 mm above the level of the top of the dormer windows, and where on slopes of roofs, to be fixed with screws to lead covered blocks fixed to roof boarding with proper lead flashing to tiles.

Waste pipes
297   Waste pipes to be medium pattern 50 mm diameter cast-iron coated pipes to conform to BS 416 and fixed as described for soil and ventilating pipes. Hopper heads to be fitted to receive water from baths and lavatory basins. The bottom of waste pipes to be jointed in cement and sand to back inlet gullies.

Hot Water Supply
Note   The choice of materials and the joining used in the installation should be based on the requirements of the Local Water Board. For the purpose of this specification it is assumed the installation is to be of the direct type in copper tubing with independent boiler, but regard should be given to the Water Boards requirements.

Design   The hot water service should be designed to give a supply of hot water at each draw-off in accordance with the Code of Practice 342 for centralised Domestic Hot Water supply.

Boiler
298   A cast-iron open domestic boiler, conforming to BS 758, with cream vitreous enamelled finish, of capacity of not less than 66 000 BTUs per hour is to be provided and fixed in the boiler-house. Boiler to be complete with set of stoking tools, safety valve and automatic damper regulator. Emptying cock together with thermometer mounted on boiler flow are also to be provided.

Smokepipe connection
299   From the smoke outlet on the boiler a short length of cast iron vitreous enamelled smokepipe fitted with necessary bends and cleaning doors to be carried to connect to the brick flue.

Storage cylinder
300   A copper hot water cylinder of not less than 80 gallons capacity to be provided and fixed on cantilever brackets in boiler room, being constructed to conform to BS 699. Cylinder to be complete with manhole and cover for cleaning purposes and the necessary screwed bosses for pipe connections. Primary connections are not to be less than 38 mm diameter bore and a valve is to be fitted on the cylinder left ready for the plumber to make cold water connections. This should not be less than 31 mm diameter bore.

Circulating mains and branches
301   The boiler and cylinder to be connected together by primary flow and return mains with secondary circulations and branches taken from the cylinder to the draw-off points specified hereafter.

All pipes to be copper tube, connected together with all necessary pipe fittings and the branches being run to connect up to fittings.

Unions or connectors to be fitted at frequent intervals to facilitate the disconnection of pipe lines in position where they are readily accessible.

Copper tubes to be in accordance with BS 2871 Table Z, with capillary joints.

Expansion
302   Provision to be made in the pipe lines for taking up expansion and contraction by the arrangement of the fittings. Where this cannot be achieved additional bends to be provided as necessary.

Supports, sleeves, etc
303   All pipes to be supported on hangers, clips and brackets and in the case of pipes passing through walls or floors, sleeves, floor or ceiling plates to be provided to allow necessary expansion and contraction.

Valves
304   A control valve or stopcock is to be fitted on each branch serving a fitting or range of fittings.

Venting
305   An open vent of not less than 25 mm bore to be provided at the highest point of the circulation where air may accumulate.

Covering
306   The hot water cylinder to be covered with 25 mm glass-fibre flexible insulating jacket of approved make securely fixed with aluminium bands.

Towel rail
307   A chrome plated towel rail having three horizontal tubes with wheel valve on flow and lockshield valve on return of easy-clean chrome plate pattern to be fitted in each bathroom. The towel rails to be not less than 1 m long x 1 m high and fixed to walls with top stays

Coil in linen store
308   A coil of two 35 mm diameter pipes is to be fitted in the linen cupboard. Provide and fix 19 mm connections complete with lockshield valve on return and coil also to be fitted with aircock.

Schedule of draw-off points
309   Ground floor

Kitchen   2 sinks   25 mm draw-off
Cloaks   lavatory basin   12 mm draw-off

First floor
Two bathrooms each comprising
1 lavatory basin   12 mm draw-off
1 bath   19 mm draw-off
1 towel rail   19 mm connections.

Linen cupboard   35 mm coil at low level.

Testing
310   The complete plant is to be hydraulically tested to ensure all pipes are sound and drip tight after which the Contractor is to carry out a full working heat test to the requirements and full satisfaction of the Architect.
   The whole installation to be left in working order.

Central Heating
System   To be designed for gravity circulation
Boiler
311   To be of the cast-iron sectional type of approved manufacture, to BS 779; of capacity not less than 117 000 BThUs per hour. Complete with one set of stoking tools, spring type safety valve, brass cased thermometer, 19 mm emptying cock complete with hose union and automatic damper regulator. The boiler is also to be provided with galvanised mild steel insulated jacket.
   Capacity to be based upon the total heating load, plus a margin of 25%.

Smokepipe connection
312   From the smoke outlet on the boiler a short length of cast-iron smokepipe, fitted with necessary bends and cleaning doors, to be carried to connect to the brick flue.

Circulating mains
313   The flow and return circulating mains to be taken from the boiler with branches to serve the various heating appliances.
   All pipework to be black medium quality tube in accordance with BS 1387, tested to a pressure of approximately 700 lb per sq in., by tube manufacturers before delivery. The pipework to be connected together with screwed and socketed joints, complete with all necessary fittings. Unions or connectors to be fitted at frequent intervals to facilitate the disconnection of pipe lines in positions where they are readily accessible.

Expansion
314   Provision to be made in the pipe lines for taking up expansion

and contraction by the arrangement of the fittings, where this cannot be achieved additional bends to be provided as necessary.

Supports, sleeves, etc
315   All pipes to be supported on hangers, clips and brackets and in the case of pipes passing through walls or floors, sleeves, floor or ceiling plates to be provided to allow necessary expansion and contraction.

Radiators
316   The radiators to be cast iron of approved pattern manufactured to comply with BS 3528 and of heights to suit positions where indicated and in accordance with accompanying schedule.

Each radiator to be fitted with vent plug, also two gunmental easy-clean pattern control valves. The valve on the flow connection being provided with a wheel for individual control of heat by the occupants of the room and the valve on the return fitted with a lockshield to be regulated by the Engineer on completion.

Expansion tank
317   Provide and fix, in a suitable position in roof space, one 30 gallon (nominal) capacity galvanised feed and expansion tank. Tank to be complete with loose drop-over cover and to conform to BS 417. Ballvalve to be fitted complete with 12 mm stop cock and left ready for plumber to connect to rising main.

Venting. Cold water feed. Emptying
318   An open vent of not less that 19 mm bore to be provided at the highest point of each circuit where air is likely to accumulate. A cold feed is to be taken direct from feed and expansion tank to a point on the main boiler return.

Emptying facilities are to be provided on all main branch circuits. Cocks to be 12 mm bore and fitted with hose unions.

Temperatures
319   The apparatus is to be designed to obtain the following temperatures in the rooms specified with a boiler temperature maintained at not less the $82°C$ ($180°F$) when the building is dry and in occupation and the external temperature is at $0°C$ ($32°F$). Calculations to be based on the computation of heat losses as recommended by the institute of Heating and Ventilating Engineers:

Ground floor

Living-room	2 radiators.	1½ air changes per hour $18°C$ ($65°F$)
Dining room	2 radiators.	2 air changes per hour $18°C$ ($65°F$)
Office	1 radiator.	2 air changes per hour $18°C$ ($65°F$)
Kitchen	1 radiator.	2 air changes per hour $15°C$ ($60°F$)
Entrance hall.	1 radiator.	2 air changes per hour $15°C$ ($60°F$)

First floor

Bedroom 1	2 radiators.	2 air changes per hour 12°C (55°F)
Bedroom 2	1 radiator.	2 air changes per hour 12°C (55°F)
Bedroom 3	1 radiator.	2 air changes per hour 12°C (55°F)
Bedroom 4	1 radiator.	2 air changes per hour 12°C (55°F)
Dressing-room	1 radiator.	2 air changes per hour 12°C (55°F)

Testing
320   The complete plant to be hydraulically tested to ensure that all joints are sound and drip-proof. A heat test is then to be carried out, for which the Contractor is to provide the necessary thermometer and fitters attendance. Fuel for the test will be provided, but Contractor is to provide attendance in firing. Test to be carried out under the conditions as laid down by Institute of Heating and Ventilating Engineers. The installation to be left in full working order.

Note   This specification covers for a hand-fired boiler, but in some instances gas-fired boilers could be substituted or oil-fired equipment added.

Gas Fitter
Gas pipes
321   Pipes to be galvanised wrought iron tubes, together with all fittings, such as bends, elbows, tees, equal or diminishing sockets, nipples, connectors, etc, and put together with tow and red lead cement.

Fixing gas pipes
322   Pipes above ground to be neatly secured with galvanised pipe clips and fixed at an inclination so that no water may lodge.

Supply of gas
323   Connection to the gas company's main to be made with ferrule or tee-piece, and gas to be laid on to suitable capacity meter, fixed where directed, upon softwood shelf and having 31 mm gas cock with loose key on company's side of meter, or arrange for the local company to do this work. From the meter a 25 mm service pipe to be laid on to the gas cooker and to one other point in kitchen, finished with plug, also to garage over bench where directed.

Testing gas supply
324   The whole of the gas services to be thoroughly tested to the satisfaction of the Architect.

Gas cooker
325   The gas cooker will be supplied by the Employer, but the Contractor must accept delivery and place in position and connect to service.

Electrical Installation

Contractor

326   The whole of the work to be carried out by a Member of the Electrical Contractors Association.

Electric supply

327   Arrangements to be made with the local Electricity Board for the installation of the necessary service cable and all charges so incurred to be included. The supply cutouts and meter are to be fixed in an agreed position in the building.

Main switch gear

328   The main switch and distribution fuseboard to be 500 volt pattern metal clad. The fuseboard being complete with single pole and neutral fuseways of appropriate capacity and complying with Home Office regulations.

The switch gear to be erected adjacent to the service fuse and main meter.

General installation

329   All wiring to be 250 volt grade PVC insulated and sheathed cables enclosed in heavy gauge screwed welded conduit where concealed in floors; where concealed in walls the cables to be protected by light gauge close joint conduit.

Wiring to be installed in the 'looping' system and the conduit installation to be complete throughout with screwed conduit accessories, the whole system being effectively earthed at the supply intake position.

The complete installation to comply with the current edition of the Institution of Electrical Engineers *Regulations for the Electrical Equipment of Buildings*. Lighting and socket outlet points to be as shown on the 'Schedule of Points'.

Lighting points

330   No conductor smaller than 1.5 sq mm is to be used and not more than eight lighting points are to be connected to any one circuit. Each lighting point is to terminate in a conduit outlet box left ready to receive the selected lighting fitting.

Socket points

331   No conductor smaller than 2.5 sq mm to be used and circuits to be arranged on the ring main system with spur connection where applicable. The socket installation to comply strictly with Regulations A30 — A41 of the aforementioned IEE Regulations.

Switches

332   To be 5 or 15 ampere flush AC pattern to BS 3676 mounted on metal boxes with adjustable grids and heavy over-lapping brass plates

finished as required. Switches in wcs and kitchen, etc, to have all insulated plates and dollies. Switches in bathrooms to be ceiling pull cord type.

Socket outlets
333   To be 13 ampere switched or non-switched type to BS 1363 mounted in metal boxes and heavy overlapping plates finished to match wall switches. Each socket to be complete with fused plug top.

Lighting fittings and lamps
334   Lighting fittings will be selected and provided by the Employer, but erection and connection to be included for by the Contractor.

Testing
335   The whole of the work to be tested on completion and left to the satisfaction of the Architects and Electricity Authority.

Schedule of Electric Points

...ition	Ceiling points	Bracket points	Lighting point watts	Total lighting point watts	Switches	13 amp socket outlets
...ound floor						
...ing room	1	2	60/200	320	3	4
...ing room	1	—	200	200	2	3
...chen	1	—	200	200	1	2
...der	1	—	60	60	1	—
	1	—	40	40	1	—
...ler room	1	—	60	60	1	1
...re	1	—	60	60	1	—
...aks	1	—	60	60	1	—
...trance hall	2	—	100	200	2 2-way	1
...bby	1	—	60	60	1	—
...ch	1	—	60	60	1	—
...ice	1	—	150	150	1	2
...n porch	2	—	60	120	2	2
...re	1	—	60	60	2 2-way	—
...rage	2	—	100	200	2	1
...chen yard	—	1	60	60	2 2-way	—
...st floor						
...nding	1	—	100	100	2 2-way	1
...hroom 1	1	—	60	60	1	—
...ssing-room	1	—	100	100	1	1

Schedule of Electric Points *(continued)*

Position	Ceiling points	Bracket points	Lighting point watts	Total lighting point watts	Switches	13 soc out
Bathroom 2	2	—	60/100	160	2	—
Bedroom 1	2	—	60/100	160	2	3
Bedroom 2	2	—	60/100	160	2	2
Bedroom 3	2	—	60/100	160	2	3
Bedroom 4	1	—	100	100	1	1
Totals	30	3	—	2,910	29 8 2-way	27

SUMMARY   33 Ceiling and Bracket Lighting Points — 2.91Kw. 27 13 amp Socket Outlets — 3Kw each on ring main circuits

Glazier
Glass
336   All glass to be of English manufacture, the full weight specified, free from bubbles, smoke wanes, air holes, scratches or other defects, to be delivered on the site in the makers' original packages and the makers' guarantee to be produced if called for by the Architect.

Fixing glass
337   All glass to be cut accurately to fit easily into the rebates, and, except in doors, to be well puttied, back puttied, and sprigged. Care to be taken to see that the putty does not show beyond the sight lines of panes.

Putty
338   Glazier's putty to be made of pure whiting and raw linseed oil, and to be used fresh except to metal windows and doors where approved metal casement putty is to be used.

Glazing
339   Windows of wcs and bathrooms to be glazed with approved obscure glass (Group 2), all other windows and doors to be glazed with 3 mm selected glazing quality, clear sheet glass.

Leave glass perfect
340   All glass broken or cracked during the progress of the works to be reinstated; all glass to be cleaned both sides, and all glazing left clean and perfect at the completion of the contract.

Painter

Paint

341   The paint to be obtained from Messrs . . . (here should be stated the particular manufacturer's name and address, together with the names of the particular brand or quality it is intended to use. As all paints vary to some extent it is essential that the Contractor should know exactly what paint is required in order that he may make all the necessary allowances for covering capacity, cost and special requirements).

Knotting

342   The wood and iron work to be properly cleaned and the woodwork to be twice knotted previous to the priming coat, and to be stopped, pumiced, and felted down between each coat.

Distinct tints

343   Each coat of paint (except white) to be of a distinct tint, to distinguish it from the previous one.

Painting

344   The paint to be put on with approved brushes, kept well bound, and well worked during its application. For ironwork fairly stiff brushes to be used. The painting to be carried out in such order as directed, and each coat to ḅ. thoroughly dry before the next coat is laid on. An interval of four clear days to be allowed between the coats where possible.

Cleaning woodwork

345   All unprimed woodwork shall be lightly rubbed down and dusted off and afterwards knotted and primed. After priming, nail holes and other imperfections shall be stopped with a hard stopping consisting of paste white lead and gold size stiffened with whiting.

Cleaning ironwork

346   All iron or steelwork delivered to the site already primed to be examined as to the quality and condition of the existing primer to ascertain that it is hard, firmly adhering and not chalking, blistered or crazed. If the quality or condition of the existing primer is not satisfactory it shall be completely removed and the surfaces thoroughly cleaned and wire-brushed and primed immediately with the appropriate primer. All iron and steelwork delivered to the site unprimed shall be chipped, scraped and wire-brushed to remove all rust and loose scale and cleaned to remove all dirt and grease and then primed immediately with the appropriate primer.

Sample tints

347   Sample tints of all finishing coats to be submitted to the Architect for approval.

Paint woodwork
348   The whole of the external and internal woodwork usually painted, except where otherwise specified, to be knotted, primed, stopped, and then painted two undercoats and one finishing coat in colours to the approval of the Architect.

Emulsion paint
349   The plastered walls and ceilings of all rooms except bathrooms and wcs to be given one coat of primer and two coats of emulsion paint.

Paint plaster
350   The walls and ceilings of bathroom and wcs to be prepared and painted four coats, finished stippled.

Stain floors
351   The whole of the oak block floor of hall to be stained with approved stain and wax polished.

Paint ironwork
352   The whole of the iron and steel work throughout, unless otherwise specified, to be primed and painted one coat before fixing and two coats after fixing.

Cement wash on steel
353   All steel joists, etc, embedded in concrete to be given two coats of thick cement wash.

Paint radiators
354   All radiators, together with all exposed hot-water pipes, to be thoroughly cleaned and painted two coats of approved metallic paint.

Cleaning on completion
355   All floors to be twice washed, all marks on paint to be sponged off, the work generally to be touched up after all other workmen have left, and the whole of the buildings left clean, perfect and watertight on completion to the satisfaction of the Architect.

INDEX TO SPECIFICATION
The numbers given refer to the clauses

FORM OF SCHEDULE OF PRICES
(Referred to in chapter X page 73)

Proposed New Residence at New Oxford for William Brown Esq

August 1973

X Y Jones Esq
Architect

Schedule of Prices
For use where quantities do not form part of the Contract

[See Clauses 3 and 11 of the Conditions of the Standard Form of Building Contract 1963 (without Quantities) Edition (July 1973 Revision)]

Item	Rate	Unit
Excavate over site to remove turf and vegetable soil to a depth of 225 mm, fill into barrows and wheel and deposit on site where directed a distance not exceeding 200 metres		Per square metre
Excavate to reduce levels and get out		Per cubic metre
Excavate to form surface trenches not exceeding 1.50 m deep and get out		Per cubic metre
Fill excavated material into barrows, wheel from spoil heaps and return, fill in and ram around foundations in 300 mm layers		Per cubic metre
Fill surplus excavated material into barrows or carts and wheel or cart from spoil heaps and deposit on site in 300 mm layers where directed a distance not exceeding 200 metres		Per cubic metre
Level and well ram bottom of trenches		Per square metre
Stout planking and strutting to sides of surface trenches not exceeding 1.50 m deep (both sides measured)		Per square metre
Ditto, ditto, but to sides of excavations to reduce levels not exceeding 3.00 m deep		Per square metre
Hardcore as described to make up levels under floors well rammed and consolidated in 300 mm layers		Per cubic metre

Item	Rate	Unit
Bed of hardcore 150 mm thick spread and levelled to receive concrete well rammed and consolidated, including levelling and ramming ground under		Per square metre
Ditto, ditto, but laid to falls and currents		Per square metre
Portland cement and 'All-in' ballast concrete (1:6) in foundations		Per cubic metre
Portland cement concrete (1:2:4) with aggregate to pass a 19 mm ring in 38 mm wide cavity in hollow wall		Per square metre
Portland cement and 'All-in' ballast concrete (1:6) in layer 125 mm thick laid on hardcore and finished spade face		Per square metre
Ditto, ditto, but in layer 150 mm thick and finished to receive cement screeds		Per square metre
Ditto, ditto, 150 mm thick but laid to falls and currents		Per square metre
Precast Portland cement concrete (1:2:4) in lintel size 75 mm x 150 mm with one 12 mm diameter mild steel rod as described		Per linear metre
Ditto, ditto, but size 103 mm x 150 mm with one 20 mm diameter mild steel rod		Per linear metre
Ditto, ditto, but size 241 mm x 225 mm twice rebated and with four 20 mm diameter mild steel rods		Per linear metre
Hack concrete to form key for plastering		Per square metre
Form or leave mortices in concrete for ends of metal balusters and grout in		Each
Sweep clean surface of concrete beds and apply two coats of waterproof cement grout		Per square metre
Formwork to soffit of suspended concrete floor slab, including strutting not exceeding 3.50 m high		Per square metre

Item	Rate	Unit
Formwork to sides and soffits of concrete beams and lintels		Per square metre
Formwork to edge of concrete 100 mm high		Per linear metre
Ditto, ditto, but 150 mm high		Per linear metre
16 mm diameter mild steel reinforcing rods as described in suspended concrete floor slab		Per kilogramme
20 mm diameter, ditto, ditto		Per kilogramme
One brick wall in local bricks as described (pc £15 per thousand delivered to site)		Per square metre
243 mm hollow wall constructed of two half brick thicknesses of local bricks in cement mortar with 38 mm cavity, tied with galvanised steel twisted wall ties as described		Per square metre
Half brick wall in local bricks in cement mortar		Per square metre
Damp proof course of two courses of stout new Welsh slates		Per square metre
Ditto, ditto, but 100 mm wide		Per linear metre
Extra over local brickwork for facing to outer half brick thickness of hollow wall in stretcher bond with facing bricks (pc £30 per thousand delivered to site)		Per square metre
Rake out joints of brickwork at least 16 mm deep to form key for plaster		Per square metre
Bed plate in cement mortar		Per linear metre
225 mm x 150 mm terra cotta air brick and build in face of external wall, including forming opening through 243 mm hollow wall and lining over cavity with thin slates		Each
Gather in chimney throat and form flue 225 mm x 225 mm in the clear, 8.00 m long with proper bends, etc, where required		Each

Item	Rate	Unit
Parge and core flue 225 mm x 225 mm in the clear		Per linear metre
Rough rendering in cement and sand around chimney stacks in roof space		Per square metre
Extra for selected facings and pointing as described to reveal half brick wide		Per linear metre
Ditto, ditto, but one brick wide		Per linear metre
Extra over one brick wall built in facing bricks finished fair face both sides for brick on edge flat arch faced and pointed both sides and soffit to match facings		Per linear metre
Extra over one brick wall built in facing bricks finished fair face both sides for brick on edge coping and two course tile creasing projecting both sides, including cement fillets and pointing to match facings		Per linear metre
38 mm granolithic paving laid to falls and currents and finished with a hard trowelled surface		Per square metre
19 mm granolithic skirting 150 mm high with cove to 25 mm radius and rounded top edge		Per linear metre
50 mm precast concrete paving slabs as described size 600 mm x 450 mm and bedding jointing and pointing in cement mortar to falls including all straight cutting		Per square metre
152 mm x 152 mm x 22 mm thick red quarry tile paving to conform to BS 1286 type A bedded jointed and pointed in cement mortar on screed (given separately), including all straight cutting, and cleaning off on completion		Per square metre
Red quarry tile skirting 152 mm high with rounded top edge and cove at bottom bedded jointed and pointed in cement mortar, including cleaning off on completion		Per linear metre

Item	Rate	Unit
50 mm hard Yorkshire stone paving in square and random slabs to detail plain dressed on surface and with square edges, and bedding jointing and pointing in cement mortar		Per square metre
Labour fair dressed edge to 50 mm York stone paving		Per linear metre
Excavate trench for 100 mm diameter drain pipe of sufficient and approved width not exceeding 1.50 m deep average 750 mm deep the bottom to be formed to required falls, return fill in and ram after drains have been laid and tested and wheel and deposit surplus excavated material as previously described. Include for all planking and strutting required and for baling or pumping out water as necessary		Per linear metre
Portland cement concrete (1:6) as described in bed 450 mm wide and 100 mm thick for 100 mm diameter drain pipe and laying in trench (given separately), including forming hollows at intervals to receive sockets of pipes and benching up sides to at least the centre of the pipe with similar concrete after the pipes have been laid and tested and include for filling in any holes or uneven places in trench with concrete		Per linear metre
100 mm diameter 'British Standard' socket jointed salt glazed stoneware drain pipe and laying to falls on concrete bed (given separately) in trench and jointing in cement mortar as described		Per linear metre
Extra only for 100 mm diameter bend and extra joint		Each
Salt glazed stoneware gully similar to Messrs Broads H 13/J with 152 mm x 152 mm galvanised grating and 102 mm diameter outlet and 102 mm vertical back inlet and setting on and including 150 mm bed of Portland cement concrete (1:6) as described size 600 mm x 600 mm x 300 mm thick and encasing with concrete 150 mm thick all round and connecting to drain, including all extra excavation required		Each

Item	Rate	Unit
Brick on edge curb to three sides of 152 mm x 152 mm gully top rendered all over in cement and sand (1:3) trowelled to a hard smooth surface with sharp arrises and cement skirting 150 mm high at back with fair edge and arris		Each
Excavate to form soakaway pit 1.00 m diameter and 2.00 m deep and fill in with hardcore up to about 300 mm below ground level. Provide 75 mm thick precast concrete slab and place in position and cover with earth and include for all necessary planking and strutting and wheel and deposit surplus excavated material as previously described		Each
100 mm diameter British Standard 'Tested' socket jointed salt glazed stoneware drain pipe and laying to falls on concrete bed (given separately) in trench and jointing in cement mortar as described		Per linear metre
Extra only for 100 mm diameter stoneware 'Tested' bend and extra joint		Each
100 mm diameter coated cast-iron spigot and socket drain pipe to conform to BS 437 with caulked lead joints and laying to falls on concrete bed (given separately) in trench in short lengths in branches		Per linear metre
Extra only for 100 mm diameter cast-iron bend, including extra joint and cutting		Each
Form or leave hole on rake through foundation of 243 mm hollow wall for 100 mm diameter drain pipe and pack around drain pipe with Portland cement concrete (1:6) as described where passing through wall		Each
100 mm diameter approved stoneware disconnecting trap with cleaning arm and stopper built into side of manhole, the stopper to be bedded in cart grease and to have galvanised iron lever and chain, the trap to be bedded on Portland cement concrete (1:6) as described size 600 mm x 600 mm x 450 mm thick and		

Item	Rate	Unit
packed around with similar concrete and jointed to drain		Each
Excavate to form manholes not exceeding 1.50 m deep and get out		Per cubic metre
Portland cement concrete (1:6) as described in bed 150 mm thick to bottom of manholes		Per square metre
100 mm pre-cast concrete slab (1:2:4) as described with aggregate to pass a 19 mm ring, including light fabric reinforcement and with rebated perforation formed in same for 610 mm x 455 mm manhole cover, including all moulds, casing, etc, and bedding in cement mortar on brickwork size 1143 mm x 1307 mm		Each
Rendering in Portland cement and sand (1:2) 19 mm thick on internal face of brickwork in manholes finished with a smooth trowelled watertight surface		Per square metre
Form or leave hole in one brick sides of manholes and build in end of 100 mm drain pipe and make good brickwork and rendering		Each
Messrs Broads 3B or other approved galvanised cast-iron manhole cover and frame size 610 mm x 455 mm weighing 38 kilogrammes the frame bedded in rebate in concrete cover in cement mortar and the cover bedded in cart grease		Each
Three layer standard grey self-finished bituminous roofing felt similar to the Ruberoid Co. Ltd's specification G3/M and fixing to insulation board (measured net) and allow for all straight cutting		Per square metre
Extra labour and material on felt roofing for dressing down into gutter		Per linear metre
Turning piece to flat brick arch 102 mm on soffit and strutting not exceeding 3.50 m high		Per linear metre
100 mm x 50 mm sawn softwood plate		Per linear metre

Item	Rate	Unit
200 mm x 50 mm sawn softwood floor joist		Per linear metre
200 mm x 50 mm sawn softwood floor joist not exceeding 1.25 m long		Per linear metre
150 mm x 50 mm sawn softwood ceiling joist		Per linear metre
100 mm x 50 mm sawn softwood rafter		Per linear metre
225 mm x 75 mm sawn softwood purlins		Per linear metre
150 mm x 50 mm sawn softwood members of roof trusses		Per linear metre
150 mm x 25 mm sawn softwood ridge		Per linear metre
50 mm x 50 mm sawn softwood herringbone strutting to 200 mm joists		Per linear metre
50 mm x 25 mm sawn softwood tilting fillet		Per linear metre
100 mm x 50 mm ditto, ditto		Per linear metre
200 mm x 50 mm sawn softwood blocking pieces in 450 mm lengths fixed and wedged between joists to receive plate for partition		Per linear metre
Bore hole through 38 mm softwood for 12 mm diameter bolt		Each
Labour notching 50 mm joists over 75 mm x 50 mm plate		Each
Labour notching and fitting ends of 200 mm x 50 mm joists over plates and into web of steel joists		Each
Ends of 100 mm x 50 mm rafters cut on splay for a length of 300 mm		Each
Hoist and fix only in position at First Floor level roof truss about 6.00 m span		Each
Casing to 200 gallon cistern size about 1170 mm x 900 mm x 900 mm formed with 19 mm		

Item	Rate	Unit
wrought softwood tongued and grooved boarding on 50 mm x 50 mm sawn softwood bearers, the 50 mm space between casing and cistern filled with slag wool tightly rammed, the lid to be moveable formed with two thicknesses of 12 mm tongued and grooved boarding and 75 mm x 12 mm ledges with thick felt between the thicknesses		Each
Supply only 38 mm x 19 mm sawn softwood tiling battens to 346 mm gauge for Double Roman tiles, including all cutting		Per square metre
38 mm x 19 mm sawn softwood counter battens and nailing to rafters at 450 mm centres		Per square metre
13 mm thick approved insulating board to BS 1142 and nailed with galvanised nails to sloping soffit of rafters (measured net and allow for all straight cutting)		Per square metre
19 mm thick approved insulating boarding to BS 1142 nailed with galvanised nails to joists to flat roofs, including firring to shallow falls (measured net and allow for all straight cutting)		Per square metre
Reinforced bitumen felt to BS 747 type 1F weighing 11.3 kilogrammes per 10 square metre roll and fixing with galvanised clout nails well lapped at edges (measured net and allow for all straight cutting)		Per square metre
25 mm wrought softwood square-edged boarding in batten widths and nailing to ceiling joists in roof space		Per square metre
19 mm wrought softwood tongued and grooved V-jointed boarding in 100 mm widths and nailing to soffit of joists		Per square metre
25 mm x 25 mm wrought softwood moulded fillet		Per linear metre
75 mm x 38 mm wrought softwood moulded fillet including mitres and fitted ends		Per linear metre

Item	Rate	Unit
13 mm wrought softwood tongued and grooved and V-jointed boarding 150 mm wide to underside of joists to form soffit board		Per linear metre
13 mm wrought softwood tongued and grooved and V-jointed boarding 300 mm wide fixed sloping to rafters		Per linear metre
175 mm x 25 mm wrought softwood beaded and splayed fascia		Per linear metre
25 mm wrought softwood tongued and grooved flooring in ordinary widths each board securely fixed to each joist with two 57 mm brads well punched in and cleaned off and protected until completion of contract		Per square metre
75 mm x 19 mm wrought softwood splayed and rounded skirting plugged and fixed to brickwork, including all short lengths, mitres, cut and fitted and returned ends		Per linear metre
100 mm x 100 mm wrought oak framed posts with four slightly rounded arrises		Per linear metre
19 mm wrought cedar tongued and grooved boarding in 150 mm widths with rebated joint to form groove on face fixed vertically externally to bearers (given separately)		Per square metre
25 mm wrought cedar tongued and grooved boarding in 150 mm widths fixed vertically externally to bearers (given separately)		Per square metre
89 mm x 63 mm wrought oak framed rebated splayed throated and rounded head		Per linear metre
125 mm x 63 mm ditto, ditto		Per linear metre
89 mm x 63 mm wrought oak framed rebated splayed and rounded frame fixed with holdfasts (given separately)		Per linear metre
125 mm x 75 mm wrought oak framed rebated weathered rounded and throated sill		Per linear metre
150 mm x 75 mm wrought oak framed rebated weathered rounded and throated sill		Per linear metre

Item	Rate	Unit
Fair returned ends to last		Each
191 mm x 25 mm wrought oak splayed nose window board grooved for plaster on the underside and screwed to brickwork, the heads of screws let in and pellated		Per linear metre
Fair notched returned and mitred ends to last		Each
Internal tongued and mitred irregular angle to last		Each
44 mm wrought softwood framed ledged and braced doors filled in with 25 mm tongued and grooved boarding V-jointed both sides		Per square metre
50 mm wrought softwood door in one large panel left open for glass, hung folding in two leaves		Per square metre
56 mm wrought softwood framed ledged and braced doors filled in with 32 mm tongued and grooved boarding V-jointed both sides hung folding in two leaves		Per square metre
44 mm wrought softwood rebated and moulded fixed fanlight in one square		Per square metre
38 mm hollow cored flush door to BS 4787 faced both sides with 5 mm interior quality plywood for painting and with solid hardwood lipped edges		Per square metre
Labour rebated and beaded joint to meeting stile to 56 mm thick softwood doors		Per linear metre
175 mm x 32 mm wrought softwood twice rounded frame fixed to and including sawn softwood grounds or fixing slips to brickwork		Per linear metre
25 mm x 16 mm wrought softwood splayed cover bead including mitres and fitted ends		Per linear metre
114 mm x 19 mm sawn softwood ground plugged and fixed to brickwork		Per linear metre
44 mm wrought oak three panel moulded on the solid both sides door with 6 mm oak solid panels		Per square metre

Item	Rate	Unit
125 mm x 50 mm wrought oak rebated and splayed frame with groove for plaster fixed with holdfasts (given separately)		Per linear metre
32 mm wrought oak treads with moulded nosing and small moulding under and 25 mm risers all tongued and grooved together and glued blocked and bracketed on and including 100 mm x 75 mm sawn softwood carriage the treads to be screwed to the risers with three brass screws to each tread from the underside		Per square metre
32 mm wrought oak tongued and grooved landing in 100 mm widths fixed on and including 100 mm x 50 mm sawn softwood bearers		Per square metre
Extra over 32 mm wrought oak landing for 75 mm x 32 mm moulded nosing tongued to edge of floor with small moulding under to match tread		Per linear metre
225 mm x 38 mm wrought oak apron lining the lower edge moulded and grooved		Per linear metre
330 mm x 50 mm wrought oak framed cross-tongued cut outer string moulded and grooved on lower edge and prepared for risers		Per linear metre
Extra for fair shaped moulded and mitred end to last		Each
Extra for splayed cut end framed to apron lining		Each
Extra for tongued and mitred internal angles and ramp raking to raking		Each
300 mm x 38 mm wrought oak cross-tongued moulded and splay rebated wall strong prepared for moulded nose treads and risers fixed upon and including sawn softwood grounds and backings plugged and fixed to brickwork or partition		Per linear metre
Extra for fair shaped moulded and mitred end		Each
Extra for short shaped ramp with part mitred fair return and heading joint to skirting		Each

Item	Rate	Unit
56 mm x 50 mm wrought oak fully moulded handrail		Per linear metre
Extra for short ramp and returned moulded end including extra joint and handrail screws		Each
Extra for quadrant angle straight to straight, including extra joint and handrail screws		Each
Extra for wreathed ramp raking to raking, including extra joint and handrail screws		Each
32 mm x 32 mm wrought oak square and turned balusters 990 mm long housed to handrail and nosing, including mortices		Each
32 mm x 32 mm wrought oak square and turned balusters 990 mm long but housed to tread and handrail, including mortices		Each
Extra for fair mitred ends to treads		Each
Ends of risers housed to string		Each
Ends of treads and risers housed to string		Each
50 mm x 32 mm wrought softwood grooved and splayed picture rail plugged and screwed to brickwork, including all short lengths and mitres		Per linear metre
38 mm wrought softwood one panel square framed both sides trap door size 762 mm x 762 mm		Each
Fit and fix only the following ironmongery to softwood:		
Pairs 100 mm steel butt hinges		Each
75 mm upright mortice lock and set of lever handles on long back plate		Each
BMA double locking pattern cylinder rimlock		Each
300 mm x 75 mm BMA push plates		Each
300 mm BB barrel bolts with sockets		Each
Double action floor spring with loose box and top centre and fill with sufficiency of oil		Each

Item	Rate	Unit
Fit and fix the following ironmongery to hardwood:		
Pairs 100 mm steel butt hinges		Each
75 mm upright mortice lock and set of lever handles on long back plate		Each
BMA double locking pattern cylinder rim lock		Each
200 mm x 19 mm BMA flush bolt and plates		Each
25 mm x 6 mm galvanised wrought iron weather bar cut to lengths and bedded in mortar in concrete		Per linear metre
19 mm diameter galvanised steel dowels 150 mm long and mortices in softwood and concrete		Each
150 mm x 25 mm sawn softwood coal boards 700 mm long with two hand holes cut in each and fixing in position in groove in frame		Each
25 mm wrought softwood cross-tongued shelving fixed to bearers (given separately), including cut and fitted ends		Per square metre
Wrought softwood slatted shelving formed of 38 mm x 13 mm slats in short lengths spaced 19 mm apart and having 50 mm x 38 mm front and back bearers with the short lengths framed in to same, the shelving screwed to bearers (given separately) with steel screws, the heads of screws let in and pellated		Per square metre
50 mm x 19 mm wrought softwood chamfered bearers fixed to and including hardwood plugs let into brickwork, including returned mitred ends		Per linear metre
100 mm x 32 mm wrought softwood rebated lining tongued at angles and fixing to backings and fixing slips to brickwork		Per linear metre
150 mm x 25 mm wrought softwood china shelf splayed recessed or grooved on top for plates fixed with screws to brackets (given separately) including mitres		Per linear metre

Item	Rate	Unit
32 mm wrought teak stopped grooved draining board size 700 mm x 500 mm set level, the fall to be in the grooves, with small rounded fillet fixed with brass screws in cups to front edge and one return and with 100 mm x 13 mm skirting tongued in on back edge and fixing to brickwork with rawlplugs and screws. The board is to be bedded in white lead to edge of sink and screwed to cantilever bearer (given separately) and the board and skirting to be twice oiled with linseed oil		Each
50 mm x 13 mm wrought iron arch bar cut to lengths with caulked ends and building in		Per linear metre
25 mm x 3 mm galvanised wrought iron holdfasts 300 mm long one end bent holed and screwed to back of softwood door frame and the other end split and built into brickwork		Each
25 mm x 3 mm ditto, ditto, but screwed to back of hardwood door and window frames		Each
Universal beam 203 mm x 133 mm x 30 kilogrammes per linear metre and hoisting and fixing in position at First Floor level		Per kilogramme
Ditto, ditto, but at Main Roof level		Per kilogramme
Rolled steel angle 102 mm x 76 mm x 9 mm x 12.5 kilogrammes per linear metre and hoisting and fixing in position at First Floor level		Per kilogramme
13 mm diameter screw bolts 140 mm long with head, nut and washer and fixing through softwood and steel (holes given separately)		Each
Unpack, assemble, hoist to position and fix only with screws provided metal window size 610 mm x 610 mm to hardwood frame and bed metal window all round in oil mastic and leave in working order		Each
Ditto, ditto, but size 1219 mm x 1321 mm		Each
Portland cement and sand (1:3) floated bed 19 mm thick laid on concrete and finished to receive tile paving		Per square metre

Item	Rate	Unit
Portland cement and sand (1:3) rendering mm thick on brick walls scored to receive wall tiling		Per square metre
Ditto, ditto, but plain face 16 mm thick on brick walls		Per square metre
Render float and set in lime plaster as described on brick walls		Per square metre
Make good lime plaster up to metal window frame		Per linear metre
Extra over lime plaster for Keene's cement rounded external angle to 10 mm radius, including two 50 mm wings		Per linear metre
Render float and set in gypsum plaster as described on brick walls		Per square metre
Labour slightly rounded arris		Per linear metre
Render and set in gypsum plaster as described on concrete soffits		Per square metre
9.5 mm *Thistle* plaster board and fixing to soffit of joists with galvanised nails the joints filled with plaster and covered with scrim finished with a skim coat of *Thistle* board plaster not less than 5 mm thick. (Measured net and allow for all straight cutting)		Per square metre
9.5 mm ditto, ditto, but fixed to bearers to sloping soffit of staircase		Per square metre
Labour arris on skim coat		Per linear metre
152 mm x 152 mm standard white glazed wall tiling 6 mm thick as dado bedded and jointed in Portland cement and sand and pointed in Keene's or Parian cement, including all straight cutting		Per square metre
152 mm x 152 mm ditto, ditto, but in splash backs		Per square metre

Item	Rate	Unit
Extra for 152 mm x 152 mm rounded edge tile as capping		Per linear metre
229 mm x 152 mm fibrous plaster louvred ventilators and securing to plastered wall face with Plaster of Paris		Each
2.24 mm milled lead and all labour in covering to trays under cistern		Per square metre
1.8 mm milled lead and all labour in flashings		Per square metre
3 mm selected glazing quality clear sheet glass and glazing in metal in putty in panes exceeding 0.10 and not exceeding 0.50 square metres		Per square metre
3 mm ditto, ditto, in panes exceeding 0.50 and not exceeding 1.00 square metre		Per square metre
3 mm ditto, ditto, in panes exceeding 1.00 square metre		Per square metre
4 mm selected quality clear sheet glass and glazing in metal in putty in panes exceeding 1.00 square metre		Per square metre
6 mm S.G. quality clear float glass and glazing in beads and washleather seatings (both given separately) in wood in panes not exceeding 4.00 square metres		Per square metre
6 mm ditto, ditto, but glazing in wood in panes exceeding 4.00 and not exceeding 9.30 square metres		Per square metre
Allow to dry out thoroughly, brush down and twice distemper plastered walls		Per square metre
Ditto, ditto, plastered soffits		Per square metre
Allow to dry out thoroughly brush down and apply two coats of emulsion paint on plastered walls		Per square metre
Ditto, ditto, plastered soffits		Per square metre
Thoroughly scrape clean, prepare and paint metal windows one coat of primer, two undercoats and one coat of enamel in large panes. (Externally)		Per square metre

Item	Rate	Unit
Ditto, ditto. (Internally)		Per square metre
Knot, prime, stop, prepare and paint wood surfaces generally two undercoats and one coat of enamel. (Externally)		Per square metre
Ditto, ditto, to moulded fillets not exceeding 100 mm girth		Per linear metre
Ditto, ditto, to moulded fillets exceeding 100 mm and not exceeding 200 mm girth		Per linear metre
Knot, prime, stop, prepare and paint wood surfaces generally two undercoats and one coat of enamel. (Internally)		Per square metre
Ditto, ditto, to moulded fillets not exceeding 100 mm girth		Per linear metre
Ditto, ditto, but to moulded fillets exceeding 100 mm and not exceeding 200 mm girth		Per linear metre
Knot, prime, stop and paint one coat of oil colour on back of frame or lining		Per linear metre
Prepare, body in, stain and wax polish hardwood plain surfaces internally to Architect's approval		Per square metre
Ditto, ditto, moulded panelled doors		Per square metre
Prepare, body in, stain and wax polish hardwood square and turned balusters exceeding 100 mm not exceeding 200 mm girth		Per linear metre
Clean and apply one coat of clear varnish (external quality) on boarding		Per square metre
Prepare and apply two coats of 'Cuprinol' liquid preservative on softwood plates and bearers before fixing		Per square metre
Clean and twice oil oak sills or frames where exposed externally with linseed oil well rubbed in exceeding 100 mm and not exceeding 200 mm girth		Per square metre

SHORT FORM OF CONTRACT
Referred to in chapter XIII, page 103

Articles of Agreement made the *7th* day *June 1943* between *Robert Z Blank Esq*, of *The Red Cottage, Brighton* (hereinafter referred to as the Employer) of the one part and *Mr John Brown*, of *147 Blank Street, Brighton* (hereinafter referred to as the Contractor) of the other part.

WHEREAS the Employer is desirous of having a *bungalow erected* at *Johnsonville, Sussex,* all in accordance with the drawings numbered *1 and 2* inclusive and the specification marked 'A' prepared by *Mr John Taylor*, of *65 Newport Avenue, Westbay* (hereinafter referred to as the Architect),

NOW IT IS HEREBY AGREED BY THE EMPLOYER AND THE CONTRACTOR AS FOLLOWS:

Amount of Contract
1   The Contractor will execute and complete the works shown upon the drawings and described in the specification with materials and workmanship of the respective kinds described in the specification to the reasonable satisfaction of the Architect for the sum of *Nine hundred and fifty pounds (£950).*

Possession of site and completion
2   Possession of the site (or premises) will be given to the Contractor on or before the *10th* day of *June 1943*. He shall begin the works immediately after such possession and shall regularly proceed with them, and shall complete the same by the *10th* day of *December 1943,* subject nevertheless to the provisions for extension of time hereafter contained.

Damages for delay
3   If the Contractor shall fail or neglect to complete the works on or before the date stated in clause 2 hereof or by any extension of time given by the Architect, the Contractor hereby agrees to pay or allow to the Employer as and by way of liquidated damages and not by way of penalty the sum of *£5* for every week or part of a week during which the completion is delayed.

Extension of time
4   If in the opinion of the Architect the works be delayed through any cause not under the control of the Contractor, the Architect shall make a fair and reasonable extension of time for completion of the works.

Schedule of Rates

5   The Contractor shall forward to the Architect a Schedule of Rates upon which his estimate has been based and the Schedule shall remain with the Architect until the works are completed.

Notices and fees

6   The Contractor shall comply with all rules, regulations and by-laws of any Local Authority, Water or Lighting Companies and shall conform to the provisions of any Acts of Parliament relating to the works and he must give all notices required by the said Acts, rules, regulations and by-laws and pay all fees legally demandable.

Variations

7   The Employer and Contractor agree that no variation shall vitiate the contract but that all variations authorised by the Architect shall be measured and valued at the rates contained in the Contractor's Schedule of Rates or where the same may not apply at rates proportionate to the prices therein contained. The amount to be allowed on either side in respect of the variations so ascertained shall be added to or deducted from the contract sum as the case may be.

Injury to Persons and Property

8   (a) Injury to Persons. The Contractor shall be liable for and shall indemnify the Employer against all loss, claims or proceedings whatsoever whether arising in Common Law or under any Acts of Parliament in respect of personal injuries to persons whether in his employment or not arising out of or in the course of the execution of the contract and against all costs and charges incurred in relation to the investigation or settling of such claims.

(b) Injury to Property. The Contractor shall be liable for and shall indemnify the Employer in respect of any liability, loss, claim or proceedings and for any injury or damage whatsoever arising out of or in the course of the execution of the contract works to any property, real or personal, due to any negligence, or omission or default of himself, his agents or his servants or of any Sub-Contractor or to any circumstances within his control.

(c) The Contractor shall secure the due performance of these indemnities by forthwith entering into proper and sufficient policies of insurance.

Insurance against fire

9   The works from the commencement until they are taken possession of by the Employer shall stand at the risk and be in the sole charge of the Contractor who shall forthwith insure them and keep them insured until they are delivered up, against loss or damage by fire in the joint names of himself and the Employer, for the full value of the works executed.

Defects
10   The Contractor shall make good at his own expense any defects, shrinkages, and other faults which may appear within *six* months from the completion of the works arising in the opinion of the Architect from materials or workmanship not in accordance with the contract.

Provisional and prime cost sums
11   All provisional sums and prime cost prices mentioned in the specification for the execution of the works or for the supply of goods are strictly net and are intended to be available in full (with the exception only of any bona-fide discount which may be allowed for cash which shall not exceed 2½ per cent) for payment to the parties appointed by the Architect.

Payment
12   The Employer will pay to the Contractor the sum mentioned in clause 1 or such other sum as shall become payable from time to time by instalments when in the opinion of the Architect work to the value of £100 (or less at the reasonable discretion of the Architect) has been executed in accordance with the contract, at the rate of *90* per cent, the balance to be paid within *six* months after the works have been finally completed and all defects made good, whichever shall last happen.

Arbitration
13   The Employer and Contractor agree that should any dispute or difference arise between them touching any matter concerning the works then either party shall forthwith give to the other notice of such dispute or difference and the same shall be referred to the Architect whose award shall be final and binding on all parties concerned.

AS WITNESS our hands this *7th* day of *June 1943*.

Witness
    Frank Smith
    Secretary

Witness
    John Jones
    Clerk

Robert Z Blank
Employer

John Brown
Contractor

FORM OF PRIME COST CONTRACT

Referred to in chapter XIII, page 103

𝕬𝕲𝖗𝖊𝖊𝖒𝖊𝖓𝖙 made the *7th* day of *June 1952*, between *R. Z. Blank Esq*, of *The Red Cottage, Brighton* (hereinafter called the Empolyer) and *John Brown* and *Thomas White*, carrying on business as *Messrs J. Brown and Sons*, of *147 Blank Street, Brighton* (hereinafter called the Contractor), for the carrying out of various building works at *The Red Cottage, Brighton.*

1   The Contractor hereby undertakes to carry out any building works (hereinafter referred to as the work) as required to the order, instructions, and satisfaction of *Mr John Taylor*, the Architect appointed by the Employer (hereinafter called the Architect).

2   The Employer agrees to pay to the Contractor a sum equal to the prime cost of the work plus *twelve and a half* per cent, calculated on such prime cost for establishment charges and profit.

3   The words 'prime cost' shall mean and include the following:

(*a*) The actual amount of wages paid by the Contractor to the foreman, timekeeper, and workmen in respect of such time as they are employed upon the works excluding any wages paid and occasioned by correcting or amending defective work or materials.
(*b*) A correct percentage to cover the Insurance of the Contractor's liability as an Employer under any Statute or at Common Law, insurance against third party risks and Employers' contributions in respect of National Insurance, holiday stamps and the like.
(*c*) The actual amounts paid by the Contractor for materials specially purchased for the work after deducting all trade, cash, or other discounts. Any surplus materials or materials condemned by the Architect to be credited at the same rate as paid for.
(*d*) The current market price of all materials, if any, supplied direct from the Contractor's stock.
(*e*) The current market price or the actual amount paid for necessary cartage of materials, plant or rubbish, except (*a*) cartage included in the price of materials supplied and (*b*) cartage of surplus materials or materials condemned by the Architect.
(*f*) The current market price of all materials for use and waste in shoring, centering, planking and strutting, other than any item particularly mentioned in clause 4.
(*g*) The actual amounts paid by the Contractor for fares, country money and lodgings of clerks previously sanctioned by the Architect, supply of water, fire insurance, artificial lighting, electric or

other power at the site, and any fees, expenses or charges of District, County or Local Surveyors or others relating to the work.

(*h*) The actual amounts paid by the Contractor to Sub-contractors or Special Tradesmen engaged by the Architect for all work done by any of them, which amounts shall be absolutely net, and no cash discount shall be required by or accepted by the Contractor.

(*j*) A sum of *£45* for the use of all necessary machinery at the Contractor's premises and yards.

(*k*) The current rates for the hire of scaffolding and plant (if any) additional to that particularly mentioned in clause 4 ordered by the Architect for the use of Sub-contractors and Special Tradesmen, such rates in no case to exceed the actual value of the materials.

4   The words 'establishment charges' shall be deemed to cover any charge or expense incurred for or in respect of the services necessary for the execution of the work, and the provision and use of full and sufficient yard staff and accommodation, power, machinery, materials, conveniences, equipment, permanent and consumable tools of every description, and any matter or thing other than the items specified and defined as prime cost necessary or requisite to enable the work to be executed in an efficient, expeditious and economical manner and in particular, by way of illustration and not so as in any wise to limit or restrict the scope or extent of the general agreement herein contained, shall include the following items, that is to say:

Rent, rates and taxes, repairs, lighting, heating, water supply, furniture, safes and equipment of Contractor's offices, premises and yards.

Fire insurance of Contractor's premises, offices and yards, and works in process of manufacture therein.

Advertising and any legal fees.

Interest on capital and bank charges.

General management and supervision.

Salaries of Clerks, Surveyors, Managers, Buyers of materials and Yard Foreman.

Books, stationery, postage, telephone and telegraph charges.

Steam engines and boilers at works, including fuel, oil, and other necessary items.

Lost, damaged and waste materials.

Upkeep, maintenance and depreciation of plant and machinery.

Sharpening of tools.

Plant and tools as follows:

Anvil and tools	Buckets
Axes	Carts
Baskets	Cleaning cloths
Benches	Clerk of Works office
Blow-lamps	Cordage
Brick augers	Cramps
Brick cleaners	Cranes and hoisting tackle

Cross-cut saws
Crowbars
Diamonds
Drain rods and fittings
Dressers
Dumpy level, tripod and
  reading staff
Dusters
Dust sheets
Feather edges
Files
Fire devils
Floating rules
Foreman's office
Gas tongs
Gauge rods
Glue-pots
Granite axes
Granite picks
Grindstone
Grubbers
Hack-saw blades
Hammers
Hods
Hose pipe and fittings
Iron ladles
Joint rakers
Jumpers
Ladder cripples
Ladders
Larries
Leathers
Levels
Lewises
Lines
Mason's hammers
Mason's lines
Measuring-rods
Melting-stoves
Mess-rooms
Mortar boards
Mortar mill, engine, etc,
  including fuel, oil, etc
Moulds
Nail-boxes
Paint-brushes of all kinds
Painter's cripples
Paint kettle

Paint pots
Pickaxes
Pins for opening ends of
  pipes
Pipe cutters
Pipe vice
Plumb bobs
Plumber's irons
Plumb rules
Portable forge
Pulleys and wheels, ropes
  and chains, etc
Pumps
Putlogs
Rammers
Rods
Sand screens
Sawing stools
Saw-sharpeners
Scaffold boards
Scaffold cords
Scaffold hammers
Scaffold poles
Scaffold ropes
Scaffold steel lashes and
  wires
Scaffold wedges
Screeds
Screens
Screw-jacks
Scrubbing-brushes
Sheds for storing materials
Shovels
Sieves
Sighting-rods
Sight rails
Slater's axes
Slater's block
Slater's hammers
Slater's punches
Slater's rips
Sledges
Sleepers
Small spades
Smoke test machines
Sponges
Staging
Steps

Stone-breaker	Tubs for mixing lime
Stirring-sticks	Tubs for scaffold poles
Straight-edges	Water-cans with roses
Strutting boards	Water cistern
Sweeping brushes	Wedges
Tarpaulins	Wheelbarrows
Templates	Wheeling planks
Travelling cradles and gear	Windlasses
Trestles and planks	Yokes and chains

5   The Contractor shall so far as necessary conform to the provisions of every Act of Parliament relating to the work, and to the regulations and by-laws of any Local Authority, and of any Water and Lighting Companies with whose systems any part of the work is proposed to be connected, and shall before making any variation from the drawings and specification that may be necessitated by so conforming, give to the Architect written notice, specifying the variation proposed to be made, and the reason for making it, and applying for instructions thereon. In case the Contractor shall not in due course receive such instructions he shall proceed with the work, conforming to the provision, regulation or by-law in question.

6   From the commencement until the delivering up of the work the care of the same shall rest entirely with the Contractor, and he shall be responsible for anything that may be lost, stolen or damaged by fire, or other accident or in any other way, and he shall insure the same against fire to the full value thereof in the joint names of the Employer and the Contractor in a Fire Insurance Office to be approved by the Architect and shall deposit with the Architect the policies and receipts for the premium paid for such insurance.

7   The wages paid by the Contractor shall be in accordance with the rules or decisions of the National Joint Council for the Building Industry and the wages of the Foreman shall be agreed by the Architect before he is engaged and shall not be varied except by the written authority of the Architect.

8   No overtime shall be worked without the previous sanction in writing of the Architect.

9   No Sub-contractor shall be employed to whom the Architect or the Contractor takes reasonable exception, and no sub-contract shall be entered into without the previous written consent of the Architect.

10   The Contractor shall allow the use of all ordinary scaffolding and plant as may be directed by the Architect to the Sub-contractors and Special Tradesmen.

11   The Contractor shall place at the disposal of the Employer and the Architect the services and the advice of himself and his firm, and of any of his or their staff of Surveyors, Managers, Buyers of materials, Foremen of trades, or other skilled person employed by him or them upon the conduct of the work and for the selection and buying of materials and arrangements for the delivery of the same at the site and otherwise as may be necessary, and shall use every endeavour to obtain materials in the cheapest market and to carry out the work with as much economy and dispatch as would be the case in a lump sum contract.

12   The Architect shall have power to order the execution of the work in any manner or place he may choose, and he may also select the source of supply of any materials and the manner of purchasing them. He shall also have power by notice in writing on behalf of the Employer to determine the Contract at any time, and any such determination shall not give rise to any claim by the Contractor except for the price of the work done at the date of the determination.

13   The Contractor shall permit the Architect or any person authorised by him to have access to the workshops of the Contractor or the places where any materials or item for use or incorporation in the work is being prepared. If any Clerk of Works is employed he shall act solely as Inspector under the Architect and the Contractor shall afford him every facility for examining the work and materials.

14   The Contractor shall keep or cause to be kept separate records, time sheets, cost books and other necessary books of account recording in detail:

(a) The actual hours worked by each man employed in the execution of the work, the rates and net amount of wages paid, together with the actual amounts disbursed on account of fares and lodgings.
(b) The prime cost of the work as defined in clause 3 hereof, including all purchases and payments made by him.
(c) All materials received on the site of the work and all material returned as surplus and all materials condemned by the Architect.
(d) Any other matter or thing requisite or necessary for the purpose of ascertaining the prime cost of the work as herein defined

and shall from time to time as and when requested so to do produce for the inspection of the Employer, the Architect and the Quantity Surveyor, *Mr John Williams*, or any person authorised by any of them all such records, time sheets, costs books or other books of account together with the original priced invoices and receipts for all materials purchased or supplied and all statements of account for the work of Sub-contractors and Special Tradesmen.

15   The Contractor shall deliver to the Architect not later than the Wednesday in each week a statement of account of the work done and payments made during the preceding week together with invoices for all materials purchased and/or supplied by the Contractor from stock referred to in the said statement of account, all of which weekly statements shall be submitted to and checked by the Quantity Surveyor, who shall report and deliver to the Architect a statement of account made up to the end of each calendar month.

16   Subject to the provisions of clause 18 the Architect shall upon receipt of the Quantity Surveyor's statement of account on or after the 15th day of each month issue his certificate of the amount due to the Contractor, which shall include as far as possible the value of all work executed up to the end of the preceding month and one half of the percentage on prime cost allowed for establishment charges and profit.

17   The Employer shall pay to the Contractor the amount included in each certificate of the Architect within *seven* days after the date of the said certificate.

18   Any invoices for materials supplied or any other charges, the amount of which is included in any certificate issued by the Architect, shall be discharged by the Contractor and the receipt thereof delivered to the Architect and no further certificate shall be issued or payment made until such receipts have been delivered.

19   Subject to the provisions of clause 21 the Contractor shall be entitled to payment of the remaining half of the percentage on prime cost mentioned in clause 2 hereof, *six* months after the date of the certificate of the Architect of the completion of the work. Provided always that if the contract is determined before the completion of the work under the provisions in clause 12 hereof the Contractor shall be entitled to payment of any balance of the price of the work done by him within *fourteen* days after the same has been ascertained and certified by the Architect.

20   The Contractor shall begin the work immediately possession of the site has been given him, and shall proceed regularly with the work and complete it by the *31st* day of *December 1952*. The work being intended for *the occupation of the Employer* and any delay in completion being a cause of loss to the Employer the Contractor hereby agrees that if the work is not completed by the date aforesaid he will pay to the Employer as and by way of liquidated damages the sum of *£20* for every week or part of a week during which the completion is delayed. Any sum payable under this clause shall be taken into account and set off against any money otherwise due to the Contractor so far as the same may extend and subject thereto shall be a debt recoverable by the Employer from the Contractor.

21   The Contractor shall make good at his own cost and expense any defects, shrinkage or other faults which may appear in the work within *six* months from the completion of the work owing to faults or defects in workmanship or materials the certificate of the Architect in regard to any such defects, shrinkage, or other faults and the cause thereof to be conclusive.

22   All materials delivered on the site will at once become the property of the Employer and no material so delivered and no old materials taken out of any existing building shall be removed without the written authority of the Architect.

23   The Contractor shall be responsible for all damage to property, and for injury to persons, animals or things caused by the work or workmen and shall indemnify the Employer against any claims or proceedings in respect thereof and shall secure the due performance of these indemnities by entering into proper and sufficient policies of insurance.

24   Any questions arising as to the admissibility or otherwise of any charges made by the Contractor under Clause 3 hereof shall be referred to the arbitration, pursuant to the Arbitration Act 1950, of a Surveyor to be agreed between the Employer and the Contractor or failing agreement to be nominated by the President of the Royal Institution of Chartered Surveyors whose decision shall be final and binding on the parties hereto.

AS WITNESS our hands this *7th* day of *June 1952.*

> *Witness*
>   *F Smith*
>   Secretary   *R Z Blank*
>   Employer
>
> Witness
>   *John Jones*
>   Clerk   *J Brown & Sons*
>   Contractors

FORM OF PARTY STRUCTURE AWARD

Referred to in chapter XXVI, page 194

> Award in the matter of the London Building Acts (Amendment) Act 1939, 2 and 3 Geo. 6, chapter XCVII, Part VI, and in the matter of a certain party structure separating the proposed new building on the site of 62 Blank Street, and premises adjoining thereto on the north side and being known as 61 Blank Street.

WHEREAS John Smith, the owner of the premises, 62 Blank Street (hereinafter called the Building Owner), did on the 14th day of June 1965, give notice in writing to William Jones, the owner of 61 Blank Street (hereinafter called the Adjoining Owner) of his intention to exercise the rights given to him by the said London Building Act to execute certain works in the erection of the said proposed new building and to do certain work to the said party wall or structure and perform any necessary works incident to the erection of a new external wall as generally mentioned in the said notice.

AND WHEREAS a difference having arisen between the Building Owner and the Adjoining Owner the Building Owner has appointed Hamilton H. Turner, of 19 Queen Anne's Gate, Westminster, SW1, Surveyor, and the Adjoining Owner has appointed William Robinson, of 364 Blank Street, New Blankton, Surveyor pursuant to and for all the purposes mentioned in Section 55 of the said London Building Act.

AND WHEREAS the said Hamilton H. Turner and William Robinson have in pursuance of the said Section 55 of the said Act selected John Brown, of 52 White Street, New Blankton, to act as Third Surveyor and in the event of the said John Brown being unable to act have agreed that, if they do not jointly decide upon a substitute, the Third Surveyor shall be appointed by the Superintending Architect of the Greater London Council.

Now we the said Hamilton H. Turner and William Robinson having surveyed the said premises do hereby award and determine as follows:

(a) The existing wall separating the proposed new premises from 61 Blank Street, between the points marked respectively A and B on the drawing attached hereto shall be treated as a party wall for the purpose of this Award and is in a substantial and sound condition and is sufficient for the purposes of the Building Owner and the Adjoining Owner.

(b) The Building Owner shall be at liberty at his own cost to raise upon, cut away, pull down, build into, strengthen, repair and underpin the party wall as shown on the drawing attached hereto and as may be necessary for the purpose of the proposed new building in good cement concrete with proper cement concrete foundations and footings of proper width projecting on either side of the wall with two layers of asphalt three-quarters of an inch thick as horizontal and vertical damp courses on the new work.

(c) During the progress of the works mentioned in clause (b) the Building Owner shall adequately shore, uphold, maintain and protect the Adjoining Owner's premises and shall erect, maintain and shift as may be required weatherproof and dust sheets for the protection and security of the Adjoining Owner's premises.

(d) The Building Owner shall raise the existing chimneys of 61 Blank Street, to the height shown upon the drawing and to the reasonable satisfaction of the Surveyor to the Adjoining Owner.

(e) The Building Owner shall construct the recess in the proposed new building opposite the recess in the existing building of 61 Blank Street, as shown in the drawing attached hereto and shall face the new recess with white glazed bricks and shall keep the glazed facings clean.

(f) The Building Owner shall take down, alter as necessary and refix the existing fire escape staircase in the new position shown on the drawing attached hereto.

(g) The Building Owner shall at his own cost on completion clear away all shoring and enclosures, together with all rubbish and materials, and shall plaster any walls and ceilings of 61 Blank Street, and make good all work disturbed, and redecorate the new and adjacent work in the same style as at present in all rooms in any way affected by the works, so that nothing disturbed may be in worse condition than it is now.

(h) The whole of the works shall be carried out by the Building Owner at his own cost and risk and he shall pay the costs of the District Surveyor and the Greater London Council in connection therewith.

(j) The Building Owner shall be responsible for any injury to persons or property which may be occasioned by or in consequence of the works and shall indemnify the Adjoining Owner in respect of any claims which may be made against him in regard to such injury.

(k) The Adjoining Owner's Surveyor or his representative shall be allowed access to the premises of the Building Owner during the progress of, and to inspect, the said works.

(l) The Building Owner shall commence the work immediately after this Award has been signed, and the works, so far as they affect the Adjoining Owner, shall be proceeded with continuously and shall be carried out with as little inconvenience to the Adjoining Owner as may be possible.

(m) The Building Owner shall forthwith pay to the Surveyor appointed by the Adjoining Owner a fee of Fifteen guineas for his costs in this matter up to the signing of this Award and for his inspection of the work herein detailed to be executed and shall also pay to the said Surveyor a further reasonable fee in connection with any damage caused to the Adjoining Owner's premises in consequence of the carrying out of the work herein mentioned and in connection with any other matter arising out of this Award and the said party wall notice.

(n) Power is reserved by the respective Surveyors to make any additional Award or Awards in the event of any different or additional work within or occasioned by the said party wall notice being found necessary or desirable before completion of the work herein mentioned.

(o) The whole of the works shall be carried out to the reasonable satisfaction of the Adjoining Owner's Surveyor and shall be completed before the expiration of six months from the date of the party wall notice.

Dated this 9th day of August 1965.

Witness to the Signature
   of Hamilton H Turner   Hamilton H Turner

      J Smith
      Clerk

Witness to the Signature
   of William Robinson   William Robinson

      T Brown
      Secretary

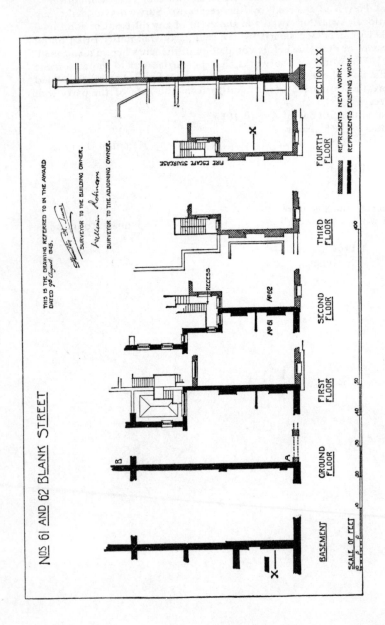

FORM OF SCHEDULE OF DILAPIDATIONS

(Referred to in chapter XXVIII, page 213)

SCHEDULE OF DILAPIDATIONS AND WANTS OF REPAIR SUFFERED TO ACCRUE IN AND UPON THE PREMISES KNOWN AS BLANK HOUSE, TAKEN IN ACCORDANCE WITH THE COVENANTS CONTAINED IN THE LEASE DATED 25 AUGUST 1899.

Thomas V. Taylor
Chartered Surveyor
Westminster, SW1

April 1920

Internally

First Floor
North-East Bedroom (over Dining-room)
Clean off small pieces of linoleum and paste from floor.
Clean, stain and varnish margin of floor.
Strip, stop, prepare and hang walls with paper of similar quality to that now hung.
Cut out cracks in ceiling, repair, wash, stop and twice whiten.
Wash, stop, prepare and paint two coats all woodwork now painted.
Reinstate missing key to lock of room door.
Renew broken pin to casement stay.
Renew cracked and broken tiles in hearth.
Repair broken back to grate.
Reinstate broken pane of glass.

North-West Bedroom (over Kitchen)
Repair defective flooring.
Clean, stain and varnish margin of floor.
Strip, stop, prepare and hang walls with paper of similar quality to that now hung.
Cut out cracks in ceiling, repair, wash, stop and twice whiten.
Wash, stop, prepare and paint two coats all woodwork now painted.
Reinstate missing key to cupboard lock.
Refix loose bolts to door to balcony.
Reinstate broken iron fanlight stay.
Reinstate missing brass cover to escutcheon on room door.
Refix loose hearth tiles.

South Bedroom (over Morning-room)

Clean, stain and varnish margin of floor.
Strip, stop, prepare and hang walls with paper of similar quality to that now hung.
Cut out cracks in ceiling, repair, wash, stop and twice whiten.
Wash, stop, prepare and paint two coats all woodwork now painted.
Renew broken panel to room door.
Renew broken sash-lines to window.
Reinstate missing brass sash lift.
Refix loose plinth to jamb of mantelpiece.

Guests' Bedroom (over Drawing-room)

Repair defective flooring.
Clean, stain and varnish margin of floor.
Strip, stop, prepare and hang walls with paper of similar quality to that now hung.
Cut out cracks in ceiling, repair, wash, stop and twice whiten.
Wash, stop and twice whiten cornice and frieze.
Wash, stop, prepare and paint two coats all woodwork now painted.
Renew broken finger-plate to door.
Reinstate missing pull-down hook to window.
Renew broken sash-fastener.
Renew cracked and broken tiles in hearth.
Reinstate broken panes of glass.
Refix coat-hooks in cupboard.

South-East Bedroom (over office)

Clean, stain and varnish margin of floor.
Strip, stop, prepare and hang walls with paper of similar quality to that now hung.
Cut out cracks in ceiling, repair, wash, stop and twice whiten.
Wash, stop and twice whiten cornice and frieze.
Wash, stop, prepare and paint two coats all woodwork now painted.
Reinstate missing knob to cupboard door.
Renew missing casement stay.
Renew tiles in hearth and surround to grate.
Reinstate cracked pane of glass.

Bathroom (over Kitchen)

Clean and wax-polish oak floor.
Remove nails and plugs from walls and make good.
Wash, stop, prepare and paint two coats all plaster-work now painted.
Cut out cracks in ceiling, repair, wash, stop and twice whiten.
Wash, stop and twice whiten cornice and frieze.
Wash, stop, prepare and paint two coats all woodwork now painted.
Renew broken coat-hook on room door.
Reinstate missing key to lock of room door.

Reinstate cracked lavatory basin and make proper connections to all pipes.

Thoroughly clean stains from inside of bath.

Clean and paint outside of bath two coats.

Reinstate glass shelf and brackets over lavatory basin.

Rewasher hot-water tap of bath.

Reinstate white glazed tiles where perforated and cracked.

Repair defective joint to towel airer.

Ground Floor

Drawing-room

Clean and wax-polish oak parquet floor.

Strip, stop, prepare and hang walls with paper of similar quality to that now hung.

Cut out cracks in ceiling, repair, wash, stop and twice whiten.

Wash, stop and twice whiten cornice and frieze.

Wash, stop, prepare and paint two coats all woodwork now painted.

Reinstate missing finger-plate to door.

Renew broken casement fastener.

Renew cracked portion of marble surround to fireplace opening.

Reinstate broken parts of register grate.

Repair defective cement hearth.

Dining-room

Clean and wax-polish oak parquet floor.

Strip, stop, prepare and hang walls with paper of similar quality to that now hung.

Cut out cracks in ceiling, repair, wash, stop and twice whiten.

Wash, stop and twice whiten cornice and frieze.

Regrain and varnish woodwork at present grained.

Ease door to verandah.

Renew missing cover-plate to lock of room door.

Reinstate broken casement stay pin.

Refix two loose casement fasteners.

Morning-room (South)

Clean and wax-polish oak parquet floor.

Strip, stop, prepare and hang walls with paper of similar quality to that now hung.

Cut out cracks in ceiling, repair, wash, stop and twice whiten.

Wash, stop and twice whiten cornice and frieze.

Wash, stop, prepare and paint two coats all woodwork now painted.

Rehang room door with new brass hinges.

Ease casements of windows.

Reinstate defective casement fasteners.

Reinstate cracked marble hearth.

Reinstate missing glass smoke-screen to fireplace.

Repair cast-iron leg to dog grate.

Reinstate cracked panes of glass in leaded lights.

Office
Repair defective flooring.
Clean, stain and varnish margin of floor.
Strip, stop, prepare and hang walls with paper of similar quality to that now hung.
Cut out cracks in ceiling, repair, wash, stop and twice whiten.
Wash, stop, and twice whiten cornice and frieze.
Wash, stop, prepare and paint two coats all woodwork now painted.
Repair bottom of room door.
Renew broken sash-lines.
Reinstate cracked fire back to grate.
Renew pointing to mantelpiece.

Hall, Staircase and Landing
Repair defective flooring.
Strip, stop, prepare and hang walls with paper of similar quality to that now hung.
Cut out cracks in ceiling and soffits, repair, wash, stop and twice whiten.
Wash, stop and twice whiten cornice and frieze.
Wash, stop, prepare and paint two coats all woodwork now painted.
Clean and polish handrail and newels.
Ease lock of door to drawing-room.
Renew five missing balusters.
Renew three defective treads.
Ease casements in staircase window.
Reinstate broken panes of glass in lead lights.

Kitchen
Clean off small pieces of linoleum and paste from floor.
Strip, stop, prepare and hang walls with paper of similar quality to that now hung.
Cut out cracks in ceiling, repair, wash, stop and twice whiten.
Wash, stop, prepare and paint two coats all woodwork now painted.
Reinstate cracked finger-plates.
Reinstate broken sash-fastener.
Reinstate cracked and broken tiles to surround of range.
Overhaul working parts of range.
Renew missing iron shelf in oven of range.
Renew fire-brick sides of range.
Reinstate missing fittings of range.
Black range and polish bright parts.
Reinstate missing knob to dresser drawer.

Scullery
Repair cement floor.
Wash, stop and twice distemper walls.
Cut out cracks in ceiling, repair, wash, stop and twice whiten.

Wash, stop, prepare and paint two coats all woodwork now painted.
Reinstate cracked earthenware sink and make proper connections to all pipes.
Reinstate decayed draining board.
Reinstate cracked white glazed tiles at back of sink.
Renew broken shelf and bearers under draining board.
Reinstate one broken pane of glass.
Repair cement rendering to top of washing copper setting.
Renew missing towel roller.

WC

Repair cracked tiles in floor.
Strip, stop, prepare and hang walls with paper of similar quality to that now hung.
Cut out cracks in ceiling, repair, wash, stop and twice whiten.
Wash, stop, prepare and paint two coats all woodwork now painted.
Reinstate missing bolt to door.
Renew defective sash-fastener.
Renew defective wc pan and make proper connection to all pipes.
Reinstate rubber buffers to wc seat.
Clean and repolish wc seat.
Clean and paint flushing cistern and pipe, two coats.
Repair damaged skirting.

Externally

Wash, stop, prepare and paint two coats all wood and ironwork now painted.
Renew cement pointing to roof over entrance porch.
Reinstate defective iron air-bricks.
Take down wood lining to porch where affected by dry-rot and reinstate with new and paint four coats.
Reinstate broken stone to coal plate.
Reinstate two stone treads to steps to scullery door.
Repair woodwork of garden door.
Repair defective stucco near window of bathroom.
Repair, cement and tile course at bottom of stucco near window of guests' bedroom.
Repoint top of kitchen stack.
Renew defective chimney-pot to flue from drawing-room.
Reset loose chimney-pots and make good flaunching.
Reinstate cracked, broken or missing tiles.
Clean out secret gutters to valleys.
Clean out all cast-iron eaves gutters.
Reinstate defective wire balloons to rain-water pipes.
Repoint door and window frames in cement.
Hack out and reinstate loose putties to windows.
Refix loose tiles in porch.
Brush down and lime-white walls where now so treated.
Reset loose stone coping.

Fences and Garden

Entrance Gate, etc

Renew oak post and fastenings to keep gate open.
Reinstate defective oak pales in fence.
Repair and straighten wire fence near gate.
Repair defective hanging stile to gate.

East and West Fences

Put oak spurs to all loose posts.
Renew length of fence near small wicket-gate.
Repair and rehang small gate.
Take out portions of fences repaired with deal boards and renew
with oak pales.
Renew oak capping where missing.
Renew defective deal gate-post with oak.
Renew all defective iron uprights.

Paths, etc

Remove weeds and top and gravel all paths and carriage-drive.

Garden

Remove concrete lily pond and reinstate ground to original con-
dition.
Repair defective wood slats of seat.
Repair defective cold frames and reputty glass.
Remove weeds and top and gravel all paths.
Clear away all weeds and suckers of trees; dig and manure the
garden: burn all rubbish and clear away débris.
Carefully prune all fruit-trees.

Generally

Reinstate all defective fastenings to doors and windows where not
previously mentioned, replacing any missing keys.
Relacquer all brass furniture, finger-plates, etc.
Sweep all flues and scrub all floors and stairs.
Black all grates and range.
Clean all windows.
Examine and leave in working order all bells, electric light and water
services, and clean out cisterns.
Clean out all gully traps and manholes, well flush all drains, and
leave sound and in good order.
Clear away all rubbish.
Paint two coats all wood and ironwork now painted, but not already
specified.
Where paintwork is bad owing to neglect bring forward with two
coats of paint in addition to that already specified.
Do all works incidental to and rendered necessary by compliance
with the covenants of the lease whether specially mentioned or not
in this Schedule of Dilapidations.

FORM OF REPORT ON PROPERTY TO BE PURCHASED
Referred to in chapter XXIX, page 222; plans of the house are given on page 356.

47 William Street
Blankton
5 June 1962

Dear Sir
re Westburton, Blankton

In accordance with your instructions I have made a careful survey of the above property in order to advise you as to its condition and value.

2   The house contains:

Ground Floor
Drawing-room
24 ft 3 in. x 12 ft 5 in. x 9 ft 0 in. high, with bay window, large recessed window having door leading out to a verandah, and large fireplace. The floor is of oak. The ceiling is very badly cracked. There is a large rain-water tank under the floor.
Lounge hall
24 ft 0 in. x 12 ft 0 in. x 9 ft 5 in. high, with very small bay window and entrance door.
Dining-room
15 ft 9 in. x 11 ft 8 in. x 9 ft 6 in. high, with large recessed window. The ceiling is badly cracked.
Pantry and store
9 ft 2 in. x 7 ft 0 in. x 9 ft 5 in. high. In this room there is a very good store fitting and shelves.
Kitchen
14 ft 0 in. x 12 ft 0 in. x 9 ft 0 in. high, with two good cupboards, a dresser, a range in good condition and rails for dish covers. The ceiling is badly cracked.
Scullery
14 ft 4 in. x 10 ft 9 in x 8 ft 6 in. high, with concrete floor, stone sink, plate rack, and washing copper.
Larder
7 ft 4 in. x 5 ft 5 in. with concrete floor, slate and wood shelves.
Servants' wc
5 ft 5 in. x 3 ft 0 in.
Workshop
31 ft 6 in. x 8 ft 0 in., with brick floor in bad condition, wood shelves and side entrance door.

First Floor

Bedroom 1 (over drawing-room)
19 ft 9 in. x 12 ft 3 in. x 9ft 0 in. high. The ceiling is badly cracked. This bedroom leads out of bedroom 2.

Bedroom 2 (over lounge hall)
21 ft 3 in. x 12 ft 3 in. x 9 ft 0 in. high, fitted with a good cupboard. The ceiling is very badly cracked.

Bedroom 3 (over dining-room)
16 ft 2 in. x 12 ft 0 in. x 8 ft 9 in. high. The ceiling is very badly cracked.

Bedroom 4 (over pantry and store)
9 ft 7 in. x 7 ft 0 in. x 8 ft 8 in. high, with trap-door to give access to underside of roof. This room is fitted with a large cupboard containing the hot-water tank.

Bedroom 5 (over kitchen)
14 ft 0 in. x 12 ft 0 in. x 8 ft 6 in. high, with two good cupboards. The ceiling is badly cracked.

Bedroom 6 (over scullery)
12 ft 0 in. x 11 ft 2 in. x 8 ft 0 in. high. The ceiling is cracked. There are five steps leading to bedroom 7.

Bedroom 7 (over workshop)
12 ft 3 in. x 7 ft 8 in. x 7 ft 4 in. high. The ceiling is very badly cracked and damp owing to faulty roof. This bedroom can only be reached through bedroom 6.

Bathroom
10 ft 0 in. x 6 ft 6 in. x 9 ft 0 in. high, fitted with enamelled iron bath and small angle lavatory basin. The ceiling is badly cracked.

WC
5 ft 0 in x 3 ft 0 in. x 7 ft 0 in. high, in a very undesirable position.

Corridor
3 ft 0 in. wide, 7 ft 10 in. high, leading to adjoining cottage.

Basement

Small billiard room (under dining room)
15 ft 8 in. x 12 ft 0 in. x 6 ft 10 in. high, with recess. The walls are plain brickwork whitened and the floor is of brick.

Coals (under lounge hall)
15 ft 6 in. x 12 ft 0 in. x 6 ft 3 in. high.

Wine cellar (under lounge hall)
12 ft 0 in. x 4 ft 0 in. x 6 ft 3 in. high, fitted with stone and wood shelves, which are in a dilapidated condition. The floor is of brick.

Cellar (under pantry)
9 ft 2 in. x 6 ft 0 in. x 5 ft 9 in. high, with access from scullery.

3   The house is built of brick, with a slate damp-proof course, and is about eighty years old. It is situated about a mile from the railway station and upon gravel soil. The property in the neighbourhood consists of small houses and artisans' dwellings. The roof to the portion

over bedroom 7 and verandah is slated and the remainder is tiled. With the exception of a damp ceiling, etc in bedroom 7, due no doubt to the bad condition of the slate roof, the house is dry. The roof, where I could inspect it, is boarded upon rafters and is in a good condition.

4 The floors, except where otherwise stated in paragraph 2, are softwood boards upon wood joists, and with one slight exception, near the stairs down to the basement, are in good condition. The underside of the floors is well ventilated with air-bricks. The air-bricks, however, to the underside of the drawing-room floor are covered with soil which should be removed. No visual evidence of dry rot was found and the floor boards appeared sound when pierced with a pen knife, but as it has not been possible for me to make a detailed examination of floor joists, wall plates, underside of floor boards or of roofing timbers and other timbers in the premises, no guarantee or assurance can be given that any timbers are free from rot, woodworm or other infestation. Arrangements can be made for a detailed examination and report by specialists if required.

5 Venetian blinds are fitted to all windows, and there is an outside roller blind to the south-east window of the drawing-room. The tenant's fixtures, which it is stated are to be taken at a valuation, consist of Venetian blinds, one outside roller blind, gas-brackets, a plate rack, and possibly the cupboard in bedroom 2. If an offer for the house is made it should be subject to an agreed valuation of the tenant's fixtures.

6 The fences to the property consist of a brick wall on the north and part of the east side, oak pale fence to Charles Street, and softwood close-boarded fences elsewhere. All these fences appear to go with the property. The softwood fences and gate require repair.

7 The garden contains a conservatory 12 ft 0 in. x 8 ft 0 in. in a dilapidated condition and a garden house 14 ft 0 in. x 10 ft 0 in. in good condition. There is also a small summer-house in a bad state of repair. The kitchen garden has been much neglected, and this also applies to the asphalt tennis court 90 ft 0 in. x 36 ft 0 in., which requires to be relaid.

8 The property has frontages to Charles Street of 225 ft 0 in., and to North Road of 100 ft 0 in., with an area of a little over half an acre.

9 **Sanitary Report**
Drainage I was only able to make a superficial examination of the drains. They are practically all outside the house, and approximately in the position shown on the plan attached to this report. There are three manholes, and from the appearance of the drains I feel sure that a satisfactory system has been provided and that no work other than thoroughly cleaning out will be required. Nevertheless, in the event of

your purchasing the property, I advise that the drainage system be tested. The manhole nearest the sewer is provided with a disconnecting trap and fresh-air inlet. The head of the system on the garden side of the house is properly ventilated, but apparently there is no ventilation on the North Road side. This would have to be provided.

Sanitary Fittings   The sanitary fittings are as follows:
On the first floor an obsolete wash-out closet in an apartment not directly connected with the external air, but having a window looking into a long corridor. I consider that the position of the wc apartment should be changed (see paragraph 15) and a new up-to-date pedestal closet and flushing cistern provided.

On the ground floor a wash-down pedestal closet and flushing cistern which are satisfactory, but the pan requires thorough cleansing with spirits of salts.

In the bathroom on first floor an enamelled iron bath, which is in a bad state of repair. This should be taken out and a new bath fixed. An angle lavatory basin which is too small, and should be taken out and replaced with a larger and more up-to-date fitting.

In the scullery on ground floor a stone sink, which is saturated with grease and should be taken out and an up-to-date stoneware sink and draining board provided. There is no trap to the waste pipe.

10   Water Supply

Water is laid on to the house from the main in North Road, and is taken to the roof, where there are two cisterns, each of about 175 gallons capacity, with wood covers and casing packed with sawdust. It is necessary that these cisterns should be thoroughly cleaned out. From these ‘cisterns water is laid on to the various points in the house, including the hot-water tank in bedroom 4.

Hot water to the bath and sink is provided in the usual manner by means of a boiler at back of the kitchen range with a 40-gallon hot-water tank in cupboard in bedroom 4. There is a safety valve on the flow pipe in the kitchen. I understand from the caretaker that a fairly good supply of hot water can be obtained when the range is understood and well·stoked. There was a very good supply when I inspected the house. If, however, a second bath is installed it will be advisable to have an independent boiler of the 'Ideal' type and a complete new system of hot-water pipes.

There are two rain-water cisterns in the following positions:

(a) Under the drawing-room floor a cistern of about 500 gallons capacity, enclosed in brick with a wood cover. Water is obtained from this cistern by means of a pump near the verandah outside the drawing-room. I recommend that this cistern should be taken out all pipes removed. There is an overflow pipe which appears to discharge into the drains, but I could not trace its direction.

(b) In the yard outside the kitchen a cistern of 360 gallons capacity with a dilapidated wood cover, which must be repaired.

11   Lighting

The house is wired for electric light, and there are a number of plug points in the principal rooms. Gas is also laid on in many places from a 22-light meter fixed in the small billiard-room. The electric wiring will have to be overhauled and many new points provided.

12   Bells

There is a system of mechanical bells, which is not efficient. I recommend that a new system of electric bells be installed.

13   Speaking Tubes

There is a speaking tube on the landing of first floor to the kitchen and also in the bedroom over drawing-room to dining-room.

14   There is a lightning conductor outside the building near the bay window of drawing-room.

15   The doorways leading from kitchen yard on ground floor and from the corridor on first floor to the adjoining property will require to be bricked up. When this is done the corridor will be free and will permit of a wc being formed at the end with access to the open air.

16   It is necessary to carry out external painting, and some repairs will be required to the rain-water pipes outside the house, part of which are in iron and part in zinc.

17   The property has been neglected in past years and will require the expenditure of something like £1500 to put it in a sanitary condition, to provide proper and efficient hot-water supply, new sink, bath, new wc, lavatory basin, and to put it in good general and decorative repair.

18   I understand that the property is freehold and that the price asked is £8000. I consider that, after an expenditure of £1500, as suggested in the last paragraph, the property would be a desirable investment and well worth £8500. I, therefore, recommend you to make an offer of £7000 for the property as it stands.

19   I attach sketch plans of the property, which show the position of the rooms, etc, and also a small site-plan showing the garden, etc, and shall be pleased to give you any further information you may require.

F. W. Jones Esq   Yours truly
The Drive   William Smith
London

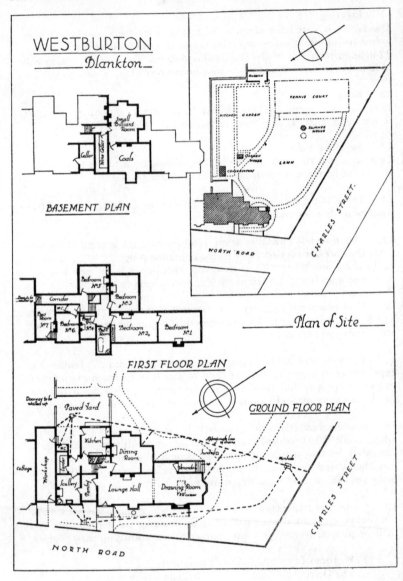

WESTBURTON
Blankton

BASEMENT PLAN

FIRST FLOOR PLAN

Plan of Site

GROUND FLOOR PLAN

FORM OF REPORT UPON THE CONDITION OF PROPERTY
Referred to in chapter XXVIII, page 357, plans of the house are given on page 369.

Report upon the condition of the House and Property known as Westlodge, Blankton, Kent, prepared by William Smith and Son, Chartered Surveyors, 342 Livingstone Street, Blankton, after an inspection made on 9 November 1943.

INTERNALLY
Ground Floor
Hall, Staircase and Landing

Floors   Deal boarded and, with the exception of some loose boards, in good condition.

Walls   Plastered and papered, the paper badly marked at foot of stairs and at dado height.

Ceilings   Plastered, lined and distempered, in good condition.

Stairs   Softwood with softwood newels, balusters and mahogany handrail. One baluster is missing and two broken. French polish in bad condition.

Door   Framed and braced oak, having small panels at back and moulded casing outside studded with iron nails, four of which are missing. Door fitted with night latch, bronze knobs and two keys, large centre bronze knob and bronze lion knocker, two brass bolts and brass chain, brass letter plate but no internal letter box. Woodwork requires re-polishing.

Windows   Single-light metal casement to Hall in good order, but the iron stay is broken. Metal casement and frame to Staircase in good condition.

Lighting   Wired for centre pendant to Hall and Landing, but no fittings. Two-way switches.

Pipe casing   Softwood painted in one angle in good condition.

Paintwork   Poor.

Sitting-room (South-west Room)

Floor   Boarded and covered with oak parquet in good condition, except where stained by ink near window, but requires cleaning and repolishing.

Walls   Plastered and papered, discoloured on west wall.

Skirting   Oak, in good condition.

Picture rail   Softwood, moulded in good condition.

Ceiling   Plastered, lined and distempered. One bad crack across centre.

Cornice   Two bad cracks and one small piece broken away.

Door   Four panelled oak, moulded both sides, fitted with mortice lock, oval brass knobs and two plain brass finger plates, all in good order. No key, and one escutcheon cover missing.

Windows   Ordinary softwood cased frames and sashes in good condition. One sash fastener broken. Two panes of ordinary clear glass cracked and two sash cords broken.

Lighting   Wired for centre pendant and two brackets over fireplace but no fittings, one switch at side of each door, on plain brass plates. Three plugs, one having socket missing.

Bells   Bell press on each side of fireplace in good order.

Heating   Three four section radiators in good order. One electric power socket.

Fireplace   Painted wood mantel with bright steel interior and tiled hearth. Interior requires re-polishing, six tiles are broken. Loose iron bottom to grate is cracked. Loose bright steel ash front in order. Plate glass blower in steel frame in good condition.

Paintwork   Good, but oakwork requires repolishing.

Dining-room (south room)

Floor   Softwood boarded. Dry rot had appeared in south-west corner but woodwork has been repaired.

Walls   Plastered, lined and distempered in good condition.

Skirting   Softwood moulded in good condition.

Picture rail   Softwood moulded in good condition.

Ceiling   Plastered, lined and distempered, some cracks which require making good.

Cornice   Bad crack on west wall.

Doors   Four panelled oak, moulded both sides, fitted with mortice lock and key, oval brass knobs and two brass finger-plates to each door, all in good condition.

Window   Ordinary softwood cased frame and sashes, one sash has been repaired. One pull-down hook missing. Two sash cords broken.

Lighting   Wired for centre pendant with switch at side of door on plain brass plate, also two plugs. No fittings.

Bells   One bell press at side of doorway and another in floor under position of dining-table, all in order.

Heating   Two four-section radiators in good order. One electric power socket.

Paintwork   Poor.

Study (leading out of dining-room)

Floor   Softwood boarded and stained, stain much worn.

Walls   Plastered and papered, paper badly scratched.

Skirting   Softwood moulded in good condition.

Picture rail   Deal in good condition.

Ceiling   Plastered, lined and distempered in good condition.

Cornice   Small piece broken away at an external angle.

Doors   Four panelled oak, moulded both sides each fitted with mortice lock, oval brass knobs and two brass finger plates. Door to outside fitted with two brass barrel bolts in addition.

Windows   Ordinary softwood cased frames and sashes, one sash cord broken and two panes of glass cracked, otherwise in good condition. Folding softwood panelled internal shutters with fittings and locking bars all in order. Outside sun blind rods and fittings to two windows in order.

Lighting   Wired for centre pendant with switch at side of door and two plugs all in order. No fittings.

Bells   One bell press at side of fireplace, out of order.

Fireplace   Cast-iron mantel register with tile surround and hearth. Four tiles in hearth are broken and fire-brick back badly cracked.

Paintwork   Poor

Lavatory and WC

Floor   Softwood boarded and stained, in good condition.

Walls   Plastered and distempered, in good condition.

Skirting   Softwood moulded in good condition.

Ceiling   Plastered, lined and distempered, in good condition.

Doors   Four panelled oak, moulded both sides, fitted with mortice lock and key, oval brass knobs, and two brass finger plates to each door, all in good condition.

Windows   Metal casements and frames in good condition.

WC apparatus   Low-down suite, with mahogany seat and cover in good order.

Lavatory   Porcelain enamelled basin 24 in. x 16 in. with chromium plated taps, chain and plug, in good order.

Paintwork   Good.

Cloaks

Floor   Softwood boarded and stained, in good condition.

Walls and ceiling   Plastered and distempered in good condition.

Doors   Four panelled oak, moulded both sides and fitted with mortice lock and key, oval brass knobs, one brass finger plate, all in good condition.

Lighting   Wired for pendant with switch at door, but no fitting.

Paintwork   Poor.

Kitchen

Floor   Red quarry tiles, ten cracked and the floor spotted with grease.

Walls   Plastered and distempered. Several bad cracks, one specially large has been badly repaired.

Skirting   Red quarry tiles in good condition.

Ceiling   Plastered and distempered. Many bad cracks and loose portions.

Doors   Four panelled softwood, moulded one side, in good order, each door fitted with mortice locks and brass knobs, no keys and no finger plates.

Window   Ordinary softwood cased frame and sashes, in good order. One sash fastener broken. Two panes of clear glass broken.

Lighting   Wired for centre pendant. No fitting.
Bells   Indicating board in good order.
Dresser   Softwood with cupboards in lower part and three shelves above. Six cup hooks and two cupboard knobs missing. No keys to cupboard locks.
Sinks   Glazed stoneware 24 in. x 16 in., the glaze much chipped, draining boards badly worn, softwood plate rack, two rods of which are missing and no tray under.
Paintwork   Very much worn in places.

Store

Floor   Red quarry tiles in good condition.
Walls and ceiling   Plastered and distempered, the plaster cracked in several places.
Door   Four panelled softwood, moulded one side, fitted with Norfolk latch, all in good condition.
Window   Single light metal casement in good condition.
Lighting   Wired for pendant, but no fitting.
Shelves   Four softwood shelves, two metal brackets are broken, several cup hooks are missing.
Paintwork   Poor.

Larder

Floor   Cement in good condition.
Walls   Plastered and distempered. Two courses of white glazed tiles over lower shelf, three tiles cracked and two are missing.
Ceiling   Plastered and distempered, in good condition.
Door   Four panelled softwood square framed, fitted with rim lock and brass knobs. Key is missing.
Window   Metal casement and frame, the stay is broken. Fly screen outside window is very defective and requires renewal.
Shelves   One slate shelf and two softwood shelves in good condition.
Paintwork   Bad.

Maids Room (adjoining Dining-room)

Floor   Softwood boarded and stained, in good condition, but many nail marks.
Walls   Canvas lined and papered, the paper discoloured.
Skirting   Softwood in good condition.
Picture rail   Softwood in good condition.
Ceiling   Plastered, lined and distempered in good condition.
Door   Softwood four panelled moulded both sides, fitted with rim lock, brass knobs and key.
Window   Ordinary softwood cased frame and sashes. Two sash cords are broken and one pane of glass cracked.
Lighting   Wired for pendant with switch at door. No fitting.
Fireplace   Cast-iron grate and mantel with tile surround and stone

hearth which is cracked, two tiles are missing, but otherwise in good condition.
Paintwork   Poor.

Boiler Room
Floor   Cement badly cracked.
Walls   Plain brick, require whitewashing.
Ceiling   Plastered and dirty.
Door   Four panelled softwood square framed, with stock lock, brass knobs and key.
Window   Single-light metal casement, glazed with rough rolled glass, all in good condition.
Lighting   Wired for centre pendant with switch in passage outside. No fitting.
Boilers and cylinder   Two independent boilers, one 'Ideal' and the other of Sectional type are in order. The lagging of hot-water cylinder requires renewing. One thermometer is missing and two handles of the doors to boilers are damaged. The heating and hot-water installations have not been tested so that the condition of the pipe system cannot be stated.
Paintwork   Bad.

Back Entrance and Service WC
Floors   Red quarry tiles, badly damaged near entrance.
Walls   Plastered and distempered.
Skirting   Red tiled squares in good condition.
Ceilings   Plastered and distempered. Several small cracks.
Doors   Four panelled softwood square framed to wc with rim lock, brass knobs and small iron barrel bolt. No key to lock. Framed and braced softwood to back entrance with rim lock, brass knobs and key, and two iron barrel bolts.
Window   Single-light metal casement glazed with obsure glass, one pane cracked, otherwise in good condition.
Lighting   Wired for pendant in wc and in passage. A lamp holder and 10 in. opal shade to passage, but no fitting in wc.
WC apparatus   Stoneware pan with cast-iron flushing cistern and lead pipe. The pan is cracked, the handle missing to chain pull. The pan and softwood seat require cleaning.
Meter cupboard   Softwood panelled with lock and key in good condition.
Paintwork   Poor.

Coals
Floor   Cement badly damaged in places.
Walls   Plain brick, require cleaning, repointing and whitewashing.
Ceiling   Plastered and dirty.
Door   Four panelled softwood square framed, one panel cracked. Stock lock and key, brass knobs.

Coal boards   Softwood slide fillets in position but boards missing.
Paintwork   Bad.

Garage
Floor   Cement paving badly cracked.
Walls   No plaster but require distempering.
Ceiling   Covered with asbestos boards, two sheets are missing.
Door to house   Four panelled softwood, fitted with *Yale* pattern lock and two keys.
Doors (large)   Softwood framed and braced. No lock. Wrought iron locking bar and padlock. Two barrel bolts, one of which is missing.
Windows   Metal casements and frames in good condition.
Lighting   Wired for one pendant, no fitting, also wired for outside light but no fitting.
Heating   Two small radiators in order.
Paintwork   Bad.

First Floor
Own Bedroom (over Sitting-room)
Floor   Softwood boarded. Some loose boards and some damaged where feet of bedstead have been placed.
Walls   Plastered, lined and distempered. Several bad cracks and damp patches. One specially large crack has been badly repaired.
Skirting   Softwood moulded in good condition.
Picture rail   Softwood moulded in good condition.
Ceiling   Plastered, lined and distempered. Many bad cracks which require immediate attention. Lining paper in bad condition distemper discoloured.
Cornice   Three bad cracks.
Doors   Four panelled softwood, moulded both sides, fitted with mortice locks with brass knobs. Lock to cupboard door is defective and key and escutcheon cover are missing. Two plain finger plates to each door which require relacquering.
Window   Ordinary softwood cased frame and sashes in good order. Sash fastener is broken and one sash lift is missing.
Lighting   Wired for dressing table pendant with two lamps and lamp over lavatory basin with switches on plain brass plates near door. No fittings. Electric plug in skirting.
Bells   Brass bell press at door in order. Hanging bell rosette over bed, the cord and press are missing.
Heating   Two four-section radiators with stop-cocks, the shank of one of which is defective, otherwise in good order. One electric power socket on brass plate.
Fireplace   Painted wood mantel with cast-iron register grate, tiled surround, and tiled hearth. Six tiles in hearth cracked and wood mantel chipped in places.

Lavatory basin   Earthenware basin 24 in. x 16 in. on white enamelled iron brackets, hot and cold water, chromium plated taps and chain and plug, earthenware splash back, and 24 in. x 18 in. mirror in painted wood surround all in good order. Plated towel rail on door in good order.
Paintwork   Fair.

South Bedroom (over Dining-room)
Floor   Softwood boarded, badly worn where over pipes in floor, and several joints open.
Walls   Plastered and distempered, in good condition.
Skirting   Softwood moulded in good condition.
Ceiling   Plastered, lined and distempered, in good condition.
Cornice   Plastered, distempered, in good condition.
Door   Softwood four panelled moulded both sides, fitted with mortice lock and bronze knobs. No key. Two brass finger plates require relacquering.
Window   Ordinary softwood cased frame and sashes in good condition. One pane of ordinary sheet glass is broken.
Lighting   Wired for dressing table pendant with two lamps and lamp over lavatory basin with switches on plain brass plates near door. No fittings. Electric plug in skirting.
Bells   Brass bell press at door in order. Hanging bell rosette over bed, the cord and press are missing.
Heating   One three-section radiator in good order. Recess for gas stove but stove missing. One electric power plug.
Lavatory basin   Earthenware basin 24 in. x 16 in. on white enamelled iron brackets, hot and cold water chromium plated taps and chain and plug, the plug wedged in overflow, with earthenware splash back and 18 in. x 24 in. mirror in painted wood frame, all in order.
Paintwork   Good.

Bedroom over Garage
Floor   Softwood boarded, stained all over, the stain much worn.
Walls   Plastered and papered with a cheap paper.
Skirting   Softwood moulded in good condition.
Ceiling   Plastered, lined and whitened. Two small cracks.
Door   Softwood four panelled moulded both sides. Mortice lock, brass knobs and key. Two plain brass finger plates require relacquering.
Window   Ordinary softwood cased frame and sashes. One sash fastener is defective and one pane of clear glass is cracked.
Lighting   Wired for pendant over dressing table, with switch on plain plated plate near door, but no fitting. Wired for plug in skirting near door.
Bells   Brass bell push at side of door in order.
Heating   Two-column radiator in good order.

Fireplace   Painted iron mantel register with tiled surround, and cement hearth which is burnt and cracked, otherwise all in good condition.

Lavatory basin   Earthenware basin 20 in. x 12 in. on white enamelled iron brackets, hot and cold water chromium plated taps and chain and plug, plate glass splash back, one corner of which is cracked, otherwise all in good order.

Paintwork   Very good, has been painted recently.

Maids Bedroom (over Larder, etc)

Floors   Softwood boarded, slightly marked by Furniture but otherwise in good condition.

Walls   Plastered, lined and distempered. Two bad cracks.

Skirting   Softwood moulded in good condition.

Picture rail   Softwood moulded in good condition.

Ceiling   Plastered, lined and distempered. Some bad cracks which require attention.

Door   Four panelled softwood, moulded both sides, fitted with mortice lock, brass knobs but no key. Two plain brass finger plates.

Windows   Ordinary softwood cased sashes and frames. Three panes of glass are cracked.

Lighting   Wired for dressing table pendant and switch on plain brass plate near door, no fitting.

Heating   Small radiator in good order.

Paintwork   Very good, had been painted recently.

Maids Bedroom (South-east room)

Floor   Softwood boarded in good condition.

Walls   Plastered and papered with a cheap paper.

Skirting   Softwood in good condition.

Ceiling   Plastered and distempered. One bad crack.

Door   Four panelled softwood, moulded one side, fitted with rim lock with brass knobs but no key. Two plain brass finger plates.

Window   Ordinary softwood cased frame and sashes, the lower part of frame has been repaired and a new oak sill inserted.

Lighting   Wired for pendant in centre of room with lamp holder and a 10 in. opal shade.

Fireplace   Painted wood mantel, with cast-iron register grate, in good condition.

Paintwork   Poor.

Bathroom over Hall

Floor   Softwood boarded and covered with linoleum in good condition (flooring unexamined).

Walls   Plastered above a white-glazed tile dado. Six tiles (6 in. x 6 in.) are cracked and one is missing. Walls above dado have been painted but are in bad condition.

Ceiling   Plastered and has been painted.

Cornice   Painted. Several small cracks and one piece broken off at an external angle.

Door   Softwood four panelled moulded both sides, fitted with mortice lock, bronze knobs and two brass finger plates which require relacquering. No key to lock. Small brass barrel bolt.

Window   Ordinary softwood cased frame and sashes, the fastener broken, otherwise in good condition. One pane of obscure glass cracked.

Lighting   Wired for pendant with plain opal shade and holder with electric lamp.

Bath   6 ft 0 in. cast-iron enamelled, the enamel on inside much worn and the hot and cold taps require plating.

Lavatory basin   Porcelain enamelled basin 24 in. x 16 in., with white marble top. The basin is cracked and the hot and cold taps, chain and plug require re-plating.

Towel-airer   Chromium plated in good order.

Paintwork   Poor.

Bathroom over Kitchen

Floor   Softwood boarded, but damaged by removal of linoleum.

Walls   Plastered, have been painted.

Ceiling   Plastered, lined and painted.

Door   Softwood four panelled, moulded one side fitted with rim lock, brass knobs and small bolt. No key to lock.

Window   Ordinary softwood cased frame and sashes, the lower portion of frame has been repaired, all in good condition.

Lighting   Wired for pendant but no fitting.

Bath   5 ft 6 in. cast-iron enamelled, the enamel on inside much worn. Hot and cold taps require relacquering.

Lavatory basin   Earthenware basin 20 in. x 12 in. on cast-iron enamelled brackets and hot and cold taps and chain and plug, all in good condition.

Paintwork   Bad.

WC (opposite main bedroom)

Floor   Softwood boarded and stained in good condition.

Walls and ceiling   Plastered, lined and painted in good condition.

Door   Softwood four panelled moulded both sides, fitted with mortice lock, bronze knobs, two brass finger plates and a 6 in. brass barrel bolt all in good condition but no key to lock.

Window   Softwood cased frame and sashes in good condition.

WC apparatus   Low-down suite all in order, except that mahogany seat and cover are loose. Toilet roll holder is badly fixed.

Lighting   Wired for centre pendant, no fitting.

Paintwork   Poor.

WC (end of passage)

Floor   Softwood boarded in good condition.

Walls and ceiling   Plastered and distempered, in good condition.

Door   Softwood four panelled, square framed, fitted with rim lock, brass knobs, and small bolt. No key, all in good condition.

Windows   Softwood cased frame and sashes, the fastener missing and one pane of obscure glass broken.

Wc apparatus   Stoneware pan and softwood seat with cast-iron flushing cistern and pipe. The chain pull is missing and the seat cracked, otherwise in good order.

Lighting   Wired for pendant but no fitting.

Paintwork   Bad

Linen Room

Floor   Softwood boarded in good condition.

Walls and ceiling   Plastered and distempered in good condition.

Door   Oak four panelled, moulded one side, fitted with mortice lock, bronze knobs and two brass finger plates, all in good condition.

Lighting   Wired for pendant, no fitting.

Heating   Coil of iron pipes in good order.

Shelves   Four rows of slat shelves in good condition.

Paintwork   Fair.

Boxroom (over boiler-room)

Floor   Softwood boarded in good condition.

Walls   Plastered and distempered, much discoloured.

Skirting   Softwood moulded, damaged where boxes have been placed.

Ceiling   Plastered and distempered in good condition.

Door   Softwood four panelled, square both sides, two panels are split. Mortice lock, no key. One brass finger plate.

Window   Ordinary softwood cased frame and sashes. One pane of glass is cracked.

Lighting   Wired for centre pendant, no fitting.

Luggage rack   In good condition.

Paintwork   Very bad.

Roof Space

Flooring   Softwood 3ft 0 in. wide, from trap door to cisterns.

Cold-water cistern   Galvanised iron water storage cistern, 150 gallons with softwood casing and loose cover. The cistern requires cleaning.

EXTERNALLY

Walls   Brickwork of west elevation and chimney stacks requires re-pointing. Top of north-west chimney requires to be rebuilt. Two chimney pots are cracked and one metal cowl at top of pot has rusted away. Cement rendering to all elevations, except the west, is in bad condition with many cracks and bad patches.

Doorways   One stone step to back entrance doorway is cracked and the top step badly worn. All door frames require re-pointing. One bracket to canopy over front entrance doorway is loose.

Windows   Two stone sills are cracked, the remainder in good condition. Window frames require re-pointing. Putties to glass require renewing.

Paving   The yard is paved with concrete slabs, six slabs are cracked, and all joints require re-pointing.

Entrance gate   Ornamental cast-iron, the lock broken and no key.

Roof   Generally in good condition, but many hand-made tiles are cracked and where repairs have been carried out, machine-made tiles have been used. Leadwork to flat has several cracks which have been repaired but otherwise is sound, flashings require pointing. One length of cast-iron eaves gutter is cracked, and two lengths of rain-water pipe are broken. Wrought iron stays to ventilating pipe are loose and all stays are badly rusted. All balloon guards are missing. One length of stone coping is broken. Snow guard at eaves is rusted away.

Paintwork   All wood- and iron-work badly needs painting, some places in woodwork are quite bare.

Drains   The drainage system has not been tested, but appears to be in good order. The manholes are dirty and require immediate attention. Manhole cover in yard is cracked and must be repaired.

THE GARDEN

Fences   The brick wall (7 ft 0 in. high) on the south boundary is in good condition except that the brick coping is damaged in about ten places. The fences on the east and west sides of the property are ordinary oak park-pale (4 ft 0 in. high) with gravel boards and oak capping. A great number of pales and a quantity of gravel boards and capping are missing and generally the fences are in a bad condition. The front fence (2 ft 0 in. high) consists of plain iron standards and three iron rails upon a dwarf brick wall all in fair condition. One large and two small iron gates are sound but the locks to the small gates are broken and there are no keys. All ironwork requires painting.

Lawns   The lawns are poor and exhausted and full of plantains, dandelions, docks and moss.

Paths   Most of the gravel and all the softwood edging has disappeared. Some box edging remains but is in a bad condition owing to neglect.

Trees   All the fruit trees in the open ground (about 60) are very old and in a neglected state, canker and lichen are abundant. On the walls are three pear, two plum, one fig, four peach and two apricot trees. Much dead wood is apparent and suckers from all the trees have almost superseded the trees themselves. Old nets are hanging and rotting on the trees.

Garden house The garden house is constructed on a brick floor of wood posts and rafters with a thatched roof and one slatted seat. The thatch has almost disappeared and the woodwork is in a bad condition.

Tool shed The tool shed is constructed of wood posts covered on the outside with elm weather boarding and a tiled roof, a four panelled door with rim lock and key, a sliding sash window and a brick floor. Two shelves and a wood bench are inside, and all is in good condition.

The foregoing report upon the condition of the house and property known as Westlodge, Blankton, Kent, was compiled by us at the inspection made on 9 November 1943, and is hereby certified as accurate and correctly represents the state of the property as regards its condition of repair.

Signed for and on behalf
of the Lessor

William Smith and Son
Chartered Surveyors
342 Livingstone Street
Blankton, Kent

Signed for and on behalf
of the Lessee

Thomas Jones and Co
Chartered Surveyors
247 William Street
Newton

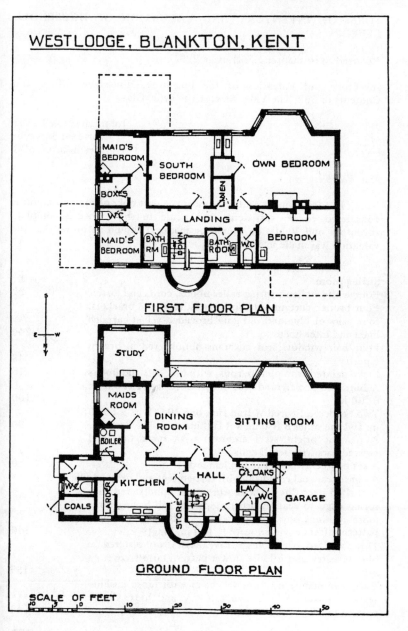

FORM OF INVENTORY AND VALUATION OF HOUSEHOLD EFFECTS

Referred to in chapter XXXI, page 229.

Inventory and Valuation of the Furniture, Household Effects and Contents of 362, The Vale, Newton-on-Tyne, Glos.

John Hamilton Turner
Chartered Surveyor
Westminster, SW1

March 1964

Note: The following inventory concerns a part only of the house, but is considered to be sufficient as a guide to show how a complete Inventory and Valuation should be made. It should be noted that the valuation was made in 1964.

	£
Sitting-room	
Four white holland spring roller blinds, cords and tassels	32
Four bronze curtain rods, spear ends, rings and brackets, four pairs of blue and old gold brocaded velvet curtains lined and inter-lined	240
Four hair window seat cushions upholstered in brown tapestry	48
Eight painted iron picture rods, with brackets and hooks	16
A bordered and figured Wilton corridor rug, 12 ft 0 in. x 6 ft 0 in.	100
Two bordered figured Wilton rugs one 10 ft 0 in. x 6 ft 0 in. and the other 8 ft 0 in. x 4 ft 0 in.	90
A pair of bright steel andirons with spear tops and twisted bars with scroll ends	20
A set of steel twisted fire implements	10
A light steel coal cauldron with shaped feet and drop handle	14
A stuffed over Chesterfield arm settee, upholstered with spring edge to seat in brown tapestry and having three loose cushions on the seat and back, also a loose flower pattern taffeta cover *en suite* (6 ft 0 in. long)	140
Three stuffed over lounge easy chairs, upholstered in blue tapestry and a loose flower pattern taffeta cover *en suite*	135
Two low mahogany fireside chairs with loose cushion seats upholstered in brown tapestry and loose flower pattern taffeta covers en suite	40

Continued £885

Continued £885

Two Hepplewhite style mahogany chairs, open railed backs, with carved decorations, seats upholstered in pig skin, finished with bronze headed nails	120
A lady's mahogany work table, lift-up top inlaid satinwood borders on square supports with stretchers	40
A light steel two-fold fire screen, 3 ft 6 in. high	14
A Queen Anne design mahogany circular two-flap table (4 ft 0 in. diameter) on claw and ball legs	40
Two mahogany wine tables, 20½ in. high, 12 in. top, each with carved pillar and shaped legs	30
A rosewood circular card table with revolving top and receptacle for packs of cards, etc, on carved pillar and shaped and carved legs	60
Two mahogany dwarf book cases, each 4 ft 0 in. long with three movable softwood shelves edged with mahogany	40
A nest of three mahogany tables, with moulded and carved legs largest size 17 in. x 13 in.	20
A low circular mahogany fireside table 2 ft 6 in. dia. with moulded legs and having loose baize covers	11
A brass water gilt French chandelier with chain, four candle holders, opaque candles, electric lamp and silk shades	150
A brass gilt picture lamp and fittings	16
Two mahogany turned and carved standard lamps each with candle holder and electric lamp, and old gold and blue brocaded velvet shade and with cord connection	80
A Bechstein Boudoir piano	300
A mahogany music stool 3 ft 0 in. long with loose hair cushion, upholstered in brown tapestry	10
A mahogany music cabinet on legs and having three drawers and a small cupboard	30
A Radiogram, 4-valve GEC set in mahogany case with six press buttons and connections	50
A Ferguson 14 in. television set with wood stand	200
A plain mahogany gramophone records cabinet with index, etc	20
Six down cushions covered with silk brocade	18
Four down cushions covered in yellow taffeta	12
Two sets of portiere curtains in blue and old gold brocade velvet and with bronze rods, brackets, etc.	80
A walnut carved and shaped wall mirror with eagle ornament at top, the mirror 22 in. wide and 3 ft 6 in. high	150

Continued £2376

Continued £2376

A Japanese four-fold screen, 5 ft 6 in. high front panels, with brocaded flowers on grey, set back panels landscape, etc	40
A painted wicker log basket, 23 in. x 17 in. x 15 in.	5
Two painted wicker waste paper baskets	3
A wrought-iron twisted shaped stand with large brass flower bowl	7
A carved ebony elephant with ivory tusks	10
Two majolica ware flower holders with figures and cupid	30
Two Oriental metal, two majolica and three glass ash trays	3
Two bright steel electric candle lamp holders and three sockets to each and rosette fronts with lamps	40
An old French gilt clock decorated in pink enamel	100
A walnut cocktail cabinet, 1 ft 6 in. wide, 15 in. deep and 3 ft 0 in. high, with cupboard, glasses, shaker, and two cut glass decanters	75

Pictures

A Landscape in gilt glazed frame with stream, cows and mountains by A. Hart 3 ft 0 in x 2 ft 0 in.	150
One water colour drawing in gilt glazed frame, of the Forum, Rome. Unknown artist	30
One water colour drawing in gilt glazed frame of the Matterhorn from Zermatt. Unknown artist	30
Two water colour drawings of mountains in Switzerland by unknown artists	40
Six small landscapes in colour Unknown artists	6

Books

Follow on with complete list of books, atlases, encyclopaedia, etc, say	250
Total for Sitting Room	£3,195

Main Bedroom	£
Four bronze casement rods with fittings, cords, etc, silk curtains and frilled top	20
Four blue union spring roller blinds, cords and acorn knobs	24
Four painted softwood valance boards on brackets, nylon runners, cords and pulleys, flowered pattern tapestry cretonne, lined and inter-lined curtains with fringed valances, *en suite*	120
Four hair window seat cushions, upholstered *en suite*	24
Four painted brass picture rods with brackets and hooks	10

Continued £198

Continued £198

A grey seamless pile carpet as laid with a thick brown felt under carpet

200

A pierced, bright steel fender with beaded edge

10

A set of bright steel fire implements, comprising poker, tongs, shovel and brush

8

A light steel coal cauldron with shaped feet and drop handle

12

A mahogany bedstead 4 ft 0 in. wide, fitted with side and end rails, box spring mattress in fancy striped tick linen valances, hair and wool mattress in white, a down bolster and four feather pillows

120

Four blankets and an eiderdown in pink and blue silk

30

A mahogany bedside pedestal cupboard with drawer

13

A mahogany kneehole dressing table on turned legs and having five drawers and mirror with bevelled edges

60

A mahogany hanging wardrobe with two doors and set of five drawers in centre and having long narrow mirrors with bevelled edges on inside

100

A mahogany cheval mirror 12 in. wide, 4 ft 0 in. high on carved legs

20

A stuffed easy chair upholstered in blue twill with a loose cretonne cover

20

Two Queen Anne reproduction chairs with walnut frames, open backs on cabriole supports, loose stuffed seats, upholstered in blue twill, and loose cretonne covers

50

A fancy wicker waste paper basket

2

Pair of heavy bronze candlesticks, 12 in. high

10

A cut glass water jug and tumbler

2

An oxidised electric table lamp and cord connection and with silk shade

6

An oxidised electric pendant with two arms, lamps and silk shades

24

A square gilt wicker linen basket

2

A mahogany chest, 3 ft 0 in. long 3 ft 9 in. high, with four long and two short drawers and secret compartment above the top drawers

60

A mahogany bow front writing table, 2 ft 3 in. wide on cabriole shaped legs and having two drawers, brass drop handles and escutcheons

60

An oil landscape decorative picture in a gilt frame over mantelpiece. Unknown artist. Size 3 ft 6 in. x 2 ft 6 in.

40

A mahogany top adjustable bed table on cast-iron frame, fitted with patent ledges, adjustable reading desk with

Continued £1047

Continued £1047

fittings and small mahogany side table	24
A mahogany bed tray with reading flap. Size 20 in. x 14 in.	6
A jewel safe (Chubbs)	72
An electro-plated biscuit box	4
A Pye 5-valve radio set and connections, with four press-button pre-set stations	40
A transistor portable radio set	15

Total for Main Bedroom £1,208

Bathroom £

A blue union spring roller blind, cords, acorn knobs	4
A painted softwood valance board on brackets, runners, cords and pulleys, flowered pattern tapestry cretonne, lined and inter-lined curtains, with a fringed valance *en suite*	30
Green linoleum as laid	12
Chromium plated electric light pendant, with lamp and silk shade	9
A painted softwood dressing mirror fitted to wall with two folding panel doors, silvered glass to back and two doors	60
A plate glass shelf on two chromium plated brackets	4
A large wall mirror in an enamelled wood frame	10
A chromium plated tooth brush holder, and tumbler, and two chromium plated hat and coat hooks	3
A painted mahogany chair to wc with wicker seat and back	25
Two painted deal small corner cupboards each with a triangular shelf	12
A cut glass water jug and tumbler	3
A chromium plated and teak bath tray for sponge and soap and chromium plated and teak bath seat	10
A cork bath mat with wood frame, 30 in. x 20 in.	3
A white enamelled bathroom chair with cork seat	3
A white enamelled bathroom table with plate glass top, drawer and undershelf	10
A chromium plated toilet roll paper holder	2
A painted wicker corner linen basket	4
A personal weighing machine, Japanned white with gold line and having boxwood height rod attached	25

Total for Bath Room £229

Kitchen

	£
Two white holland spring roller blinds, cords and acorns	6
Two casement curtains of printed linen with rods, hooks, etc	6
Brown linoleum as laid	30
An electric light pendant with two arms, lamps and opal shades	6
An electric hand lamp with cord and plug	4
A 5 ft 0 in. softwood kitchen table with drawer at each end	12
A 4 ft 0 in. softwood table with drawer at one end	9
A softwood pastry board 24 in. x 16 in., a towel roller with back board and brackets, a mahogany butler's tray and stand, a hardwood knife box in two divisions, and a plate cleaning board padded and covered with leather 22 in. x 14 in.	15
A painted white deal flour bin	4
A three-division plate basket	3
A hardwood tray rack 2 ft 0 in. long on chromium plated brackets	4
A set of scales with metal dish and weights	6
A 4 ft 0 in. dwarf painted cupboard with shelves and with shaped top and glass doors	15
Two Windsor chairs	6
A softwood painted chest of drawers 2 ft 6 in. wide, 4 ft 0 in. high	14
A coffee grinding mill for fixing to table	3
A japanned anthracite coal hod	
A kitchen coal scuttle with hand scoop	3
A canister rack with twelve gilt lettered canisters	4
A radiogram set	15
Four Britannia metal dish covers on rail	20
A Minton black key on gold band and gold line earthenware dinner service comprising 64 pieces	35
A Minton white china tea service comprising 40 pieces	20
A Doulton dark blue design with gilt edge china breakfast set comprising 29 pieces	18
Two white stoneware hot-water jugs with metal covers	4
A kitchen tea, breakfast and dinner service, comprising 76 pieces	18
Sundry articles as pudding basins, jugs, moulds, pots, pie dishes, etc.	15
Six hardwood tea trays with chromium plated handles	16
Three light oak trays	3
Three oblong handled mahogany trays	8
Sundry cooking utensils	15

Continued £337

Continued £337

A 10in. dial kitchen clock in mahogany case   12

A ceiling clothes airer 16 in. wide with four wood laths,
pulleys, iron brackets and cords complete   4

Total for Kitchen £353

Linen   £

6 Pairs of linen sheets for single beds   48

3 Pairs of linen sheets for double beds   42

12 Pillow slips   8

6 Linen bed-spreads   18

6 Toilet covers and mats   10

36 Face towels   16

36 Bath towels, various sizes   30

etc, etc   —

Total for Linen £172

Silver

SILVER PLATE ELECTRO-PLATE Complete list and valuation
followed by all personal effects and wearing apparel.

FORM OF PROOF OF EVIDENCE
Referred to in chapter XXVIII, page 213.

Thomas V. Taylor will say:

My name is Thomas Vincent Taylor. Age 55. I am a Fellow of The Royal Institution of Chartered Surveyors, and am in practice at Victoria Street, Westminster. I have had much experience in building works and have prepared many schedules of dilapidations.

I received instructions from Mr John B Williams, solicitor, to prepare a schedule of dilapidations and estimate in connection with the termination of a lease for twenty-one years of a house in North Street, Yarmouth. I inspected the property on 29 August 1945, exactly one week before the expiry of the term, and again on 22 September 1945.

I have perused and considered the lease of the property giving special attention to the repairing covenants and I consider that the schedule of dilapidations I have submitted has been prepared in strict accordance with the terms of the lease, but am fully aware that the lessee does not share my opinion.

The repair of the property has been neglected for many years and I could find no evidence of any recent repair. As an example of neglected repair the following items, referred to among many others in my schedule of dilapidations, will show that the lessee has seriously neglected to carry out repairs necessary to comply with his obligations.

(a) No internal painting or papering has been done for many years and certainly not during the last year of the term as provided for in the lease. Wall paper is badly discoloured in the drawing-room and portions of the paper on the walls of the dining-room have been marked by ink splashes and parts stripped off. Owing to the action of the sun the paintwork of the dining-room is badly blistered and in many places the wood itself is exposed. This also is the case in many of the other rooms.

(b) External painting of both wood and iron has been neglected, particularly on the external door and frame of the side entrance and there are many instances of decayed oak window-sills in consequence, and iron eaves gutters are rusted.

(c) The window sashes in at least twenty cases have decayed owing to lack of paint. An attempt to avoid renewal has been made by screwing small iron plates over the joints, but the sashes do not close properly. Several sash-fasteners are broken.

(d) The putties to the window sashes have perished and in many cases the pointing between the window frame and the brickwork has fallen away.

(e) Many panes of glass in the windows of outbuildings are cracked or missing and six sash cords are broken.

(f) With the exception to the locks of the front and back doors there are no keys and at least five of the brass knobs to the doors have been dented by rough usage.

(g) The marble surround to fireplace in drawing-room is cracked and the tiles in the hearth in dining-room are also cracked.

(h) There is evidence of dry-rot in some of the flooring of the dining-room. The dry-rot is due to air bricks being blocked up by flower beds.

(j) The lavatory basin is cracked and the sink in the scullery is badly chipped.

(k) One six feet length of rain-water pipe at the north-east end of the house is missing.

(l) There are fifty ordinary tiles missing or cracked on the main roof alone, the result of which is that wet has penetrated into the roof space and caused decay to several rafters and ceiling joists, the ceilings and walls of two bedrooms are discoloured owing to wet coming through.

(m) The lead gutter on the main roof has been unsuccessfully repaired by the application of a bituminous compound. This form of repair provides only a temporary repair.

(n) One chimney pot is missing from the centre stack. The upper part of the kitchen stack requires re-pointing.

(o) One sheet of corrugated iron is missing from the roof of the cow-shed.

(p) The concrete paving in the yard is badly cracked. In one place I could put my two foot rule well into the crack.

(q) The wire guards at the top of the ventilating pipes have wasted away and only a few wires remain.

(r) One manhole cover is cracked and one other has been taken out and replaced by a wood cover.

(s) The entrance gates and pillars have been damaged and the stone cap of one pillar is missing.

(t) The park pale fences have been allowed to decay and in two bays to collapse. The feet of many of the posts have perished and no attempt has been made to repair. Many of the original oak pales have disappeared and been replaced by softwood boards.

(u) A concrete lily pond has been constructed in the garden for which no permission has been sought or given, so far as I know.

(v) The garden paths are covered with weeds and the timber edges are missing in several cases.

The estimate of £450 I have submitted is based on current prices and when tenders are obtained for carrying out the work I am convinced that the amount of the estimate will be required to make good the damage caused to the property to the prejudice of the lessor.

Thomas V. Taylor

Chartered Surveyor

15 January 1946

FORM OF LIST OF MARKET PRICES

Referred to in chapter XIII, page 103

Chemistry Laboratories, 1973

Schedule of market prices referred to in clause 31A of the Standard Form of Building Contract 1963 edition (July 1973 revision) as issued to contractors with the Bills of Quantities. The rates shown are those entered in the schedule and submitted to the Architect by the Contractor with his tender.

Note: The Contractor must state the actual cost of the various materials upon which his prices in the Bills of Quantities are based. References only to standard lists, control rates, etc, are not to be used.

Description	Rate £	Unit
38 mm coarse aggregate	1.95	per m^3
19 mm coarse aggregate	2.57	per m^3
Fine aggregate	2.65	per m^3
Building sand	2.46	per m^3
Portland cement	9.32	per tonne
White cement	18.63	per tonne
Hydrated hydraulic lime	11.20	per tonne
Common bricks	12.25	per 1000
Second quality Stock bricks	35.25	per 1000
Southwater engineering bricks, No.2	33.00	per 1000
Blue Staffordshire engineering bricks	54.25	per 1000
Asbestos base bitumen damp proof course to BS 743. Type C	0.51	per m^2
75 mm Clinker concrete block partitions	0.75	per m^2
100 mm Ditto, ditto	0.93	per m^2
100mm British Standard stoneware drain pipes	0.31	per m
100 mm British Standard 'Tested' stoneware drain pipes	0.43	per m
100 mm British Standard stoneware bends	0.28	each
100 mm British Standard 'Tested' stoneware bends	0.42	each
610 mm x 455 mm galvanised cast iron solid top manhole cover and frame to BS 497 Grade B weighing 143 kg.	22.00	each

Description	Rate	Unit
6 mm Gauge granite chippings	3.70	per tonne
229 mm x 229 mm x 32 mm Buff coloured quarry tiles	4.50	per m^2
Portland stone	30.65	per m^3
150 mm Corrugated asbestos cement sheeting	0.81	per m^2
25 mm Thick cork insulation slabs	0.72	per m^2
50 mm Thick ditto, ditto	1.45	per m^2
25 mm normal quality wood wool building slabs	0.50	per m^2
76 mm Thick, ditto, ditto	0.93	per m^2
Sawn softwood	42.00	per m^3
Joinery softwood	60.00	per m^3
6 mm Diameter steel reinforcing rods cut to lengths	67.62	per tonne
8 mm Ditto, ditto	65.40	per tonne
12 mm Ditto, ditto	61.81	per tonne
25 mm Ditto, ditto	56.84	per tonne
203 mm x 102 mm Rolled steel joist cut to lengths	81.80	per tonne
Rolled steel angle	84.40	per tonne
Steel fabric to BS 4483 Ref C503-4.34 kg	0.63	per m^2
76 mm Diameter painted cast iron rainwater pipe	0.70	per m
Plasterers' sand	2.46	per m^3
Keene's cement (white)	20.89	per tonne
Carlite plaster	20.00	per tonne
Carlite metal lathing plaster	21.89	per tonne
152 mm x 152 mm x 6 mm Standard white glazed wall tiles	1.68	per m^2
24 Gauge expanded metal lathing	0.47	per m^2
3 mm Selected glazing quality clear sheet glass	1.50	per m^2
3 mm patterned glass (Group 2)	1.87	per m^2
6 mm Georgian wired cast glass	2.26	per m^2
Emulsion paint	2.95	per 5 litre
Ready mixed red lead primer	2.12	per 5 litre
Ready mixed white lead undercoating	3.45	per 5 litre
Ready mixed white lead gloss finish	3.50	per 5 litre
Boiled linseed oil	1.45	per 5 litre

Note: The Contractor should note that adjustments due to fluctuations of the prices of materials used under this Contract will be limited to those materials priced in the foregoing schedule. Any other materials which the Contractor wishes to be subject to fluctuation should be stated and priced in the space below.

Description	*Rate*	*Unit*
75 mm Hollow clay floor blocks	57.00	per thousand
100 mm Ditto, ditto	66.00	per thousand
51 mm York stone sawn paving in random sizes	10.32	per m^2
3 mm Hardboard	1.85	per m^2

Signature of Contractor.................................

Address ....

....

Date ....

GENERAL INDEX

Note   Full index to Type Specification appears on pages 299-308

Mitchell's Building Construction

The volumes in this series of standard text
books have been thoroughly re-written,
re-illustrated, and amplified in order to bring
them into line with the present-day needs of
students of Architecture, Building, and
Surveying.
All quantities are expressed in SI units and
there are tables giving imperial conversions.
Also included are the main CI/SfB
classifications on which are indicated the
relevant volumes and chapters in Mitchell's
Building Construction.
There are five related volumes:

Environment and Services
Peter Burberry Dip Arch ARIBA

Materials
Alan Everett ARIBA

Structure and Fabric Part 1
Jack Stroud Foster FRIBA

Structure and Fabric Part 2
Jack Stroud Foster FRIBA

Part 2 is an extension and development of the
material in Part 1 and with it forms a complete
work in the area of its subject title.

Components and Finishes
Harold King ARIBA
and Alan Everett ARIBA

Elements of Estimating

David S. M. Hall provides students of
Estimating, Quantity Surveying and Building
Management with the fundamentals of the
complex art of estimating for building work.

The book covers the examination requirements
of the Institute of Building Final Part 1 and the
Estimating examinations of the Royal
Institution of Chartered Surveyors and the
Institute of Quantity Surveyors.

The 21 chapters include: Introduction to Price
Analysis; The Labour Rate; Excavation and
Earthwork; Concrete Work; Brickwork and
Blockwork; Rubble Walling; Roofing;
Carpentry; Joinery; Structural Steelwork and
Metalwork; Plumbing; Plasterwork and
Finishings; Glazing; Painting and Decorating;
Drainage; Preliminaries; Completion of the
Tender; Approximate Estimating; The
Examination Approach; Examination Papers;
Basic Prices of Materials.

At the end of each chapter examples of typical
price build-ups are given. These reflect the
orderly approach and layout which the author
advises and adopts.

David S. M. Hall, AIQS, AIArb, was for ten
years a Quantity Surveyor with John Laing
Construction Limited and has for twenty years
been an Estimator with this well-known
company. He also lectures to post-graduate
building management trainees at The London
Polytechnic.